Lecture Notes in Computer Science 9674

Commenced Publication in 1973
Founding and Former Series Editors:
Gerhard Goos, Juris Hartmanis, and Jan van Leeuwen

More information about this series at http://www.springer.com/series/7411

Lefteris Mamatas · Ibrahim Matta
Panagiotis Papadimitriou
Yevgeni Koucheryavy (Eds.)

Wired/Wireless Internet Communications

14th IFIP WG 6.2 International Conference, WWIC 2016
Thessaloniki, Greece, May 25–27, 2016
Proceedings

 Springer

Editors
Lefteris Mamatas
University of Macedonia
Thessaloniki
Greece

Ibrahim Matta
Boston University
Boston
USA

Panagiotis Papadimitriou
Leibniz University Hannover
Hannover
Germany

Yevgeni Koucheryavy
Tampere University of Technology
Tampere
Finland

ISSN 0302-9743   ISSN 1611-3349   (electronic)
Lecture Notes in Computer Science
ISBN 978-3-319-33935-1   ISBN 978-3-319-33936-8   (eBook)
DOI 10.1007/978-3-319-33936-8

Library of Congress Control Number: 2016937946

LNCS Sublibrary: SL5 – Computer Communication Networks and Telecommunications

Printed on acid-free paper

This Springer imprint is published by Springer Nature
The registered company is Springer International Publishing AG Switzerland

Preface

On behalf of the WWIC committee members, we welcome you to the proceedings of the 14th International Conference on Wired and Wireless Internet Communications (WWIC 2016), which was held in Thessaloniki, Greece, during May 25–27, 2016.

WWIC is a well-established conference in Internet communications, covering research topics such as the design and evaluation of network protocols, experiences from the design and implementation of wireless systems, network modeling, wireless network security and management, mobile network services, and emerging technologies such as software-defined radio and network function virtualization.

This year the conference received submissions from 20 countries in Europe, Asia, North America, and North Africa on a wide range of Internet communication aspects. After a rigorous review process, the Program Committee selected 27 papers out of 54 submissions, based on criteria such as relevance with the conference scope, originality, timeliness, technical correctness, and presentation quality. The conference program, which includes eight technical sessions, reflects this high quality level and topic diversity.

We would like to thank our keynote speakers Scott Burleigh (NASA Jet Propulsion Laboratory, USA), George Pavlou (University College London, UK), and Vassilis Tsaoussidis (Democritus University of Thrace, Greece) for delivering excellent talks on information-centric and mobile networking.

We further thank all authors for their submissions and their contribution to the technical excellence of WWIC 2016. We are also thankful to the Program Committee and all reviewers for their tremendous effort and commitment during paper reviewing, as well as to the rest of the conference organizing team for their support.

Last but not least, we would like to thank the University of Macedonia in Greece, especially the Department of Applied Informatics and its Graduate Program, and the International Federation for Information Processing (IFIP) for sponsoring the conference.

We hope that all attendees enjoyed the technical program and social activities during the conference and look forward to the next edition of WWIC.

May 2016

Lefteris Mamatas
Ibrahim Matta
Panagiotis Papadimitriou
Yevgeni Koucheryavy

Organization

Steering Committee

Torsten Braun	University of Bern, Switzerland
Georg Carle	TU München, Germany
Geert Heijenk	University of Twente, The Netherlands
Peter Langendorfer	IHP Microelectronics, Germany
Ibrahim Matta	Boston University, USA
Vassilis Tsaoussidis	Democritus University of Thrace, Greece

Conference Chairs

General Co-chairs

Lefteris Mamatas	University of Macedonia, Greece
Ibrahim Matta	Boston University, USA

TPC Co-chairs

Panagiotis Papadimitriou	Leibniz University Hannover, Germany
Yevgeni Koucheryavy	Tampere University of Technology, Finland

Technical Program Committee

Ahmed Abujoda	Leibniz University Hannover, Germany
Mari Carmen Aguayo-Torres	University of Malaga, Spain
Sami Akin	Leibniz University Hannover, Germany
Francisco Barcelo-Arroyo	Universitat Politecnica de Catalunya, Spain
Paolo Bellavista	University of Bologna, Italy
Nikolaos Bezirgiannidis	Democritus University of Thrace, Greece
Fernando Boavida	University of Coimbra, Portugal
Zdravko Bozakov	EMC Research Europe, Ireland
Torsten Braun	University of Bern, Switzerland
Scott Burleigh	NASA JPL/California Institute of Technology, USA
Maria Calderon	Universidad Carlos III de Madrid, Spain
Zhen Cao	Leibniz University Hannover, Germany
Georg Carle	Technische Universität München, Germany
Ana Cavalli	Telecom SudParis, France
Eduardo Cerqueira	Federal University of Para/UCLA, Brazil
Marinos Charalambides	University College London, UK
Periklis Chatzimisios	Alexander TEI of Thessaloniki, Greece

Organizing Committee

Local Organization

Committee Chair

Sofia Petridou   University of Macedonia, Greece

Proceedings Chair

Ageliki Tsioliaridou   Foundation for Research and Technology, Greece

Publicity Chair

Giorgos Papastergiou   Simula Research Laboratory, Norway

Web Master

Antony Tsioukas   LiveEvents, Greece

Additional Reviewers

S. Agrawal   Dan Noyes
Carlos Anastasiades   Cristian Olariu
Jose Carrera   André Riker
Karl-Johan Grinnemo   Christos-Alexandros Sarros
Adriana Hava   Vitor Souza
Sotirios Kontogiannis   Giacomo Tanganelli
Yizhen Liu   Tryfon Theodorou
Eva Marn-Tordera   George Violettas
Israel Martin-Escalona   Artemios Voyiatzis
Sarwar Morshed   Fanzhao Wang

Sponsoring Institutions

International Federation for Information Processing TC6

University of Macedonia, Greece

Applied Informatics Department/Graduate Program in Applied Informatics, University of Macedonia, Greece

Contents

Network Applications and Tools

Network Protocols

Network Modeling

Wireless Sensor Networks

Resource Management and Optimization

Wireless Technologies and Systems

High-Performance Wideband SDR Channelizers

Islam Alyafawi[1], Arnaud Durand[2], and Torsten Braun[1(✉)]

[1] University of Bern, Bern, Switzerland
{alyafawi,braun}@inf.unibe.ch
[2] University of Fribourg, Fribourg, Switzerland
arnaud.durand@unifr.ch

Abstract. The essential process to analyze signals from multicarrier communication systems is to isolate independent communication channels using a channelizer. To implement a channelizer in software-defined radio systems, the Polyphase Filterbank (PFB) is commonly used. For real-time applications, the PFB has to process the digitized signal faster or equal to its sampling rate. Depending on the underlying hardware, PFB can run on a CPU, a Graphical Processing Unit (GPU), or even a Field-Programmable Gate Arrays (FPGA). CPUs and GPUs are more reconfigurable and scalable platforms than FPGAs. In this paper, we optimize an existing implementation of a CPU-based channelizer and implement a novel GPU-based channelizer. Our proposed solutions deliver an overall improvement of 30 % for the CPU optimization on Intel Core i7-4790 @ 3.60 GHz, and a 3.2-fold improvement for the GPU implementation on AMD R9 290, when compared to the original CPU-based implementation.

Keywords: SDR · CPU · GPU · Channelizer

1 Introduction

Different wired/wireless systems, such as the Global System for Mobile Communications (GSM), use frequency-division multiplexing (FDM) techniques [12]. In FDM-based systems, the signal is divided into multiple channels without cross-synchronization among themselves. In [3], we developed a single-band passive receiver that can capture, decode, and parse uplink messages of different GSM Mobile Devices (MDs). The proposed receiver is implemented as a GNURadio (GR) module with definite input and output interfaces. The output from multiple receivers (MD identity and received signal power) was sent to a centralized system to perform the localization process as described in [4]. However, since GSM MDs in a certain area may connect to multiple GSM Base Transceiver Stations (BTSs) operating at different frequencies, it is required to support the proposed Software-Defined Radio (SDR) receiver with wideband capturing capabilities. To do so, we use a channelizer, which splits the wideband spectrum into a set of independent channels fed to different instances of the single-band receiver as shown in Fig. 1.

© IFIP International Federation for Information Processing 2016
Published by Springer International Publishing Switzerland 2016. All Rights Reserved
L. Mamatas et al. (Eds.): WWIC 2016, LNCS 9674, pp. 3–14, 2016.
DOI: 10.1007/978-3-319-33936-8_1

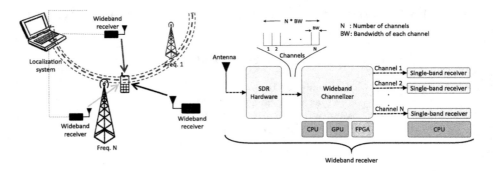

Fig. 1. Architecture of a wireless localization system using the wideband GSM receiver.

Polyphase Filterbanks (PFB) channelizers are powerful tools that (i) split the wideband signal into equispaced channels and (ii) filter the split channels with a given filter. The channelizer performance varies based on the underlying processing hardware architecture. While FPGA-based approaches can provide the required processing performance, they lack the run-time flexibility of GPP-based approaches [5]. The authors in [1,2,8,14] show the possibility to perform a PFB channelizer with a GPU underlying processing unit. However, these solutions are (i) not implemented as GR modules, (ii) not provided as an open-source and (iii) not optimized with respect to throughput and latency for data transfer between system memory (RAM) and GPU memory.

The contribution of this paper is optimizing an existing GR CPU-based channelizer using advanced CPU instructions and implementation of a new high-performance GPU-based channelizer suited for GR (c.f., Sects. 3 and 4). Our proposed solutions are provided as GR open-source modules [6] with optimized data transfer between RAM and GPU memory. An evaluation of the proposed solutions is presented in Sect. 5.

2   Problem Formulation

Our focus is to improve the PFB channelizer performance as a GR module. The channelized streams can then be sent to a centralized or a distributed system for signal processing and data acquisition. Our solution starts by understanding the signal processing and conversions between the antenna and the processing machine holding the channelizer.

2.1   SDR Hardware

Our proposed solution is hardware agnostic and, hence, it is possible to use any SDR equipment from any vendor that meets the minimum performance requirements. The Universal Software Radio Peripheral (USRP) is a series of SDR-enabled devices [19]. We use a set of USRP N210 devices (we call them

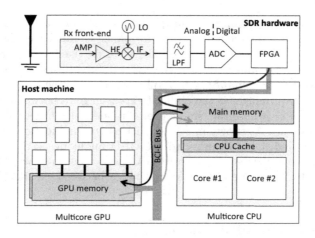

Fig. 2. SDR system architecture.

N210 for simplicity). A simplified architecture of the N210 is illustrated in Fig. 2. The received radio signal will be amplified before being converted from the High-Frequency (HF) to the Intermediate-Frequency (IF) band. Then, it will be filtered using a Low-Pass Filter (LPF) with a bandwidth up to 20 MHz. The filtered signal is digitized inside the Analog-to-Digital Converter (ADC), which has 14-bit precision for each In-phase and Quadratic (I/Q) samples. The ADC digitizes the signal with a fixed sampling rate equal to 100 Msps (Mega samples per second). The FPGA changes the data to 32-bit samples when configured in 16-bit mode (16 bit I and 16 bit Q). The UHD driver is used to control I/O communication between the USRP and the host computer [22]. It is configured to transfer up to 25 Msps in 16-bit mode over a Gigabit Ethernet (GbE) interface. The UHD driver converts sampled signals obtained from the USRP to IEEE 754 floating point numbers and store them in the host memory.

2.2 Wideband Channelizer

GR is an open-source framework to build SDR systems. Radio samples are typed *gr_complex* in GR, but are in fact only a redefinition of the C/C++ std :: complex data type. Complex numbers are represented as two consecutive single-precision Floating-Point Units (FPUs), thus taking 64 bits. The default GR PFB channelizer makes use of the host CPU to process the entire bandwidth signals, which can take advantage of CPU-specific SIMD (Single Instruction Multiple Data) operations. Without any up-/down sampling operations, the overall output sample rate of a PFB channelizer is equal input sample rate. Nevertheless, the available processing resources will reach their limits with the increasing width of the channelized spectrum. Hence, there is a need for alternative optimized (or newly implemented) PFB solutions within the same processing platform [9].

GPUs are fine grain SIMD processing units suited for general-purpose processing with a relatively low cost compared to other specialized architectures [18]. GPUs contain a large number of computing units. Hence, they can be used to implement a high-performance channelizer. There are several technologies available to realize GPUs, such as the CUDA programming model or the OpenCL framework [24]. However, to integrate such solutions with the GR framework, it is mandatory to implement the channelizer as a GR module. An essential requirement is the ability to transfer data between CPU (where GR works) and GPU (where the channelizer can be implemented) at high bandwidth and low latency. As shown in Fig. 2, existing communication methods that transfer data through CPU memory to the GPU might be used. Additional to the original data transfer between the FPGA and system memory (RAM), data must cross the PCI Express (PCIe) switch twice between the RAM and GPU memory.

2.3   Polyphase FilterBank Channelizer

A PFB channelizer is an efficient technique for splitting a signal into equally-spaced channels [12]. A PFB is mainly composed of two main modules: M FIR (Finite Impulse Response) filters (the filterbank) and an M-point FFT (Fast Fourier Transform). A basic implementation of the PFB channelizer is illustrated in Fig. 3, which represents the input with M FDM channels that exist in a single data stream and the resulting M Time Division Multiplexed (TDM) output channels. The fundamental theory of polyphase filters is the polyphase decomposition [16]. We discuss here the two principal components of the decomposition process.

FIR filters are digital filters with a finite impulse response. The transfer function of FIR filter samples is expressed in Eq. 1.

$$f[n] = \sum_{k=0}^{N-1} h[k]x[n-k] \tag{1}$$

N is the number of FIR filter coefficients (known as filter taps), $x[k]$ are FIR filter input samples, $h[k]$ are FIR filter coefficients and f$[n]$ are FIR filtered samples.

A **Fast Fourier Transform (FFT)** is a fast way to calculate the Discrete Fourier Transform (DFT) of a vector x. The FFT operation transforms the input signal from the time domain into the frequency domain. The M-point FFT transfer function is expressed in Eq. 2.

$$y[k] = \sum_{m=0}^{M-1} f[m]e^{-2\pi jmk/M} \tag{2}$$

f$[n]$ is the input and $y[k]$ is the output. The time it takes to evaluate an FFT on a computer depends mainly on the number of multiplications involved. FFT only needs $Mlog_2(M)$ multiplications.

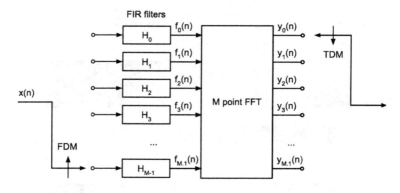

Fig. 3. PFB channelizer.

3 Enhanced CPU-Based PFB

GR takes advantage of architecture-specific operations through the Vector Optimized Library of Kernels (VOLK) machine [23]. The VOLK machine is a collection of GR libraries for arithmetic-intensive computations. Most of the provided VOLK implementations are using x86 SIMD instructions, which enable the same instruction to be performed on multiple input data and produce several results (vector output) in one step. The FFT operations are computed through the fftw3 library [10]. This open source library takes advantage of modern CPU architectures by making use of specific SIMD operations. As we consider this library to be optimal for CPU usage when used correctly, we will not consider further FFT optimizations. FIR filters are accumulators that perform a lot of multiply-accumulate operations. Thus, the PFB channelizer relies heavily on the VOLK multiply-and-add routine and most of the CPU cycles are spent inside this function [20]. The fastest multiply-and-add routine available in the VOLK machine for our CPU (Intel Haswell) is `volk_32fc_32f_dot_prod_32fc_a_avx` using the Advanced Vector Extensions (AVX) instruction set [15]. In the following, we present a set of optimizations by the available AVX PFB implementation.

Memory Alignment: CPUs access memory in chunks. Depending on the memory access granularity, a CPU may retrieve data in 2, 4, 8, 16, 32-bytes chunks or even more. Depending on the particular instruction, it may or may not be allowed to load data from memory into registers using addresses not being multiple of the memory access granularity [7]. Indeed, if allowed, loading unaligned data requires more operations as the register must execute shifting and merging operations of different memory chunks. AVX are extensions to the x86 instruction set. They allow operations on 256-bit registers, enabling eight single-precision floating point numbers to be stored side-by-side in the same register and processed simultaneously. AVX uses relaxed memory alignment requirements. It means that using unaligned data is allowed for most instructions, but this comes with a performance penalty. When allocating memory using `malloc()`, compilers are in charge of the alignment, and we cannot assume that the returned

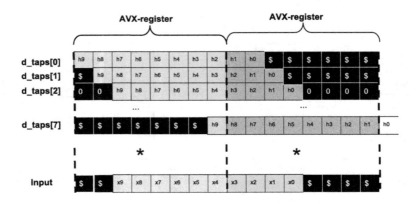

Fig. 4. GR FIR taps alignment and AVX dot product.

address is aligned. However, it is possible to force alignment when desirable. GR provides such facility through the `volk_malloc()` function [11]. Such a function allocates a slightly bigger amount of memory (desired size + granularity - 1) and moves the pointer to the next aligned address. However, the FIR filters from the PFB channelizer cannot use this function because GR buffers are not necessarily aligned. Instead, GR generates a set of aligned taps d_taps for each possible architecture alignment as shown in Fig. 4. In the illustrated example of Fig. 4, we have a FIR filter with a history of 10 samples $h[0]$, ..., $h[9]$. By measuring the alignment of the input samples, we can select the correctly aligned taps. For example, if the input register is aligned with two floats, GR will choose to multiply with d_taps[2] (a set of taps aligned with two floats). $ indicates unaligned data and $x[0]$, ..., $x[9]$ are the input samples. GR performs SIMD operations on aligned data and non-SIMD operations on the remaining input samples. To avoid non-SIMD operations, one solution is to make the number of filter taps as a multiple of 8. Then, we can fill taps corresponding to unaligned data with zeros as shown in Fig. 4 (**d_taps[2]**). We then consider the data aligned in GR buffers because zeros will discard unaligned input values.

Fused Multiply-Add (FMA) Operations: FMA operations are AVX2 instructions to 128 and 256-bit Streaming SIMD Extensions (SSE) instructions [13] (AVX2 is an expansion of the AVX instruction set). AVX2 FMA operations are floating point operations similar to c ← (a * b) + c, which performs multiply and add in one step (c.f. Fig. 5). These operations are compatible with the GNU compiler collection. However, AVX performs (a * b) + c in two steps (first a * b, then + c). Benchmarks of pure multiply and accumulate operations on Intel Haswell CPUs show double performance using AVX2 FMA compared to AVX. The PFB implementation uses the product of complex and float vectors. This implementation requires some further operations like deinterleaving an input block of complex samples into M outputs.

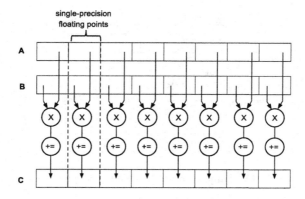

Fig. 5. FMA SIMD operation.

Better Pipelining: complex numbers are just two consecutive floats as defined in `complex.h` of the C standard library. From the previous example c ← c + (a * b), a is a complex number representing an input sample and b is an integer representing a FIR filter coefficient. Consider that a is a tuple of (r, qi): r is the in-phase part of a, q is the quadrature part of a, and i is the complex number $\sqrt{-1}$. Complex arithmetic rules define a*b = (r + qi) * b = (r + qi) * (b + 0i) = (rb + qbi). As the GR FIR filters are not specifically designed for AVX operations, the coefficients are just stored as consecutive floats. Unfortunately, feeding 256-bit registers with consecutive floats is a costly process because it requires a for-loop operating over all input sample to perform the (r + qi) * b instructions. The best we can do is to create a more compatible layout of filter taps to benefit from AVX2-FMA operations. To do this we load (_mm256_loadu_ps), unpack (_mm256_unpackXY_ps) and then permute (_mm256_permute2f128) FIR coefficients before operations. The behavior of unpack does not allow to permute coefficients across 128-bit boundaries. This behavior is inherited directly from the legacy SSE unpack operation. However, by re-shuffling the taps during the creation of the PFB as illustrated in Fig. 6, we can create a layout that enables the taps to be in the right order when unpacked (without permutation). Then, we can perform four (r + qi) * b instructions in one step.

4   GPU-Based PFB

We can make PFB processing faster by taking advantage of massively parallel architectures, such as GPUs [18]. There are several technologies available to perform GPU processing. OpenCL is an open framework for heterogeneous computing [21]. It is open by design and, therefore, best suited to the philosophy of GR. For this reason, we will implement a PFB channelizer using OpenCL. In our test setup, we use a discrete graphics card, meaning that the CPU and GPU do not share the same memory (c.f. Fig. 2). There are several techniques to transfer data between the CPU and GPU, with various transfer speeds [17]. However, when using physically shared memory between the GPU and CPU using

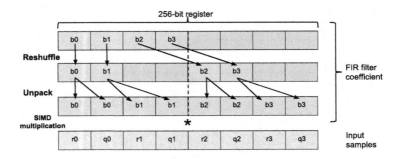

Fig. 6. AVX unpack operation and multiplications.

fused architectures, e.g., using Intel Integrated Graphics Processors (IGP), we are not required to transfer data. Data could be copied using the CPU or GPU direct memory access (DMA). However, IGPs are generally less powerful than discrete GPUs and thus, not used in our research. To process data in real-time, we have strict requirements for transfer speeds. Since GR has no built-in support for coprocessors, buffers could only be transferred to/from the GPU inside the work() function (where we want our code to be implemented). Every time work() is called by the GR scheduler, we should (i) transfer a portion of input samples (decided by the GR scheduler) from the main memory to the GPU, (ii) perform the PFB channelizer on the GPU and (iii) transfer the channelizer output from the GPU to the main memory. This situation is not optimal as the (i) and (iii) lead to a low throughput and high latency data transmission. For real-time processing, data transfer between CPU and GPU is a time critical action. The time spent transferring data is time lost for processing. It is important to obtain a balance between transfer delay and processing delay. As a solution to this situation, we proposed the following: First, to avoid inefficient data transfer to a single stream, we perform the FDM operation of Fig. 3 inside work(). This is simply done using the **stream_to_streams** (s2ss) function, which converts a stream of M items into M streams of 1 item. Hence, we get the inputs of the FIR filters on different streams with different buffers and transfer data more efficiently. Second, to avoid inefficient data transfer (small amount of data with high transferring latency), we batch the s2ss transferring buffers using **clEnqueueWriteBuffer()** with non-blocking write transfer. With the non-blocking write transfer, control is returned immediately to the host thread, allowing operations to occur concurrently in the host thread during the transfer between host and device proceeds. On the GPU device, as illustrated in Fig. 7, our filter taps are copied to the GPU memory once at the startup of our PFB channelizer. Each GPU FIR filter (inside the PFB channelizer) runs in parallel inside an independent GPU computing unit. Once we get the output from the FIR filters, we pass the output of the FIR filters to the input sequencer such that we can perform the M-point FFT. There are several OpenCL FFT libraries available like AMD clFFT (an open source library). clFFT usage is straightforward. Here, we take advantage of the functions `bakePlan()` to apply device optimizations and `setPlanBatchSize()` to handle several clFFT operations concurrently.

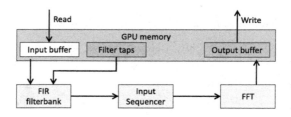

Fig. 7. PFB Channelizer on GPU.

5   Experimental Results

In this section, we consider the GR CPU-based implementation of the PFB channelizer as a reference. We are using GR version 3.7.5. All experiments are performed on a Linux-based machine with Intel Core i7-4790 @ 3.60 GHz CPU, AMD R9 290 (Tahiti) GPU (4 GB video memory), and 32 GB RAM. We use a simple benchmark experiment illustrated in Fig. 8. The signal source is a GR block used to generate continuously a certain type of a signal, such as sine, cosine or constant. In this experiment, we used *gr_complex* defined in GR as an output to emulate the behavior of a USRP N210. The head block stops the signal source when N items of the gr_complex type are processed. Hence, we can configure experiments' duration through N. The s2ss block performs the FDM operation in Fig. 3. We used three implementations for the PFB channelizer: (i) original GR with AVX instructions, (ii) our optimized GR implementation with AVX2-FMA instructions, and (iii) our GPU implementation. The channelized streams are sent to a null sink because our target is to evaluate the performance of the PFB channelizer only.

5.1   A Running Example

To measure the performance of our solutions proposed in Sects. 3 and 4, we will use a running example based on our passive GSM receiver [3]. Each GSM receiver requires a precise sample rate R for each GSM channel: $R = 1625000/6 = 270833$ complex samples per second (sps), which is equivalent to the data rate of the GSM signal itself. From these numbers, we can calculate a few elements for a wideband GSM receiver:

– We need a wideband sampling rate $R_b = R * M_{ch}$, where M_{ch} is the number of GSM channels.
– We can capture up to $M_{ch} = 25 \times 10^6/R = 92$ channels using a N210 USRP device with 16 bit precision.

Fig. 8. PFB channelizer benchmark overview.

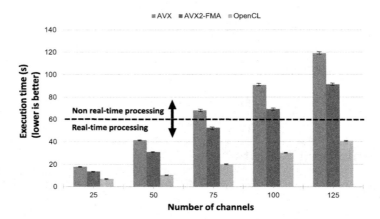

Fig. 9. Real time processing of PFB channelizer.

5.2   AVX vs AVX2-FMA vs GPU

In these experiments, we want to measure the improvement provided by the optimized AVX2-FMA PFB (presented in Sect. 3) and the proposed GPU-based PFB (shown in Sect. 4) compared to the default GR AVX implementation. We use a pre-designed filter of 55 taps, and we want to test the performance for different numbers of channels. The channelizer performance is agnostic to the data content, i.e., feeding a generated signal to the channelizer is the same as feeding a USRP input stream. For each number of channels shown in Fig. 9, we generate a signal equivalent to 60 s of data. For example, in experiments with 50 channels, we use a signal source block (a producer of data) with sampling rate $R_b = 50R$ and a number of samples $X = 60R_b$. The benchmark output is the total runtime, and the presented results are the arithmetic mean of 5 runs. If the processing time exceeds the 60 s, it means that the PFB channelizer cannot process data in real-time. As illustrated in Fig. 9, the improvement using our optimized AVX2-FMA ranges from 30 % to 33 %. Our optimized filter can process in real-time up to 76 channels. It is, however still, lower than what a USRP N210 device can support (c.f., Sect. 5.1: 92 channels). Compared to the reference channelizer, there is an average of 3.2-fold improvement by the GPU-based PFB implementation. That means we can channelize more than 125 GSM channels, more than what the USRP N210 can capture.

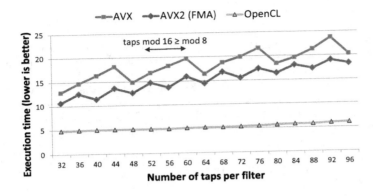

Fig. 10. Taps impact on PFB channelizer.

5.3   Taps per Filter

In this experiment, we run the same benchmark as in Sect. 5.2 with a constant number of channels equal to 25, but varying the number of taps per FIR filter (channel). Again, the results present the arithmetic mean of 5 runs. As illustrated in Fig. 10, the execution time increases with the increasing number of FIR taps. The different zig-zag behavior for AVX and AVX2 implementations is because AVX2 registers have the double size of AVX registers. Extra samples in both implementations are processed using standard non-SIMD operations. This behavior is not noticed in the OpenCL implementation due to the different mechanisms for data transfer from/to GPU. Note that it is important to use a multiple of 2^N so that the compiler can optimize the costly division operation to a bit shifting operation.

6   Conclusions

GR is the framework of choice for many SDR projects. We demonstrated that it was possible to create high-performance GSM channel processing by reusable components for wideband applications. The channelizer technique is applicable for any distributed system with a set of independent channels. The polyphase filterbank channelizer is not only useful for FDM-based technologies but is a critical component in many SDR systems. Our AVX2 optimizations improve the performance by up to 30 % using recent CPU instructions, namely fused multiply-add operations, compared to the AVX implementation. Moreover, the GPU implementation opens up opportunities for applications, where expensive specialized hardware was required previously. The GPU-based implementation is a GR-like module with 3.2-fold improvement when compared to the original GR implementation on CPU only. Our proposed solutions are available as independent GR modules [6].

References

1. Adhinarayanan, V., Feng, W.C.: Wideband channelization for software-defined radio via mobile graphics processors. In: International Conference on Parallel and Distributed Systems (ICPADS) (2013)
2. Adhinarayanan, V., Koehn, T., Kepa, K., Feng, W.C., Athanas, P.: On the performance and energy efficiency of FPGAs and GPUs for polyphase channelization. In: International Conference on ReConFigurable Computing and FPGAs (2014)
3. Alyafawi, I., Dimitrova, D., Braun, T.: Real-time passive capturing of the GSM radio. In: ICC (2014)
4. Alyafawi, I., Schiller, E., Braun, T., Dimitrova, D., Gomes, A., Nikaein, N.: Critical issues of centralized and cloudified LTE-FDD radio access networks. In: ICC (2015)
5. Awan, M., Koch, P., Dick, C., Harris, F.: FPGA implementation analysis of polyphase channelizer performing sample rate change required for both matched filtering and channel frequency spacing. In: Asilomar Conference on Signals, Systems, and Computers (2010)
6. Channelizer. http://cds.unibe.ch/research/hp_sdr_channelizer.html
7. Intel Corperation: Intel C++ compiler intrinsics reference (2006)
8. del Mundo, C., Adhinarayanan, V., Feng, W.C.: Accelerating fast fourier transform for wideband channelization. In: ICC (2013)
9. Durand, A. (2015). http://cds.unibe.ch/research/pub_files/internal/du15.pdf
10. FFTW. www.fftw.org
11. GNURadio. https://gnuradio.org
12. Harris, F.J.: Multirate Signal Processing for Communication Systems. Prentice Hall PTR, Upper Saddle River (2004)
13. Jain, T., Agrawal, T.: The haswell microarchitecture - 4th generation processor. IJCSIT **4**(3), 477–480 (2013)
14. Kim, S.C., Bhattacharyya, S.S.: Implementation of a high-throughput low-latency polyphase channelizer on GPUs. EURASIP J. Adv. Signal Process. **1**, 1–10 (2014)
15. Lomont, C.: Introduction to intel advanced vector extensions. Intel Corperation (2011)
16. Madisetti, V.K.: The Digital Signal Processing Handbook, 2nd edn. CRC Press, Boca Raton (2009)
17. Munshi, A.: The opencl specification, version 1.1. Khronos OpenCL Working Group (2010)
18. Plishker, W., Zaki, G.F., Bhattacharyya, S.S., Clancy, C., Kuykendall, J.: Applying graphics processor acceleration in a software defined radio prototyping environment. In: International Symposium on Rapid System Prototyping (2011)
19. Ettus Research. http://www.ettus.com/
20. Rondeau, T.W., Shelburne, V.T., O'Shea, V.T.: Designing anaylsis and synthesis filterbanks in GNU radio. In: Karlsruhe Workshop on Software Radios (2014)
21. Tsuchiyama, R., Nakamura, T., Iizuka, T., Asahara, A., Son, J., Miki, S.: The OpenCL Programming Book. Fixstars, Tokyo (2010)
22. UHD. http://code.ettus.com/redmine/ettus/projects/uhd/wiki
23. VOLK. https://gnuradio.org/redmine/projects/gnuradio/wiki/volk
24. Wilt, N.: The CUDA Handbook: A Comprehensive Guide to GPU Programming. Addison-Wesley Professional, Boston (2012)

Location Based Transmission Using a Neighbour Aware-Cross Layer MAC for Ad Hoc Networks

Jims Marchang[✉], Bogdan Ghita, and David Lancaster

Centre for Security, Communications and Network Research (CSCAN), School of Computing, Electronics and Mathematics, Plymouth University, Plymouth PL4 8AA, UK
{jims.marchang,bogdan.ghita,david.lancaster}@plymouth.ac.uk,
http://cscan.org/

Abstract. In a typical Ad Hoc network, mobile nodes have scarce shared bandwidth and limited battery life resources, so optimizing the resource and enhancing the overall network performance is the ultimate aim in such network. This paper proposes anew cross layer MAC algorithm called Location Based Transmission using a Neighbour Aware – Cross Layer MAC (LBT-NA Cross Layer MAC) that aims to reduce the transmission power when communicating with the intended receiver by exchanging location information between nodes in one hand and on the other hand the MAC uses a new random backoff values, which is based on the number of active neighbour nodes, unlike the standard IEEE 802.11 series where a random backoff value is chosen from a fixed range of 0–31. The validation test demonstrates that the proposed algorithm increases battery life, increases spatial reuse and enhances the network performance.

Keywords: Power controlled transmission · MAC · Ad hoc networks

1 Introduction

In a resource-constrained Ad Hoc network, interference is a significant limiting factor in achieving high throughput. As the interference range is directly proportional to the transmission range, controlling transmission range of the active nodes dictates the density of parallel or simultaneous communication, subsequently, the overall network performance. Using a large transmission range does have its benefits, as it reduces the path length and increases link stability and throughput, but the resulting interference increases heavily and the network performance degrades as the number of the active nodes increases. On the other hand, when the transmission range is low, the overall interference decreases, but path length between the source and the destination increases; as a result the end-to-end throughput may decrease since throughput decays as the communicating path length increases as discussed by authors of [1], but the reuse factor in terms of frequency and space increases, thereby increasing the probability of parallel transmission. In this paper mobility is not taken into account, so route maintenance is not considered, but focuses on the power controlled Medium Access Control (MAC) using a single hop communication and tested extensively with both fixed and random topologies with random sources and destinations.

Published by Springer International Publishing Switzerland 2016. All Rights Reserved
L. Mamatas et al. (Eds.): WWIC 2016, LNCS 9674, pp. 15–27, 2016.
DOI: 10.1007/978-3-319-33936-8_2

Authors of [2–4] provides a thorough study on different power control MAC for wireless Ad Hoc networks, but most of the approaches uses a fixed maximum power transmission for control frames like RTS and CTS, and uses a low transmission range for Data and ACK frames, the flaw in such approach is that the probability of concurrent transmission is less, since a higher degree of neighbouring nodes will be disturbed by the RTS and the CTS control frames. Some other technique uses a set of power levels as described in [5], where the power level is increased step by step until the next hop neighbour is discovered or maximum power is reached, whichever is earlier; the flaw of such approach is that each node will try with different transmission power levels without knowing whether it will result in successful discovery of next hop neighbour or not.

When a pair of communicating nodes is close to each other, using a fixed transmission power leads to a significant interference and waste energy unnecessarily, as shown in Fig. 1(I). On the other hand, if a node communicates with the next hop destination uses only the required minimum transmission power as shown in Fig. 1(II), then the area of interference decreases, probability of parallel transmissions increases and prolongs battery life, which is the notion of this paper. This paper also focuses on drawing a relationship between the amount of energy spent by an active node and the distance between the communicating nodes. In order to decrease waiting time during low congestion, a new MAC with a dynamic backoff ranges based on the number of active neighbours is also considered in this paper rather than using a fixed backoff ranges.

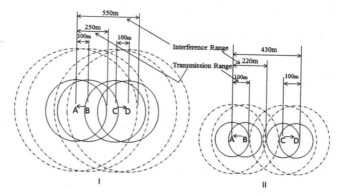

Fig. 1. Using a fixed transmission range (I) and using a location based power controlled transmission (II).

2   Transmission Power Control in Ad Hoc Networks

Different approaches were investigated by various authors to reduce interference and improve the performance of the overall network by controlling the transmission power. A power controlled MAC called POWMAC is discussed in [7], which is an extension of their previous work done in [6]; the author uses the RTS and the CTS control frames for exchanging the signal strength and it exchanges N number of RTS/CTS pairs for securing N concurrent transmissions, so this approach involves a significant control overhead. In order to reduce the signaling burden, authors of [8] proposed an adaptive power control MAC by using only the RTS and CTS for collecting transmission power of the active neighbours and interference level; in order to validate its claims, the study assumes that the transmission range and the carrier sensing range are identical, but in reality, the carrier sensing range is much greater than the transmission range. To reduce the degree of collision in such approaches, a new power controlled MAC is proposed in [9] which utilizes the fragmentation mechanism of IEEE 802.11 and controls the transmission power based on the fragmentation technique. The limitation of such approach is that fragmentation does not occur always unless the packet size reaches the Maximum Transfer Unit (MTU) of the link. All these papers consider sending RTS/CTS and/or ACK frames with maximum power and Data with minimum power.

A cross layer technique combining scheduling, routing and power control transmission is proposed in [10], based on the Time Division Multiple Access (TDMA) mechanism; but synchronization could be an issue with such approach in a distributed Ad Hoc networks. Authors of [11] shows that in optimal power control mechanism approaches to improve spatial reuse, senders should not send with just enough power to reach the next hop node, but it should use higher transmission power. A power control transmission based on the interference and distance estimation is designed in [12], but such approach suffers from distinguishing the differences between the low power transmissions for short distance from high power transmission with long distance. Authors of [13] designed a collision avoidance MAC by adjusting the appropriate power level of the source node, so that the active neighbour can withstand its interference level. Another power control MAC where the RTS/CTS are sent with maximum power and the Data/ACK are sent with minimum power is proposed in [14], but the Data packet is send with maximum power periodically, such approach may save power, but the potential probability of areal space reuse is low. To avoid such problems, the authors of [15] introduce a new method where the RTS messages are not sent with a constant maximum power; instead, transmission starts with a lower transmission power, which is also advertised in the message, but the CTS are sent with maximum power to alert any neighbours that have Data to send. Such mechanism tends to lead to varying transmission ranges from a same node, so active neighbours experiences an uneven degree of interference which may lead to unfair end-to-end throughput. Authors of [16] introduce a mechanism where the transmission power is reduced based on the degree of contention by monitoring the contention window. A trade-off between the bandwidth, latency and network connectivity during transmission power control Ad Hoc networks is proposed in [17]. As such, transmission power control can lead to battery durability and space reuse for parallel transmission, but authors of [18] suggest that obtaining an optimal transmission power is an NP-hard problem even if the node has the entire knowledge of the network. So, this paper uses a deterministic approach to optimize the durability of the battery life and enhances the network performance by considering a minimum power needed by each node during data transmission with the help of location information and by observing its neighbour activity. In a multiple channel approach, authors of [19] divides the channels and assigned one for control frames and Data packet, and the other channels for transmitting busy tone and receiver busy tone, but such approach of considering multiple channel consumes too much resources. In order to increase throughput, a joint power and rate control scheme is discussed in [20], which also maximizes the energy efficient, but such approach considers a cognitive radio which allows secondary users to access licensed spectrum band. The authors of [21] designed a power control MAC by considering an optimal hop distance in a dense single cell network, but the approached considers an existence of no hidden nodes. In order to improve the average signal-to-interference ratio, outage probability, and spatial reuse, the authors of [22] studied if discrete power control is better than no power control when the nodes of the Ad Hoc networks are in the form of a Poison-distribution.

The remainder of the paper is structured as follows. The proposed MAC is described in detail in Sect. 3. Section 4 provides the evaluation of the results, and then Sect. 5 concludes the paper by proposing a number of future directions.

3   Power Control Cross Layer MAC

As highlighted by prior research, the transmission power does have a significant influence on the network capacity, particularly for relatively high node density, due to interference. To reduce the impact of these issues, this paper proposes a new cross layer MAC called Location Based Transmission using a Neighbour Aware – Cross Layer MAC for Ad Hoc Networks (LBT-NA Cross Layer MAC). The proposed protocol consists of two parts: calculation and transmitting any Data and control frames using an exact minimal needed power using location information and secondly calculation of a new backoff value which depends on the number of active neighbour nodes. The detail work of the proposed cross layer MAC is described in the following subsections:

3.1   Proposed Power Calculation Model

The proposed model assumes that each node knows its location information, with the help of a Global Positioning System (GPS) and they are exchanged to calculate the distance (d) and the required minimum transmission power between the communicating nodes. This leads to a twofold advantage from an efficiency perspective. Firstly, it uses only the minimal required power between the communicating nodes, so it extends battery lifetime. Secondly, the interfering range changes dynamically depending on the distance of communication, so the probability of simultaneous transmissions without interference increases.

The proposed protocol embeds the location information in Request-To-Send (RTS) and Clear-To-Send (CTS) control frames to avoid additional control overheads. This paper considers only 2D topologies. When a node has a data to send, it starts by broadcasting RTS frame at full power and the intended next hop receiver replies with a CTS control frame to reserve the channel. When the intended Destination node N_D with coordinates $(X_D, Y_D, 0)$ receives an RTS frame from a Source node N_S with a coordinate $(X_S, Y_S, 0)$, it extracts the location information and calculates the corresponding Euclidian distance $d = \sqrt{(X_D - X_S)^2 + (Y_D - Y_S)^2}$ of two nodes. Likewise, upon receiving a

CTS frame, the sender also calculates the distance between the two nodes. So, the source and the next hop destination are aware of their distances upon receiving the first RTS and the first CTS frames.

In this paper, the maximum transmission power used is $(P_t) = 0.28183815$ W, a power that can cover a maximum fixed transmission range of 250 m. The interference range covers a radial distance of 2.2 times of the transmission range (default value in NS2). The threshold value of the signal strength to be considered within a transmission range is 3.652e-10 W and a signal received up to 1.559e-11 W is considered to be within an interference range.

$$Cross\_Over_{distance} = 4\pi h_t h_r / \lambda \tag{1}$$

$$P_t = P_r (4\pi d)^2 L / G_t G_r \lambda^2 \tag{2}$$

$$P_t = P_r d^4 L / G_t G_r h_t^2 h_r^2 \tag{3}$$

In this paper a Dumb Agent routing technique is used as it discovers a one hop path length. Initial route discovery packets are always sent with maximum transmission power since the node has no information about the location until RTS/CTS packets are exchanged. If the location information received through the exchanged control frames is unchanged for the communicating pair, then the distance need not be re-calculated. Based on the distance information and the minimum receiving signal strength i.e. RXthresh_, new transmission power is calculated using (2) for the Friss propagation model and uses (3) for Two Ray Ground propagation model. The Friss model is more efficient to Two Ray Ground propagation model when a distance of communication is short. Here in this paper both the propagation models are considered and the node activates to one of the propagation models based on the distance between the communicating pair. A crossover distance between the two communicating nodes is calculated using (1). Crossover distance is a critical distance after which the received power decays with an order of d^4, so whenever the distance crosses the crossover distance Two Ray ground propagation model is used, otherwise Friss model is considered. Authors of [23] analyse and concludes that the Two Ray Ground propagation model also has its own limitations in real life application in comparison to basic Freespace model like Friss and the authors introduces a new propagation model based on the phase difference of interfering signals and a reflection coefficient which yields to a better results for an unobstructed communication between the sender and the receiver.

The algorithm for adjusting the transmission power for a routing packets using Dumb Agent, any MAC control frames RTS/CT/ACK and Data packets is described in Table 1 and a record of the RTS/CTS frames of all the active neighbour nodes is maintained by each node as shown in Table 2. The node records the IDs of the source-destination pair of the active neighbours, the timestamp of the frame, the position information of the active neighbour, and the NAV duration information. During updating the active neighbour table, records with a timestamp older than T second from the current time are removed from the list, and here in this paper T = 1 s is considered, it is done in order to maintain the freshness of the network condition and remove the entry of those nodes which are no longer active.

Table 1. Algorithm for adjusting the transmission power.

When node i has to transmit to node j

$\texttt{If}\,[Pkt_{type} == Routing]\,\texttt{then}$
$\quad\texttt{If}\,[(ID_i^{Sent_{cts}} \rightarrow ID_j) == Yes\,|\,|\,(ID_j^{Received_{cts}} \leftarrow ID_i) == Yes\,]\,\texttt{then}$
$\quad\quad\quad Transmission\_Power_i = Power_{New}$
$\quad\texttt{Else}$
$\quad\quad\quad Transmission\_Power_i = Power_{Max}$

$\texttt{Else If}\,[Pkt_{type} == PT_{MAC}\&\&PT_{MAC} = RTS\,||\,PT_{MAC} = CTS\,]\,\texttt{then}$
$\quad\texttt{If}\,[RTS\_CTS\underset{i\,to\,j}{\xrightarrow{Sent}} \geq 1]\,\texttt{then}$
$\quad\quad\quad Transmission\_Power_i = Power_{New}$
$\quad\texttt{Else}$
$\quad\quad\quad Transmission\_Power_i = Power_{Max}$
$\texttt{Else If}\,[Pkt_{type} == PT_{MAC}\&\&PT_{MAC} = ACK\,||\,PT_{MAC} = DATA]\,\texttt{then}$
$\quad\quad\quad Transmission\_Power_i = Power_{New}$

Table 2. Algorithm for collecting active neighbour information

---

When node i overheard packet/frame from node j

$\texttt{If}\,[Power_{recv} \geq RXthresh\_\&\&Dst_j \neq ID_i\&\&Pkt_{type} == RTS/CTS]\,\texttt{then}$
$\quad\texttt{If}\,[Record\_Count\_Neigh_i == 0]\,\texttt{then}$
$\quad\quad\quad Active_i^{Neighbour}[0] \leftarrow \{ID_j, Dst_j, Time_j, x_j, y_j, z_j, NAV_j\}$
$\quad\quad\quad\quad Record\_Count\_Neigh_i + +;$
$\quad\texttt{Else}$
$\quad\quad\texttt{For}\,[i = 0\,;\,i < Record\_Count\_Neigh_i\,;\,i + +]$
$\quad\quad\texttt{Do}$
$\quad\quad\quad\texttt{If}\,[Active_i^{Neighbour}[i].ID == ID_j\&\&Active_i^{Neighbour}[i].Dst == Dst_j]\,\texttt{then}$
$\quad\quad\quad\quad Active_i^{Neighbour}[i] \leftarrow \{Time_j, x_j, y_j, z_j, NAV_j\}$
$\quad\quad\quad\quad\texttt{Break};$
$\quad\quad\quad\texttt{Else If}[\,i + 1 == Record\_Count\_Neigh_i]$
$\quad\quad\quad\quad Active_i^{Neighbour}[i + 1] \leftarrow \{ID_j, Dst_j, Time_j, x_j, y_j, z_j, NAV_j\}$
$\quad\quad\quad\quad Record\_Count\_Neigh_i + +;$
$\quad\quad\quad\quad\texttt{Break};$
$\quad\quad\quad\texttt{Else}$
$\quad\quad\quad\quad\texttt{Continue};$
$\quad\quad\texttt{Done}$

3.2 Proposed Exponential Backoff Mechanism

The new backoff mechanism is designed based on active neighbour information. Each active node maintains three-level of degree of contention (C_d); where $C_d = 0$, if $Active_i^{Neighbour} = 0$; $C_d = 1$, if $Active_i^{Neighbour} \leq 2$; and $C_d = 2$, if $Active_i^{Neighbour} \geq 3$. The degree of contention (C_d) and the retrial number (r) controls the exponential contention window size as shown in (4). The contention random backoff value doubles whenever the transmission fails. When the number of active nodes within its transmission range is Low, Average and High, the maximum allowable contention window value is 255, 511 and 1023 respectively. If the calculated $CW_{C_d,r}$ goes beyond the given maximum contention window sizes then it takes the provided maximum values.

$$CW_{C_d,r} = \begin{cases} 2^{(3+C_d)} - 1; \; r = 0 \\ 2^{(3+C_d+r)} - 1; \; r \geq 1 \end{cases}$$

$$\text{Where: } C_d = \{\text{Low} = 0, \; \text{Average} = 1, \; \text{High} = 2\}$$

$$r = \{0, 1, 2, \ldots \ldots, 7\}$$

(4)

4   Evaluation and Discussion

The proposed cross layer transmission power controlled MAC was tested in different scenarios and benchmarked against the IEEE 802.11 and IEEE 802.11e standards. All simulations were carried out with NS2, version 2.35. with the network parameters listed in Table 3 and an antenna parameters such as Transmitter Gain ($G_t = 1.0$ dBd), Receiver Gain ($G_r = 1.0$ dBd), Height of Transmitter ($h_t = 1.5$ m), Height of receiver ($h_r = 1.5$ m), Frequency ($f = 914.0e6$ Hz), wavelength (λ) of the corresponding frequency, System Loss ($L = 1.0$) are considered.

Table 3. Network simulation setup.

Parameter	Value/protocol used
Grid Size	2000 m × 2000 m
Routing Protocol	DumbAgent
Queue Type	DropTail
Queue Size	100
Bandwidth	2 Mbps
SIFS	10 μs
DIFS	50 μs
Length of Slot	20 μs
$Power_{Max}$	0.28183815 W
Default RXThresh_	3.652e-10 W for 250 m
Default CSThresh_	1.559e-11 W for 550 m
CPThresh_	10.0
Max_{Retry}	7
Simulation Time	1000 s
Traffic Type	cbr
Packet size	1000 bytes

4.1   One Hop with a Single Source-Destination Pair

Since, LBT-NA Cross Layer MAC is a power control communication mechanism, when the communicating nodes are closer, the amount of energy spend is less compared to the situation when the communicating nodes are of greater distance. It is also considered that if a node is in a sleep mode then the amount of power consumed in a second is 0.001 W, when a node goes to an idle state from a sleep state it requires 0.2 W of power and the time required to wake up is 0.005 s. Each node is charged with 1000 Joules of energy and simulation is carried out for 1000 s. The transmission power of a node for LBT-NA Cross Layer MAC is adjusted as per the location of the destination node, but for the standard IEEE 802.11b and IEEE 802.11e, a fixed transmission power of 0.28183815 W is used.

By using the network parameters listed in Table 3 and a cbr traffic with an offered load of 2000 kb/s, Fig. 2 depicts the level of remaining energy of a source node when the communicating nodes are static with an initial distance of 50 m and then the communicating distance is increased by a factor of 10 m after every n rounds of simulations up to a maximum distance of 250 m.When the communicating nodes are separated only by 50 m, then the amount of energy the source saves using LBT-NA Cross Layer MAC is 38 % over IEEE 802.11b, 35 % over IEEE 802.11e with highest priority traffic and 40 % over IEEE 802.11e with lowest priority traffic. Even when the source and the distance is 250 m away from each other, a node using LBT-NA Cross Layer MAC still uses less energy due to the use of new backoff mechanism where a node with less active neighbours backs off with smaller value as described in Sect. 3.2.

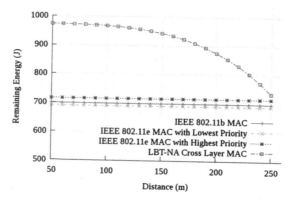

Fig. 2.   Remaining energy of data traffic generator vs distance of communication.

Figure 3 shows the remaining level of energy of a destination node when the distance of communication with the source increases. IEEE 802.11b and IEEE 802.11e use a constant energy unlike LBT-NA Cross Layer MAC due to the fixed transmission power method. The new protocol performs better in terms of saving energy even at the destination node. A small range of backoff value (0–7) is used in LBT-NA Cross Layer MAC when there are no active neighbours and in that of IEEE 802.11e with highest priority traffic, so it saves more energy to that of IEEE 802.11b and IEEE 802.11e with lowest priority traffic since sensing and waiting time is reduced. In a long distance communication, IEEE 802.11e with highest priority traffic saves more energy to that of LBT-NA Cross Layer MAC. When the distance of communication is short, the amount of energy saved by a destination node using LBT-NA Cross Layer MAC is 8 % over the standard IEEE 802.11b, 4 % over the node using IEEE 802.11e with traffic flowing with lowest priority.

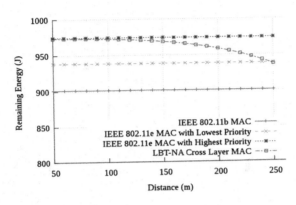

Fig. 3. Remaining energy of a receiver vs distance of communication.

4.2 Multiple Sources with Parallel Communication

Considering the topology shown in Fig. 1, where node B sends to node A and node C sends to node D, both the sources are exposed to each other, when the nodes uses a fixed transmission range of 250 m, so the bandwidth is shared. But when the proposed LBT-NA Cross Layer MAC is used, parallel communication is possible because node B's interference range (220 m for a transmission range of 100 m) does not disturb the sending activity of node C, and vice versa, so the overall network performance enhances.

Figure 4, confirms that using a fixed maximum transmission power methods like IEEE 802.11 cannot exhibit parallel transmission for a topology arrangement shown in Fig. 1 and the network saturates faster when the offered per flow loads are 710 kb/s and 450 kb/s for IEEE 802.11b and IEEE 802.11e respectively, unlike the newly proposed MAC which saturates at a very high data rate 1425 kb/s. It shows a performance gain of above 100 % over IEEE 802.11b and a gain of above 300 % over IEEE 802.11e MAC. Since the numbers of active nodes around each active source are few, the new backoff mechanism further enhances the overall network performance.

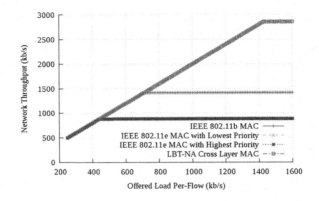

Fig. 4. Network performance with parallel transmission.

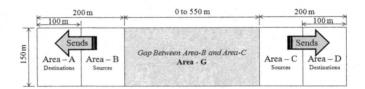

Fig. 5. Random topology with fixed boundaries

4.3 Random Topology

Since, IEEE 802.11e MAC is not competitive in terms of network performance; hereafter the proposed MAC, LBT-NA Cross Layer MAC is compared only with IEEE 802.11b MAC. In order to validate the robustness and test the performance of the proposed technique, a more realistic random topology with a defined space boundary is considered as shown in Fig. 5, using the network parameters listed in Table 3. The topology space is divided into four 150 m × 100 m sections with same areal space called Area-A, Area-B, Area-C and Area-D, with each section containing 10 nodes which are placed randomly. The fifth areal section called Area-G is considered with its areal length varied from (0 m to 550 m) × 150 m to separate Area-B and Area-C. Destination nodes are selected randomly, from Area-A and Area-D for the random sources which are picked from Area-B and Area-C respectively. The space divided as shown in Fig. 5 allows any node deployed in one section can communicate with a node deployed with the next consecutive sectional area with one hop communication, considering that the maximum transmission range is 250 m. The Area-G which separates the areal sections Area-B and Area-C is increased by a factor of 10 m and analysed the overall network performance using a UDP connection with cbr application as well as TCP traffic with same packet sizes of 1000 bytes. The per flow data rate offered in the network is 2000 kb/s in case of cbr traffic.

Figure 6 shows the network performance of a random network topology setup of Fig. 5. As the Area-G widens the network performance of the proposed protocol LBT-NA Cross Layer MAC increases rapidly unlike a fixed transmission range methods where the performance increases only after the length of the Area-G is greater than 270 m. When the length of the Areal-G is 200 m, the performance gain of cbr and tcp traffic of the proposed method against the IEEE 802.11b is 73 % and 63 % respectively. Such increased in performance is due to increase in probability of parallel transmission of the exposed sources. During network saturation and areal reused, use of low contention window for less active neighbours leads to a gain of 30 kb/s in case of cbr traffic in LBT-NA Cross Layer MAC over IEEE 802.11b, but for tcp traffic such method leads to reduction of sliding window and results in lowering the performance.

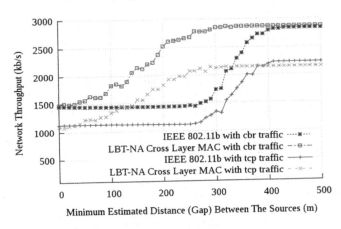

Fig. 6. Network performance of random sources and destinations

5 Conclusion and Future Direction

This paper proposed a new MAC called LBT-NA Cross Layer MAC where transmission power is controlled based on the location and uses a new random backoff values based on the number of the active neighbour around the node. In such mechanism, the performance of the network in terms of spatial and bandwidth reuse are better compared to a fixed transmission range methods. The durability of the battery life increases since, the system uses only the required transmission power during communication, and moreover the backoff values is directly proportional to the number of active neighbours, there is a performance gain of 30 kb/s when cbr traffic is used at a saturation region. The proposed protocol is also tested with random topologies to validate and investigate its efficiency.

Future work will be focussed on estimating power instead of using location information and considers signal strength of active neighbour's transmission to provide fairness and uses a dynamic Extended Inter Frame Spacing (EIFS) instead of using a fixed one as considered in IEEE 802.11 series when packet error or collision or capture occurred; since packets are generally of different sizes.

References

1. Marchang, J., Ghita, B., Lancaster, D.: Hop-based dynamic fair scheduler for wireless ad-hoc networks. In: 2013 IEEE International Conference on Advanced Networks and Telecommunications Systems (ANTS), pp. 1–6, 15–18 December 2013. doi:10.1109/ANTS.2013.6802873
2. Douros, V.G., Polyzos, G.C.: Review of some fundamental approaches for power control in wireless networks. Comput. Commun. **34**(13), 1580–1592 (2011). doi:10.1016/j.comcom.2011.03.001. ACM Digital Library
3. Pradhan, N.L., Saadawi, T.: Power control algorithms for mobile ad hoc networks. J. Adv. Res. **2**(3), 199–206 (2011). Science Direct
4. Patnaik, L.M., Hasan Raza Naqvi, S.: A review of medium access protocols for mobile ad hoc networks with transmission power control. Microprocess. Microsyst. **28**(8), 447–455 (2004)
5. Zhao, Z., Zhang, X., Sun, P., Liu, P.: A transmission power control MAC protocol for wireless sensor networks. In: Sixth International Conference on Networking, ICN 2007, vol. 5, p. 5, 22–28 April 2007
6. Muqattash, A., Krunz, M.: A single-channel solution for transmission power control in wireless ad hoc networks. In: Proceedings of the 5th ACM International Symposium on Mobile ad hoc Networking and Computing (MobiHoc 2004), pp. 210–221. ACM, New York (2004)
7. Muqattash, A., Krunz, M.: POWMAC: a single-channel power-control protocol for throughput enhancement in wireless ad hoc networks. IEEE J. Sel. Areas Commun. **23**(5), 1067–1084 (2005)
8. Li, P., Geng, X., Fang, Y.: An adaptive power controlled MAC protocol for wireless ad hoc networks. IEEE Trans. Wireless Commun. **8**(1), 226–233 (2009)
9. Kim, D., Shim, E., Toh, C.K.: A power control MAC protocol based on fragmentation for 802.11 multi-hop networks. In: Chong, I., Kawahara, K. (eds.) ICOIN 2006. LNCS, vol. 3961, pp. 227–236. Springer, Heidelberg (2006)
10. Li, Y., Ephremides, A.: A joint scheduling, power control, and routing algorithm for ad hoc wireless networks. Ad Hoc Netw. **5**(7), 959–973 (2007). Science Direct
11. Wei, W., Srinivasan, V., Chua, K.-C.: Power control for distributed MAC protocols in wireless ad hoc networks. IEEE Trans. Mob. Comput. **7**(10), 1169–1183 (2008)
12. Seth, D.D., Patnaik, S., Pal, S.: EPCM – an efficient power controlled MAC protocol for mobile ad hoc network. Int. J. Electron. **101**(10), 1443–1457 (2014). Taylor & Francis Online
13. Shih, K.-P., Chen, Y.-D.: CAPC: a collision avoidance power control MAC protocol for wireless ad hoc networks. IEEE Commun. Lett. **9**(9), 859–861 (2005)
14. Jung, E.-S., Vaidya, N.H.: A power control MAC protocol for ad hoc networks. Wireless Netw. **11**(1–2), 55–66 (2005). Springer
15. Varvarigos, E.A., Vasileios, G., Nikolaos, K.: The slow start power controlled MAC protocol for mobile ad hoc networks and its performance analysis. Ad Hoc Netw. **7**(6), 1136–1149 (2009). Science Direct
16. Cui, M., Syrotiuk, V.R.: Time-space backoff for fair node throughput in wireless networks using power control. Ad Hoc Netw. **8**(7), 767–777 (2010). ACM Digital Library
17. Chen, Y., Sirer, E.G., Wicker, S.B.: On selection of optimal transmission power for ad hoc networks. In: Proceedings of the 36th Annual Hawaii International Conference on System Sciences, January 2003

18. He, J., Yang, J., An, C., Li, X.: Transmission power selection for ad hoc networks. In: Proceedings of the 4th Annual International Conference on Wireless Internet (WICON 2008). ICST (Institute for Computer Sciences, Social-Informatics and Telecommunications Engineering), Brussels, Belgium, Article 18, p. 9 (2008)
19. Cui, H., Wei, G., Zhang, Z., Zhang, J.: Medium access control scheme supporting real-time traffic with power control in wireless ad hoc networks. IET Commun. 4(4), 377–383 (2010)
20. Sánchez, S.M., Souza, R.D., Fernandez, E.M.G., Reguera, V.A.: Rate and energy efficient power control in a cognitive radio ad hoc network. IEEE Signal Process. Lett. 20(5), 451–454 (2013)
21. Ramaiyan, V., Kumar, A., Altman, E.: Optimal Hop Distance and Power Control for a Single Cell, Dense, Ad Hoc Wireless Network. IEEE Trans. Mob. Comput. 11(11), 1601–1612 (2012)
22. Liu, C.-H., Rong, B., Cui, S.: Optimal discrete power control in poisson-clustered ad hoc networks. IEEE Trans. Wireless Commun. 14(1), 138–151 (2015)
23. Sommer, C., Dressler, F.: Using the right two-ray model? A measurement based evaluation of PHY models in VANETs. In: Proceedings of 17th ACM International Conference on Mobile Computing and Networking (MobiCom 2011), Poster Session, Las Vegas, NV, September 2011

Message Transmission Scheduling on Tandem Multi-hop Lossy Wireless Links

Agussalim$^{(\boxtimes)}$ and Masato Tsuru

Graduate School of Computer Science and System Engineering,
Kyushu Institute of Technology, Fukuoka, Japan
agussalim@infonet.cse.kyutech.ac.jp,
tsuru@cse.kyutech.ac.jp
http://nmlab.cse.kyutech.ac.jp

Abstract. This paper proposes a framework for message transmission scheduling on a simple tandem multi-hop transmission model with lossy unreliable wireless links, where each of N nodes periodically generates a message every T time-slots. Such a model is of practical importance, e.g., in low-cost serially-arranged sensor networks in the wild. Each message can be transmitted to an adjacent in a single time-slot, and should be relayed in a store-wait-and-forward manner from its source node to one of gateways at the edges of the tandem within T time-slots. Our framework consists of: (i) a static global time-slot assignment over all links analytically derived by a central server; and (ii) a local message selection for transmission with a simple XOR network coding-based proactive recovery over assigned time-slots on each link. Simulation results show the probability that all messages are successfully delivered to the server (via gateways) by the proposed framework is comparable to or even better than that by ACK-based reactive recovery schemes.

Keywords: Transmission · Scheduling · Tandem · Multi-hop · Lossy · Wireless · Networks

1 Introduction

Multi-hop wireless networks consist of multiple wireless nodes collaborating to provide communications between sources and destinations distributed in geographically different places. Such networks are of practical importance due to their lower cost, rapid deployment, and flexibility compared with wired networks in connecting or covering nodes in an area where single-hop wireless networking is not sufficient. Moreover, transmission over multiple "short" links might require less transmission power and energy than over "long" links.

Due to the nature of wireless radio communications, there are two fundamental issues in multi-hop wireless networks that significantly impact on data transmission performance; lossy unreliable wireless radio links, and conflicts (interferences) among simultaneous transmissions on adjacent links (or links within

© IFIP International Federation for Information Processing 2016
Published by Springer International Publishing Switzerland 2016. All Rights Reserved
L. Mamatas et al. (Eds.): WWIC 2016, LNCS 9674, pp. 28–39, 2016.
DOI: 10.1007/978-3-319-33936-8_3

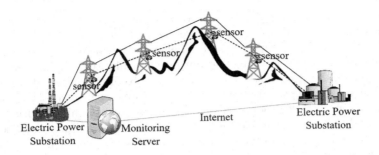

Fig. 1. Real-world facility monitoring scenario

an interference range) using the same radio frequency channels [3], especially in using non-directional (omnidirectional) antenna.

Recovery of lost messages can be considered either in a reactive manner, i.e., ACK and NACK-based re-transmission (ARQ), or in a proactive manner i.e., message-level forward erasure correction (FEC) and bit-level forward error correction. On the other hand, two types of Media Access Control (MAC) schemes can be considered to avoid/reduce simultaneous transmission conflictions, the contention-based such as CSMA/CA and the scheduling-based such as Time Division Media Access (TDMA).

Fang, et al. [4] proposed XOR-based network coding to the loss recovery of reliable broadcast transmission in wireless networks. Sagduyu, et al. [5] implemented network coding in tandem network case, they considered the problem of network coding in wireless queuing networks with tandem topology. In earlier work of TDMA scheduling, it is based on distributed implementation, i.e., [6] proposed a distributed implementation of RAND, a randomized time slot scheduling algorithm, called DRAND. Otherwise, the shortest schedules is proposed in [7], which introduced two centralized algorithms. Zeng, et al. [8] proposed a new scheduling algorithm based on the collaboration of nodes to resolve the slot collision when nodes try to assign slots to them.

In this paper, we target a tandem multi-hop transmission model on static (stationary) nodes with lossy unreliable wireless links, which can be seen in facility monitoring scenarios where multiple stationary nodes (sensors that can relay messages) are serially arranged along a road, river, or power transmission tower network as shown in Fig. 1. In this example, a stationary sensor node located at each power transmission tower monitors the facility and periodically generates a monitoring message. Each message is relayed on a lossy unreliable wireless link between two neighbour sensor nodes, which is eventually bound for a single central management server via one of the gateways at the both edges of the network, e.g., electric power substations.

We propose a framework for message transmission scheduling on tandem multi-hop lossy wireless links that consists of; (i) a static global time-slot assignment over all links to avoid unnecessary interferences, (ii) a local message selection for transmission including a naive XOR network coding-based redundant transmission for proactive recovery over assigned time-slots on each link to recover lost messages. Item (i) is analytically derived by a central high-performance server based on each individual link's message loss rate (which is assumed to be stable over some time duration), while item (ii) is light-weight and simply done by each node. We do not need to assume any advanced but complicated physical layer and MAC layer functions such as adaptive moderation, interference cancellation, CSMA/CA, high-dimensional network coding, and ACK/NACK-based reactive recovery. On the other hand, to realize item (i), we need to assume a protocol between the server and each node by which the server can estimate the loss rate of each link averaged over some time interval and can inform each node of the global scheduling decision. This mechanism is not treated in this paper and remains as future work.

The rest of this paper is organized as follows. In Sect. 2, we describe a system model used in this paper. In Sect. 3, we provide the proposed message transmission scheduling scheme. Section 4 presents evaluation and discussion through simulation results. Finally, Sect. 5 concludes the paper. This paper is an extended version of [1,2].

2   Tandem Multi-hop Transmission Model

A simplified tandem multi-hop transmission model (Fig. 2) is used in which n nodes ($j = 1, 2, \ldots, n$) are connected in tandem and each node periodically generates a message at the beginning of every "one circle" (consisting of T time-slots [e.g., sec]). A message generated at source node k is denoted as message k ($k = 1, \ldots, n$). Each message can be transmitted on a link from a node to an adjacent in a single time-slot, should be relayed in a store-wait-and-forward manner from its source node to either of two gateways (X and Y) at the edges of the tandem, and then will be forwarded from the gateway to central server S via a reliable network. Link j connects two nodes j and $j - 1$ with loss rate q_j ($0 < q_j < 1$) that is the probability of message loss on link j. We assume that each message should reach either node X or Y within T time-slots (i.e., within the current time circle).

We adopt a single directed model in which, for some separation node m, messages generated at nodes $1, 2, \ldots, m$ will be destined for X and those generated at nodes $m + 1, m + 2, \ldots, n$ will be destined for Y. We call it m-$(n - m)$ separation model. Figure 2 shows 3-$(n - 3)$ separation model where messages generated at nodes N_1, N_2, and N_3 are sent to gateway X and other messages

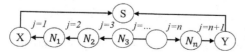

Fig. 2. Two-gateways single-directed model

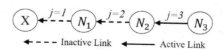

Fig. 3. Interference avoidance condition

are sent to Y. In this single directed model, we can treat each direction (each side of the separation model) independently after deciding a separation model. Therefore, in the proposed scheme, for a given separation model, we analytically derive a good (possible best) performance static global time-slot assignment for each side and compute the total performance by combining both sides, i.e., both directions, of the model. By examining the best performance of each possible separation model in this way and comparing them, we can finally select the best performed one among all possible global time-slot assignments with all possible separation models in response to environmental conditions.

3 Proposed Message Transmission Scheduling

The proposed framework consists of:

- a static global time-slot assignment over all links with a choice of separation model, and
- a local message selection for transmission including a naive XOR network coding-based redundant transmission for proactive recovery over assigned time-slots on each link,

which should be appropriately combined in order to statically avoid conflicts among simultaneous transmissions on adjacent links or links within an interference range, and at the same time, to redundantly but efficiently send messages on lossy links.

3.1 Static Global Time-Slot Assignment

A static global time-slot assignment is considered to avoid conflicts among simultaneous transmissions on adjacent links as well as to give more chances to redundant transmission to worse (i.e., more lossy) links. At each time-slot, one or more links are assigned as active, and on each active link, a message can be transmitted in this time-slot. The active links are statically and globally determined, and not changed regardless of each transmission result. We assume that wireless transmission of a message at node j affects two adjacent nodes $j-1$ and $j+1$. For example, in Fig. 3, N_1 and N_3 should not send messages to the next nodes at the same time-slot to avoid interference at N_2. This simple and homogeneous assumption is for conciseness and can be changed accompanied with a more complicated constraint condition on time-slot assignment.

To derive an "optimal" static time-slot assignment with static message selection for re-transmission of original messages, we adopt the product of the success delivery probabilities for each individual node as the objective function to be maximized. This objective function can be interpreted as the probability that all messages are successfully delivered to the server if the message losses on links are independent. Although there are diverse possible patterns for static global time-slot assignment that can avoid conflicts among simultaneous transmissions on adjacent links, we can consider "the links far from the destination (upper-side links) first" restricted patterns without loss of generality in optimization for the above objective function.

Given (fixed) node k, we focus only on message k (a message generated by node k) that is destined for gateway X. Like Fig. 4, the message transmission scheduling according to a static time-slot assignment with static message selection for re-transmission of original messages is as follows.

1. First, send the message on the first hop link, i.e., link k, to node $k-1$ during u_k time slots repeatedly.
2. Next, on the second hop link (link $k-1$), send the message to node $k-2$ in u_{k-1} times similarly,
3. Do it in a similar manner to descendant of the link and so forth, and
4. Finally on the last hop link (link 1), send it to X in u_1 times.

For conciseness, we explain the optimization in one direction (i.e., on one side of a separation model) with an example in 5-node case shown in Fig. 5. Note that this optimization example for 5-nodes can be reduced to 4 nodes and be extended to more than 5 nodes accompanied with different condition analysis.

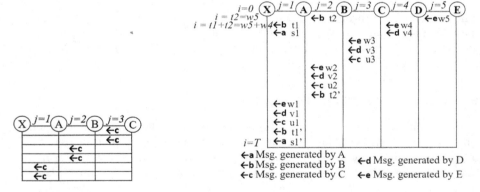

Fig. 4. An assignment pattern for message C

Fig. 5. Five-nodes case example

In this case, since the number of nodes in a single direction exceeds three, there are two or more links that can be active at the same time-slot (i.e., they can transmit messages simultaneously) because they are displaced and not interfered. This makes the possible assignment patterns more complicated than a very simple one like Fig. 4. For example, messages generated at nodes E and B can be transmitted simultaneously at the same time slot. As a result, messages generated at node B may be transmitted on link 2 and link 1 with two separated durations. In such situations, we introduce a term "early-stage transmission", for the transmission in possible time-slots (stage) earlier than the normally assigned time-slots, to be distinguished from "normal-stage transmission". If the number of nodes in one direction increases, there can be more than one early-stages for some links close to the gateway.

The whole static scheduling is represented as follows.

- s_1, s_1': the number of time-slots on link 1 for a message from A (message A in short) for early-stage transmission and for normal-stage transmission, respectively.
- t_1, t_1': the number of time-slots on link 1 for message B, for early-stage transmission and for normal-stage transmission, respectively.
- t_2, t_2': the number of time-slots on link 2 for message B, for early-stage transmission and for normal-stage transmission, respectively.
- u_j ($j = 1, 2, 3$): the number of time-slots on link j for message C.
- v_j ($j = 1, 2, 3, 4$): the number of time-slots on link j for message D.
- w_j ($j = 1, 2, \ldots, 5$): the number of time-slots on link j for message E.

On the above assignment pattern, the success delivery probabilities of each node, $M_1, M_2, \ldots, M_5$ have explicit forms by using $q_1, \ldots, q_5$ ($0 < q_j < 1$) which are message loss rates on links $1, \ldots, 5$, respectively.

The optimization problem to find $\mathbf{x} = (s_1, s_1', t_1, t_1', t_2, t_2', u_1, u_2, u_3, v_1, \ldots, w_5)$ is as follows.

$$\max_{\mathbf{x}} \prod_{k=1}^{5} M_k(\mathbf{x}), \tag{1}$$

$$\text{subject to } s_1' + t_1' + t_2' + u_1 + u_2 + u_3 + v_1 + v_2 + v_3 + v_4$$
$$w_1 + w_2 + w_3 + w_4 + w_5 = T, \tag{2}$$

$$t_2 = w_5, \tag{3}$$

$$s_1 + t_1 = w_4 + v_4, \tag{4}$$

where

$$M_1 = 1 - q_1^{s_1 + s_1'}$$
$$M_2 = (1 - q_1^{t_1 + t_1'})(1 - q_2^{t_2}) + (1 - q_1^{t_1'})(1 - q_2^{t_2'})(q_2^{t_2})$$
$$M_3 = (1 - q_1^{u_1})(1 - q_2^{u_2})(1 - q_3^{u_3})$$
$$M_4 = (1 - q_1^{v_1})(1 - q_2 v_2)(1 - q_3^{v_3})(1 - q_4^{v_4})$$
$$M_5 = (1 - q_1^{w_1})(1 - q_2^{w_2})(1 - q_3^{w_3})(1 - q_4^{w_4})(1 - q_5^{w_5})$$

This can be numerically solved by a greedy approach in Integer Programming in general. However, as a more efficient way, we first apply Lagrange optimization method to a "relaxed" version allowing real number solutions, and obtain a real number solution of this relaxed problem. Then we search a good integer solution around the above real number solution. See Appendix for more details.

3.2 XOR Network Coding-Based Message Selection

Network coding is an approach that allows each network (relay) node to generate a new message by combining more than one relayed messages. In a proactive

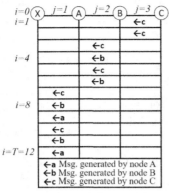
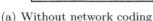

(a) Without network coding

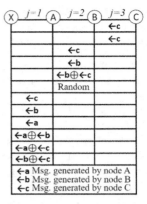

(b) With network coding

Fig. 6. Simple XOR network coding

recovery scheme for lost messages, network coding can be used as dynamic and inter-flow forward erasure correction (FEC) in multi-hop wireless transmission. After deciding a static time-slot assignment by the procedure in Subsect. 3.1, we adopt a fair message selection with naive XOR network coding-based message transmission, in which each node can send an encoded message that is an XOR-combination of available original messages at the node.

Table 1. Link loss rate setting examples

Case	q_1	q_2	q_3	q_4	q_5	q_6	q_7	q_8	q_9
1	0.1	0.2	0.3	0.2	0.3	0.3	0.2	0.1	0.2
2	0.6	0.1	0.1	0.3	0.3	0.2	0.3	0.2	0.1

At each time-slot assigned to the link, one of original or encoded messages is selected to be sent on the link. To make sure that each message has the same chance to be selected, the transmission counter for each message records how many times the message is selected. Original messages, or messages with the lowest value of transmission counter have high priority to select first, then encoded messages will be selected randomly according to the transmission counter value. When all messages have the same transmission counter value, one message will be randomly selected. Figure 6(a) and (b) shows message transmission scheduling examples without and with network coding implementation.

4   Evaluation and Discussion

For model-based numerical simulation and evaluation, the proposed framework is implemented by Java, and a 8-nodes tandem multi-hop lossy wireless network

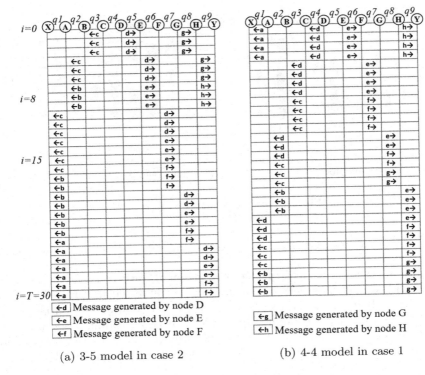

(a) 3-5 model in case 2

(b) 4-4 model in case 1

Fig. 7. Slot assignment and separation model

is examined with two different link loss rate settings (Cases 1 and 2) in Table 1. The total number (T) of time-slots for one time circle is set to 30, 45 and 60.

4.1 Static Slot Assignment with Separation Model

As explained in Sect. 2, we can find a "good (possibly best)" static global time-slot assignment with a "good (possibly best)" separation model by applying the proposed optimization in one direction explained in Subsect. 3.1 for each setting (i.e., Cases 1 and 2 in Table 1 using $T = 30, 45, 60$). Figure 7(a) and (b) shows the obtained good static time-slot assignments for 3–5 model in Case 2, and for 4-4 model in Case 1, respectively, in case of $T = 30$. In the following simulation evaluation (i.e. Subsects. 4.2 and 4.3), we use Case 2 which is an example of sever situations with imbalanced link loss rates. In Case 2, the best separation is 3–5 model shown in Fig. 7(a).

4.2 Performance of Static Slot Assignment with Simple XOR Network Coding-Based Message Selection

We introduce a comparative static time-slot assignment method in which the number assigned slots for each link is proportional to both the number of message

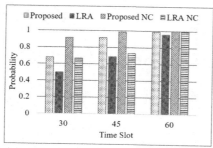
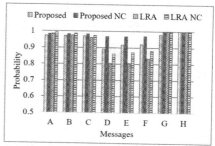

(a) All messages in different static time-slot assignments

(b) Each message in different static time-slot assignments with $T = 30$

Fig. 8. Success delivery probability

paths passing the link and the loss rate of the link. We call it Loss Rate Aware (LRA).

Figure 8(a) shows the performance comparison of static time-slot assignment method with static message selection using $T = 30, 45, 60$ in term of success delivery probability of all message. Our proposed method always outperforms the LRA method. Next, we employ simple XOR network coding-based message selection scheme (NC) to all of static slot assignment methods (proposed, and LRA). In general implementation of NC improves the performance all of static time-slot assignment methods.

Figure 8(b) shows success delivery probability of each message using $T = 30$. In general, the message generated at the upper-side nodes (the nodes far from its gateway) suffer from a more opportunities of message loss in traveling multiple lossy links. On the other hand, the balance among messages (i.e., source nodes) varies depending on the time-slot assignment. In LRA NC method which also gives importance on link loss rate, message A and B have higher success delivery probabilities. In Proposed NC method, a most fair balance among messages is exhibited.

4.3 Performance Comparison with ACK-Based Methods

As comparative approach, Acknowledgement (ACK)-based reactive recovery is considered. We introduce two ACK-based message transmission methods; Limited-ACK (L-ACK) and Unlimited-ACK (U-ACK). In L-ACK, the sender-side node will attempt to transmit a message on a given link until either an ACK for the message is returned or the number of transmissions reach the total number of time-slots consecutively assigned to the link by the static assignment. When two different messages should be sent on a link within an assigned number of consecutive time-slots, if transmissions of the first message exhaust the assigned time-slots, then the second message cannot be sent at all. In contrast, U-ACK is independent of a given static time-slot assignment. In U-ACK, the sender-side node will attempt to transmit a message on a given link until ACK for the message is returned, and repeat this process until ACKs for all messages are returned. This process will be repeated from the source node to each downstream node, i.e., upper-side links first until all T time-slots in one time-circle are exhausted. There is no limitation on the number of re-transmissions both for each message and for each link.

In addition, to reflect realistic conditions, we implement a reverse direction loss and delay of ACK by artificially increasing the loss rate value for each link by multiplying 1.2 and 1.4 for U-ACK and decreasing the total number (T) of time-slots by multiplying 0.8 for U-ACK and L-ACK, respectively. We also consider "ideal" ACK with no overhead and no loss to investigate the upper bound performance. In ideal ACK, when a message is successfully received by the receiver-side node, the sender-side node immediately knows that without any time delay and error.

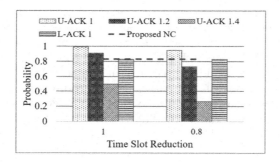

Fig. 9. Success delivery probability of all messages for ACK-based methods and proposed NC method with $T = 30$

Figure 9 compares the success delivery probability of all messages by the proposed NC method and ACK-based methods. The ideal condition (with no loss and delay of ACK) are identified as time-slot reduction of 1 by indicating the x-axis and the legend names of U-ACK 1 and L-ACK 1. The realistic conditions (with reverse loss and delay) is identified as time-slot reduction of 0.8 (that is $T = 24$ instead of 30) and legend names U-ACK 1.2 and U-ACK 1.4. When there is no time slot reduction, U-ACK 1 outperforms Proposed NC and L-ACK 1, in consistent with our expectation that the "ideal" U-ACK 1 will show the upper-bound performance in terms of the success delivery probability of all messages.

On the other hand, Proposed NC achieves the same performance of L-ACK 1 with no loss and no delay. Then, in realistic conditions (i.e., the number of time slots is reduced from 30 to 24, and the link loss rates are increased) for ACK-based methods, Proposed NC achieves the same performance of U-ACK 1.2. These results suggest that Proposed NC is comparable to or better than ACK-based methods in realistic conditions.

In ideal condition, ACK-based reactive recovery of lost packets is resource efficient in theory compared to proactive recovery. However, implementation of ACK-based retransmission model will increase the cost and complexity of each node of a real system. In contrast, our scheme can assume very low-cost nodes while assuming a centralized management.

5   Conclusion and Future Work

In this research, we have proposed a framework for message transmission scheduling on tandem multi-hop transmission model with lossy wireless links. By applying mathematical optimization, we can obtain a static assignment solution for the number of time-slots that assigned to each link. We also have introduced a simple XOR network coding-based scheme for proactive message transmission on proposed static time-slot assignment. Simulation results showed the probability that all messages are successfully delivered to the server (via gateways) by our proposed framework is comparable to and sometimes even better than that by ACK-based reactive recovery schemes which are more complex and costly. This suggests the effectiveness of our approach that combines a static global time-slot assignment (to avoid unnecessary interferences) and a local message selection for transmission with a simple network coding-based proactive message re-transmission (to recover lost messages). For large adaptability, we need to extend the model that can treat different scenarios such as heterogeneous message generation rates and more than two gateways (e.g., on a tree topology).

Acknowledgments. This work is supported by Directorate General of Resources for Science, Technology and Higher Education of Indonesia Government and partly supported by JSPS KAKENHI (25330108).

Appendix: Five Nodes Case Example

Applying Lagrangian method to the optimization problem consisting of Eqs. (1) – (4), we obtain:

$$
u_1 = v_1 = w_1 = -\frac{\log(1 - \alpha \log q_1)}{\log q_1},
$$

$$
u_2 = v_2 = w_2 = -\frac{\log(1 - \alpha \log q_2)}{\log q_2},
$$

$$
u_3 = v_3 = w_3 = -\frac{\log(1 - \alpha \log q_3)}{\log q_3},
$$

$$
v_4 = w_4 = -\frac{\log(1 - \alpha \log q_4)}{\log q_4},
$$

$$
t_2 = w_5 = -\frac{\log(1 - \alpha \log q_5)}{\log q_5} \tag{5}
$$

In addition, we can assume the solution satisfies:

- $s_1' + t_1'$ is minimized as long as $s_1 + s_1' \geq w_1$,
- if $t_2 = w_5 \geq w_2$ then an additional t_2' is not necessary any more.

The derivation procedure to get an optimal solution changes according to the relationship among q_1, q_2, q_4, q_5. More precisely, there are four conditions to be considered – (i) $q_2 \leq q_5$ and $q_1 > q_4$, (ii) $q_2 \leq q_5$ and $q_1 \leq q_4$, (iii) $q_2 > q_5$ and $q_1 > 2q_4$, (iv) $q_2 > q_5$ and $q_1 \leq 2q_4$.

In condition (ii),

- $q_2 \leq q_5$ implies $w_2 \leq w_5$ and $t_2' = 0$.
- $q_1 \leq q_4$ implies $w_1 \leq w_4$, suggesting $t_1 = w_1$, $s_1 = 2w_4 - w_1$ and $t_1' = s_1' = 0$.

Therefore α in Eq. (5) can be numerically determined by solving an irrational equation derived from Eq. (2) by substituting Eq. (5) and the above auxiliary relations.

In conditions (i) and (iii), a similar derivation can be applied. However, in condition (iv), the condition analysis becomes more complicated and there is no single irrational equation to decide a best solution. Instead, each of possible sub-conditions should be examined by solving a corresponding equation, and finally a best solution is decided by comparison. Note that, to apply the derivation to the right-hand side of a separation model, the node indexes are swapped accordingly. When considering the right-hand side of 3–5 separation model in Table 1, (q_9, q_8, q_7, q_6) will be renamed as (q_1, q_2, q_3, q_4).

References

1. Umar, F., Agussalim, Tsuru, M.: Message scheduling for tandem multi-hop wireless networks. In: Proceedings of IEEE APWiMob 2014, Indonesia, pp. 201–207, August 2014
2. Agussalim, Tsuru, M.: Static slot assignment with transmission scheduling on tandem multi-hop lossy wireless links. In: Proceedings of the IEICE Society Conference, Japan (2015)
3. Jain, K., Padhye, J., Padmanabhan, V., Qiu, L.: Impact of interference on multi-hop wireless network performance. In: Proceedings of the ACM MobiCom 2003, USA, pp. 66–80 (2003)
4. Fang, W., Liu, F., Liu, Z., Shu, L., Nishio, S.: Reliable broadcast transmission in wireless networks based on network coding. In: Proceedings of the IEEE INFOCOM Workshops 2011, Shanghai, pp. 555–559 (2011)
5. Sagduyu, Y.E., Ephremides, A.: Network coding in wireless queueing networks: Tandem network case. In: Proceedings of the IEEE International Symposium on Information Theory, USA, pp. 192–196 (2006)
6. Rhee, I., Warrier, A., Min, J., Xu, L.: DRAND: distributed randomized TDMA scheduling for wireless ad-hoc networks. IEEE Trans. Mob. Comput. **8**(10), 1384–1396 (2009)
7. Ergen, S.C., Varaiya, P.: TDMA scheduling algorithms for wireless sensor networks. Wireless Netw. **16**(4), 985–997 (2010)
8. Zeng, B., Dong, Y.: A collaboration-based distributed TDMA scheduling algorithm for data collection in wireless sensor networks. J. Netw. **9**(9), 2319–2327 (2014)

Influence of Backoff Period in Slotted CSMA/CA of IEEE 802.15.4

Ahmed Naseem Alvi[1(✉)], Safdar Hussain Bouk[2], Syed Hassan Ahmed[2],
and Muhammad Azfar Yaqub[2]

[1] Department of Electrical Engineering,
COMSATS Institute of Information Technology, Islamabad, Pakistan
naseem_alvi@comsats.edu.pk
[2] School of Computer Science and Engineering,
Kyungpook National University, Daegu, Korea
{bouk,hassan,yaqub}@knu.ac.kr

Abstract. Low rate wireless applications are under attraction since last decade. For such applications, IEEE designed a standard known as IEEE 802.15.4. The standard operates at 868, 915 and 2400 MHz with or without using super frame structure. Most of the low rate Wireless PAN applications follow superframe structure. A superframe structure comprises of contention based and contention free periods by offering slotted CSMA/CA and TDMA like operation respectively. This paper analyzes the performance of slotted CSMA/CA algorithm. CSMA/CA algorithm highly depends upon backoff period that is why its impact is analyzed in this work. The performance analysis is based on probability determined by using discrete markov chain model. The performance analysis comprises of nodes waiting time before transmission, channel busy probability and ultimately throughput and reliability is calculated. Results show that network reliability along with throughput of a wireless network increases gradually with the increase in backoff period at the cost of increase in average wait time of nodes.

Keywords: IEEE 802.15.4 · CSMA/CA · Markov chain · Backoff period

1 Introduction

Wireless technologies are developing swiftly as demand of wireless Sensor Networks (WSN) increases. There are number of WSN applications such as surveillance and monitoring. Wireless nodes in WSN are tiny in size having limited energy, computation, processing and communication capabilities. These limitations are not addressed at once by well known IEEE 802.11 and IEEE 802.16 as they consume more energy during idle listening. ZigBee is the most prominent alliance supporting low-power embedded systems and facilitates multiple

© IFIP International Federation for Information Processing 2016
Published by Springer International Publishing Switzerland 2016. All Rights Reserved
L. Mamatas et al. (Eds.): WWIC 2016, LNCS 9674, pp. 40–51, 2016.
DOI: 10.1007/978-3-319-33936-8_4

applications. It uses IEEE 802.15.4 standard at its physical and MAC (Medium Access Control) layer. IEEE 802.15.4 standard is suitable for energy efficient and low data rate applications. Some of these applications are environmental monitoring, light control systems, agricultural monitoring, automatic metering, industrial and security alarm system [1]. The standard suits well for static and low cost mobile wireless nodes having limited battery power with high reliability, as discussed in [2–4].

IEEE 802.15.4 runs at 868 MHz, 915 MHz and 2.4 GHz frequency bands. The standard operates in *Beacon* as well as in *Non-Beacon* enabled modes. Beacon mode comprises of Contention Access Period (CAP) and optional TDMA based Contention Free Period (CFP). During CAP, nodes follow slotted CSMA/CA mechanism. CSMA/CA depends upon multiple parameters, however, the most prominent one is the *backoff period* length. This paper contributes in analyzing the impact of varying backoff periods to determine the IEEE 802.15.4 performance. A comprehensive study of different backoff period lengths and their impact in slotted CSMA/CA, where all wireless nodes contend to access the medium and chances of collision are maximum, is also done in this work. The analysis is performed with fixed number of nodes and similar load variations.

Rest of the paper is organized as follows: In Sect. 2, the performance analysis of different authors in this field is discussed. Next Sect. 3 discusses the brief overview of IEEE 802.15.4 standard. Sections 4 and 5 illustrates slotted CSMA/CA algorithm and markov chain model respectively. Section 6, evaluates the effect of different parameters against varying backoff period and conclusion is described in Sect. 7.

2   Related Work

Contention access period of IEEE 802.15.4 is quite similar to IEEE 802.11. The only differences are that IEEE 802.15.4 starts sensing the availability of medium at the end of the backoff period and also it confirms the channel availability twice before transmitting its packets. Authors in [5–7] analyzed the performance of heterogeneous traffic under non saturated mode of IEEE 802.11 Distributed Coordination Function (DCF). In [5], authors presented an extended Bianchi model [8] for unsaturated heterogeneous data traffic of IEEE 802.11 DCF. Authors in [6] used discrete Markov chain model to find out the probability of utilization factor, throughput and delay for diverse traffic in a wireless LAN of IEEE 802.11e. Tickoo *et al.* in [7], considered homogeneous as well as heterogeneous data traffic to analyze the service time distribution of IEEE 802.11.

Many authors have analyzed IEEE 802.15.4 in different scenarios by highlighting its duty cycle and less energy consumption. Performance analysis of unslotted CSMA/CA in different prospects of the standard is analyzed by authors in [9,10]. In [11–13], many simulation based studies are discussed to evaluate the performance of the standard in different prospects. Pollin et al. in [14], used Markov chain model to determine the performance of slotted CSMA/CA of the standard with saturated traffic load. In [15], authors have analyzed the throughput of slotted CSMA/CA by applying enhanced Markov Chain model during un-saturated region. In this work we have explored the importance of backoff period in CSMA/CA operation of IEEE 802.15.4 and analyzed the effect of varying backoff period in novel way by following discrete Markov channel model described in [16].

3 IEEE 802.15.4 Overview

The standard is designed for both Physical and MAC layers by offering duty cycle even less than 0.1 %. The standard operates in three different frequency bands. Detail of all these frequency bands is shown in Table 1.

Table 1. Frequency Bands with Data Rate

Frequency Band (MHz)	Modulation Scheme	Symbols/sec	Bits/symbol	Symbol Duration (sec)	Data rate (bits/sec)
868 - 868.6	BPSK	20000	1	50*e-6	20000
902 - 928	BPSK	40000	1	25*e-6	40000
2400 - 2483.5	O-QPSK	62500	4	16*e-6	250000

IEEE 802.15.4 uses un-slotted CSMA/CA algorithm during non beacon enabled mode. However, superframe structure is applied in beacon enabled mode. Superframe structure comprises of active and inactive period. Beacon frame, Contention Access Period (CAP) and optional Contention Free Period (CFP) are part of active period as shown in Fig. 1, whereas the node remains in sleep mode during inactive period. Active period consists of 16 slots, out of these 16 slots, maximum 7 slots may be allocated for CFP and the rest consists of Beacon frame and CAP. All beacon enabled nodes contend to access the medium in transmitting data to its coordinator during CAP by following slotted CSMA/CA algorithm as shown in Fig. 3.

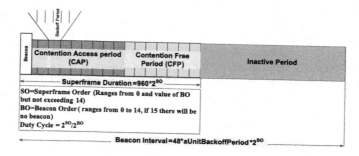

Fig. 1. Superframe structure with CAP and CFP

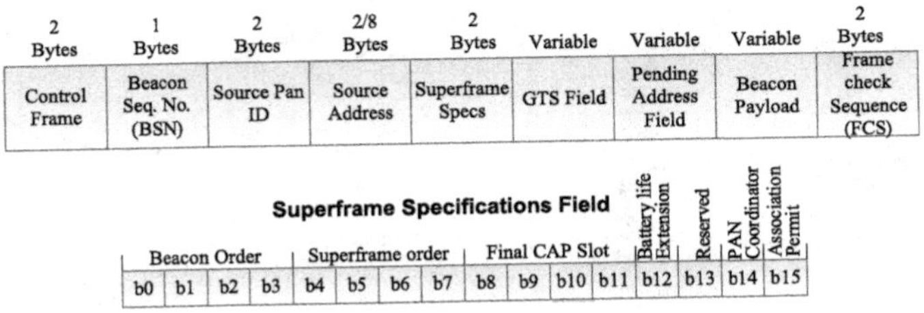

2 Bytes	1 Bytes	2 Bytes	2/8 Bytes	2 Bytes	Variable	Variable	Variable	2 Bytes
Control Frame	Beacon Seq. No. (BSN)	Source Pan ID	Source Address	Superframe Specs	GTS Field	Pending Address Field	Beacon Payload	Frame check Sequence (FCS)

Superframe Specifications Field

Beacon Order				Superframe order				Final CAP Slot				Battery life Extension	Reserved	PAN Coordinator	Association Permit
b0	b1	b2	b3	b4	b5	b6	b7	b8	b9	b10	b11	b12	b13	b14	b15

Fig. 2. Beacon frame with superframe specification field description

PAN coordinator is responsible for generating beacon frames in the network after regular intervals. These beacon frames are used to synchronize all the associated nodes in that WPAN. Information about active Superframe duration and arrival of next Beacon frame can be calculated from different parameters highlighted in the superframe specification field present in beacon frame. Superframe Duration (SD) and Beacon Interval (BI) is calculated as:

$$SD = 48 \times 2^{SO} \times aUnitBackoffPeriod \tag{1}$$

$$BI = 48 \times 2^{BO} \times aUnitBackoffPeriod \tag{2}$$

Expressions (1) and (2) show that the Superframe duration and Beacon Intervals mainly depend on $aUnitBackoffPeriod$ length. Varying the length of $aUnitBackoffPeriod$ highly affect the performance of CSMA/CA operation during active period of Superframe. That's why, the impact of varying backoff period is evaluated in this work (Fig. 2).

4 Slotted CSMA/CA Mechanism

During CAP of IEEE 802.15.4, slotted CSMA/CA mechanism is used that mainly comprises of three parameters as NB,BE and CW. NB is number of times, node should wait for backoff periods. Value of NB ranges from 0 to 4. This allows a node to attempt for maximum of 5 times in order to access the channel. If a node fails to find the channel idle for maximum allowed attempts, then it reports failure to its upper layer.

Parameter BE stands for *Backoff Exponent* and it describes the random range of backoff periods, a node should wait before assessing the channel availability. It ranges from 0 to $2^{BE} - 1$ and default value of BE ranges from 3 to 5 by following the parameters of $macMinBE$ and $aMaxBE$, respectively. This results in backoff period initial range from 0 to 7 and last backoff period range from 0 to 31.

Contention Window (CW) is related to idle channel availability by using Clear Channel Assessment (CCA). Initial value of CW is 2, that is node needs to pass the channel availability for two successive times before declaring the channel idle. Detailed flow diagram of CSMA/CA is shown in Fig. 3.

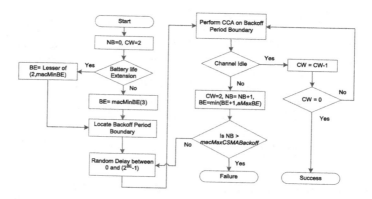

Fig. 3. Flow diagram of slotted CSMA/CA

Packets are transmitted only if computed frame's length along with its acknowledgment and inter-frame spacing can be completed within same active period.

A complete frame duration (CFD) consists of time required to transmit data with acknowledgment and is calculated as:

$$CFD = T_{BO} + T_D + 2T_P + T_{TA} + T_{Ack} + T_{IFS}$$

where,

T_{BO} = Waiting time during Backoff Periods,
T_D = Frame's transmitting time,
T_P = Propagation delay from source to destination,
T_{TA} = Turn around time,
T_{Ack} = Time for Acknowledgment frame, and
T_{IFS} = Time for Inter frame space.

5   Markov Chain Model for Slotted CSMA/CA of IEEE 802.15.4

The operation of slotted CSMA/CA is analyzed with the help of discrete Markov chain model. The model is implemented by considering such states where changes occur. Slotted CSMA/CA algorithm based on three basic parameters, NB, BE and CW as mentioned in Sect. 4. Similarly in this model, each state (A) defines NB(t), BC(t) and CW(t). Here NB(t) is the value of NB at time t and it ranges from 0 to m, where m = macMaxCSMABackoff. BC(t) indicates backoff counters in each state and its value ranges from 0 to W_{i-1}, where $W_i = 2^{BE}$ and can be computed as shown in Eq. 3. CW(t)[0, 2] represents contention windows. The state k, b, 2 represents that node is in its (k+1)th backoff period, where b represents backoff counter and 2 means node requires to perform CCA for two times. A discrete Markov chain model is shown in Fig. 4.

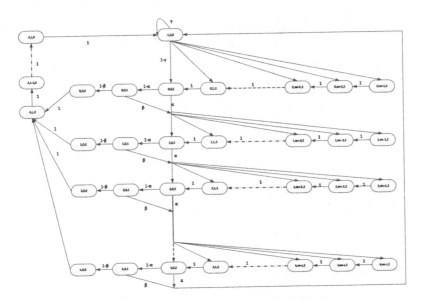

Fig. 4. Discrete time Markov chain model.

$$W_i = 2^{macMinBE} \times 2^{min\{aMaxBE-macMinBE,i\}} \tag{3}$$

Some of the states mentioned in the model are described as under.

{-1, 0, 0} idle state {k, 0, 2} node is going to perofrm CCA1 during (k+1)th time {k, 0, 1} node is about to perform CCA2 during (k+1)th time {k, 0, 0} node successfully passed the CCA1 and CCA2 {k, b, 2} node needs to wait for b backoff counter before performing CCA1 α busy medium probabilty during CCA1 β busy medium probabilty during CCA2 γ probability of node having no data to send

Suppose stationary probabilities of Markov chain is: $b_{k,b,c} = P\{NB(t) = k, BC(t) = b, CW(t) = c\} \forall$ k,b,c

From the markov chain model, we obtain

$$b_{k,0,2} = \alpha b_{k-1,0,2} + \beta b_{k-1,0,1} k\varepsilon[1, m] \tag{4}$$

From the Markov chain, we know that:

$$b_{-1,0,0} = p_{cf} + b_{-1,t,0} + \gamma b_{-1,0,0} \tag{5}$$

Here, p_{cf} is probability of channel access failure,

$$p_{cf} = \alpha b_{m,0,2} + \beta b_{m,0,1} \tag{6}$$

All these states are determined by following Eqs. 7 to 14

$$b_{k,0,0} = (1 - \beta)b_{0,0,1} \tag{7}$$

$$b_{k,0,2} = b_{0,0,2}(\alpha + \beta - \alpha\beta)^k \tag{8}$$

$$b_{k,0,1} = b_{0,0,2}(1 - \alpha)(\alpha + \beta - \alpha\beta)^k \tag{9}$$

Similarly $b_{k,0,0}$ is calculated as:

$$b_{k,0,0} = b_{0,0,2}(1 - \beta)(1 - \alpha)(\alpha + \beta - \alpha\beta)^k \tag{10}$$

$$b_{k,0,0} = b_{0,0,2}(1 - (\alpha + \beta - \alpha\beta)^{k+1}), k\varepsilon[0, m] \tag{11}$$

$$b_{k,0,0} = b_{-1,t,0} = b_{-1,t-1,0}, t\varepsilon[2, T] \tag{12}$$

$$b_{0,0,2} = b_{-1,0,0}(1 - \gamma) \tag{13}$$

$$b_{-1,0,0} = (b_{0,0,2})/(1 - \gamma) \tag{14}$$

$b_{k,p,2}$ can be represented with $b_{0,0,2}$ as:

$$b_{k,p,2} = b_{0,0,2}(\alpha + \beta - \alpha\beta)^k(W_k - p)/(W_k), k\varepsilon[1, m], p\varepsilon[1, W_k - 1] \tag{15}$$

Similarly $b_{0,p,2}$ can be represented with $b_{0,0,2}$ as:

$$b_{0,p,2} = b_{-1,0,0}(W_0 - p)(1 - \gamma)/(W_0) \tag{16}$$

By simultaneously solving 13 and 16, we get:

$$b_{0,p,2} = b_{0,0,2}(W_0 - p)/(W_0), Here p \varepsilon[1, W_0 - 1] \tag{17}$$

As sum of all the probabilities of the states is always one, we have:

$$b_{-1,0,0} + \sum_{k=0}^{m} b_{k,0,1} + \sum_{k=1}^{m} b_{k,0,2} + \sum_{k=1}^{m} \sum_{p=1}^{W_k-1} b_{k,p,2} \tag{18}$$
$$+ \sum_{p=1}^{W_0-1} b_{0,p,2} + \sum_{t=1}^{T} b_{-1,t,0} = 1$$

By replacing values of each state mentioned in Eq. 18 and by simplifying, we get:

$$b_{0,0,2} = \cfrac{1}{\frac{1}{1-\gamma} + (1 - (\alpha + \beta - \alpha\beta)^{m+1})T + \frac{(2-\alpha)(1-(\alpha+\beta-\alpha\beta)^{m+1})}{(1-(\alpha+\beta-\alpha\beta))}} \\ + \sum_{k=0}^{m}(\frac{W_{k-1}}{2})(\alpha + \beta - \alpha\beta)^k \tag{19}$$

6   Analysis with Results

It is evident from (1) and (2) that SD and BI depend on $aUnitBackoffPeriod$. As per CSMA/CA flow chart in Fig. 3, each transmitting node has to wait for random number of backoff period. Due to the significance of backoff period length, the performance of CSMA/CA is analyzed by varying the backoff period's length. The simulation analysis includes node's average wait time before transmitting, probability of channel access busy during CCA1 and CCA2. Analysis also comrises of throughput, reliability and transmission failure probability. All these results are analyzed by increasing load. The simulation parameters are briefly summarized in Table 2.

Table 2. Simulation Parameters

Parameters	Value
Number of Nodes	10
Data Rate	250 Kbps
Offered Load (bits)	484 to 6776
$aUnitBackoffPeriod$ (Symbols)	10:10:50
Turnaround time (Sec)	0.000192
$macAckWaitDuration$	0.000864
$macMaxCSMABackoff$	4
$aMaxFrameRetries$	3

6.1   Busy Channel Probability During CCA1

Each data transmitting node senses the medium availability after completing its random backoff count. If τ is the probability of transmitting a packet which is computed by markov chain as:

$$\tau = \sum_{t=1}^{T} b_{-1,t,0}(1 - (\alpha + \beta - \alpha\beta)^{m+1}) \times T \times b_{0,0,2} \tag{20}$$

then busy channel probability during first attempt (α) is computed as:
$$\alpha = [L(1 - (1 - \tau)^{N-1})(1 - \alpha)(1 - \beta)] + \cdots$$

$$L_{ack}\frac{N_\tau(1 - \tau)^{N-1}(1 - (1 - \tau)^{N-1})(1 - \alpha)(1 - \beta)}{1 - (1 - \tau)^N} \tag{21}$$

$$\alpha = (1 - \alpha)(1 - \beta)(1 - (1 - \tau)^{N-1})\cdots$$

$$[L + \frac{L_{ack}(N_\tau(1 - \tau)^{N-1})}{1 - (1 - \tau)^N}] \tag{22}$$

where L is data frame length in slots, L_{ack} is length of Acknowledgment frame and $[1 - (1 - \tau)^{N-1}]$ is collision probability. It happens when one of the remaining nodes also transmit data in same backoff slot.

Results shown in Fig. 5 illustrates that increase in traffic load increases the α probability. This is because of busy channel for most of the time. The results further show that reduced backoff period length increases the busy channel probability during CCA1 and vice versa.

6.2   Channel Assess Busy Probability During CCA2

CSMA/CA algorithm describes that value of CW is decremented by 1 when a node finds the channel idle during CCA1. At the start of next backoff period,

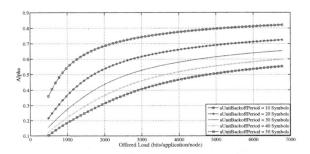

Fig. 5. Busy channel probability during CCA1

node senses the medium availability for the second successive time. CCA2 is computed as:

$$\beta = \frac{1 - (1 - \tau)^{N-1} + N\tau(1 - \tau)^{N-1}}{2 - (1 - \tau)^N + N\tau(1 - \tau)^{N-1}} \tag{23}$$

Here β is probability to find medium busy during CCA2.

Figure 6 illustrates that there is comparably less probability of finding channel busy during CCA2 as of CCA1. This happens because CCA2 sensed the medium in very next slot instead of waiting for backoff period. Here probability of finding channel busy are similar for different backoff period lengths however it rises more with applied load where backoff period length is higher.

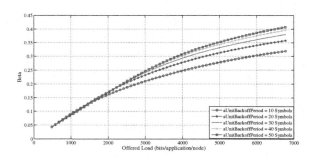

Fig. 6. Busy channel probability during CCA2

6.3   Wait Time

Average wait time of a network is the time for which networking nodes have to wait before transmitting the data packets due to busy medium. It is noted that node's waiting time is more when backoff period length is higher as shown in Fig. 7. This is due to the fact that nodes have to wait for longer time due to longer backoff period as of the shorter backoff period length.

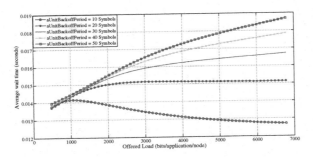

Fig. 7. Average wait time before transmitting

6.4   Reliability

Reliability of a network is based on the successful transmission of data packets from source towards destination. Following are the two reasons of data packet failure.

1. A node could not transmit its data packet as medium remains busy for such time when NB>macmaxcsmabackoff.
2. A node transmits the data packet again and again until the retry limits (Pcr) exceeds $aMaxFrameRetries$ and no acknowledgment frame is received.

Reliability of a network is calculated as:

$$Reliability = 1 - P_{cf} - P_{cr} \qquad (24)$$

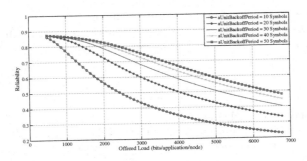

Fig. 8. Network Reliability

Results in Fig. 8 show that a network is more reliable with reduced load and less reliable with increased load. Longer Backoff Period length increases the reliability of successful transmission.

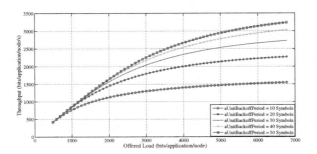

Fig. 9. Network Throughput

6.5 Average Throughput

Average throughput is defined as number of successful data over total time through a medium. Figure 9 shows that the larger backoff period length achieves higher throughput compared to the smaller backoff period length.

7 Conclusion

The paper analyzed the effect of varying backoff period on the performance of slotted csma/ca. Discrete Markov chain model is used to determine different probabilities of slotted CSMA/CA. Effect of same load variation has been analyzed by finding the probability during CCA1, CCA2. In addition failure probability along with reliability and throughput are also analyzed. Results show that the reliability of successful transmission increases with the increase in backoff period length due to less probability of collisions. However, it increases the node's waiting time before transmitting its frame in the medium. Therefore, reduction in chances of collision increases the power efficiency of nodes, which results in longer network life-time at the cost of longer waiting time.

References

1. Zigbee Alliance. www.zigbee.org
2. Callaway, E., et al.: Home networking with IEEE 802.15.4: a developing standard for low-rate wireless personal area networks. IEEE Commun. Mag. **40**(8), 70–77 (2002)
3. Gutierrez, J., et al.: IEEE 802.15.4: a developing standard for low-power low-cost wireless personal area networks. IEEE Network **15**(5), 12–19 (2001)
4. Zheng, J., et al.: Will IEEE 802.15.4 make ubiquitous networking a reality?: a discussion on a potential low power, low bit rate standard. IEEE Commun. Mag. **42**(6), 140–146 (2004)
5. Malone, D., et al.: Modeling the 802.11 distributed coordination function in nonsaturated heterogeneous conditions. IEEE/ACM Trans. Netw. **15**(1), 159–172 (2007)

6. Engelstad, P.E., et al.: Non-saturation and saturation analysis of IEEE 802.11e EDCA with starvation prediction. In: Proceedings of the ACM SIGMETRICS International Conference Measurement Modeling Computer System, Banff, AB, Canada, 6–10 June 2005, pp. 224–233 (2005)
7. Tickoo, O., et al.: Queueing analysis and delay mitigation in IEEE 802.11 random access MAC-based wireless networks. In: Proceedings of the IEEE Conference on Computer and Communication, China, pp. 1404–1413 (2004)
8. Bianchi, G.: Performance analysis of the IEEE 802.11 distributed coordination function. IEEE J. Sel. Areas Commun. **18**(3), 535–547 (2000)
9. Latré, B., et al.: Throughput and delay analysis of unslotted IEEE 802.15.4. J. Netw. **1**(1), 20–28 (2006)
10. Kim, T.O., Kim, H., Lee, J., Park, J.S., Choi, B.D.: Performance analysis of IEEE 802.15.4 with Non-beacon-enabled CSMA/CA in non-saturated condition. In: Sha, E., Han, S.-K., Xu, C.-Z., Kim, M.-H., Yang, L.T., Xiao, B. (eds.) EUC 2006. LNCS, vol. 4096, pp. 884–893. Springer, Heidelberg (2006)
11. Zayani, M.-H., et al.: A joint model for IEEE 802.15.4 physical and medium access control layers. In: 7th International Wireless Communications and Mobile Computing Conference in (IWCMC), pp. 814–819, July 2011
12. Koubaa, A., et al.: A comprehensive simulation study of slotted CSMA/CA for IEEE 802.15.4 wireless sensor networks. In: IEEE International Workshop on Factory Communication Systems, pp. 183–192 (2006)
13. Jurcik, P., et al.: A simulation model for the IEEE 802.15.4 protocol: delay/throughput evaluation of the gts mechanism. In: 15th International Symposium on Modeling, Analysis, and Simulation of Computer and Telecommunication Systems, MASCOTS 2007, pp. 109–116, October 2007
14. Pollin, S., et al.: Performance analysis of slotted carrier sense IEEE 802.15.4 medium access layer. IEEE Trans. Wireless Commun. **7**(9), 3359–3371 (2008)
15. Jung, C., et al.: Enhanced Markov chain model and throughput analysis of the slotted CSMA/CA for IEEE 802.15.4 under unsaturated traffic conditions. IEEE Trans. Veh. Technol. **58**(1), 473–478 (2009)
16. Park, P., et al.: A generalized Markov chain model for effective analysis of slotted IEEE 802.15.4, mobile adhoc and sensor systems. In: IEEE 6th International Conference on MASS 2009, pp. 130–139, October 2009

Middleboxes and Addressing

Multipath TCP Proxy: Unshackling Network Nodes from Today's End-to-End Connection Principle

Christos Pollalis[✉], Paris Charalampou, and Efstathios Sykas

Computer Networks Laboratory, School of Electrical and Computer Engineering,
National Technical University of Athens, Zografou, Greece
pollalisbelg@yahoo.gr, {pchara,sykas}@cn.ntua.gr

Abstract. Nowadays, mobile devices are equipped with multiple radio inter-faces, data centers provide redundant routing paths, and multihoming is the new tendency in existing, extensive server farms. Meanwhile, the unending growth rate of Internet traffic generation raises difficulties in meeting end user demands regarding bandwidth availability and Quality of Service standards, while TCP itself persists as a single-path transport protocol. Multipath TCP, as a set of extensions to legacy TCP, permits the simultaneous utilization of the available interfaces on a multihomed host, while preserving the standard TCP socket API. Consequently, smart terminals possess the distinct capability of leveraging path diversity in order to provide robust data transfers and enhance the overall connec-tion performance. However, the implementation of Multipath TCP is still at a premature state. Ergo, we propose and evaluate a Multipath TCP Proxy as a mechanism towards the incremental adaptation of the extended protocol by service delivery platforms. Particularly, we examine the use of an HTTP Proxy as a protocol converter that will allow MPTCP-enabled clients to benefit from Multipath TCP even when communicating with legacy servers.

Keywords: Multipath TCP · Protocol conversion · Congestion control · Policy routing · Bandwidth throttling

1 Introduction

Computer networks are continuously evolving. When the TCP/IP stack was originally designed, hosts were equipped with a single network interface. On modern epoch termi-nals, however, multiple wired and/or wireless interfaces are available. Despite its age, the Transmission Control Protocol (TCP) remains the dominant transport mechanism on the Internet in an era when smart devices crave to exploit their numerous, usually underutilized, interfaces and harvest the available network resources.

A number of protocols have been proposed to provide multihoming functionalities to end user devices without the use of legacy routing protocols, such as BGP. Two main categories can be identified: (a) host based solutions – where modifications should be implemented on user handsets and devices, and (b) router based solutions – where end devices are left unchanged and new protocol implementations are fulfilled on router

© IFIP International Federation for Information Processing 2016
Published by Springer International Publishing Switzerland 2016. All Rights Reserved
L. Mamatas et al. (Eds.): WWIC 2016, LNCS 9674, pp. 55–65, 2016.
DOI: 10.1007/978-3-319-33936-8_5

networking stack. Since multihoming and simultaneous usage of network interfaces should be agnostic of the basic network connectivity, solutions that are based on the introduction of middle-boxes seem more appropriate in multivendor and multi-ISPs environments. In this paper we try to address the issues imposed from higher bandwidth requirements, especially on mobile nodes.

The first and more widely adopted approach is the SCTP (Stream Control Transmission Protocol). SCTP is a message-oriented protocol like UDP that requires SCTP associations over diverse network paths. SCTP is based on delivering chunks of information from different network interfaces, transported on different paths inside an IP network and finally multiplexed on host level. Even though SCTP is adopted from the vast majority of Operating Systems and is already used in the telecom industry as a replacement to the SS7 signaling protocol, SCTP cannot be consider as the optimal way forward for end-devices. The main drawback of SCTP implementations [1] is the high complexity and the negative effect on computing resources, which are relatively expensive on mobile nodes. Furthermore, existing experimental analysis of SCTP in heterogeneous networks demonstrates poor performance in high packet and bandwidth rates.

Another approach is the Loc/ID (Locator and Identity) separation method. In this context, the nodes have both an identity that uniquely distinguishes the end host and an associated locator that describes the network connectivity structure. This concept separates the two name spaces (identities and addresses), which are combined in traditional IP networks. In Loc/ID separation architectures the IDs are used for end to end communications, whereas the locators are assigned to different network interfaces. The main representative in this category is the LISP implementation for mobile nodes, described as Lisp-MN [2]. LISP is not yet implemented on large scale networks and requires significant changes in the infrastructure of Internet Service Providers (ISPs). Furthermore, it lacks the functionality to parallel use multiple interfaces on the same dialogue maximizing throughput and user experience.

A third approach is Multipath TCP (MPTCP) [3]. Multipath TCP enables an Internet device to efficiently use its multiple interfaces by installing a set of extensions on top of traditional TCP, which permit the establishment of additional TCP subflows under the umbrella of a single MPTCP session. Consequently, supplementary capabilities are introduced to the protocol's core functionality empowering features such as enhanced robustness against network malfunction, bandwidth aggregation, as well as dynamic data offloading. Moreover, cellular networks leveraging MP-TCP can enhance Quality of Experience (QoE) by providing robustness towards data communication technology availability and cell-to-cell service degradation. At the same time, MPTCP preserves the standard socket API and maintains backward compatibility with Legacy TCP at both the network and application levels. This fallback procedure serves also as a fail-safe mechanism, since MPTCP deployment is at a premature state and/or middle-boxes may strip down the MPTCP signaling options.

In an attempt to achieve effective "resource pooling" [4] and aggregate the bandwidth available, MPTCP implements a congestion control mechanism coupled at the MPTCP-level of the transport layer [5], consequently creating a coalescence of links effectively behaving as a shared channel of higher capacity. As a result, hosts are able to ceaselessly monitor the dynamic state of the network routes involved in data transfers and shift

Internet traffic from degraded paths to more efficient ones according to the available bandwidth per utilized link. On the other hand, in order to ensure continuous packet transmissions, unaffected by individual malfunctioning connections or link-related congestion phenomena, a unique receive window shared across all the TCP subflows is implemented at the recipient. Additionally, a buffer of adequate space is required [6], so as to assure in-order delivery of the information segments to the application layer. The buffering space should accommodate an increased amount of packets, compared to legacy TCP systems, in an effort to cope with the head-of-line blocking caused by the dissimilar transmission delays of the diverse routing paths.

Nonetheless, the deployment of MPTCP solutions is still lagging behind. Currently, a host can benefit from Multipath TCP only if its peer possesses MPTCP-capability as well. This requirement raises barriers in the deployment of MPTCP, since service delivery platforms dawdle as far as protocol installation is concerned [7]. While the multipath functionality can be introduced quite seamlessly to user equipment due to the frequent OS updates of personal computers and smart devices, such changes are more complex to conduct inside an Internet Service Provider's core infrastructure, especially on application servers handling a myriad of requests on a constant basis. The inset of an intermediate node as a protocol converter, aiming at the creation of a split TCP-MPTCP connection between the MPTCP-enabled clients and MPTCP-unaware systems, as illustrated in Fig. 1, may serve as a stepping stone towards the gradual incorporation of MPTCP, partially sidestepping initial compatibility issues and consequently user QoE degradation.

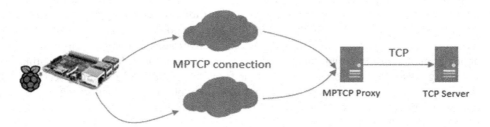

Fig. 1. Creation of the split TCP-MPTCP connection, after insertion of the MPTCP Proxy in between the communication ends.

2   Multipath TCP Proxy

Deploying proxies as a middle-box is often not considered best practice by researchers [8] regarding traditional network architectures and datacenter topologies [9]. Such deployments reduce the overall service availability, downgrade service performance by creating bandwidth bottlenecks, and increase the operational costs. Even though middle-boxes impose all these drawbacks, service providers are still keen on deploying them as a way to enforce network policies for charging or traffic steering purposes. Furthermore, installing middle-boxes is relatively common in order to benefit from new technologies without waiting to be adopted by terminals and network devices [10, 11].

Our proposal aims at the introduction of a protocol converter in the form of a Multipath TCP Proxy in order to provide multipath functionality on behalf of traditional TCP systems, bypassing compulsory protocol adaptation in the ISP core infrastructure [12]. As a result, MPTCP-capable hosts will be able to effectively take advantage of their enhanced, multipath features, while the established path redundancy will give network operators the opportunity to more efficiently distribute traffic load and mitigate bottleneck occurrences.

In addition, our MPTCP Proxy is enhanced with a bandwidth throttling [13] mechanism as a reactive means for network traffic regulation and congestion minimization. The bandwidth manipulation algorithm, which runs inside the MPTCP Proxy, permits the application of load control policies, compatible with the specifications of Multipath TCP with regard to traffic engineering and billing purposes, while aiming at the satisfaction of Quality of Service (QoS) standards. The mechanism utilizes a Scapy [14] sniffer, which is responsible for monitoring the characteristics of incoming connections by parsing the options field of the TCP header. As soon as an MPTCP connection is established consisting of at least two active TCP subflows, the MPTCP Proxy throttles the desired TCP connection based on pre-determined criteria. The eventual traffic redirection is feasible due to the insertion of packet mangling rules on top of the Netfilter Framework [15].

The overall scheme allows operators to get in the middle of the process of outgoing data scheduling by virtually sub-dividing a packet queue into multiple ones and re-configuring them using classful queuing disciplines. Each independent queue is responsible for the management and forwarding of packets of a predetermined destination, allowing network operators to manipulate Internet traffic by assigning the most fitting packet queue to specific TCP subflows based on routing policy criteria. The concurrent utilization of diverse wired and/or radio access technologies in conjunction with the application of capacity limitation techniques creates the illusion of less suitable routing paths, ergo resulting in a force-steering of the forwarded traffic. As a result, it becomes possible to re-allocate network load and alleviate bottleneck phenomena, while harnessing the excess, available bandwidth, as well as offer MPTCP-enabled clients enhanced QoE due to the traversal of less congested areas.

3   Experimental Evaluation

We have evaluated our proposal in an experimental environment similar to the aforementioned Fig. 1, consisting of a Raspberry Pi Model B running Debian Wheezy on top of a custom, MPTCP-compatible 3.12.35 + Linux kernel, an MPTCP Proxy with kernel version 3.14.0 and Squid Proxy installed, equipped with the stable release v0.89.2 of the extended protocol, and a MPTCP-unaware HTTP server with Apache2 running on port 80. During our experimental scenarios we have disabled Squid's caching mechanism in order to measure pure forwarding performance. In particular, we examined the impact of memory space allotment with regards to the MPTCP attainable bandwidth, the responsiveness of our bandwidth throttling mechanism, as well as the packet forwarding delay inserted due to the protocol conversion process.

3.1   Baseline Scenario

In our initial experimental scenario, we depict the performance accomplished by Legacy TCP during direct communication between our Raspberry Pi and the MPTCP-unaware HTTP server. Since the MPTCP Proxy is not explicitly introduced to our client-side device, the negotiation of multipath functionality fails between the end hosts. As the MPTCP options embedded inside the TCP header cannot be interpreted by the legacy server-side system, multipath support is not advertised by the HTTP server causing the RPi to fall back to regular TCP and only establish a single – traditional – TCP connection. Figure 2 illustrates the achieved throughput for two types of TCP sessions, a wired and a wireless connection, respectively.

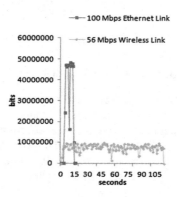

Fig. 2. Legacy TCP performance

3.2   Dynamic Load Balancing

Since in our current setup the MPTCP-enabled Raspberry Pi is still unable to simultaneously utilize both its network interfaces, we inset our MPTCP Proxy as an intermediate node in order to provide multipath functionality on behalf of the legacy TCP server. The MPTCP session terminates on the client-side of the protocol converter, while a regular TCP connection is initiated on the server-side towards the desired destination. Figure 3 depicts the aggregated throughput achieved under MPTCP's modified congestion control algorithm.

As the Ethernet interface offers a higher link capacity alongside a smaller Round Trip Time (RTT) value compared to the wireless connection, the respective subflow's congestion window tends to inflate faster, ergo allowing for the largest percentage of packets to be forwarded via the wired routing path. On the other hand side, the wireless link remains almost fully underutilized, since MPTCP perceives it as an inferior alternative for load balancing or data offloading in the absence of congestion on the wired connection. Therefore, the observations above come to confirm MPTCP's capability to strip data across the most efficient of the available paths, while offering no less capacity compared to a legacy TCP session.

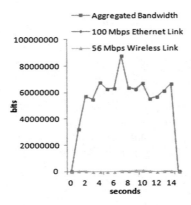

Fig. 3. Multipath TCP performance

3.3   TCP Buffer Size Impact on MPTCP Performance

TCP Memory Allocation. One of the major challenges arising as a consequence of the deployment of MPTCP solutions is the allocation of adequate buffering space in order to cope with the increased demands regarding packet reordering at the receiver [16]. The disparate propagation delays along the utilized network links create discontinuities in the re-assembled information stream, since TCP segments often reach their final destination out of sequence. In such case, the head-of-line blocking effect becomes quite noticeable, temporarily interrupting the final in-order delivery to the application layer.

Figure 4 illustrates the performance of MPTCP corresponding to two distinct receive buffer configurations. According to MPTCP specifications, the required accommodation space for TCP segments amounts to a maximum of 0.48 MB. As clearly shown in Fig. 4a, adopting a lower bound results in data loss at the receiver, leading to unavoidable packet retransmissions and an overall service degradation.

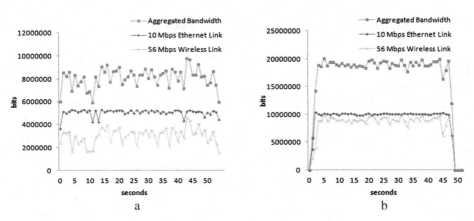

Fig. 4. MPTCP performance based on different receive buffer configurations. Max memory allocation set at (a) 0.18 MB, (b) 0.72 MB

On the other hand, Fig. 4b depicts a much more efficient data transfer. Besides the naturally stable behavior of the wired access link, the wireless interface achieves a satisfactory throughput rate, as well, especially if we additionally consider the potential randomness of the wireless transmission environment resulting in elevated propagation delays. The TCP memory allocation is adequate enough to sustain a constant delivery rate of segments to the application layer, minimizing the impact of head-of-line blocking. In general, MPTCP paths of commensurate delays tend to decrease receiver memory consumption even close to zero, since packets routed over different paths arrive timely at their destination without causing extensive gaps in the packet sequence at the recipient.

Maximum Transmitted Unit Size Adjustment. Similar considerations apply in case of Maximum Transmitted Unit (MTU) size variations. Intuitively, a large MTU size leads to higher data rates, since the number of interrupts, which need to be processed by the receive system, diminishes. On the other hand, a small MTU size compels the recipient to handle an increased amount of TCP segments provoking packet dropping, as depicted in Fig. 5, and overall destabilizing the MPTCP session compared to Fig. 4b. Default MTUs carry enough payload so as to cause no impairment during the data transmission, while gradual size reduction leads more swiftly to service degradation compared to legacy TCP systems. This more abrupt impact derives from a combination of reasons, including the increased number of packets that need to be handled and their dissimilar transfer delays. Since more packets are accommodated inside the receive buffer, the re-ordering process becomes more intense due to the different arrival periods of consequent segments. Practically, in case of MTU size variations, a proportionate TCP memory extension should be allocated in order to cope with buffering demands and avoid service quality downgrading.

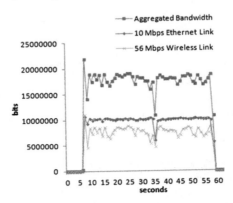

Fig. 5. MPTCP performance degradation as a result of decreasing MTU size down to 1000 bytes, while keeping buffer size at 0.72 MB

3.4 Bandwidth Throttling Mechanism

While Multipath TCP is capable of pooling the accessible network resources per interface, spreading load over a wider network, as well as achieving dynamic data offloading, the parallel application of bandwidth throttling allows for further traffic manipulation. Administrators are capable of further managing the MPTCP sessions and force-shifting data across eclectic routing paths, while offering the multipath connection no less capacity than a single-path TCP session. This is all feasible via the prioritization of the TCP subflows by applying the desired levels of bandwidth restriction per available network interface, ergo outsmarting MPTCP into perceiving select TCP connections as less efficient paths for packet routing, even though their potential link capacity indicates otherwise. As a result, packet flows can be redirected away from congested areas, while concurrently alleviating bottlenecks.

Figure 6a illustrates the effect of the bandwidth restriction introduced on the Ethernet interface of our Raspberry Pi. The process completion delay alongside the moderate utilization of the available resources tends to cause a miniature impact on delivery time. However, even if the queuing disciplines are not configured timely in case of transfers of minimal size, a tolerable scenario for network-friendly communications in terms of congestion, the desired control policies will be already installed in order to support future multipath transmissions without the original process overhead, as depicted in Fig. 6b.

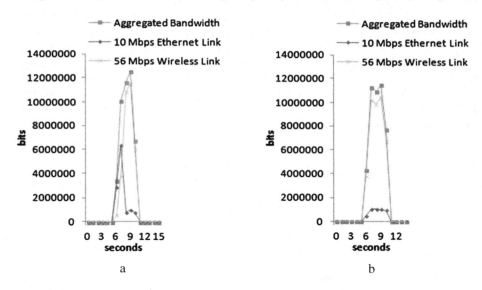

Fig. 6. Application of bandwidth throttling on the wired network interface (a) initial 5 MB file transfer, (b) 5 MB file re-transmitted

Finally, Fig. 7 exhibits the bigger picture of leveraging MPTCP with our bandwidth throttling mechanism, as well as the generic behavior of the involved TCP subflows. As soon as the control policies have been established, the MPTCP congestion control algorithm tends to offload data to the wireless connection, which manages to achieve a higher throughput rate compared to throttling-free transmissions (Fig. 4b). Moreover, the overall connection performance becomes slightly inferior to regular data transfers (Fig. 4b) due to the extreme underutilization of the Ethernet link, a differentiation that can be undone by the proper reconfiguration of the capacity limitation levels.

Nevertheless, the bottom line is that MPTCP still outperforms legacy TCP, as well as meets its design goals.

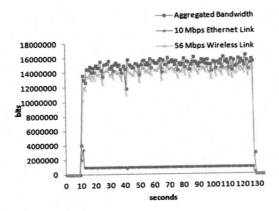

Fig. 7. Application of bandwidth throttling on the wired network interface during the transfer of a 200 MB file

3.5 Protocol Conversion Delay

Table 1 presents the chain-performance of the MPTCP Proxy regarding protocol conversion and packet forwarding. The measurements were attained via the insertion of IPtables mangling rules on top of the Netfilter Framework, which targeted corresponding packets of specific characteristics on both communication ends. As a matter of fact, our middle-box tends to synchronize one session at a time. Therefore, the MPTCP-to-TCP SYN segment conversion delay is equivalent to the time between the client-side connection establishment and the server-side 3-way-handshake initialization. Moreover, data segments are reconstructed internally, meaning they are converted and forwarded, after they have been received by the application layer. Of course, such interaction between low-level kernel and user space tends to introduce additional conversion delay, as packets are processed along the entire TCP/IP stack. Furthermore, since the system is actually hosted inside an ESXi hypervisor, the server is also running on constrained memory resources and computation power, ergo its proportionate underperformance. Undoubtedly, an application-level solution cannot ensure effective service delivery in real world networks compared to – preferably application agnostic – highly performing kernel module implementations [17]. Such solutions can provide efficient protocol conversion by minimizing unnecessary memory allocations and costly `read()` – `write()` system calls.

Table 1. Conversion time within the MPTCP Proxy between the MPTCP and TCP connections

	SYN	Data
Time (sec.)	0.0078341 ± 0.0006805	0.0153311 ± 0.0080645

4 Conclusion

The traditional TCP protocol obeys rigorously to the end-to-end connection principle, thus deterring smart terminals from efficiently exploiting their numerous network access interfaces. While TCP is upper bounded by the available capacity of the bottleneck link, Multipath TCP permits the concurrent distribution of traffic load over a wider network. As a consequence, MPTCP enhances user experience by providing improved performance alongside redundancy, as well as mitigates congestion via dynamic data offloading between the available network links.

Since MPTCP capability still remains to be implemented on the server side, the deployment of a MPTCP Proxy at the ISP infrastructure can provide multipath functionality on behalf of legacy TCP systems, as well as allow MPTCP-enabled clients to achieve effective "resource pooling", without the requirement for service providers to undergo major changes inside their core network. However, technical and economic concerns emerge regarding protocol adaptation, such as increased buffer space demands, which may lead to infrastructure upgrades and more expensive implementations; re-evaluation of existing mechanisms, such as TCP's re-ordering algorithm in order to effectively handle re-ordering events and lessen head-of-line blocking phenomena, as well as revision of today's routing policies in order to cope with MPTCP path utilization.

Thereupon, we emphasized the importance of memory allocation sufficiency and how inadequate buffer space can lead to performance degradation. In addition, we introduced a bandwidth throttling technique as a means to apply traffic engineering schemas compatible with MPTCP path utilization without downgrading service quality. Finally, we underlined the importance of application-agnostic, kernel module implementations in order to efficiently cope with real world networks' demands by minimizing superfluous system processes and overall protocol conversion overhead.

References

1. Dainotti, A., Loreto, S., Pescape, A., Ventrem, G.: SCTP performance evaluation over heterogeneous networks. Special Issue: Perform. Anal. Enhancements Wirel. Netw. **19**(8), 1207–1218 (2007). doi:10.1002/cpe.1159
2. Menth, M., Klein, D., Hartmann, M.: Improvements to LISP mobile node. In: 22nd International Teletraffic Congress (ITC22), Amsterdam, The Netherlands, September 2010
3. ICTEAM: MultiPath TCP – Linux Kernel Implementation. http://www.multipath-tcp.org/. Accessed Oct 2014
4. Wischik, D., Handley, M., Braun, M.B.: The resource pooling principle. ACM SIGCOMM **38**(5), 47–52 (2008). doi:10.1145/1452335.1452342
5. Wischik, D., Raiciu, C., Greenhalgh, A., Handley, M.: Design, implementation and evaluation of congestion control for multipath TCP. In: Proceedings of the 8th USENIX Conference on Networked Systems Design and Implementation, Lombard, IL, USA, pp. 99–112, April 2011
6. Raiciu, C., Paasch, C., Barre, S., Ford, A., Honda, M., Duchene, F., Bonaventure, O., Handley, M.: How hard can it be? Designing and implementing a deployable multipath TCP. In: Proceedings of the 9th USENIX Conference on Networked Systems Design and Implementation, San Jose, CA, USA, pp. 29–42, April 2012

7. Mehani, O., Holz, R., Ferlin, S., Boreli, R.: An early look at multipath TCP deployment in the wild. In: Proceedings of the 6th International Workshop on Hot Topics in Planet-Scale Measurement, Paris, France, pp. 7–12, September 2015. doi:10.1145/2798087.2798088

8. Sherry, J., Hasan, S., Scott, C., Krishnamurthy, A., Ratnasamy, S., Sekas, V.: Making middleboxes someone else's problem: network processing as a cloud service. In: Proceedings of the ACM SIGCOMM Conference on Applications, Technologies, Architectures, and Protocols for Computer Communication, Helsinki, Finland, pp. 13–24, August 2012. doi: 10.1145/2342356.2342359

9. Potharaju, V, Jain, N.: Demystifying the dark side of the middle: a field study of middlebox failures in datacenters. In: Proceedings of the Conference on Internet Measurement Conference, Barcelona, Spain, pp. 9–22, October 2013. doi:10.1145/2504730.2504737

10. Yap, K.-K., Huang, T.-Y., Kobayashi, M., Yiakoumis, Y., McKeown, N., Katti, S., Parulkar, G.: Making use of all the networks around us: a case study in android. In: Proceedings of the ACM SIGCOMM Workshop on Cellular Networks: Operations, Challenges, and Future Design, Helsinki, Finland, pp. 19–24, August 2012. doi:10.1145/2342468.2342474

11. Fayazbakhsh, S.K., Chiang, L., Sekar, V., Yu, M., Mogul, J.C.: Enforcing network-wide policies in the presence of dynamic middlebox actions using flowtags. In: Proceedings of the 11th USENIX Symposium on Networked Systems Design and Implementation, Seattle, WA, USA, pp. 533–546, April 2014

12. Pollalis, C., Charalampou, P., Sykas, E.: HTTP data offloading using multipath TCP proxy. In: Proceedings of the 15th IEEE Conference on Computer and Information Technology, Liverpool, UK, pp. 777–782, October 2015. doi:10.1109/CIT/IUCC/DASC/PICOM. 2015.114

13. Wikipedia: Bandwidth Throttling. https://en.wikipedia.org/wiki/Bandwidth_throttling. Accessed Mar 2015

14. SECDEV: Scapy. http://www.secdev.org/projects/scapy/. Accessed Mar 2015

15. Netfilter Core Team: netfilter: firewalling, NAT, and packet mangling for Linux. http://www.netfilter.org/. Accessed Mar 2015

16. Barré, S., Paasch, C., Bonaventure, O.: MultiPath TCP: from theory to practice. In: Domingo-Pascual, J., Manzoni, P., Palazzo, S., Pont, A., Scoglio, C. (eds.) NETWORKING 2011, Part I. LNCS, vol. 6640, pp. 444–457. Springer, Heidelberg (2011)

17. Detal, G., Paasch, C., Bonaventure, O.: Multipath in the middle(Box). In: Proceedings of the 2013 Workshop on Hot Topics in Middleboxes and Network Function Virtualization, Santa Barbara, CA, USA, pp. 1–6, December 2013. doi:10.1145/2535828.2535829

SDN-Based Source Routing for Scalable Service Chaining in Datacenters

Ahmed Abujoda[✉], Hadi Razzaghi Kouchaksaraei,
and Panagiotis Papadimitriou

Institute of Communications Technology,
Leibniz Universität Hannover, Hanover, Germany
{ahmed.abujoda,panagiotis.papadimitriou}@ikt.uni-hannover.de,
razzaghi.kouchaksaraei@stud.uni-hannover.de

Abstract. The migration of network functions (NFs) to datacenters, as promoted by Network Function Virtualization (NFV), raises the need for service chaining (*i.e.,* steering traffic through a sequence of NFs). Service chaining is typically performed by installing forwarding entries in switches within datacenters (DCs). However, as the number of service chains in DCs grows, switches will be required to maintain a large amount of forwarding state. This will raise a dataplane scalability issue, due to the relatively small flow table size of switches. To mitigate this problem, we present a software-defined network (SDN) based source routing architecture for scalable service chaining, at which the NF-path is encoded into the packet header obviating the need for any forwarding state and lookup in the switches. We assess the feasibility and efficiency of our architecture using a prototype implementation.

1 Introduction

Network Function Virtualization (NFV) is an emerging concept aiming to replace special-purpose and hardware-based middleboxes with software-based network functions (NFs) deployed on virtualized infrastructures [7,8,21,22,24]. Inspired by the success of cloud computing, NFV strives to introduce new business models to the network operators (*e.g.,* NF as a service (NFaaS)), enabling the migration of middleboxes to Network Function Providers (NFPs) in a pay-per-use manner. This can lead to a significant reduction in capital and operational expenses, while enabling elastic provisioning based on service demand. Opting to support NFV and offer NFaaS, many Internet Service Providers (ISPs) have already started to deploy micro-datacenters on their networks for NFaaS offerings to their clients [9].

To implement security and access control policies, middleboxes are deployed in certain locations in enterprise networks, such that traffic can traverse them in a particular order (*e.g.,* a firewall should be deployed before a load balancer to

© IFIP International Federation for Information Processing 2016
Published by Springer International Publishing Switzerland 2016. All Rights Reserved
L. Mamatas et al. (Eds.): WWIC 2016, LNCS 9674, pp. 66–77, 2016.
DOI: 10.1007/978-3-319-33936-8_6

filter malicious traffic). This order needs to be maintained when migrating NFs to NFPs' datacenters (DCs). In other words, there is a need for steering traffic through NFs deployed in DCs to ensure compliance with the client's policy. The so-called *service chaining* can be performed in DCs via the installation of forwarding entries in switches, such that the traffic traverses the NFs in the exact order specified by the client (*i.e.,* as prescribed in the service chain [10,20]). We refer to this approach as *rule-based service chaining*. Several studies have investigated rule-based service chaining in enterprise and wide-area networks [5, 19,25]. However, an increasing number of service chains will require a substantial amount of forwarding state in switches, which, in turn, will raise a dataplane scalability issue for NFPs, due to the relatively small flow table size of switches (*i.e.,* a switch flow table can typically store a few thousand entries).

To mitigate this problem, we employ source routing to steer traffic through the NFs of a service chain. In particular, the NF-path is encoded into the packet header obviating the need for any forwarding state and lookup in the switches, *i.e.,* switches forward packets based on the information carried in the packet header. Source routing is an attractive solution for DCs where the number of hops is relatively small (typically there are three switches between access gateways and any server in a DC) in comparison to ISP and enterprise networks [4,11,23]. Furthermore, as opposed to the wide-area, source routing does not raise any serious security concerns within DCs, since only switches and hypervisors (on virtualized servers) managed by the DC network operator can insert or remove paths from packet headers. However, source routing raises a set of challenges in terms of scalability and performance. More specifically, the encoded path may increase the packet size beyond the maximum segment size (*e.g.,* 1500 bytes for Ethernet). As such, there is a need to minimize the packet header space used for source routing. Furthermore, source routing should yield packet forwarding rates as high as in rule-based forwarding.

Service chaining with source routing raises the following requirements: (i) the discovery of switch output ports based on the NF-path in order to compose the source routing header, (ii) the encapsulation of the source routing header into the incoming packets, and (iii) traffic steering based on the source routing header. To meet these requirements, we present a software-defined network (SDN) based source routing architecture for scalable service chaining in DCs. We rely on a centralized controller to collect information about the switch ports and subsequently derive the sequence of output ports for each service chain. In this respect, we assume the presence of service mapping techniques, *i.e.,* the assignment of service chains to DC networks [1,6]. The controller uses OpenFlow [13] to insert the service routing header in the incoming packets at the core switches. We have further implemented a datapath using Click [12] for packet forwarding using the source routing header. We study the feasibility of our architecture using a prototype implementation. Our experimentatal results show that our source-routing based approach for service chaining yields high packet forwarding rates, low header insertion delay (*i.e.,* flow setup time), and a significant reduction in the control communication overhead in DCs.

The remainder of the paper is organized as follows. Section 2 presents our architecture for source routing within DCs using SDN. Section 3 discusses the implementation of our architecture components. In Sect. 4, we evaluate the performance of our source routing datapath and controller. Finally, Sect. 5 highlights our conclusions.

2   Service Chaining Architecture

In this section, we elaborate on our source routing based approach for service chaining. Consider the example in Fig. 1 where traffic needs to be routed through three NFs deployed on servers within a DC for service chaining. A straightforward approach is to install a forwarding entry in each switch on the path connecting the NFs, for each service chain. Despite its simplicity, this approach requires maintaining the state of each service chain on multiple switches (in this example, 7 entries for one chain are required) which restricts the number of service chains that can be deployed on a DC (given the small flow table size in switches). Using source routing instead, the path between the NFs can be encoded into the packet header at core switches, eliminating the need for inserting forwarding state on each switch on the path.

Along these lines, we propose to encode the sequence of switch output ports into the header of each packet. For instance, to steer traffic through NF1 and NF2, each packet should carry the port numbers 1, 3, and 5. As such, each switch can merely extract the output port number from the packet and forward it accordingly (*e.g.,* switch A will extract and forward to port number 1). To allow the switches to identify the corresponding port numbers (out of a sequence of port numbers encoded into the packet), we add a counter field to the routing header. This counter identifies the next port number to be read by the next switch on the path, *i.e.,* the counter field specifies the location of the corresponding port number from the beginning of the routing header. For example, when reaching switch B, the counter will carry the value of 6 indicating that switch B should read the sixth field on the port number starting from the beginning of the routing header (Fig. 1). The value of the counter is decremented at each switch to indicate the next port number to be read.

In the following, we describe a source routing based architecture for service chaining leveraging on SDN. Our architecture consists of four main components (Fig. 2):

- **Source Routing Encapsulation (SRE) switch** is an OpenFlow [13] switch which inserts the source routing header into each incoming packet based on the configuration provided by the source routing controller. In a DC we consider SRE switch functionality at the core level.
- **Source routing controller** provides support for: (i) topology discovery to keep track of the different links and switches on DC network, (ii) path-to-ports translation to identify the corresponding switch output ports for the NF-path, and (iii) flow table configuration on SRE switches for the insertion of source routing headers on incoming packets.

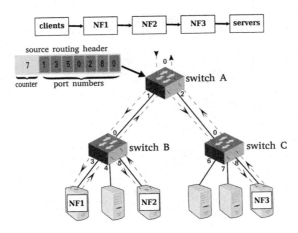

Fig. 1. Example of service chaining using source routing.

- **Source routing switch** extracts the output port from the source routing header and forwards the packet accordingly. This role is mainly fulfilled by aggregation and top-of-the-rack (ToR) switches.
- **Southbound interface** provides an interface for the controller to install flow entries on SRE switches and perform topology discovery (*i.e.,* collect information about the switch port numbers and active links).
- **Northbound interface** enables the NFV orchestrator to submit the service chain mapping to the source routing controller.

Inserting the port numbers of the entire path on the packet headers may significantly increase the packet size leading to high bandwidth consumption and/or packet sizes beyond the maximum segment size (MSS). For instance, a service chain consisting of 10 NFs which are assigned to different racks requires a routing header with 30 port numbers. Assuming each port number is carried on 8-bits field, a routing header adds 31 extra bytes (1 byte is needed for the counter field) to each incoming packet. This would lead to the consumption of 48 % more bandwidth for packets with the size of 64 bytes and the fragmentation of packets with a size larger than 1470 bytes (with Ethernet).

To mitigate this problem, we use more than one SRE switches along the path. In this respect, the service chain is subdivided into pathlets where each pathlet starts and ends with an SRE switch. The location and number of SRE switches are identified by the DC network operator based on the DC network topology and the employed service mapping algorithm. Minimizing the number of racks used for each service chain reduces the number of hops and consequently, the number of SRE switches per chain.

An alternative approach is to deploy both SRE switch and source routing functionality within all DC switches, allowing the DC operator to dynamically install routing headers on packets in different locations of the network. To identify packets reaching the end of their pathlet, we use the zero value of the counter

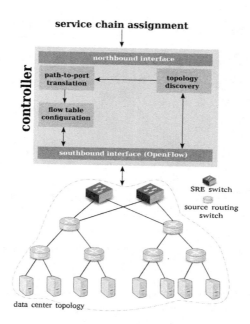

Fig. 2. Source routing architecture.

field (indicating no further ports to read). While this approach provides more flexibility, it increases the complexity of the switch design.

To quantify the benefits of source routing, we calculated the amount of forwarding state required to steer traffic across a service chain's path using source routing (with a single and multiple SRE switches – 1 SRE switch for 10 hops) and rule-based forwarding. According to Fig. 3, source routing with a single and multiple SRE switches achieves a significant reduction in the state compared to rule-based forwarding.

3 Implementation

In this section, we discuss the implementation of our architecture components:

– **Source routing header.** To insert the routing header into the incoming packets, we use the destination MAC address and further add a VLAN tag and a MPLS label stack to each packet. In particular, we encode the port numbers in the destination MAC address, the VLAN ID, and the MPLS label (OpenFlow 1.0, which we use for our implementation, does not allow modifying other VLAN and MPLS fields). By combining these fields, we can store 10 port numbers per packet, where each field is 8-bit long and supports switches with up to 256 ports. To store the counter value, we use the TTL field of the MPLS header. We can further increase the number of encoded ports by inserting more MPLS stack labels in each packet.

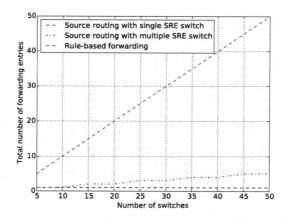

Fig. 3. Forwarding state with source routing and rule-based forwarding.

- **Source routing controller.** We use POX [18] to implement the different components of our controller. Using OpenFlow, the controller collects and stores the port numbers of each switch. Based on this information, the controller extracts the switch ports for each service chain path. Subsequently, the controller inserts the port numbers into a bit vector. This bit vector is further broken down into the MAC destination address, the VLAN ID and the MPLS label. Next, a flow entry is installed in the SRE switch using OFPT_VENDOR [15] message. This message carries the flow matching fields (*e.g.,* source/destination IP, source/destination port numbers and protocol), the VLAN tag, the MPLS stack, the destination MAC address as well as the output port number.
- **SRE switch.** We rely on OpenvSwitch [16] to insert routing headers on the arriving packets. OpenvSwitch exposes an OpenFlow interface to the controller to install forwarding rules. As such, the controller inserts the routing headers on the packets by adding a VLAN tag and a MPLS label stack to each packet and updating its destination MAC address.
- **Source routing datapath.** We extend Click Modular Router [12] with a new element, SourceRouter, which extracts the values of the VLAN ID, MPLS label, MPLS TTL, and the destination MAC address and subsequently combines them into the routing header (see Fig. 1). Based on the counter value, the element reads the corresponding port number through which the packet is forwarded. Combining our element with existing Click elements for packet I/O, we implement a source routing datapath (Fig. 4).

4 Experimental Evaluation

In this section, we evaluate the performance of our source routing datapath and controller. In particular, we use our emulab-based testbed to measure the

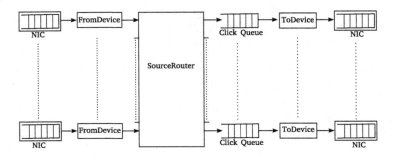

Fig. 4. Source routing datapath implementation with Click.

packet forwarding rate and the computational requirements of our source routing switch, as well as the setup time and communication overhead of our controller. We run our experiments on 4 servers equipped with an Intel Xeon E5520 quad-core CPU at 2.26 GHz, 6 GB DDR3 RAM and a quad 1 G port network interface cards (NICs) based on Intel 82571EB.

4.1 Source Routing Switch Performance

To measure the packet forwarding rate, we deploy our source routing datapath on one server and use two other servers as traffic source and sink. The switch and destination servers run Click modular router 2.0 in kernel space on Linux kernel 2.6.32. To generate traffic, we use a NetFPGA-based [14] packet generator which is installed on and controlled through our source server. Since the switch on our testbed filters packets with VLAN and MPLS header, we encapsulate our packets in IP-in-IP header. We measure the forwarding rate of our switch with packet sizes of 85 bytes including the source routing header and the IP encapsulation header. We further compare our switch performance with rule-based forwarding where we forward packets based on packets' destination IP address using a routing table with 380 K entries. Figure 5 shows that our source routing switch achieves more than 30 % higher forwarding rate than rule-based routing. This performance is achieved using a single CPU core.

Furthermore, we use Oprofile 1.1.0 [17] to measure the computational overhead of our switch in terms of CPU cycles per packet. As depicted in Table 1, our source routing datapath consumes less than 8 % of the total CPU cycles per packet. On the other hand, packet I/O operations represent the dominant share of the CPU cycles/packet. Similar results for packet I/O operations are shown in [2].

4.2 Controller Performance

To evaluate the performance of our controller, we use 4 servers, two of which act as traffic source and sink, while the other two servers host the controller and the SRE switch. Initially, we measure the flow setup time (*i.e.,* the time required to

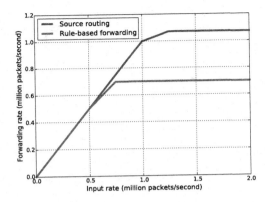

Fig. 5. Packet forwarding rate of our source routing datapath with a single CPU core.

Table 1. Average CPU cycles/packet

Element	Cycles/packet	Percentage
Source Routing Switch	156	7.9 %
Packet I/O	1008	51.3 %
Encapsulation	259	13.2 %
Decapsulation	81	4.2 %
Others	458	23.4 %
Total	1965	100 %

insert the source routing header at the SRE switch) which we define as the time elapsed from the flow's first packet arrival at the SRE switch ingress port till its departure from the egress port.

As depicted in Fig. 6, the flow setup time does not change significantly across the various flow arrival rates. We further break down the setup time into multiple components. In particular, we measure the time required for the source routing header computation, the time the control packet takes to traverse the POX and kernel stack on the controller server in both directions (between the controller and the switch), the RTT (between the controller and the SRE switch) and the SRE switch processing time. As shown in Table 2, source routing header computation consumes less than 29 % of the total setup time. Instead, most of the setup time is spent in POX, kernel stack, and the SRE switch processing.

We also compare source routing with rule-based forwarding in terms of control communication overhead. We first measure the communication overhead on a single switch for different flow arrival rates. In this respect, we measure the control traffic between the switch and controller per direction (noted as uplink and downlink overhead). Our measurements show that both source routing and rule-based forwarding consume the same amount of bandwidth at the uplink (Fig. 7(a)), since both approaches use the same packet size and format

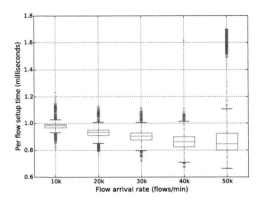

Fig. 6. Setup time per flow.

Table 2. Flow setup time

Element	Time (milliseconds)
Source routing header computation	0.25
POX processing + kernel stack	0.24
RTT	0.1
SRE switch processing	0.3
Total	0.89

(*i.e.,* OFPT_PACKET_IN [15]) to transfer the packet fields to the controller. On the other hand, for downlink, source routing consumes more bandwidth than rule-based forwarding (Fig. 7(b)), due to the extra packet fields (*i.e.,* VLAN and MPLS) required to install the source routing header.

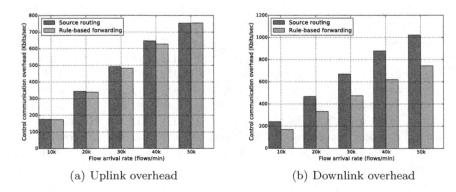

(a) Uplink overhead   (b) Downlink overhead

Fig. 7. Controll overhead for a single switch.

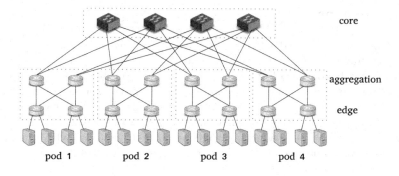

Fig. 8. Fat tree DC network topology.

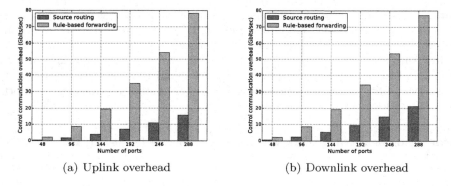

(a) Uplink overhead   (b) Downlink overhead

Fig. 9. Control overhead for multiple switches.

Using the results we obtained for a single switch, we further calculate the communication overhead with a diverse number of switches. For our calculation, we consider DCs with a fat-tree topology [3] (Fig. 8). The DC components in a fat-tree topology can be modeled based on the number of ports per switch. More precisely, a fat-tree topology with k-port switches has $(5(k^2))/4$ switches where $(k/2)^2$ of these switches are core switches and k^2 are aggregation and edge switches.

We calculate the control overhead of source routing and rule-based forwarding for fat-tree topologies with a diverse number of ports per switch. As shown in Fig. 9, source-routing introduces significantly lower communication overhead in comparison to rule-based forwarding. We observe that the savings in communication overhead increase with the size of the DC network, since the source routing controller needs to communicate only with the core switches of the DC (Sect. 1).

5 Conclusions

In this paper, we presented a SDN-based source routing architecture for service chaining within DCs. Our architecture encodes the path of each service chain into the packet headers leading to significant reduction in the forwarding state per switch and better dataplane scalability. To insert the source routing header into the incoming packets, we implemented a centralized controller that extracts switch output ports from the chain's path and subsequently encodes the port numbers into the packet headers by configuring SRE switches with OpenFlow. We further implemented a source routing datapath for packet forwarding based on the source routing header.

Using our prototype implementation, we showed that our source routing datapath achieves high packet forwarding rates and incurs low computational overhead. In addition, we showed that our controller incurs low flow setup delay and achieves a significant reduction in communication overhead in comparison with rule-based forwarding, for different DC network sizes.

In future work, we will seek to coordinate service mapping (*e.g.*, using our service chain-to-DC mapping algorithm in Nestor [6]) with SRE switch placement to achieve additional savings in terms of forwarding state and provide support for NFV deployments at massive scale.

Acknowledgments. This work was partially supported by the EU FP7 T-NOVA Project (619520).

References

1. Abujoda, A., Papadimitriou, P.: DistNSE: Distributed Network Service Embedding Across Multiple Providers
2. Abujoda, A., Papadimitriou, P.: Profiling packet processing workloads on commodity servers. In: Tsaoussidis, V., Kassler, A.J., Koucheryavy, Y., Mellouk, A. (eds.) WWIC 2013. LNCS, vol. 7889, pp. 216–228. Springer, Heidelberg (2013)
3. Al-Fares, M., Loukissas, A., Vahdat, A.: A scalable, commodity data center network architecture. ACM SIGCOMM Comput. Commun. Rev. **38**(4), 63–74 (2008)
4. Ashwood-Smith, P., Soliman, M.: SDN State Reduction. https://tools.ietf.org/html/draft-ashwood-sdnrg-state-reduction-00
5. CISCO Policy-based routing. Technical report. http://www.cisco.com/c/en/us/td/docs/switches/lan/catalyst6500/ios/15-0SY/configuration/guide/15_0_sy_swcg/policy_based_routing_pbr.pdf
6. Dietrich, D., Abujoda, A., Papadimitriou, P.: Network service embedding across multiple providers with nestor. In: IFIP Networking Conference (IFIP Networking). IEEE (2015)
7. Dobrescu, M., et al.: RouteBricks: exploiting parallelism to scale software routers. In: Proceedings of the ACM SIGOPS 22nd Symposium on Operating Systems Principles, Big Sky, USA, pp. 15–28, October 2009
8. ETSI Network Function Virtualization. http://www.etsi.org/technologiesclusters/technologies/nfv

9. Frank, B., et al.: Collaboration opportunities for content delivery and network infrastructures. In: Haddadi, H., Bonaventure, O. (eds.) Recent Advances in Networking, vol. 1, pp. 305–377 (2013)

10. Gember, A., et al.: Stratos: Virtual middleboxes as first-class entities. UW-Madison. 15, TR1771 (2012)

11. Hari, A., Lakshman, T.V., Wilfong, G.: Path Switching: Reduced-State Flow Handling in SDN Using Path Information

12. Kohler, E., et al.: The click modular router. ACM Trans. Comput. Syst. **18**(3), 263–297 (2000)

13. McKeown, N., et al.: OpenFlow: enabling innovation in campus networks. ACM SIGCOMM CCR **38**(2), 69–74 (2008)

14. NetFPGA. http://netfpga.org

15. OpenFlow Switch Specification v1.0. http://archive.openflow.org/documents/openflow-spec-v1.0.0.pdf

16. OpenvSwitch. http://openvswitch.org

17. Oprofile. http://oprofile.sourceforge.net

18. Pox. www.noxrepo.org/pox

19. Qazi, Z.A., et al.: SIMPLE-fying middlebox policy enforcement using SDN. In: SIGCOMM (2013)

20. Quinn, P., Nadeau, T.: Problem Statement for Service Function Chaining, RFC 7498 (2015). https://tools.ietf.org/html/rfc7498

21. Sekar, V., et al.: The design and implementation of a consolidated middlebox architecture. In: USENIX NSDI, San Jose, April 2012

22. Sherry, J., et al.: Making middleboxes someone elses problem: network processing as a cloud service. In: ACM SIGCOMM, Helsinki, Finland, pp. 13–24, August 2012

23. Soliman, M., et al.: Exploring source routed forwarding in SDN-based WANs. In: IEEE International Conference on Communications (ICC), pp. 3070–3075, Australia (2014)

24. T-NOVA Project. http://www.t-nova.eu

25. Zhang, Y., et al.: StEERING: a software-defined networking for inline service chaining. In: ICNP (2013)

An Efficient Geographical Addressing Scheme for the Internet

Bernd Meijerink$^{(\boxtimes)}$, Mitra Baratchi, and Geert Heijenk

University of Twente, Enschede, The Netherlands
{bernd.meijerink,m.baratchi,geert.heijenk}@utwente.nl

Abstract. Geocast is a scheme which allows packets to be sent to a destination area instead of an address. This allows the addressing of any device in a specific region without further knowledge. In this paper we present an addressing mechanism that allows efficient referral to areas of arbitrary size. The binary representation of our addressing mechanism fits in an IPv6 address and can be used for route lookup with simple exclusive-or operations. We show that our addressing mechanism can be used to address areas accurately enough to be used as a mechanism to route packets close to their destination.

Keywords: Geocast · Addressing · IPv6

1 Introduction

Geocast is the concept of sending a message to a geographical location instead of a (fixed) address. All devices on a certain network that are in the specified area and are interested in the offered data can subscribe and receive this data. When combined with the use of multicast this can lead to an efficient way of addressing all nodes in a certain area.

An important application area of geocast or geographically addressed multicast, is in the area of vehicular networks [6] or mobile systems in general. There are several situations, such as the transmission of traffic information where it is unimportant to address specific nodes, but it is important that all nodes in a certain area receive a message. For example, cars on a specific road might need to know that an ambulance is approaching so that they can make room, while a car on a parallel road does not need to receive this information.

Although most of the currently proposed geocasting systems focus on ad-hoc networks or vehicular networks more specifically [1], only few have been proposed from a fixed network point of view [2,8]. The main downside of the ad-hoc model is that it only works from inside the ad-hoc network, which limits scalability. It would be beneficial to be able to send a message from anywhere in a fixed network (for example the Internet) to a specific region. One of the main

© IFIP International Federation for Information Processing 2016
Published by Springer International Publishing Switzerland 2016. All Rights Reserved
L. Mamatas et al. (Eds.): WWIC 2016, LNCS 9674, pp. 78–90, 2016.
DOI: 10.1007/978-3-319-33936-8_7

use-cases for such a system would be to target cars on public roads to inform them of locally relevant information.

In this paper, we present an addressing method that can be used to efficiently address arbitrary areas with low computational cost. The resulting address fits in the IPv6 address space and can be used as a destination address for a packet and as a route entry for routers. Route lookup can be performed based on prefix matching already used in the Internet today. We consider the following requirements for such a system based on the requirements for an Internet-wide geo-networking system [4]:

- **Accuracy.** The proposed system needs to be relatively accurate in large as well as small areas. Inaccuracy would cause messages to be delivered to locations that are not within the destination area, or in the opposite case not to be delivered at all.
- **Minimal delay.** Routers will need to be able to quickly forward packets, preferably by a system similar to currently used unicast longest prefix matching. Large tables containing complex forwarding entries should be avoided.
- **Scalability.** Scaling to a worldwide system should be possible without impacting routing performance. It should be possible to aggregate addresses to minimize the growth of route table entries.

The main contribution of this paper is proposing an addressing method in which neighbouring areas can be specified with a single address. This addressing method has a binary representation that can be used to perform route lookups based on prefix matching, avoiding the need to do costly calculation on destination polygons [9].

The structure of the rest of the paper is as follows: In Sect. 2, we present and evaluate related work done on geocasting. Section 3 describes our method to address regions. In Sect. 4, we describe how arbitrary areas can be fitted into a single address. Section 6, explains the applications of our addressing scheme in the Internet. Finally, we conclude and explore possible directions of future work in Sect. 7.

2   Related Work

A number of papers have been published about geocasting protocols in ad-hoc networks, allowing data to be sent to other location in the wireless ad-hoc network based on the location of the destination node(s). Papers describing geocasting systems for large fixed IP networks are however, rare. In this section, several past proposals will be described.

Navas and Imielinski proposed a system that adds an overlay network on top of the existing IP infrastructure to support geocasting [8]. This system requires special routers and modification of the sending and receiving nodes. In their system routers are responsible for a certain area and can forward messages to other routers, if this destination is outside of their coverage area. Addressing in this system is based on GPS coordinates. The same authors proposed a system to use a worldwide geo-network to send and receive messages from geo-networking capable devices [3]. In this paper, the authors propose to divide the world into 3 dimensional partitions with their own individual multicast address. Communication to and from these so called 'dataspaces' is based on multicast trees between responsible routers. This addressing approach would require a unique multicast address for each area. While this approach is certainly not impossible with the IPv6 addressing space, it would lead to a large amount of route table entries. Navas and Imielinksi have also proposed a routing algorithm that uses full network knowledge to route geographic packets [9]. In this paper, the cost of calculating the forwarding links for a packet is evaluated. It is concluded that destination areas should be simplified in forwarding routers to reduce routing time at the cost of accuracy.

GPS based Multicast is based on smallest possible sections (an atom) that can be mapped to a multicast address. Each atom and each possible partition are assigned a multicast address. A sender would have to know the address of its destination area to target it. This system allows for a geocasting system that can work in any IP multicast capable network. The main addressing disadvantage is that the target region must be predefined.

The eDNS platform is a modified DNS system that can perform reverse location queries [2]. The system can be queried for all records that are in a specified area. This system allows the implementation of an application layer geocast solution. A device first looks up all the addresses of the devices in the region it wants to geocast to. When the query returns the data can be sent to all those devices. This approach has the benefit that it can be deployed on top of the existing IP infrastructure and can work with both IPv4 and IPv6. The main downside is that every device in the target area needs to be addressed individually and all devices must periodically update their location in a central database.

To the best of our knowledge, there are no more recent papers concerning geocasting in fixed networks. More recent publications generally focus on the specific ad-hoc wireless use case, specifically on sensor networks.

Georouting protocols for wireless environments are based on several assumptions that are not necessarily true in a wired setting. In a wireless setting, georouting protocols try to be 'greedy', routing packets to the neighbour node nearest to the destination [5]. The most fundamental difference is that in wireless ad-hoc networks, there is a strong relation between the physical distance between two nodes and the network distance, e.g., number of hops between nodes, data rate of a link, or error probability of a link. In a fixed network this relation is only very limited. Furthermore, in a fixed network the relation between the direction a packets needs to travel in to reach its destination does not necessarily correspond to the location of the next hop router.

When traffic volume grows efficiency becomes important, routing should preferably be done in a manner resembling the current IP routing system with no routing cost depending on the destination. Another large difference is that fixed infrastructure is generally relatively static compared to an ad-hoc environments. This gives us the possibility to consider the distribution of routing information over multiple hops, or even the entire network.

Geohash [10] is a method for efficiently indexing geographical coordinates with arbitrary precession. While Geohash is not directly related to geocast routing, it is an interesting approach to look at. The geohash system splits the world into halves based on latitude and longitude and represents them in a short form. Locations near to each other share a common prefix although this does not work near the Greenwich meridian, the 180° meridian and the poles (due to the closeness of the longitude coordinates). Due to the nature of Geohash to represent nearby coordinates with identical prefixes and the ability to use arbitrary precision, we feel that Geohash is an interesting concept to explore for routable geographic addresses.

3   Addressing

In this Section, we will describe the method we use to address sections of the planet. To represent a single section on the planet we divide the Earth into four sections based on the latitude and longitude of the wgs84 projection [7]. The latitude ranging from 90 to −90 (North to South) and longitude from −180 to 180 (East to West). The resulting four rectangles (which we refer to as level 1) meeting at (0,0) are themselves divided into four sections. This process continues for the number of steps that are needed for an optimal description of the area that we are interested in. Due to the nature of the wgs84 projection, the rectangles in our system have half the height of their width in terms of degrees. Figure 1, shows an overview of these rectangles.

The major difference between our approach and GeoHash [10] is in the way we number these rectangles. As we will examine in Sect. 3.2, it is possible to combine neighbouring rectangles into a single area description. This allows us to address arbitrary areas on the globe based on these rectangles. With the ability to combine neighbouring rectangles into a single description we can resolve one of the main limitations of addressing single rectangles.

This form of specifying areas allows fast forwarding of geographically addressed packets though the Internet. This system should be accurate enough to get packets relatively close to their destination where a more accurate but slower routing method could take over.

3.1   Size of the Rectangles

Rectangles that are split into four identical sections logically have half the height and width of their parent rectangle. We define the level of a rectangle as the number of times we need to split the initial rectangle to reach it. With this definition there are 4 rectangles at level 1, 16 at level 2 and 64 at level 3 (Fig. 1). The number of rectangles in a certain level is thus given by Eq. 1. In this equation, N is the number of rectangles that are present at a certain *level*.

The resulting height and width of a rectangle at a specific level depends on the size of the earth and the location of the rectangle on it. Due to the size in meters depending on the latitude, all calculation related to size are done in degrees. Equation 2 gives us the width of a rectangle at a specific *level* where W is the width. Equation 3 gives us the height of a rectangle at a specific *level*, where H is the height.

$$N = 4^{level} \tag{1}$$

$$W(level) = \frac{360}{2^{level}} \tag{2}$$

$$H(level) = \frac{180}{2^{level}} \tag{3}$$

As noted, the actual size of a rectangle depends on the latitude of the rectangle. Assuming the earth has a circumference of 40,075 km this gives us an upper bound on the size of a rectangle as $40,075/360 = 111$ km per degree. In practice, every line of a rectangle will be smaller per degree unless one of the lines is exactly on the equator.

3.2   Numbering the Rectangles

We number the rectangles that result from the process above in a way resembling a horseshoe (see Fig. 1). We start numbering from the centre of the rectangle that the new rectangles appear in with *1*. We then move to the side with *2*. Number *3* is the rectangle below that and we move back to the inside to place number *4*.

This system can be described mathematically by using Eqs. 4–6. We input the *longitude* and *latitude* of a location in Eqs. 4 and 5 respectively, together with the *level* we want to know the number of. We now use the resulting x and y values in Eq. 6 to find the corresponding number.

To find a complete representation of a rectangle with a certain level of precession the equation will have to be used once for each level of accuracy. A formal description of the use of these equations to find a complete description of a point can be found in Eqs. 7 and 8. In Eq. 7, $S_{level}(lat, lon)$ is the number on a specific level, with L the matrix in Eq. 6. Equation 8 represents the entire description for each level with $S(lat, lon)$ being the full description. Algorithm 1 provides the pseudo-code to perform this lookup using Eqs. 2–6.

$$x(lon, level) = \left\lfloor \frac{lon + 180}{W(level)} \right\rfloor \mod 4 \tag{4}$$

$$y(lat, level) = \left\lfloor \frac{90 + lat}{H(level)} \right\rfloor \mod 4 \tag{5}$$

$$L_{x,y} = \begin{bmatrix} 3 & 4 & 4 & 3 \\ 2 & 1 & 1 & 2 \\ 2 & 1 & 1 & 2 \\ 3 & 4 & 4 & 3 \end{bmatrix} \tag{6}$$

$$S_{level}(lat, lon) = L_{x(lon,level),y(lat,level)} \tag{7}$$

$$S(lat, lon) = (S_1(lat, lon), S_2(lat, lon), ..., S_{maxLevel}(lat, lon)) \tag{8}$$

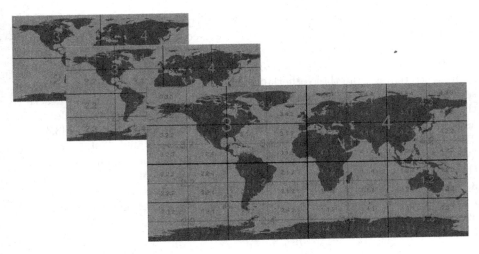

Fig. 1. Worldmap with rectangles up to level 3

The benefit of this numbering schema is that rectangles on the same level will neighbour rectangles with the same number in neighbouring parent rectangles. We will show later that this is helpful in aggregating rectangles to cover arbitrary areas.

We have chosen to represent a rectangle in this quaternary notion by separating each level with a dot. For example, a rectangle on level 2 with number *3* that has a rectangle with number *1* as its parent is represented by 1.3. Figure 1 shows rectangles with their number up to level 3 overlayed on a map of the world. Note that on each level rectangles with similar suffixes neighbour each other when their parent rectangles are neighbours.

3.3 Addressing Multiple Rectangles

Enclosing arbitrary areas in just a single rectangle would lead to a very inefficient system as it would enclose much more than just the requested area. To solve this

---

Input : *lat* and *lon* (Coordinates of point); *level*; L (Lookup matrix)
Output: List *result* with rectangle representation of length *level*
1 List *result*;   // Initialize list
2 **for** $i \leftarrow 1$ **to** *level* $+ 1$ **do**
3     $x \leftarrow (lon + 180)/(360/2^{level}) \mod 4$;   // Eq. 4 and 2
4     $y \leftarrow (90 + lat)/(180/2^{level}) \mod 4$;   // Eq. 5 and 3
5     $number_{level} \leftarrow L[x][y]$;   // Eq. 6 lookup
6     $result$.add($number_{level}$);
7 **end**

Algorithm 1. Coordinate lookup algorithm

problem, it would be beneficial to address multiple lower level rectangles that together better describe the area. To do so we need a method to address multiple rectangles at once. Because the way the rectangles are numbered it is relatively easy to address neighbouring rectangles at once. Imagine an area we want to address stretching from the Netherlands to the centre of Russia. In Fig. 1, we can see that we would likely need the rectangles 4.4.2 and 4.4.1. We can now describe this in a single address as 4.4.[1,2]. An area that crosses parent rectangles, such as the one covering the Netherlands and the UK would be described as [3,4].4.2. This notation means that we want to address both rectangle 3.4.2 and 4.4.2. We describe these rectangles as having level 3. We describe the amount of levels that a rectangle diverges from a single rectangle as its depth: [3,4].4.2 has depth 3, while 4.4.[1,2] has a depth of 1. A formalised expression of combining two rectangles can be seen in Eq. 9, where $\oplus$ denotes the operation of combining two areas.

$$(S_1^A, S_2^A, ...) \oplus (S_1^B, S_2^B, ...) = (S_1^A + S_1^B, S_2^A + S_2^B, ...) \tag{9}$$

Due to the nature of this method to 'mirror' lower level areas into higher levels, the description regularly incorporates more areas than just the components it is constructed of. An example would be extending the area covering the Netherlands and the UK eastward. This would add 3.4.1 to the group leading to the area [3,4].4.[1,2], but this also includes the 4.4.1 area. However, the numbering method has been designed to avoid this as much as possible.

3.4   Binary Representation

To enable the address to be encoded into an IPv6 address and perform route lookups based on our rectangle representation, it would be beneficial to have a binary notation that enables combining rectangles. Each level represents four possible rectangles. Because we want to address destinations that possibly overlap multiple rectangles, we cannot simply represent the numbers of the rectangles in a binary fashion. We represent each level as a 4 bit block: $1 = 1000$, $2 = 0100$, $3 = 0010$ and $4 = 0001$. Example: $2.4.2 = 0100.0001.0100$. This example can still be represented with two bits per level, but once we need to combine multiple rectangles the four bit system becomes needed. If for example we would want to address the region surrounding $(0,0)$ at level 3, this would require us to address the following rectangles: 1.1.3 (1000.1000.0010), 2.1.3 (0100.1000.0010), 3.1.3 (0010.1000.0010), and 4.1.3 (0001 1000 0010), or [1,2,3,4].1.3 (1111.1000.0010). The binary representation of rectangles that can be combined is a binary OR over the individual rectangles that cover the area.

With this binary representation it becomes possible to map the rectangle addresses to IPv6 multicast addresses. If we take the 16 bit multicast prefix into account, we will be left with 112 bits for addressing. With 4 bits per level this allows us to address a total of 28 levels. At the equator 28 levels corresponds to a rectangle of 7.5 by 3.7 cm. As this is a unrealistic small area to address it is likely that fewer levels can be used, saving space for other information in the address. We will evaluate the number of levels (and thus bits) needed for realistic scenarios in Sect. 5.

4   Area Calculation

Combining neighbouring rectangles that share a parent rectangle is trivial. It is possible to simply combine the addresses of the rectangles with a binary OR as explained in Sect. 3.4. In this section, we will explain how we can find the area between arbitrary points to build a complete representation of any rectangle.

A line can be represented by two points on the same latitude or longitude. As shown in Sect. 3, we can find the representation of these points at any level. To complete our line representation, we will however also need to include the rectangles that are between the rectangles that represent our start and end points. Consider the line between the points $(60, -55)$ 3.4.1 and $(60, 55)$ 4.4.1. As we can see in Fig. 1 the rectangles 3.4.2 and 4.4.2 are between them, to accurately represent the line we need a method to find these rectangles. To extend this idea to areas that also differ in latitude we need to also take into account the rectangles in two directions (instead of one).

We can modify Algorithm 1 to accept two coordinates and calculate the area between them. The distance of the two coordinates in the lookup matrix (Eq. 6) is calculated by subtracting the values of Eqs. 4 and 5 for both coordinates from each other per level. We can now simply 'walk' over the matrix within the calculated range for each level and add the found numbers to our value for that level. Algorithm 2 shows the procedure in pseudo code. Note that we make use of Eqs. 2–5 again. It is important that coordinate 1 is the north-western corner of the rectangle and coordinate 2 the south-eastern.

An extra check is added to the algorithm to see if the parent rectangles do not border in the East - West (*line 9*) or North - South (*line 14*) direction. When this is not the case (distance is greater or equal to 4) we need to make at least one 'loop' in that direction over the matrix in Eq. 6 to ensure we cover all rectangles between the two points at that level. If we do not do this, rectangles on that level between the points might not be included in our description.

5   Accuracy

To determine the accuracy of the system we performed an evaluation with random areas on the world map. We generated a set of 10.000 random coordinates $(lat, lon)_N, N \in [1, 10000]$. These coordinates have formed the basis of several sets of rectangles. These rectangles all have one of the generated coordinates as their north-western corner. The south-eastern corner is generated based on a random value between 0 and s. Sets $((lat, lon)_N, (lat + \Delta lat, lon + \Delta lon)_N)$ were created with randomly generated deltas starting at 0 going to $s = 0.1$, 0.5, 1, 2, 5, 10, 15 or 20°. These ranges were chosen as they would cover most realistic scenarios we can envision. As reference: on the equator 0.1° equals 11 km. Additionally, six sets were generated with separate latitude and longitude ranges to

---

Input : *(lat1,lon1),(lat2,lon2)* (2 coordinates); *level*; L (Lookup matrix)
Output: List *result* with rectangle representation of length *level*
1 List *result*;   // Initialize list
2 **for** $i \leftarrow 1$ **to** $level + 1$ **do**
3      $\quad x1 \leftarrow (lon1 + 180)/(360/2^{level})$;   // Equation 4 and 2
4      $\quad y1 \leftarrow (90 + lat1)/(180/2^{level})$;   // Equation 5 and 3
5      $\quad x2 \leftarrow (lon2 + 180)/(360/2^{level})$;   // Equation 4 and 2
6      $\quad y2 \leftarrow (90 + lat2)/(180/2^{level})$;   // Equation 5 and 3
7      $\quad dX \leftarrow (x2 - x1) \mod 4$;
8      $\quad dY \leftarrow (y2 - y1) \mod 4$;
9      $\quad$ **if** $|dX| \geq 4$ **then** // Are parents East-West neighbours?
10     $\quad\quad | \quad dX \leftarrow (dX \mod 4) + 4$;
11     $\quad$ **else**
12     $\quad\quad | \quad dX \leftarrow dX \mod 4$;
13     $\quad$ **end**
14     $\quad$ **if** $|dY| \geq 4$ **then** // Are parents North-South neighbours?
15     $\quad\quad | \quad dY \leftarrow (dY \mod 4) + 4$;
16     $\quad$ **else**
17     $\quad\quad | \quad dY \leftarrow dY \mod 4$;
18     $\quad$ **end**
19     $\quad temp \leftarrow 0$;
20     $\quad$ **for** $y \leftarrow y1$ **to** $y1 + dY + 1$ **do**
21     $\quad\quad$ **for** $x \leftarrow x1$ **to** $x1 + dX + 1$ **do**
22     $\quad\quad\quad | \quad temp \leftarrow temp \lor L[x \mod 4][y \mod 4]$;
23     $\quad\quad$ **end**
24     $\quad$ **end**
25     $\quad result.\mathrm{add}(temp)$;
26 **end**

Algorithm 2. Rectangle lookup algorithm

ensure wide and tall rectangles. These values were as $(\Delta lat, \Delta lon)$ in degrees: (1,3), (3,1), (2,5), (5,2), (2,10) and (10,2). The reason is that these areas are difficult to fit into a single rectangle without sacrificing accuracy.

To calculate the accuracy we find the area covered by our generated rectangle and divide it by the area covered by the most accurate rectangle we can find in our numbering scheme. The result is a number between 0 and 1, 1 being exact coverage by the calculated rectangle.

5.1   Lookup Level Accuracy

To find the optimal level at which the system can accurately describe most areas, we calculate the accuracy at different levels for each rectangle in our test set. We start at level 1 (One or multiple rectangles of 180 by 90°), and go up to level 18 (a single level 18 rectangle would measure 152 by 76 m on the equator). From Fig. 2 we can conclude that for each rectangle size tested, level 18 is enough to provide the maximum accuracy possible.

We can also see that larger areas need less levels before the accuracy does not increase any more, compared to smaller areas that require more levels to reach

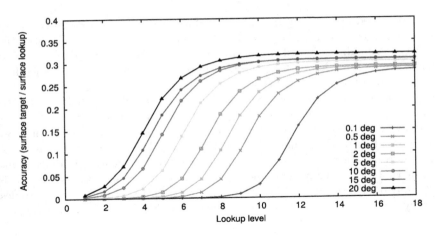

Fig. 2. Accuracy per level of different sized rectangles

the same accuracy. This is a logical result of the amount of space a rectangle of a certain level covers. We can also conclude that the maximum accuracy seems to be 0.3, meaning that the target area covers 30 % of the most accurate rectangle our system could generate.

5.2   Lookup Depth Accuracy

In Fig. 3, we examine the depth needed to accurately represent an area. We define the depth as the number of levels below the point at which the description starts covering multiple rectangles. At depth 0 the address represents a single rectangle, at depth n at most 4^n rectangles appear of that depth. Figure 3a shows that a depth of 12 is sufficient to accurately cover even small areas. In the case of larger areas the lookup can be limited to a depth of 8.

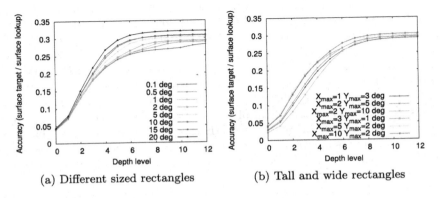

(a) Different sized rectangles   (b) Tall and wide rectangles

Fig. 3. Accuracy per lookup depth

As mentioned, we have specifically looked at very tall and wide rectangles to see their accuracy. Figure 3b shows that the performance of the description for these areas is equal to that of fully random areas. It is even possible to achieve better accuracy with less depth in these cases, likely due to the fact the these areas cover many rectangles at the lower levels.

Based on Fig. 3a and b we can conclude that calculating rectangles after depth 10 does not result in much further gain. We can also see that the tall and wide areas need on average a greater depth to gain the same accuracy compared to the completely random ones. This effect is caused by the fact that these areas require more smaller rectangles to accurately represent them. Approaches like Geohash that only represent a single rectangle perform similar to depth 0 in Fig. 3a and b, significant gains can be made by addressing multiple rectangles. Accuracy is increased at least a factor 6 as compared to the single rectangle case.

6   Application to Internet-Wide Geocasting

In this section, we explore the applicability of our addressing approach. As an example we will take a packet addressed to the country of the Netherlands.

In its binary representation, our addressing scheme could be used to lookup routes for packets in the Internet. Routing could be performed based on the four bit groups that specify one or more rectangles on a given level. A router can perform a bitwise exclusive or on an address and its routing entries to find entries that have overlap.

A route entry is represented in the same way as a destination address. We take the country of The Netherlands as an example: The country covered by the rectangle with the North-West corner (3.3750933,53.6724828) and South-East corner (7.2230957,50.6266868). It is contained in the level 7 rectangle [4].[4].[2].[3].[2].[1,2,3,4].[1,4]. At level 7 these 8 rectangles represent an area 5.625° wide and tall. The binary representation of this rectangle is 0001.0001.0100.0010.0100.1111.1001.

Now consider a router that has a route entry to this exact area. Also consider a packet addressed to the northern part of the country with the following destination address: [4].[4].[2].[3].[2].[1,2,3,4].[1] or 0001.0001.0100.0010.0100.1111.1000. The router can now perform the exclusive-or operation on the address and entry to obtain the overlap:
0001.0001.0100.0010.0100.1111.1001 $\oplus$ 0001.0001.0100.0010.0100.1111.1000 = 0001.0001.0100.0010.0100.1111.1000. The resulting value has at least a single 1 in each group of four bits, so the entry is a valid forwarding route for this address.

This approach puts the burden of most calculations at the sending system. This system will have to calculate the destination address of its packets based on Algorithm 2. Routers must initially calculate (or be provided with) the rectangle description of the area they cover, but no computationally intensive operations are necessary during forwarding.

We determined in the previous section that a description of level 18 can accurately cover most areas. A rectangle of level 18 can be encoded into 72 bits.

This means that it can be used in a IPv6 multicast address while leaving 56 bits unused.

7 Conclusion and Future Work

In this paper, we have presented a method for addressing geographic regions using rectangles. Multiple rectangular regions can be addressed with a single address. This system allows areas of any size to be specified with relative accuracy. We show our approach is in some cases a factor 6 more accurate than conventional methods such as Geohash. The binary representation of our addressing method can fit within an IPv6 address with space to spare, while maintaining good accuracy. The representation can also be used for route lookup in an IP-based network. We show that our approach has potential as a system to transmit geocast packets close to their destination, where a more accurate but computationally expensive routing method can take over.

For future work we will focus on more accurately representing areas by using multiple addresses, finding a balance between multiple packets and more accuracy. For this paper, we focussed on rectangular destinations. In practice most areas will not be rectangles but other shapes, such as polygons and circles. We will extend our work to use these other shaped which will allow greater flexibility. Furthermore, we would like to focus on routing based on the presented addressing method.

Acknowledgements. The authors would like to thank the financial support provided by the SALUS project, co-funded by the EU under the 7th Framework Programme for research (grant agreement no. 313296).

References

1. Di Felice, M., Bedogni, L., Bononi, L.: Group communication on highways: an evaluation study of geocast protocols and applications. Ad Hoc Netw. **11**(3), 818–832 (2013)
2. Fioreze, T., Heijenk, G.J.: Extending the domain name system (DNS) to provide geographical addressing towards vehicular ad-hoc networks (VANETs). In: Altintas, O., Chen, W., Heijenk, G.J. (eds.) VNC, pp. 70–77. IEEE (2011)
3. Imielinski, T., Goel, S.: DataSpace - querying and monitoring deeply networked collections in physical space. In: MobiDE, pp. 44–51. ACM (1999)
4. Karagiannis, G., Heijenk, G., Festag, A., Petrescu, A., Chaiken, A.: Internet-wide geo-networking problem statement (2013). https://tools.ietf.org/html/draft-karagiannis-problem-statement-geonetworking-01
5. Karp, B., Kung, H.T.: GPSR: greedy perimeter stateless routing for wireless networks. In: Proceedings of the 6th Annual International Conference on Mobile Computing and Networking, pp. 243–254. ACM (2000)
6. Khaled, Y., Ben Jemaa, I., Tsukada, M., Ernst, T.: Application of ipv6 multicast to vanet. In: 9th International Conference on Intelligent Transport Systems Telecommunications (ITST 2009), pp. 198–202. IEEE (2009)

7. National Geospatial-Intelligence Agency: World Geodetic System (2015). https://www.nga.mil/ProductsServices/GeodesyandGeophysics/Pages/ WorldGeodeticSystem.aspx. Accessed 14 January 2016
8. Navas, J.C., Imielinski, T.: GeoCast - geographic addressing and routing. In: Pap, L., Sohraby, K., Johnson, D.B., Rose, C. (eds.) MOBICOM, pp. 66–76. ACM (1997)
9. Navas, J.C., Imielinski, T.: On reducing the computational cost of Geographic Routing. Rutgers University, Department of Computer Science, Technical report DCS-TR-408 (2000)
10. Niemeyer, G.: Geohash (2008). http://geohash.org/

Energy Efficiency

On the Energy Inefficiency of MPTCP for Mobile Computing

Mohammad Javad Shamani[1]([✉]), Weiping Zhu[1], and Saeid Rezaie[2]

[1] School of Engineering and Information Technology, UNSW, Canberra, Australia
m.shamani@student.unsw.edu.au, w.zhu@adfa.edu.au
[2] School of Computer, West Tehran Islamic Azad University, Tehran, Iran
s.rezaie@wtiau.ac.ir

Abstract. Mobile devices have embraced Multi-Path TCP (MPTCP) for leveraging the path diversity. MPTCP is a double-edged sword since mobile phones are suffering excessively from short battery life span. In order to find energy efficiency of MPTCP, the signal quality and the transferred file size have been taken into account. We formulate the above problem as a Markovian Decision Process (MDP) for symmetric and asymmetric network traffic. Numerical and simulation results surprisingly show that MPTCP is not efficient in any selected scenarios and the proposed scheme can save 56 % of energy compared to the conventional MPTCP.

Keywords: MPTCP · Mobile device · Energy · MDP

1 Introduction

Wide coverage oriented cellular base stations and WiFi hot-spots coverage go hand in hand with arming mobile phones by different transmission interfaces such as cellular and WiFi, enhance the users' ubiquitous connectivity. Due to the error-prone nature of wireless channels, poor wireless signal quality is frequently experienced spatially and temporally by end users. It has been shown that the signal quality in WiFi or cellular-based networks dips in most cases. For instance, 43 % and 21 % of mobile phone data traffic is transmitted during low cellular and WiFi signal strength, respectively [2]. In addition, low signal strength could drain the mobile device battery. Due to the limited nature of mobile phone batteries, meeting high quality of service (QoS), while maintaining reasonable level of energy consumption, is of great importance for end-users. It is noteworthy that reaching high QoS and energy efficiency is not possible, in many cases, due to their conflicting requirements. Thus, designing a proper scheme to obtain reasonable levels of QoS and energy efficiency is critical.

Recently, MPTCP is introduced to enhance TCP performance by exploiting the path diversity [3,12]. However, base MPTCP suffers from energy inefficiency

L. Mamatas et al. (Eds.): WWIC 2016, LNCS 9674, pp. 93–105, 2016.
DOI: 10.1007/978-3-319-33936-8_8

in mobile phones. For instance, when a mobile phone experiences poor signal quality, not only is an adverse effect on energy consumption inevitable, but also QoS degradation is unavoidable. In [11] we show that the available bandwidth could be estimated by getting the signal quality as an observation and applying hidden Markov model; however, throughput is a more trustworthy metric to understand the different platforms energy consumption. In order to estimate the throughput accurately it is also important to consider the transferred file size. We explore how file size affects the throughput and how to estimate the file size by queue dynamics. The objective of this paper is to investigate whether MPTCP is more energy efficient than WiFi and LTE in real scenarios by leveraging simultaneous uploads and downloads in symmetric and asymmetric traffic pattern. Therefore, we proposed Signal Aware MPTCP (SA-MPTCP) to enhance MPTCP energy efficiency. The contribution of this paper is threefold as follows:

- We make a tight relation between signal quality, file size and energy consumption; besides the optimization problem is formulated as a Markovian decision making problem by employing buffer size dynamics to better understand transferring file sizes.
- We endeavor to minimize energy consumption by exploiting diverse characteristics of interfaces, and for the first time we have found that MPTCP is not energy efficient in real scenarios, particularly in simultaneous uploading and downloading.
- We investigate the effect of energy consumption on asymmetric and symmetric data traffic for a mobile user facing variety of signal strength on different interfaces.

The paper is organized as follows. Section 2 introduces the energy model, and shed light on the effect of file size on MPTCP throughput. Section 3 describes the problem formulation. Section 4 outlines the simulation results, and Sect. 5 reviews the related works. Finally, we conclude in Sect. 6.

2   Proposed Model

The proposed model aims to optimize the transmission energy consumption as a utility function based on signal strength and transferring file size. In the following, we describe the underlying network model and assumptions for the problem at hand.

2.1   Energy Model

The energy model used here addresses energy consumption for uploading and downloading by taking throughput into account. Where throughput would be estimated in our optimization problem by the interface's signal-to-noise ratio (SNR) and the transferring file size. To the best of our knowledge, the energy model introduced in [4] is the only proposed model that analyses energy consumption for WiFi, cellular networks and MPTCP. Considering this, we use the same concept in describing network model. We assume that the mobile device is equipped with two interfaces to transmit data. Let i denote the interface, where $i = w$ and $i = l$ represent the WiFi and LTE interface, respectively. Available uplink and downlink throughput for interface i is denoted by $Th_{u,i}$ and $Th_{d,i}$, respectively. The energy consumption in uploading data for interface i which is based on Joule (J) per byte (B), and is defined by E_i^u

$$E_i^u = (\alpha_i^u \times Th_{u,i}^{\beta_i^u})\ (\mu J/B), \tag{1}$$

where α_i^u and β_i^u are upload packet transfer coefficients of interface i, which are obtained through regression model in [4]. Similarly, for downloading, we have

$$E_i^d = (\alpha_i^d \times Th_{d,i}^{\beta_i^d})\ (\mu J/B), \tag{2}$$

where α_i^d and β_i^d are download packet transfer coefficient in interface i. Hence, total energy consumption of interface i in downlink and uplink can be formulated as $\mathcal{E}_i$ which is equal to

$$\mathcal{E}_i = E_i^u \times L_i^u + E_i^d \times L_i^d\ (J), \tag{3}$$

where L_i^u and L_i^d are the size of uploading and downloading files in bytes for interface i, respectively. In [4], it has been shown that due to the concurrent use of interfaces (WiFi and LTE) in MPTCP, the energy consumption is less than total energy consumption of WiFi and LTE, if they are not used jointly. MPTCP energy consumption, denoted as $\mathcal{E}_m$, can be written as

$$\mathcal{E}_m = (\mathcal{E}_w + \mathcal{E}_l) - \theta, \tag{4}$$

where θ represents the shared component energy. In MPTCP about 13 %–16 % energy would be consumed simultaneously [4]. Thus, in this paper we consider θ as a fixed number 14.5 %. Packet transfer coefficients for different platforms based on uplink and downlink are shown on Table 1.

2.2   Effect of File Size on Throughput

Estimating the available bandwidth by knowing the signal quality is possible. For instance, Fig. 1 shows the uplink and downlink throughput as a function

Table 1. Packet transfer coefficients [4]

		LTE	WiFi
Download	α^d	10.04	4.64
	β^d	−0.89	−0.81
Upload	α^u	13.34	3.61
	β^u	−0.83	−0.66

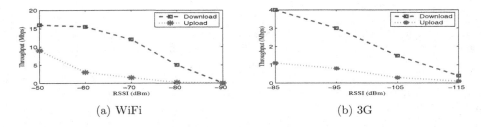

(a) WiFi   (b) 3G

Fig. 1. Average throughput based on signal strength

of received signal strength indicator (RSSI), where data is extracted from [2,5,9]. However, the amount of transfer size has a significant effect on MPTCP throughput. In Figs. 2 and 3 throughputs for MPTCP, WiFi and LTE have been plotted based on the transferred file size if the WiFi and LTE RSSI are $(-76, -90)$ and $(-106, -135)$, respectively. As it can be seen as the file size increases, the throughput reaches to the maximum capacity, which is the available bandwidth. Based on the available signal quality state and file size, the uplink and downlink throughputs could be estimated by a regression model. We have calculated the uplink and downlink coefficient for the noted RSSI states in Tables 2 and 3. The uplink throughput for interface i is defined as

$$Th_{u,i} = \kappa_i^u * (L^u)^{\eta_i^u} + \iota_i^u, \tag{5}$$

where κ_i^u and η_i^u are uplink coefficients for interface i. Downlink throughput is equal to

$$Th_{d,i} = \kappa_i^d * (L^d)^{\eta_i^d} + \iota_i^d, \tag{6}$$

where κ_i^d and η_i^d are defined as downlink coefficients for interface i. It is noteworthy that the number of selected states uplink and downlink tables should be calculated prior to the simulation.

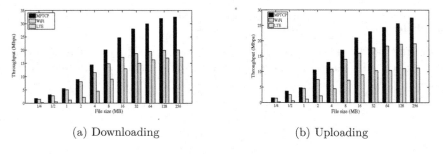

(a) Downloading   (b) Uploading

Fig. 2. Platforms throughput for different file sizes

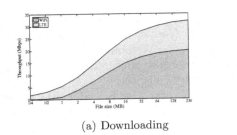
(a) Downloading

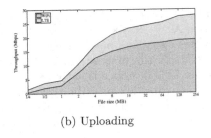
(b) Uploading

Fig. 3. MPTCP throughput for different file sizes

Table 2. Upload coefficients

	κ^u	η^u	ι^u
TCP over WiFi	-23.35	-0.16	29.48
TCP over LTE	-27.38	-0.08	29.62
MPTCP over WiFi	-27.58	-0.14	32.57
MPTCP over LTE	205.7	0.0052	-203.3

Table 3. Download coefficients

	κ^d	η^d	ι^d
TCP over WiFi	-24.1	-0.17	30
TCP over LTE	541	0.0055	-539
MPTCP over WiFi	-95	-0.039	98.22
MPTCP over LTE	-14.05	-0.15	18.59

3   Problem Formulation

3.1   Definitions

A mobile device decision making is based on the assumption that the system dynamics are determined by an MDP. MDP consists of the following elements: decision epochs, states, states transition probabilities, actions and costs. The mobile device can make a decision about tuning one or both interfaces from idle to active mode in each time epoch, where $\mathcal{T} = \{1, 2, .., y\}$ represent a set of decision epoch. The signal quality states are introduced by the following: firstly, a set of signal quality states for interface i, $\mathcal{R}_i = \{r_i^1, r_i^2, ..., r_i^n\}$, where r_i^1 is minimum and r_i^n is maximum signal quality state. It is worth adding here that each signal quality corresponds to specific uplink and downlink bandwidth. Secondly, signal quality states transition probability matrix for interface i, $P^{r_i} = [p^{r_i}(r_i^k | r_i^j), r_i^1 \le r_i^j, r_i^k \le r_i^n]$. In [11] we have shown that how to find the most probable signal quality states by getting RSSI as an observation and in this paper we assume the signal quality state is known. Let $\mathcal{S} = \mathcal{R}^1 \times \mathcal{R}^2 =$

$\{(r_1^1, r_2^1), (r_1^1, r_2^2), ..., (r_1^n, r_2^n)\} = \{s_1, s_2, ..., s_N\}$ represent the total state space, where $\mathcal{N} = |\mathcal{R}_1| \times |\mathcal{R}_2|$. The action space $\mathcal{A} = \{(on, on), (on, off), (off, on)\}$ denotes a set of all possible actions for both interfaces. Without loss of generality, let LTE be the first interface and WiFi be the second; consequently, (on, off) means LTE interface is active and the WiFi interface is idle.

The transition probability for the next state is $p(s_{t+1}|s_t, a_t)$. Since the state transition probability is the product of all state transition probabilities, we can rewrite it as

$$p(s_{t+1}|s_t, a_t) = p^{r_i}(\zeta(s_{t+1})|\zeta(s_t))p^{r_j}(\zeta(s_{t+1})|\zeta(s_t)), \qquad (7)$$

where $\zeta(s_t)$ gives the signals quality state of the compound state s_t. At time-slot t, when the action a_t is taken, the system shifts to the state s_{t+1}; therefore, the system incurs costs expressed as $c(s_t, a_t, s_{t+1})$.

Before discussing decision rules and policies, we have to shed light on cost calculation. In order to get the benefit of high accuracy of throughput estimation we need to have information about file size. Therefore, we use the backlog queue to have a better understanding of transferring file size.

Consider the proposed scheme operates n slotted times with time slots $t \in \{0, 1, 2, ...\}$. The uplink and downlink queues as defined as $\mathcal{Q}^u$ and $\mathcal{Q}^d$, respectively. At the beginning of each time slot, new packets arrive randomly. Let $\lambda_t = (\lambda_t^1, \lambda_t^2, \lambda_t^N)$ be the arrival rate vector. The service rate vector at each time slot t is defined as $\mu_t = (\mu_t^1, \mu_t^2, ..., \mu_t^N)$. The service rate is calculated based on the selected action at time t. Let's define the queue backlog as $\mathcal{Q}_t$, then the next backlog state are driven by stochastic arrival and service rates. Thus, the backlogs dynamics are given by

$$\mathcal{Q}_{t+1} = \max[\mathcal{Q}_t - \mu_t, 0] + \lambda_t. \qquad (8)$$

In the proposed scheme at each time slot we only observe the arrival rate and the quality of signal strength. Then we employ $\mathcal{Q}_{t+1}$ to estimate the transfer file size in uploading and downloading. Let's define the expected immediate cost as

$$c_t(s_t, a_t) = \begin{cases} \mathcal{E}_w + \mathcal{E}_l & a = (on, on) \\ \mathcal{E}_l & a = (on, off). \\ \mathcal{E}_w & a = (off, on) \end{cases} \qquad (9)$$

In the explained MDP problem, the objective is minimizing the expected long-term cost which is defined as

$$v^\pi(s) = \min_\pi \mathbb{E}^\pi \{\sum_{t=1}^{T} \gamma^t c_t^\pi(s_t, a_t^\pi(s_t))\}. \qquad (10)$$

Solving (10) would be computationally expensive; therefore, Let's define a policy by π, which maps states to actions. MDP endeavorers to find a policy π that minimizes some cumulative function of the stochastic costs. Given a cost criterion, a policy has an expected value for every state, specifying the cost of mobile phone receiving from following a policy in that state. Policy π^* is an best policy if there is no policy π', and no state s such that value of π' be lower than the value of π. Letting value of being at state s_{t+1} as $v_{t+1}(s_{t+1})$, then in each time step we aim for an action which has the minimum cost. let's express it as

$$a_t^*(s_t) = \arg \min_{a_t \in A_t} (c_t(s_t, a_t) + \gamma v_{t+1}(s_{t+1}), \tag{11}$$

where γ is a discount factor $(0 \leq \gamma < 1)$. Because this value shows the cost a mobile device incurs during one time period in the future, we may discount it by a factor γ. By using optimal action $a_t^*(s_t)$, the optimal value is equal to

$$v_t(s_t) = \arg \min_{a_t \in A_t} \left(c_t(s_t, a_t) + \gamma v_{t+1}(s_{t+1}(s_t, a_t)) \right) \tag{12}$$
$$= c_t(s_t, a^*(s_t)) + \gamma v_{t+1}(s_{t+1}(s_t, a^*(s_t))).$$

Because the problem is a decision problem with stochastic components and the new information would be available after The decision is made, we need to add uncertainty to (12)

$$v_t(s_t) = \min \left\{ c_t(s_t, a_t) \right.$$
$$\left. + \gamma \sum_{s_{t+1} \in S} p(s_{t+1}|s_t, a_t) v_{t+1}(s_{t+1})) \right\}. \tag{13}$$

(13) is widely known as the standard bellman equation [8]. We seek the best action in each state minimizing over policies. Thus, the expected cost provided by a policy π from time t onward is defined as

$$F_t^\pi(s_t) = \mathbb{E} \left[\sum_{t+1}^{T-1} c_{t+1}(s_{t+1}, a_{t+1}^\pi(s_{t+1})) + c_t(s_t) \Big| s_t \right], \tag{14}$$

where $F_t^\pi(s_t)$ represents the expected total cost in state s followed by a policy π from time t onward. To find (14) solution, we need to recursively calculate v_t^π. It has been shown that (14) is equal to $v_t^\pi(s_t)$ [7]. By letting $v_t(s_t)$ as a solution for (13), we will have

$$F_t^* = \min_{\pi \in \Pi} F_t^\pi(s_t) = v_t(s_t). \tag{15}$$

There are several ways to solve the infinite horizon optimization problems. For example, value iteration, or policy iteration algorithms [7]. The value iteration algorithm estimates the value function iteratively. At each iteration the best decision will be selected by a policy. In fact, value iteration begins at the end, and then goes backward to find out the best policy. The iteration counter starts at 0, and goes up until the algorithm satisfies the left-hand-side of (16). Thus, v is the largest absolute value, and the value iteration algorithm stops if the largest modify in the value of being in any state is less than the right-hand-side of (16).

$$\|v_n - v_{n-1}\| < \epsilon(1 - \gamma)/2\gamma, \tag{16}$$

where ϵ is an error tolerance parameter [7].

ALGORITHM 1. *SA-MPTCP Algorithm*

Input : λ_t^u , λ_t^d
Input : ϵ, *a tolerance parameter*
Output: *Best Policy for each state*
Begin
$set \rightarrow v_0=0$
$set \rightarrow n=1$
$set \rightarrow \lambda_u=\lambda_t^u$, $\lambda_d=\lambda_t^d$
$L_{t+1}^u = \max[L_t^u - \mu_t^u, 0] + \lambda_t^u$
$L_{t+1}^d = \max[L_t^d - \mu_t^d, 0] + \lambda_t^d$
for $s \ni S$ **do**
  $\quad v_n(s_t) = \max(c(s_t, a_t)) + \gamma \sum_{s_{t+1} \in s_t} P(s_{t+1}|s_t, a_t) v_{n-1}(s_{t+1}))$
  $\quad$ **if** $\|v_n - v_{n-1}\| < \epsilon(1 - \gamma)/2\gamma$ **then**
$$\pi^\epsilon = \pi^*, v_\epsilon = v_n$$
  $\qquad$ **else**
  $\qquad\quad n = n + 1$
  $\quad$ **end**
end
if *action a = (on,off)* **then**
  $\quad$ Enable MPTCP in backup mode
  $\quad$ Establish LTE sub-flow, postpone WiFi sub-flow establishment
else if *action a = (off,on)* **then**
  $\quad$ Enable MPTCP in backup mode
  $\quad$ Establish WiFi sub-flow, postpone LTE sub-flow establishment
else
  $\quad$ Enable MPTCP in full mode
end
End

4 Simulation and Results

In order to appraise the proposed algorithm, we have performed the simulations by ns-3 (https://www.nsnam.org). The simulation parameters are included in Table 4. We have considered three LTE and three WiFi signal quality states. Based on the selected states, we found nine spots on the simulation field as it noted in Fig. 4. We calculated nine upload and download tables as in Tables 2 and 3. Before the simulation the best policy in each state for different arrival rates have been calculated. After that the traffic has been generated between two nodes, and the mobile node (UE-1) moves from one spot to another by using the most efficient policy in each state.

In order to compare the proposed scheme to other platforms, we have simulated the same scenario using MPTCP, WiFi, and LTE in all spots. Also to have a practical perspective and general view of how the system works, two different file sizes have been selected for uploading and downloading in symmetric and asymmetric traffic scenarios.

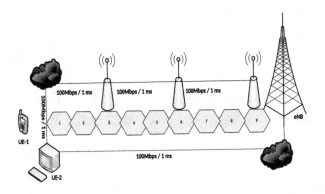

Fig. 4. Simulation topology

Table 4. Simulation parameters

LTE RSSI states	$(-45, -75), (-76, -105), (-106, -135)$
WiFi RSSI states	$(-50, -61), (-62, -75), (-76, -90)$
Point to Point bandwidth	100 Mbps
Point to Pint delay	1 ms
Direct Code Execution (DCE)	version 1.7

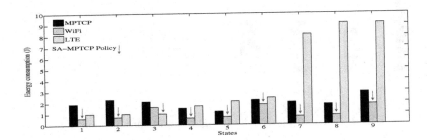

Fig. 5. 256 KB upload and 256 KB download energy consumption

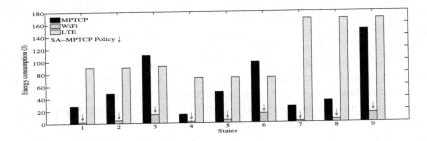

Fig. 6. 256 KB upload and 32 MB download energy consumption

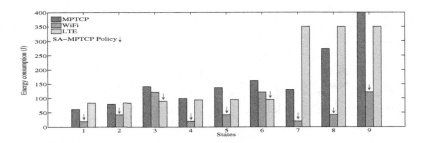

Fig. 7. 32 MB upload and 256 KB download energy consumption

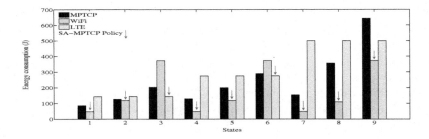

Fig. 8. 32 MB upload and 32 MB download energy consumption

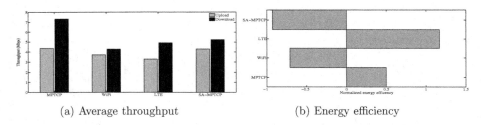

(a) Average throughput   (b) Energy efficiency

Fig. 9. Different platforms throughput and energy efficiency

From Figs. 5, 6, 7 and 8, the optimal policies have been marked by a red arrow. Taking the advantage of the packet capture feature of NS3, we have plotted the energy consumption behavior of other policies in each state. SA-MPTCP optimal decision was completely compatible with real simulation and surprisingly MPTCP has not been chosen in any scenario. In fact, this is the first time that uploading and downloading have been considered together, and the results contrast prior research such as [4,6]. Most of the time either WiFi or LTE are the best policy and even according to Fig. 6 WiFi is the best option for uploading small file size and downloading large file size. SA-MPTCP energy consumption outperforms other platforms.

Comparing SA-MPTCP to MPTCP, WiFi, and LTE, SA-MPTCP saves 56 %, 16 % and 65 % energy, respectively. On the other hand, MPTCP is 23 % more throughput efficient than SA-MPTCP. However, SA-MPTCP achieves a higher throughput compared to WiFi and LTE (Fig. 9).

5 Related Works

MPTCP has been investigated widely from different perspective; nonetheless, energy efficiency attracts the growing interest of researchers. Comparison of TCP over LTE and WiFi with MPTCP in terms of energy efficiency have been discussed in [6] by modeling, measuring and simulating. The authors proposed eMPTCP, which manages subflows expected energy efficiency based on available throughput. In fact eMPTCP is the most similar work to us, but the difference is eMPTCP only considered the downloading case and doesn't take the uploading energy into account. In addition, to estimate the available throughput eMPTCP sampled downloaded bytes, which introduces the overhead to a network.

GreenBag [1] was proposed as a bandwidth aggregate middleware on wireless links. It estimates the available bandwidth on wireless links and specifies the amount of traffic allocation while taking QoS into account. GreenBag reduces energy consumption between 14 % to 25 %; however, it needs major applications modification which is not feasible. Peng et al. [6] designed a MPTCP algorithm, decreasing energy consumption up to 22 % by intelligently compromising between throughput and energy. However, they only considered bulk data applications such as video streaming and file transfer, and they did not consider the effect of signal strength on throughput.

Markov decision process has been applied by [7] to utilize the optimal interface for different applications. Nevertheless, authors only considered throughput and stationary applications which is infeasible in dynamic environment. For instance, each application has different traffic patterns, and modeling all applications traffic is not practical. Furthermore, the optimal throughput performance is only achieved by one path, and more importantly the system performance would dwindle immensely when the optimal path is the most congested one. Energy aware MPTCP is proposed in [8] to balance the increasing throughput with the energy consumption. Unfortunately, data has been offloaded simply to WiFi whenever possible since they assumed WiFi consumes less energy than LTE. That assumption may not be true in many scenarios. In fact, when a mobile device experiences a weak WiFi signal, not only a huge amount of packet loss and delay would be irrefutable [5], but also as we showed, energy cost would increase sharply.

Lim et al. [5] proposed an inspiring algorithm, MPTCP-MA, which manages the path establishment by taking cross layer information, such as Mac layer behavior. They endeavored to increase the WiFi throughput efficiency up to 70 %; nonetheless, energy efficiency hasn't been taken into account, and they haven't addressed cellular networks behavior. In contrast to most studies, Tailless MPTCP (TMPTCP) [10] showed that MPTCP energy efficiency could be enhanced by the tail energy minimization. Since the tail energy has a enormous impression on the energy contribution, TMPTCP optimizes jointly energy and delay. However, TMPTCP deals with static bandwidth and the offline experiment demands more investigation.

6   Conclusion

In this paper, we studied the problem of energy efficiency in the context of multipath TCP. We proposed a control mechanism based on Markov Decision Process to distribute traffic over diverse paths while optimizing energy. Performance of the proposed control mechanism was evaluated and compared with the different platforms. The results indicate that the proposed control mechanism significantly outperforms other schemes in all considered scenarios and MPTCP is not energy efficient in any selected cases. Even though we have applied our approach to LTE, the model could simply extend to 3G networks. The effect of delay would be investigated in future work.

References

1. Bui, D.H., Lee, K., Oh, S., Shin, I., Shin, H., Woo, H., Ban, D.: Greenbag: energy-efficient bandwidth aggregation for real-time streaming in heterogeneous mobile wireless networks. In: IEEE 34th Real-Time Systems Symposium (RTSS 2013), pp. 57–67. IEEE (2013)
2. Ding, N., Wagner, D., Chen, X., Pathak, A., Hu, Y.C., Rice, A.: Characterizing and modeling the impact of wireless signal strength on smartphone battery drain. ACM SIGMETRICS Perform. Eval. Rev. **41**, 29–40 (2013). ACM
3. Ford, A., Raiciu, C., Handley, M., Barre, S., Iyengar, J., et al.: Architectural guidelines for multipath TCP development. IETF, Informational RFC 6182, 2070-1721 (2011)
4. Lim, Y.S., Chen, Y.C., Nahum, E.M., Towsley, D., Gibbens, R.J.: Improving energy efficiency of MPTCP for mobile devices. arXiv preprint arXiv:1406.4463 (2014)
5. Lim, Y.S., Chen, Y.C., Nahum, E.M., Towsley, D., Lee, K.W.: Cross-layer path management in multi-path transport protocol for mobile devices. In: Proceedings of INFOCOM, pp. 1815–1823. IEEE (2014)
6. Peng, Q., Chen, M., Walid, A., Low, S.: Energy efficient multipath TCP for mobile devices. In: Proceedings of the 15th ACM International Symposium on Mobile Ad hoc Networking and Computing, pp. 257–266. ACM (2014)
7. Powell, W.B.: Approximate Dynamic Programming: Solving the Curses of Dimensionality, vol. 703. Wiley, New York (2007)
8. Puterman, M.L.: Markov Decision Processes: Discrete Stochastic Dynamic Programming. Wiley, New York (2014)
9. Schulman, A., Navda, V., Ramjee, R., Spring, N., Deshpande, P., Grunewald, C., Jain, K., Padmanabhan, V.N.: Bartendr: a practical approach to energy-aware cellular data scheduling. In: Proceedings of the Sixteenth Annual International Conference on Mobile Computing and Networking, pp. 85–96. ACM (2010)
10. Shamani, M.J., Zhu, W., Naghshin, V.: TMPTCP: Tailless Multi-path TCP. In: 10th International Conference on Broadband and Wireless Computing, Communication and Applications (BWCCA), pp. 325–332 (2015). doi:10.1109/BWCCA.2015.103

11. Shamani, M.J., Zhu, W., Rezaie, S., Naghshin, V.: Signal aware multi-path TCP. In: 2016 Proceedings IEEE/IFIP of WONS, pp. 104–107. IEEE/IFIP (2016)
12. Wischik, D., Raiciu, C., Greenhalgh, A., Handley, M.: Design, implementation and evaluation of congestion control for multipath TCP. In: NSDI, vol. 11, p. 8 (2011)

Buffering... Energy for Mobile Devices: A "Store and Rendezvous" Approach

Dimitris Vardalis[✉], Christos-Alexandros Sarros, and Vassilis Tsaoussidis

Space Internetworking Center, Department of Electrical and Computer Engineering, Demokritos University of Thrace, 67100 Xanthi, Greece
dvardali@ee.duth.gr

Abstract. We exploit the traffic shaping potential of network storage and improve energy efficiency for mobile devices through the creation of idle communication intervals. We model the activity patterns between the WIRED/wireless gateway and the wireless battery-powered receiver, and employ a rendezvous mechanism that utilizes periods of inactivity created by the traffic shaping function of the network. In case multiple receivers are simultaneously active, a scheduling algorithm limits overlaps of buffer flushes. Our scenarios are based on the DTN paradigm, however, our approach is not DTN-specific. The presented simulation study involves three main types of Internet traffic (i.e. file transfer, streaming and web browsing) and demonstrates that our proposed scheme achieves significant energy conservation for mobile receivers involving, under most circumstances, only mild performance cost.

Keywords: Energy efficiency · 802.11 · Internetworking · DTN

1 Introduction

Mobile devices have become a powerful tool for communication, storage and entertainment, and often undergo several hours of daily use, which stretches their energy storing capabilities. They are equipped with increasingly more powerful CPUs, larger memory capacities, faster wireless network adapters, and a set of applications that require internetworking capabilities. However, advances in battery technology have not been able to match the increased energy demand. For applications that heavily rely on the networking subsystem, the related functions may account for as much as 60 % of the total power necessary for the mobile device operation [1]. Consequently, improving the energy efficiency of the networking subsystem has drawn significant attention from the research community and has led to the implementation of energy-saving features in a number of wireless networking applications.

The research leading to these results has received funding from the European Union's (EU) Horizon 2020 research and innovation programme under grant agreement No. 645124 (Action full title: Universal, mobile-centric and opportunistic communications architecture, Action Acronym: UMOBILE). This paper reflects only the authors' views and the Community is not liable for any use that may be made of the information contained therein.

Published by Springer International Publishing Switzerland 2016. All Rights Reserved
L. Mamatas et al. (Eds.): WWIC 2016, LNCS 9674, pp. 106–120, 2016.
DOI: 10.1007/978-3-319-33936-8_9

The ubiquitous 802.11 standard [2] confronts the energy efficiency problem by providing a power-save mechanism, which is, however, limited by the probabilistic nature of incoming data as well as the relatively small buffer space at the access point. This has led many researchers into looking for alternative methods, typically involving buffering at a "base station" (operating at the network layer and above) rather than an "access point" (operating at the MAC layer), thus highlighting that the device operation extends in higher network layers.

Our solution to the energy efficiency problem demonstrates the potential of Delay/Disruption-Tolerant Networking (DTN) [3] to shape internetwork traffic in a manner that allows mobile devices to balance their energy expenditure with minimal cost on throughput. We employ DTN in order to improve the energy efficiency of mobile devices in an infrastructure, wired-cum-wireless Internet setting with a last-hop 802.11 connection. The DTN functionality is extended with a rendezvous mechanism (first described here [4]) that allows mobile receivers to switch their Wireless Network Interface Cards (WNIC) to the sleep state during idle intervals.

In the current work, we study the operation of our DTN overlay for various types of Internet activity in terms of both the energy efficiency improvements for the mobile devices as well as possible deterioration of the user experience. Additionally, we explore alternative rendezvous scheduling aimed at minimizing transmission overlaps when multiple devices are active, further enhancing the device energy efficiency. In order to better interpret the simulation outcome, we also provide a simple mathematical formulation of the buffering process.

The rest of the paper is organized as follows: In Sect. 2 we present related work focusing on energy efficient networking and DTN. In Sect. 3 we describe our proposed solution and provide a mathematical formulation of the buffering mechanism. In Sect. 4 we present the experimental methodology and in Sect. 5 the simulation results. Finally, in Sect. 6 we summarize our conclusions and discuss future research plans.

2   Related Work

The design of energy-efficient networking protocols has long been the focus of scientific research. In [5] Jones et al. provide a comprehensive survey of energy-efficient protocols across the network stack and summarize the design principles for achieving energy efficiency. At the lower network layers, substantial effort in the energy efficiency research involves the WLAN standard 802.11 [2]. The 802.11 protocol provides a power-save mode of operation (PSM) that buffers incoming data at the access point, allowing the mobile devices to temporarily switch their wireless interfaces to the sleep state. The energy conservation potential of 802.11 is limited by the relatively small buffer space at the access point and the lack of visibility at higher network layers, leading many researchers into examining alternative methods based on the same core principle.

In [6] Chandra and Vahdat highlight the limitations of the 802.11 PSM and propose an application-specific traffic shaping proxy for multimedia streaming that can be implemented either on the server (source of the stream) or at the access point. In [7], Adams and Muntean propose an Adaptive-Buffer Power Save Mechanism (AB-PSM), again for multimedia streaming, which hides data from the base station and allows for longer idle intervals. Energy-saving strategies when streaming from a single server to multiple clients are explored by Acquaviva et al. in [8]. Zhu and Cao in [9] expand on the proxy idea by introducing a scheduler service at the base station and a proxy at the mobile terminal. Finally, in [10] the authors exploit windows of opportunities for optimal transmissions, while in [11] transmission behavior is adjusted according to network characteristics. Most of the described solutions target streaming applications and involve the installation of specialized components, such as proxies, schedulers and local services in order to operate. The network *per se* does not participate in the effort for energy efficiency.

Our contribution lies in the use of the DTN computer networking architecture for improving the energy efficiency of mobile devices. DTN was designed to cope with long propagation delays and lack of continuous end-to-end connectivity. Despite its original conception as space-communications architecture, DTN has been proposed for applications in various settings, including wired or wired-cum-wireless networks on the edges of the well-connected Internet. The DakNet [12] network employs DTN to provide Internet connectivity by physically transferring data using appropriately equipped vehicles. Significant attention from the research community has also been drawn by DTN applications related to vehicular communications [13, 14] and pocket-switched networks [15], which aim at providing Internet connectivity to commuters and mobile users respectively. More recently, DTN has been combined with resource pooling techniques that share private broadband connections in order to provide Less-than-Best-Effort, free Internet services to all users [16].

In our proposal we rely on the inherent capabilities of DTN for shaping internetwork traffic so that mobile receivers may suspend their WNICs with minimal cost on throughput. In our previous work [17] we have extended the DTN bundle protocol [18] with a cross-layer rendezvous mechanism employed between the base station and the receiving DTN nodes. The performance of our solution was evaluated for a single active file transfer. In this work we extend our study by quantifying the energy efficiency improvements achieved for the three main types of Internet traffic (i.e. file transfer, media streaming and web browsing) and assessing the impact of our solution on the user experience for each such traffic type. Furthermore, we propose alternative rendezvous mechanisms in case multiple mobile receivers are simultaneously active and evaluate the performance of these alternatives. In order to better grasp the potential and the limitations of our approach, we also formulate the operation of the rendezvous mechanism in mathematical terms.

3   Energy-Efficient Internetworking Overlay

Our energy-efficient DTN overlay is deployed on a traditional internetworked wired-cum-wireless topology with a last-hop WLAN connection, aiming to improve energy efficiency for mobile devices. The proposed overlay exploits the inherent DTN capability for shaping internetwork traffic in a manner that allows mobile devices to balance their energy expenditure. A minimum deployment of the proposed energy-efficient DTN overlay involves employing DTN on three nodes: Source, Base

Station (BS) and Mobile Receiver (MR). In our previous work [17], transmission scheduling from the BS to each MR was carried out independently of the transmissions to other MRs with active incoming flows. In this work, we extend the BS functionality so that transmission scheduling considers the incoming traffic for all active MRs, further improving the energy efficiency of the receivers.

3.1 Buffering Energy-Saving Potential

In order to assess the potential of the energy-efficient overlay as well as identify the practical limitations of the proposed solution, we developed a mathematical formulation describing the energy-saving potential of the buffering mechanism. Due to space scarcity we include an abbreviated description of the formulation; a detailed derivation of the formulation can be found here [19]. The formulation is based on the following simplifying assumptions: The incoming and outgoing data rates at the BS are constant, wireless traffic is one-way from BS to MR, and the data to be transferred are of a certain predefined amount.

The diagram of Fig. 1 depicts an example scenario where the output rate (OutRate) at the BS (i.e. the wireless channel) is double the incoming rate (InRate) at the BS (i.e. the Internet connection) and the transfer size (Size) is three times the buffering size (Buffer). The WNIC is assumed to be initially active and immediately switched to the sleep state, allowing for the buffer at the BS to fill (i.e. for a time period of Buffer/InRate). The WNIC must commence the switch to the active state at a time equal to the transition time between the idle and active states (TransTime) prior to the buffer flush, so that it will be fully operational when the BS starts transmitting.

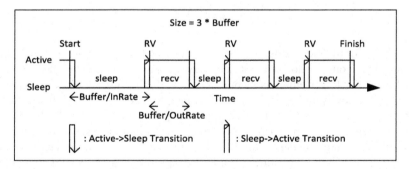

Fig. 1. Example scenario of a 3*Buffer size transfer when OutRate equals 2*InRate at the BS.

Based on the above example, the main measures in a general case can be summarized as follows:

- The total transfer duration is:

$$Duration = \frac{Size}{InRate} + \frac{Buffer}{OutRate}$$

- The receiving time for the WNIC of the MR is:

$$RecvTime = \frac{Size}{OutRate}$$

- The actual sleep time considering the WNIC transition time is:

$$SleepTime = \frac{Size}{InRate} - \frac{Size - Buffer}{OutRate} - 2 * \frac{Size * TransTime}{Buffer}$$

- Finally, the energy spent during the transfer at the MR can be calculated as:

$$Energy = 2 * \frac{Size * TransTime}{Buffer} * TransPower +$$

$$\left(\frac{Size}{InRate} - \frac{Size - Buffer}{OutRate} - 2 * \frac{Size * TransTime}{Buffer} \right) * SleepPower +$$

$$\frac{Size}{OutRate} * RecvPower$$

The above formulation leads to a number of observations that highlight the tradeoff between energy-conservation and data delivery latency, as dictated by the amount of buffered data. For larger amounts of buffered data, the energy savings are higher, but the delivery latency is higher as well. Furthermore, the amount of data that need to be buffered for the scheme to work is dictated by the specifications of the WNIC (i.e. state transition time) and the amount of excess rate of the outgoing vs. the incoming data flows at the BS. Large transition times and small outgoing-incoming data rate differences require large buffering values in order to exploit the energy-saving potential. In case of multiple active mobile receivers, the perceived OutRate for each flow becomes smaller, leading to increased energy expenditure.

3.2   The Rendezvous Mechanism

Statistical Internet traffic is shaped into tactic data delivery by the integration of our rendezvous mechanism into the DTN overlay. During idle periods the BS refrains from routing incoming bundles to their final destination and simply stores them locally. As first described in [17], the next rendezvous time is calculated as follows:

- $BP = \frac{RB}{TBO}$: Ratio of the received bytes over the desired buffer occupancy (where BP = Buffer Portion, RB = Received Bytes and TBO = Target Buffer Occupancy).
- $SBP = BP - \frac{BP-1}{2}$: Smoothed BP value for faster convergence (where SBP = Smoothed Buffer Portion).
- $NextRV = \frac{RI}{SBP}$: The interval until the next rendezvous. If 0 bytes were received during the previous interval, the NextRV is set to twice the duration of the previous interval (where NextRV = Next Rendezvous Time and RI = Reception Interval).

Once the NextRV has been calculated, the BS fragments all bundles that were partially received during the last rendezvous interval and sends the fragmented bundles to the MR. The last bundle of the burst contains the NextRV value in its DTN header. When the MR receives a bundle with a next rendezvous value, it checks if the time to the rendezvous is sufficient for switching to the sleep state and then back to the active state in time to receive the next data bulk and, if so, it suspends the WNIC.

In this work we extend the rendezvous mechanism for the case where multiple receivers are present. We experiment with alternative rendezvous strategies at the BS, seeking to improve the energy efficiency of mobile receivers by limiting overlaps among transmissions to different receivers. The analysis in the previous section suggests that by limiting transmission overlaps, each individual flush would be expedited allowing the receiver to remain active for shorter periods of time. In our study we consider three alternative rendezvous mechanisms: an isolated mechanism, which sets the rendezvous with each receiver individually based on the previously described algorithm, a combined mechanism, which takes into account scheduled rendezvous' of other receivers, and a time-based mechanism, which schedules rendezvous in a purely time-based fashion.

The combined mechanism is a variation of the isolated mechanism. Detection of overlaps among transmissions to different receivers is achieved by estimating the average flushing duration, based on the wireless link nominal bandwidth and the TBO (i.e. $FlushingDuration = \frac{OutRate}{TBO}$). At rendezvous time, each buffer's NextRV is calculated according to the original mechanism as described in the beginning of this section. Based on the flushing duration estimation, the BS detects possible overlaps with scheduled transmissions to other receivers and tries to reposition the rendezvous earlier or later in time so that overlaps are avoided. The rendezvous may be repositioned earlier than the first scheduled transmission, between two scheduled transmissions or later than the last scheduled transmission. The final choice is made so that the time shifting of the rendezvous is minimized (Fig. 2).

In the time-based mechanism, the rendezvous scheduling is based purely on time and the buffer flushes alternate in equal time intervals. Thus, overlaps are readily avoided since the flushes are scheduled adequately far apart. In this version of the mechanism, the intervals are predetermined based on the average rendezvous time for the combined algorithm for each TBO value. In future versions, however, the mechanism could be modified so that it dynamically adjusts to changing network conditions.

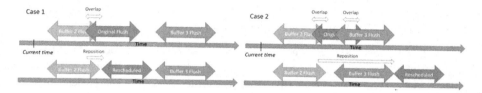

Fig. 2. Two cases of flush overlap avoidance using the combined mechanism

4 Experimental Methodology

The simulation experiments were carried out using our DTN simulation model, comprising a set of classes implemented in the ns-2 network simulator framework [20]. The model supports both TCP and UDP underlying protocols through a DTN agent, which acts as a store-and-forward module between the application and the transport layers. Simulation experiments were conducted in two main directions: Firstly, we employed a single wireless receiving device and experimented with different application protocols; secondly, we employed multiple wireless receivers and experimented with different transmission scheduling strategies at the BS, focusing on file transfers.

In all experimental scenarios, the BS is connected with the MRs on an 802.11 WLAN, with a data rate of 11 Mbps and a basic rate of 1 Mbps (the rate to be used for protocol-specific operations). The TCP packet size is 1460 and the maximum window size 100 packets, while the UDP packet size is explicitly specified in each set of experiments. The energy expenditure for the WNIC of a mobile device is tracked through the inherent energy model of ns-2. The parameters necessary for the energy expenditure calculations are set as follows [21]: transmit power = 1.400 W, receive power = 0.950 W, idle power = 0.805 W, sleep power = 0.060 W and transition time = 10 ms [22].

The simulation topology used for our experiments is depicted in Fig. 3. Nodes with the DTN suffix host a DTN agent instance, whereas Rel-IP relays IP traffic. The bandwidth and delay values for the topology links are kept constant for all the experiments at the following values: Src– Rel-IP: 1.5 Mbps bandwidth for single data transfers and 1 Mbps for multiple simultaneous data transfers, 100 ms delay, Rel – IP – BS: 1.5 Mbps bandwidth, 100 ms delay.

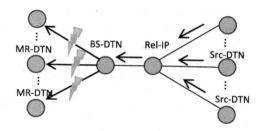

Fig. 3. Simulation topology

In the first set of experiments we employ the DTN agent in order to evaluate the energy conservation vs. delivery delay tradeoff from a user experience perspective, across the three main types of Internet applications: large file transfers (FTP), media streaming (CBR), and web browsing (HTTP). Data transfers on the overlay follow the Src-DTN → Rel-IP → BS-DTN → MR-DTN path over connections between adjacent DTN nodes. In the end-to-end scenarios a connection is setup directly between a source and a mobile receiver. The traffic characteristics for each application are: FTP – A file size of 10 MB, CBR – A flow sending 500 B every 5 ms (800 Kbps) for 1 min, and HTTP – A flow continuously sending files of 20 KB for 2 min and 40 s, where each file is sent as soon as the previous file has reached the destination. HTTP is simulated using a simple application model that assumes no request pipelining [23] and a constant small file size.

In the second set of simulations, multiple simultaneous FTP flows are active, each transferring a file of 10 MB between a DTN source and a DTN-enabled mobile receiver. Namely, the file transfers take place along the network paths: Src-DTN1 → Rel-IP → BS-DTN → MR-DTN1, Src-DTN2 → Rel-IP → BS-DTN → MR-DTN2, etc. Simulation results are reported for 2, 3 and 4 simultaneous file transfers and for all three rendezvous strategies described in Sect. 3.2 (isolated, combined, time-based). The rendezvous in the time-based case for each TBO are set based on the average measured rendezvous interval for the isolated case for that TBO.

5   Experimental Results

5.1   Single Receiver Multiple Application Protocols

The chart in Fig. 4 depicts the energy consumption and the delay for the completion of a 10 MB FTP data transfer for various TBO values, ranging from 10 to 80 KB. The end-to-end case is denoted as E2E and plotted as the first point on the energy and delay lines. The additional delay imposed by the data buffering at the BS reaches a maximum of only 0.4 s or 0.7 % of the transfer duration for a 80 KB TBO. The energy line on the same chart shows that the consumption drops from 55.5 J in the E2E case to a minimum of 36.2 J for the 80 KB TBO case, yielding a reduction of approximately 34 %. These results confirm our previous results [17] that, for relatively large file transfers, substantial energy conservation can be achieved at a negligible performance cost.

Table 1 provides information on the number of sleep intervals and the total sleep time and transition time for all TBO values. For the smallest TBO of 10 KB the overall idle time (sum of the sleep and transition time durations) is only 7 s. Due to the small TBO, the interval until the next rendezvous time is generally too short and does not allow enough time for transitioning to and from the sleep state. For TBO values of 20 KB and larger, the overall idle time is consistently higher than 25 s. Maximum sleep time is achieved for the TBO of 80 KB, which also yields the lowest energy consumption as shown in the energy chart.

In terms of the user experience, file transfers are only marginally affected by the deployed DTN overlay and the buffering at the BS introduced by the rendezvous

Table 1. FTP with no competing traffic, sleep and transition information.

TBO	Sleep count	Sleep time	Trans time
E2E	0	0	0
10	232	2.39	4.62
20	521	14.93	10.36
30	348	19.93	6.9
40	262	22.47	5.18
50	212	23.04	4.16
60	176	22.74	3.48
80	134	26.42	2.62

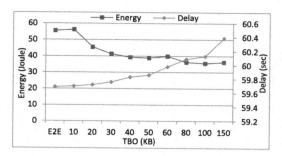

Fig. 4. FTP with no competing traffic energy and delay vs. the TBO.

mechanism. The TBO value is usually much smaller than the application ADU (i.e. the transferred file) and so the additional delay is negligible.

Figure 5 includes the energy consumption and the average delay of delivered datagrams for a CBR flow producing a 500-Byte datagram every 5 ms (800 Kbps) for 1 min. It is apparent that even for the smallest tested TBO value of 10 KB the energy saving is substantial. Specifically, the energy consumption drops from 54.14 J in the E2E case to 36.15 in the 10 KB TBO case, achieving conservation of 33 %. The corresponding average delay values for these experiments are 0.2 s for the E2E and 0.27 s for the 10 KB cases respectively; an increase in the order of 26 %. In the 30 KB case the energy expenditure drops to 30.32 J (44 % reduction), while the average delay is doubled with respect to the E2E case (0.41 s). The energy conservation reaches a maximum of 47 % for the 80 KB TBO case, when the delay is 3.7 times that of the E2E case.

Table 2. CBR with no competing traffic, sleep and transition information.

TBO	Sleep count	Sleep time	Trans time
E2E	0	0	0
10	587	24.15	11.64
20	297	30	5.84
30	199	31.98	3.9
40	153	32.92	2.94
50	123	33.26	2.34
60	100	33.93	1.96
80	77	34.44	1.48

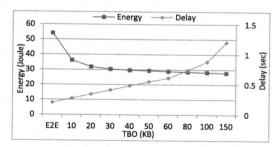

Fig. 5. CBR with no competing traffic energy and delay vs. the TBO.

The information displayed in Table 2 shows how the overall idle time (sum of sleep and transition times) remains almost identical (35–36 s) for all tested TBO values.

The additional energy conservation achieved for higher values of the TBO results from the decrease in the overall number of sleep intervals and the consequent reduction of the time spent in the energy-consuming transition state.

The simulation results show that the energy-efficient DTN overlay creates significant energy conservation potential for CBR streaming flows at the expense of a delay increase at the datagram level. However, the additional delay could be compensated in a straightforward way by a small increase in the buffering amount of the client buffering mechanism that is part of most streaming applications. For the 30 KB TBO, where the consumed energy is almost halved, the additional delay was measured at 200 ms, duration that is hardly noticeable by the end-user. Therefore our proposed solution can be applied for most streaming applications with limited adverse effect on the end-user experience.

The chart contained in Fig. 6 depicts the energy consumption and the ADU delay for a 160-second web browsing session vs. the same TBO values as the FTP and CBR examples. What becomes immediately obvious from the energy-delay chart is that the potential for energy saving is tremendous as the energy consumption drops from 134.1 J in the E2E case to 36.18 J in the 20 KB TBO case, a reduction of 73 %. The average ADU delivery latency is, respectively, increased from 0.27 s in the E2E case to 0.47 s in the 20 KB TBO case. The large energy saving potential is attributed to the long idle periods between transmissions of successive ADUs that may be readily turned into sleep periods when the rendezvous mechanism is employed. For TBO values larger than 20 KB, the energy consumption only slightly improves with a significant deterioration of the introduced delay. The key value of 20 KB for the TBO coincides with the file size of 20 KB selected for this set of experiments.

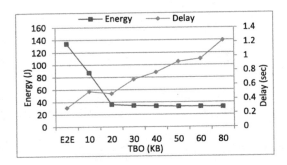

Fig. 6. HTTP with no competing traffic energy and delay vs. the TBO.

Contrary to file transfers and streaming applications studied in the previous subsections, the web browsing user experience is sensitive to the application responsiveness. Furthermore, the additional delay of 200–300 ms introduced by the buffering at the overlay will be actually multiplied by the number of elements included in a web page, resulting in a, potentially unacceptable overall delay. However, modern browsers simultaneously open multiple TCP connections so that the web page elements can be more quickly downloaded reducing the overall delay. All these connections in the DTN overlay are handled collectively so that the TBO refers to the total data amount belonging to all active flows, destined to the same node, mitigating the total delay. In any case, this type of proposed buffering in web browsing applications may deteriorate user experience and, thus, it should be employed with prudence. A possibility would be to only enable this feature with the user's consent, in cases the battery level of the device is running low. This way the device operation could be extended at the expense of an inferior web browsing user experience.

5.2   Multiple Receivers File Transfers

The charts in this section depict the average energy consumption during an FTP transfer for all active mobile receivers for TBO values ranging from 10 to 80 KB, including the end-to-end (E2E) case. Figure 7 plots the energy consumption for the three rendezvous strategies when two mobile receivers are simultaneously active on the wireless network. For TBO values under 30 KB, the isolated and time-based mechanisms require the same amount of energy in order to complete the transfer, while the combined mechanism achieves an improvement of approximately 10 %. For higher TBO values the combined mechanism generally stays between the lines of the isolated and the time-based mechanisms, achieving an average improvement of roughly 5 J compared to the isolated mechanism. For these values of the TBO, the time-based mechanism consistently achieves an improvement of over 15 % with respect to the isolated case.

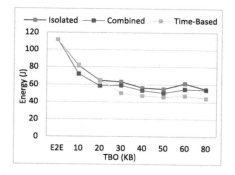

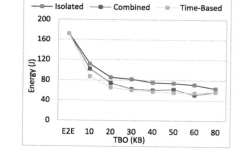

Fig. 7. Energy consumption for 2 mobile receivers.

Fig. 8. Energy consumption for 3 mobile receivers.

The results are similar, but somewhat more pronounced, for the case with three mobile receivers as may be seen on Fig. 8. Here, the effect of the mechanisms that limit the overlaps of the buffer flushes to the mobile receivers (i.e. the time-based and combined cases) are even more substantial, improving the energy efficiency of the receivers up to 25 % for TBO values between 30 and 60 KB. Moreover, the performance of the combined mechanism largely coincides with that of the time-based mechanism, showing that the flush fitting algorithm effectively limits contention on the wireless LAN.

Figure 9 depicts the average energy expenditure in the four-receiver case. Again, the time-based mechanism achieves significant energy conservation as compared to the isolated mechanism for TBOs of 30–60 KB. On average, the energy efficiency improves by 30 % when the time-based mechanism is in place. On the other hand, the combined mechanism does not exhibit a consistent behavior, although it generally achieves better energy efficiency than the isolated mechanism.

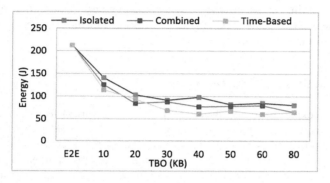

Fig. 9. Energy consumption for 4 mobile receivers.

The important conclusion that is drawn from the simulation results presented in this section is that, indeed, minimizing overlap of the buffer flushes on the wireless LAN significantly improves the energy efficiency of the mobile receivers. This becomes evident by the performance of the time-based mechanism in all 2, 3 and 4 mobile receivers cases. The combined mechanism also improves energy efficiency over the isolated mechanism to a good extent, despite its relatively inconsistent performance. It is evident that, under certain circumstances, the buffer flushing overlaps are not fully eliminated.

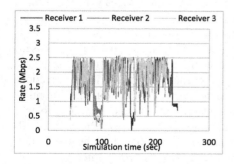

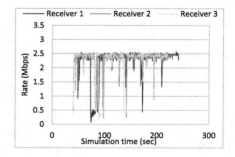

Fig. 10. Buffer flush output rate for the isolated mechanism with 3 mobile receivers and 40 KB TBO.

Fig. 11. Buffer flush output rate for the time-based mechanism with 3 mobile receivers and 40 KB TBO.

In order to visualize the effect of an overlap limiting vs. the isolated rendezvous mechanism we plotted the actual goodput achieved for each buffer flush in the isolated and time-based cases for 3 mobile receivers and a TBO of 40 KB. The results of Figs. 10 and 11 show how, for the most part, the goodput of the isolated mechanism fluctuates within a wide range, whereas the goodput of the time-based mechanism is contained within a narrow band slightly below the 2.5 Mbps maximum value. In the isolated case, multiple buffer flushes may be simultaneously active, resulting in lower goodput and, thus, longer duration for each flush, forcing the WNIC to stay active for longer periods of time at each rendezvous. On the contrary, rapid buffer flushes of the time-based mechanism achieve better energy efficiency of the receiver by minimizing the time spent in the idle state.

6 Conclusions and Future Work

Our simulation experiments are in-line with the mathematical formulation and older results in that file transfers are only marginally affected by the DTN overlay operation. Therefore, the proposed energy-efficient solution does not affect the end-user experience and can be unconditionally applied to file transfer applications. With respect to streaming flows, significant energy conservation can be achieved, introducing, however, substantial delays at the datagram level. Since the buffering amount is, generally, larger than the stream datagram, delays are introduced due to the data buffering at the base station. Nevertheless, most streaming applications employ buffering on the client side in order to cope with data rate fluctuations, so the effect of the rendezvous buffering on the end-user experience should be fairly limited, and could be compensated by a slight increase in the client buffering amount. In contrast to file transfers and streaming applications, the user experience during web browsing depends highly on the application responsiveness. Our proposed buffering scheme in the DTN overlay may deteriorate user experience in web browsing applications and, thus, it should be employed with prudence, possibly soliciting the user's consent when the battery level of the device is running low.

When multiple mobile receivers are present, our simulations confirm the implications of the mathematical description that a smart scheduling mechanism that limits overlaps of the buffer flushes further improves energy efficiency as compared to an isolated scheduling approach. Our combined mechanism improves on the isolated approach, but it does not achieve the consistent improvements of the time-based mechanism, suggesting that further development of the mechanism is necessary. It is part of our imminent plans to refine the combined mechanism, mainly in the direction of increasing its flexibility and adaptiveness to changing network condition. Currently, buffer flushing overlap avoidance depends mainly on calculations according to the nominal duration of each flush. We have strong evidence that energy efficiency could be significantly increased if the calculations dynamically adjust based on the load of the WLAN as well as the expected data amount available at rendezvous time.

References

1. Acquaviva, A., Simunic, T., Deolalikar, V., Roy, S.: Remote power control of wireless network interfaces. In: Chico, J.J., Macii, E. (eds.) PATMOS 2003. LNCS, vol. 2799, pp. 369–378. Springer, Heidelberg (2003)
2. Telecommunications and Information Exchange Between Systems: Local and metropolitan area networks – specific requirements, Part 11: wireless LAN medium access control (MAC) and physical layer (PHY) specifications. IEEE Standard for Information technology (2007)
3. Cerf, V., Burleigh, S., Hooke, A., Torgerson, L., Dust, R., Scott, K., Fall, K., Weiss, H.: Delay-Tolerant Networking Architecture, IETF RFC 4838 (2007). http://tools.ietf.org/html/rfc4838.txt
4. Vardalis, D., Tsaoussidis, V.: Energy-efficient internetworking with DTN. J. Internet Eng. 5 (1) (2011). Klidarithmos Press
5. Jones, C., Sivalingam, K., Agrawal, P., Chen, J.: A survey of energy efficient network protocols for wireless networks. ACM J. Wirel. Netw. 7(4), 343–358 (2001). ACM Journal
6. Chandra, S., Vahdat, A.: Application-specific network management for energy-aware streaming of popular multimedia formats. In: Proceedings of the General Track of the Annual conference on USENIX, Monterey CA, USA (2002)
7. Adams, J., Muntean, G.M.: Adaptive-buffer power save mechanism for mobile multimedia streaming. In: Proceedings of the IEEE International Conference on Communications, Glasgow, UK (2007)
8. Acquaviva, A., Lattanzi, E., Bogliolo, A.: Design and simulation of power-aware scheduling strategies of streaming data in wireless LANs. In: Proceedings of the 7th ACM International Symposium on Modeling, Analysis and Simulation of Wireless and Mobile Systems (MSWiM), Venice, Italy (2004)
9. Zhu, H., Cao, G.: A Power-aware and QoS-aware service model on wireless networks. In: Proceedings of the 23rd Annual Joint Conference of the IEEE Computer and Communications Societies (INFOCOM), Hong Kong (2004)
10. Tsaoussidis, V., Badr, H.: TCP-probing: towards an error control schema with energy and throughput performance gains. In: The 8th IEEE Conference on Network Protocols, ICNP 2000, Osaka, Japan (2000)
11. Mamatas, L., Tsaoussidis, V.: Effort/gains dynamics in heterogeneous networks. Int. J. Commun. Syst. (IJCS) 21, 361–382 (2007). Wiley
12. Pentland, S.A., Fletcher, R., Hasson, A.: DakNet: rethinking connectivity in developing nations. IEEE Comput. Soc. 37(1), 78–83 (2004)
13. Morris, R., Jannotti, J., Kaashoek, F., Li, J., Decouto, D.: CarNet: a scalable ad hoc wireless network system. In: Proceedings of the 9th ACM Special Interest Group on Operating Systems (SIGOPS) European Workshop, New York, NY, USA (2000)
14. Ott, J., Kutscher, D.: From drive-thru internet to delay-tolerant ad-hoc networking. In: Conti, M., Crowcroft, J., Passarella, A. (eds.) Mobile Ad-hoc Networks: From Theory to Reality, pp. 241–277. Nova Science Publishers Inc., New York (2007)
15. Hui, P., Chaintreau, A., Gass, R., Scott, J., Crowcroft, J., Diot, C.: Pocket switched networking: challenges, feasibility and implementation issues. In: Stavrakakis, I., Smirnov, M. (eds.) WAC 2005. LNCS, vol. 3854, pp. 1–12. Springer, Heidelberg (2006)
16. Lenas, S.-A., Tsaoussidis, V.: Enabling free internet access at the edges of broadband connections: a hybrid packet scheduling approach. ACM SIGMOBILE Mob. Comput. Commun. Rev. (MCR2R) 18(1), 55–63 (2014)

17. Vardalis, D., Tsaoussidis, V.: Exploiting the potential of DTN for energy-efficient internetworking. J. Syst. Softw. **90**, 91–103 (2014)
18. Scott, K., Burleigh, S.: Bundle Protocol Specification, IETF RFC 5050 (2007). http://tools.ietf.org/html/rfc5050.txt
19. Vardalis, D.: Design and implementation of algorithms exploiting properties of the delay-disruption tolerant networks. Ph.D. dissertation. Department of Electrical and Computer Engineering, Democritus University of Thrace (2015)
20. Vardalis, D.: DTN agent for ns-2, Space Internetworking Center (2012). https://www.spice-center.org/dtn-agent/
21. Shih, E., Bahl, P., Sinclair, M.: Wake on wireless: an event driven, energy saving strategy for battery operated devices. In: Proceedings of the 8th ACM International Conference on Mobile Computing and Networking (MobiCom), Atlanta, GA, USA (2002)
22. Jamieson, K.: Implementation of a power-saving protocol for ad hoc wireless networks. Master thesis, Department of Computer Science and Engineering, MIT (2002)
23. Fielding, R., Gettys, J., Mogul, J., Frystyk, H., Masinter, L., Leach, P., Berners-Lee, T.: Hypertext Transfer Protocol – HTTP/1.1 IETF RFC 2616 (1999). http://tools.ietf.org/html/rfc2616.txt

Data Aware Communication for Energy Harvesting Sensor Networks

Mohamed S. Hefeida[1](✉) and Fahad Saeed[2]

[1] American University of the Middle East, Eqaila, Kuwait
mohamed.hefeida@aum.edu.kw
[2] Western Michigan University, Kalamazoo 49008, USA
fahad.saeed@wmich.edu

Abstract. We propose a Data Aware Communication Technique (DACT) that reduces energy consumption in Energy Harvesting Wireless Sensor Networks (EH-WSN). DACT takes advantage of the data correlation present in household EH-WSN applications to reduce communication overhead. It adapts its functionality according to correlations in data communicated over the EH-WSN and operates independently from spatial and temporal correlations without requiring location information. Our results show that DACT improves communication efficiency of sensor nodes and can help reduce idle energy consumption in an average-size home by up to 90 % as compared to spatial/temporal correlation-based communication techniques.

Keywords: Sensor networks · Energy harvesting · Energy efficiency · Data collection · Data redundancy

1 Introduction

With continuous and rapid advancements in microelectronics and wireless communications, smart devices have become an integral and critical part of our everyday lives. From smart phones to smart fridges, almost every part of our daily routine involves an electrical/electronic device that consumes some form of energy, mainly electricity. However, due to various behavioral, technological, and social reasons, most of us do not have a clear idea of the amount of energy required to sustain our daily habits. Part of this is due to the lack of a clear and real-time measure for the effect of our daily habits and behavior on energy usage. An example of this lack of awareness is leakage power (a.k.a. standby power), which results from leaving electrical devices connected to the power outlet. According to [13], the average US household looses $100 every year on leakage power. On a national level these losses reach up to US $100 billion and a carbon footprint equivalent to 26.2 million tons of CO_2 emissions in the US alone.

© IFIP International Federation for Information Processing 2016
Published by Springer International Publishing Switzerland 2016. All Rights Reserved
L. Mamatas et al. (Eds.): WWIC 2016, LNCS 9674, pp. 121–132, 2016.
DOI: 10.1007/978-3-319-33936-8_10

Studies have shown that about 71 % of consumers are willing to change their energy-related habits if they had clear information about their real-time energy usage/cost [13]. Therefore, a quantitative method is required to raise awareness among consumers about their energy consumption habits.

The continual scaling of transistors allows today's electronic circuits to operate at a fraction of the power of their counterparts a few years ago, allowing electronics to be completely powered by ambient energy. In addition, wireless communication technology has grown exponentially, allowing unprecedented wireless communication amongst devices & access to the Internet through various protocols (e.g. Wifi, ZigBee, Bluetooth). The combination of these two main advancements in microelectronics and wireless communication paves the road for developing Energy Harvesting Wireless Senor Networks (EH-WSN) that partially or completely run on scavenged energy [13]. An EH-WSN can harvest power from surrounding environments while consuming very little power. Therefore, optimization of power consumption at the lowest possible level is essential for EH-WSN to operate by using idle power from other devices.

Like other WSN applications, an EH-WSN involves data gathering, in-network information processing and data aggregation (e.g. [4,9,10,21]). However, the EH-WSN application at hand has a unique feature, where correlations in the data space are not necessarily due to spatial and/or temporal correlations in the sensed phenomenon. Therefore, communication schemes that take advantage of spatial and/or temporal correlations [12,17] will not be effective in the energy monitoring EH-WSN application at hand. Physical phenomena usually result in similar data due to spatially and/or temporally correlated fields (e.g. monitoring temperature), but this may not necessarily be true for energy usage monitoring. For example, a household where one power outlet is idle while the one right next to it is plugged to a power-hungry microwave is an example of spatial correlation that does not lead to data correlation. We take advantage of this independence in data, temporal, and spatial correlations in EH-WSN and propose a communication scheme that will selectively communicate data based on its significance compared to other data.

In this paper, we tackle the problem of redundant data communication in EH-WSN from a collaborative communication perspective and evaluate the operation of the Information Processing and Communication Reduction (IPCR) scheme proposed in [10]. In contrast to other schemes [6,7,9,10,12,17] relies only on data similarity rather than on underlying field correlations. It employs a clever mechanism that compares a node's current sensed data to that communicated over the channel, based on which a decision of transmission or suppression of data is made. That is, if each node processes the information transmitted over the channel (by other nodes) to check its similarity with other sensed data, it can make a more informed decision on whether to transmit its sensed value.

The remainder of this paper is organized as follows: Sect. 2 is an overview of related studies that focus on reducing energy consumption in WSN. In Sect. 3, we map the problem to a well known collaborative sequential spectrum sensing problem based on which our problem is formulated. Section 4 describes the proposed scheme and the effect of data similarity on its operation. Finally, we evaluate the proposed scheme in Sect. 5, followed by the conclusion in Sect. 6.

2   Related Work

The majority of research efforts in improving energy efficiency of EH-WSN focus on communication operations. This is due to that communication operations consume orders of magnitude more energy as compared to computation operations (e.g. 2000X [14]). However, information processing can greatly improve the significance of the communicated data.

Few investigations have focused on joint solutions to MAC schemes and information processing [12,17]. Our previous work in [10] proposed a joint solution to reduce communication operations via collaborations between the underlying MAC scheme and a field estimation technique. We take advantage of [10] and modify it to be utilized in our EH-WSN application.

3   Problem Statement and Assumptions

3.1   Overview

Consider a household EH-WSN where standby power is monitored by a group of electro-magnetic radiation sensor nodes. Each node is required to report its sensed idle power to a central node (sink). The sink is connected to the Internet and is responsible for processing the results of all nodes and reporting energy consumption data sending alerts to a smart phone when a preset threshold of consumption is detected. Assume a total of N_p electro-magnetic radiation sensor nodes monitoring power outlets in the EH-WSN, operating in a non-data aware manner (i.e. each node is unaware of other data but its own), each of the N_p nodes transmits its sensed data independently to the sink node. According to the *similarity* of the sensed field, this can result in up to $N_p - 1$ redundant (*similar*) messages. Moreover, many collaborative communication reduction techniques tie their performance to underlying field correlations [6,12,17]. While this can be effective in applications encountering some spatially and/or temporally correlated fields (e.g. monitoring physical phenomena), it falls short when the underlying field encounters spatially and/or temporally uncorrelated *similar* values such as the case of a household where one power outlet is idle while the one right next to it is plugged to a power-hungry microwave.

Several studies proposing efficient collaborative communication techniques have been presented in the literature [5,22]. The main goal of these studies is to detect when the channel is not being used by primary users so that secondary users can utilize it during that time. In our problem, nodes sense the channel in order to detect ongoing transmissions and determine whether they have useful information to send. Moreover, all nodes have an equal opportunity and capability of acquiring the channel. Nodes listening to the channel during an ongoing transmission determine the relevance of their sensed values to those being transmitted over the channel. Therefore, the channel is monitored by non-transmitting awake nodes for other transmissions, based on which they decide whether to send their data. We tailor common representations of the collaborative communication problem in [5,10,22] to formulate our problem and the proposed solution.

3.2   Formulation

Consider N_p electro-magnetic radiation sensor nodes placed at the power outlets of a home to monitor its electricity usage, within each others' communication range and reporting to a sink node. The nodes are attempting to collectively solve a binary hypothesis testing problem, where each of the N_p nodes is required to decide between transmitting its local sensed data (hypothesis H_1) to the sink node or not (hypothesis H_0). We assume that time is divided into discrete slots of equal durations, τ_s, in which a node can transmit/receive data. We assume that all nodes listen to each others' transmissions (i.e. each transmission is a broadcast). The term slot and observation interval are used interchangeably. Let $O_i(t)$ be the observed value at node i during slot t, and $S_i(t)$ be the sensed value at node i during the same slot, where $i = 1, 2, \ldots, N_p$. Notice that the observed value at node i is that transmitted by any of the other $N_p - 1$ nodes in the network, while the sensed value is that sensed by node i itself. Elements constructing the sets of observed and sensed values at node i over a time span of T slots, $\{O_i(t)\}_1^T$ and $\{S_i(t)\}_1^T$, respectively, are independent given each hypothesis and are assumed to be identically distributed. Equation 1 represents $O_i(t)$ under the two hypotheses.

$$H_0 : S_i(t) - Thr_i(t) + W_i(t) \leq O_i(t) \leq S_i(t) +$$
$$Thr_i(t) + W_i(t), \qquad t = 1, 2, \ldots, T \qquad (1)$$
$$H_1 : otherwise$$

where Thr_i is the permissible threshold between the observed and sensed values, which reflects the level of energy consumption reporting accuracy required by the consumer. W_i is additive white Gaussian noise with a power of σ^2, assumed to be similar at all nodes.

As in [5,10,11] and without loss of generality, the primary signal $S_i(t)$ is assumed to be a real zero-mean Gaussian random variable. Moreover, the conditional probability distributions of $O_i(t)$ given H_1 and H_0 are represented by $f_{O_i(t)}(o_t|H_1)$ and $f_{O_i(t)}(o_t|H_0)$, respectively. Each of them can be represented as follows:

$$f_{O_i(t)}(o_t|H_0) \sim \mathcal{N}(0, \sigma^2)$$
$$f_{O_i(t)}(o_t|H_1) \sim \mathcal{N}(0, \sigma^2 + \sigma_{s_i}^2) \qquad (2)$$

where $\mathcal{N}(0, \sigma^2)$ and $\mathcal{N}(0, \sigma^2 + \sigma_{s_i}^2)$ are normal distributions with zero means and variances of σ^2 and $\sigma^2 + \sigma_{s_i}^2$, respectively. $\sigma_{s_i}^2$ represents the average received primary signal at the ith node, which is assumed to be fixed over the time slot duration [11]. Therefore, any local observation at a node i can be expressed as:

$$Y_i = \sum_{t=1}^{T} log \left[\frac{f_{O_i(t)}(o_t|H_1)}{f_{O_i(t)}(o_t|H_0)} \right] \qquad (3)$$

where Y_i is the Log-Likelihood Ratio (LLR), computed by node i [22]. The signal-to-noise ratio (SNR) can be defined as $\psi_i = \sigma_{o_i}^2/\sigma^2$. This will result in an LLR computed at node i as follows:

$$Y_i = \frac{\psi_i}{2\sigma^2 + 2\psi_i\sigma^2} \sum_{t=1}^{T} |O_i(t)|^2 - log(1 + \psi_i)\frac{T}{2} \qquad (4)$$

Both [5, 11] propose approximations for the above likelihood functions of Y_i given either H_0 or H_1, which are shifted scaled chi-square distributions with T degrees of freedom.

4   Proposed Technique

In this section, we describe the details of DACT, its realization of the Information Processing and Communication Reduction (IPCR) scheme presented in [10] and study the effect of data similarity on its operation.

4.1   Operation

Consider the same EH-WSN in Sect. 3. Each node $i \in N_p$, sets a backoff (BO) timer according to its locally computed LLR, such that $BO \propto 1/|LLR|$. Moreover, each node i checks the condition given in (1) to determine whether it will transmit or not. That is, if a node determines that it has highly informative information, based on the value of the BO timer (reflecting the LLR value), but it doesn't satisfy the condition in (1), it will decide *not* to transmit. This will repeat $\forall i \in N_p$. Table 1 shows the pseudo code of DACT's utilization of IPCR, the details of IPCR operation have been omitted and can be found in [10].

   Each node senses the field and sends its value if the channel is sensed idle (i.e. empty). If the channel is sensed busy, a node compares its sensed value and that being communicated over the channel according to (1). Note that this a comparison of the received data (communicated over the channel) and that locally sensed by the node. Based on this comparison, a node either decides to send (H_1) or discard (H_0) its data. The degree of information accuracy is controlled via the threshold (Thr_i) set by the user according to their habits/preference. That is, if users set the threshold to a lower value, that will result in more communication and hence less energy savings and vice versa. A detailed example of DACT's utilization of IPCR is discussed in Sect. 5.

   To avoid deadlocks, if none of the N_p nodes in the network transmits in communication round r, the first node to acquire the channel in communication round $r + 1$ will transmit its locally sensed value regardless of the current similarity check as in (1).

Table 1. Basic DACT-IPCR operation

Initialization: $\forall i \in N_p$
   1. *iter* $\leftarrow 0$ /*set counter*/
   2. $Thr_i \leftarrow Threshold$ /*set Threshold*/
Begin
   3. $S_i \leftarrow sensed\ value$
   4. *listen to chnnel*
   5. *If channel is idle*
   6.   *transmit* S_i
   7. *Else*
   8. $O_i \leftarrow ongoing\ transmission$
   9. $If(|O_i - S_i| \leq Thr_i)$ /*according to (1)*/
  10.   *discard* S_i
  11.   *exit*
  12.   *Else*
  13.   Repeat
  14.   *iter++*
  15.   *goto line 4*
  16.   Until *iter* $\leq T$ /*T is the max number of
                  slots in any frame*/
End

4.2 Communication Cost

The operation of DACT requires evaluation of neighbors' transmitted data, which involves significant communication overhead. We identify different sources of energy consumption and their dependence on network and application parameters, such as collisions and queue utilization. Our analysis is based on common channel assumptions that have been used in the literature [6,9,10].

In duty-cycled MAC schemes for WSNs, there are two main states for a node: active and sleep. During its active state, a node can transmit, receive or listen to the channel. The node turns off its radio during its sleep state. Each node is assumed to have a queue of finite length Q, and each packet in the queue has an average length L_{DATA} bits. We assume that data packets are generated following a Poisson process with a rate equal to λ packets/second (i.e. inter-packet times are independent and have an exponential distribution with a mean = $1/\lambda$). However, more complex traffic models can also benefit from our technique but with different distributions of trade-offs between energy consumed in channel sensing and that saved from collision avoidance and conditional message transmissions. Each packet is assumed to spend an average of T_{delay} before leaving the queue, which is the sum of queuing delay and service time computed by:

$$T_{delay} = \tau_s N_s + (A - 1)(\tau_s N_s + T_C) \tag{5}$$

where τ_s is the average slot duration, N_s is the average number of slots skipped before acquiring the channel on each transmission attempt (Back off window),

A is the average number of transmission attempts needed per packet, and T_C is a collision duration. A can be represented as a function of the collision probability P_C and the maximum number of retransmission attempts R_A such that $A = \frac{(1-P_C^{(R_A+1)})}{1-P_c}$. The collision probability is related to the number of nodes in the network, N_p, where $P_C = 1 - (1 - P_r)^{N_p-1}$ and P_r is the probability of a node, having a packet ready to be sent, to transmit in a random slot. P_r can be related to the queue utilization factor ρ by $P_r = \rho/(N_s + 1)$, where $\rho = \lambda/\mu$ and μ is the mean service time. T_C is deduced from IEEE 802.11 as well as the values of the guard periods, SIFS (Short Inter-Frame Space), DIFS (Distributed Inter-Frame Space), and EIFS (Extended Inter-Frame Space) [18]. $T_C = DIFS + SIFS + L_{RTS}/r$ and $T_S = \frac{L_{RTS}+L_{CTS}+L_{DATA}+L_{ACK}}{r} + DIFS + 3SIFS$ is the time needed to successfully transmit one data packet. Note that for a uniformly distributed back off window over the maximum contention window will lead to $N_s = \frac{CW_{max}}{2}$. The throughput of the queue can be computed as $\gamma = \lambda(1 - P_B)$ and $P_B = \frac{(1-\rho)\rho^Q}{1-\rho^{Q+1}}$ is the blocking probability (i.e. probability that the buffer is full).

We assume possible channel states with respect to the sending node to be: (a) empty (neighbor nodes are idle listening or sleeping), (b) sending/receiving, and (c) collision. Each state has a corresponding probability of (a) $P_e = (1-P_r)^{N_p-1}$, (b) $P_{s/r} = P_r(N_p - 1)(1 - P_r)^{N_p-2}$, and (c) $P_c = 1 - P_{s/r} - P_e$, respectively. The total energy consumption of a node is due to transmitting, receiving, and overhearing. Each one of these energy components has a certain successful and collision component in it. This leads to:

$$E_{total} = E_{tx}^s + E_{tx}^c + E_{rx}^s + E_{rx}^c + E_{oh}^s + E_{oh}^c \qquad (6)$$

where E_{tx}^s, E_{rx}^s, and E_{oh}^s are the energies consumed in successful transmission, reception and overhearing, respectively. E_{tx}^c, E_{rx}^c and E_{oh}^c are the energies consumed in collided (unsuccessful) transmission, reception and overhearing, respectively. The value of each one of these energy components will vary according to the MAC protocol behavior. Each of the above energy components suffers an amount of idle listening as well (e.g. during DIFS and SIFS). We refer to the energy consumed in a node's radio states, transmission, reception and idle as E_{radio}^{TX}, E_{radio}^{RX}, and E_{radio}^{IDLE}, respectively. Radio sleep state is assumed to consume no energy, therefore:

$$E_{tx}^s = E_{radio}^{TX} \frac{L_{RTS} + L_{DATA}}{r} + E_{radio}^{RX} \frac{L_{CTS} + L_{ACK}}{r}$$
$$+ E_{radio}^{IDLE}(DIFS + 3SIFS + N_s P_e \epsilon) \qquad (7)$$

$$E_{tx}^c = E_{radio}^{TX} \frac{L_{RTS}}{r} + E_{radio}^{IDLE}(DIFS + 2SIFS +$$
$$N_s P_e \epsilon + \frac{L_{CTS}}{r}) \qquad (8)$$

where ϵ is the duration of an empty slot. The energy consumed in successful and unsuccessful receptions can be represented by (9) and (10), respectively.

$$E_{rx}^s = E_{radio}^{RX} \frac{L_{RTS} + L_{DATA}}{r} +$$
$$E_{radio}^{TX} \frac{L_{CTS} + L_{ACK}}{r} + E_{radio}^{IDLE}(3SIFS) \qquad (9)$$

$$E_{rx}^c = E_{tx}^c - (E_{radio}^{TX} - E_{radio}^{RX})\frac{L_{RTS}}{R} \qquad (10)$$

4.3 Data Similarity

In order to offset the communication overhead encountered in DACT, a certain level of data similarity is required. Fortunately, this is the usual case when people are not at home and standby power is being wasted. DACT utilizes data similarity to detect and reduce redundant information communicated over the channel. We have used a similar scheme to exploit data redundancy in genomic data for efficient transmission [2]. Note that this distinguishes the energy consumption monitoring EH-WSN applications from other WSN applications, since similarity in sensed values does not necessarily reflect any spatial correlation, as discussed in Sect. 3.1. To represent data similarity, like in previous studies [9,10], we define a similarity factor $F_p = \frac{N_p}{N_S}$, $1 \le N_S \le N_p$, where N_S is the number of sets representing the field which has a total of N_p nodes and S_{V_x} is the set of nodes in a neighborhood with a sensed field value V_x, $min(f) \le V_x \le max(f)$, where $min(f)$ and $max(f)$ are the minimum and maximum values of the sensed field, respectively. Note that $\forall V_x \ne V_y$, $S_{V_x} \cap S_{V_y} = \emptyset$.

4.4 Discussion

Consider a building with 100 power outlets that are being monitored for idle power consumption via electro-magnetic radiation sensor nodes and a sink node, forming an EH-WSN. Assume that all sensors are calibrated to sense power on a scale of 1 to 100. At one extreme, all 100 nodes sense 90 and thus belong to one set S_{90}, therefore $F_p = N_p$, which is the maximum value for S in a neighborhood of size N_p. At the other extreme, all 100 nodes report 100 different values which results in 100 different sets and thus $F_p = 100/100 = 1$, which is the minimum possible value for F_p indicating no similarity in the sensed field.

DACT's strength lies in exploiting data similarity and redundancy that is absent in other studies [6,12,17]. In a best case scenario, when the field is highly similar (highly correlated in data space and thus low values of F_p), significant communication savings are expected, as illustrated by the previous example. However, if the field is highly dissimilar (high values of F_p), DACT will perform comparable to field correlation-based collaborative scheme [6,12,17] or non-collaborative data gathering/aggregation techniques [20]. We refer to both as conventional techniques.

Since DACT gives each node in the network an equal opportunity of acquiring the channel, load balancing is implicit. Since it is the reporting node's responsibility to assess its similarity to the data currently communicated over the channel, and the worst case scenario performance (i.e. no similarity between sensed data) will be comparable to that of conventional techniques. This greatly reduces the load required by the sink node, which is usually responsible for aggregating the unconditionally transmitted data (from reporting nodes), by distributing the effort over the entire neighborhood.

5   Evaluation

In this section, we evaluate DACT via ns-2 simulations [1]. Each node in our simulations has a single omni-directional antenna and follows ns-2's commonly used combined free space and two-ray-ground reflection propagation model for wireless sensor networks. The underlying MAC scheme is Sensor MAC (SMAC) [18], and we assume that nodes follow a single sleep/wakeup schedule. The transmission range and carrier sensing range are modeling a 914 MHz Lucent WaveLAN DSSS (Direct Sequence Spread Spectrum) radio interface which was used in several previous studies [8, 16]. Although this radio is not typical for a low power WSN node, but we use its parameters to make our results comparable to those reported in previous work [8, 16]. Furthermore, measurements have shown that similar proportions of the carrier sensing range to the transmission range are observed in some nodes [3, 16].

We test DACT on a 100 node randomly deployed electro-magnetic radiation sensor network, where sensors are deployed following a uniform random distribution, covering a total area of 10,000 square feet. The network has a randomly selected sink to which all nodes are required to report. All nodes are assumed to be in each other's communication range (forming a single neighborhood). One way of extending this to multiple neighborhoods is to have border nodes of each neighborhood follow multiple schedules as in SMAC [18]. Each simulation is an average of 15 runs, each lasting for 7000 s. Key network simulation parameters are summarized in Table 2.

Table 2. Simulation parameters

Parameter	Value	Parameter	Value
Bandwidth	20 kbps	Comm. Range	250 m
Rx Power	22.2 mW	Interference Range	550 m
Tx Power	31.2 mW	DIFS	10 ms
Idle Power	22.2 mW	SIFS	5 ms
Sleep Power	3 μW	Contention Window	64 ms
Data Pckt	100 B	MAC scheme cycle (IPCR-SMAC)	4544 ms
ACK	10 B	Duty Cycle)	50 %

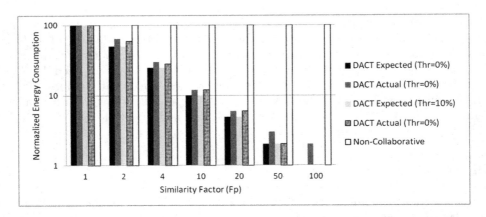

Fig. 1. Comparing DACT to non-collaborative communication solutions on a 100-node EH-WSN

In order to accurately study DACT's performance, we need to minimize the influence of the underlying MAC scheme for our simulation results. To do so, we keep the duty cycle relatively high (at 50 %) and the data rate relatively low (at 1 packet every 50 s). These values ensure that the underlying MAC protocol (IPCR in our case) is operating under relaxed conditions and allows accurate evaluation of DACT strategy.

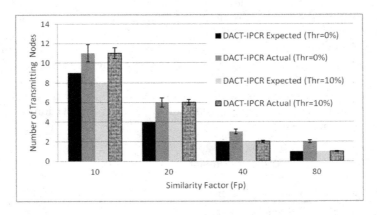

Fig. 2. Comparing Analytical and Simulation Results of IPCR on DACT for the 100-node EH-WSN (Figure reproduced based on information from [10])

Figure 1 shows the normalized energy consumption for different similarity factors at different threshold levels. When the threshold is 0 % (set by the consumer indicating maximum accuracy requirement) as shown in Fig. 1, the average energy consumed is at its maximum. This is expected due to maximum accuracy requirement. Since techniques that rely solely on spatial and/or temporal field correlations in their operation (e.g. [11,17]) do not realize field similarity occurring only in the data space, their message complexity is not affected by uncorrelated field similarity and remains at its maximum. Figure 1 also reflects the result of increasing the threshold to 10 %, which decreases the average number of reporting nodes by approximately 10 %, which is directly reflected in total energy consumption.

In Fig. 2, we take a closer look at the effect of IPCR on DACT for larger similarity factor F_p. Our experimental results show reduction in the communication complexity and is in agreement with the theoretical analysis in Sect. 4.3. Minor deviation from the average is also shown in the figure using error bars.

6   Conclusion

In this paper, we explored potential gains from monitoring energy consumption in real-time by utilizing in-network collaborative information processing to reduce information redundancy and communication operations in Energy Harvesting Wireless Sensor Networks (EH-WSN). We introduced a Data Aware Communication Technique (DACT), which exploits similarities in the sensory data to reduce communication redundancy via a clever similarity assessment technique. DACT is designed without any spatial or temporal assumptions about the data and can be applied to any energy monitoring and reduction application. DACT detects such similarities in the data space and takes advantage of them to reduce communication complexity and hence reduce energy consumption by up to 90 %.

References

1. UC Berkeley, LBL, USC/ISI and Xerox Parc, NS-2 documentation and software, Version 2.29, October 2005. http://www.isi.edu/nsnam/ns
2. Aledhari, M., Saeed, F.: Design and implementation of network transfer protocol for big genomic data. In: IEEE International Congress on Big Data (IEEE Big Data Congress 2015). IEEE (2015)
3. Anastasi, G., Falchi, A., Passarella, A., Conti, M., Gregori, E.: Performance measurements of motes sensor networks. In: Proceedings of the ACM International Symposium on Modeling, Analysis and Simulation of Wireless and Mobile Systems, MSWiM 2004, pp. 174–181 (2004)
4. Bajwa, R., Rajagopal, R., Varaiya, P., Kavaler, R.: In-pavement wireless sensor network for vehicle classification. In: Proceedings of the IEEE International Conference on Information Processing in Sensor Networks (IPSN), pp. 85–96 (2011)
5. Blum, R., Sadler, B.: Energy efficient signal detection in sensor networks using ordered transmissions. IEEE Trans. Signal Process. 56(7), 3229–3235 (2008)
6. Cano, C., Bellalta, B., Sfairopoulou, A., Oliver, M., Barcel, J.: Taking advantage of overhearing in low power listening WSNs: A performance analysis of the LWT-MAC protocol. Mob. Netw. Appl. 16, 613–628 (2011). http://dx.doi.org/10.1007/s11036-010-0280-4

7. Chen, Z., Khokhar, A.: Self organization and energy efficient TDMA MAC protocol by wake up for wireless sensor networks. In: IEEE SECON, pp. 335–341 (2004)
8. Du, S., Saha, A., Johnson, D.: RMAC: a routing-enhanced duty-cycle MAC protocol for wireless sensor networks. In: Proceedings of the IEEE International Conference on Computer Communications (INFOCOM), pp. 1478–1486, May 2007
9. Hefeida, M., Khokhar, A.: A cross-layer approach for context-aware data gathering in wireless sensor networks. In: Global Communications Conference (GLOBECOM), 2012 IEEE, pp. 238–243 (2012)
10. Hefeida, M., Khokhar, A.: Energy conservation in WSNs: a collaborative information processing approach. In: Wireless Communications and Mobile Computing Conference (IWCMC), 2014 International, pp. 1118–1123, August 2014
11. Hesham, L., Sultan, A., Nafie, M., Digham, F.: Cooperative sensing with sequential ordered transmissions to secondary fusion center. In: 2011 IEEE International Conference on Acoustics, Speech and Signal Processing (ICASSP), pp. 2988–2991, May 2011
12. Iima, Y., Kanzaki, A., Hara, T., Nishio, S.: Overhearing-based data transmission reduction for periodical data gathering in wireless sensor networks. In: International Conference on Complex, Intelligent and Software Intensive Systems, 2009, CISIS 2009, pp. 1048–1053, March 2009
13. Lee, V.C.: Energy harvesting for wireless sensor network. Ph.D. thesis, University of California, Berkeley (2012)
14. Lin, X., Kwok, Y., Wang, H.: Cross-layer design for energy efficient communication in wireless sensor networks. Wirel. Commun. Mob. Comput. 9(2), 251–268 (2009)
15. Sartipi, M., Fletcher, R.: Energy-efficient data acquisition in wireless sensor networks using compressed sensing. In: 2011 Data Compression Conference, pp. 223–232. IEEE (2011)
16. Sun, Y., Du, S., Gurewitz, O., Johnson, D.: DW-MAC: a low latency, energy efficient demand-wakeup MAC protocol for wireless sensor networks. In: Proceedings of the ACM International Symposium on Mobile Ad Hoc Networking and Computing (MobiHoc), pp. 53–62 (2008)
17. Vuran, M., Akyildiz, I.: Spatial correlation-based collaborative medium access control in wireless sensor networks. IEEE/ACM Trans. Netw. (TON) 14(2), 329 (2006)
18. Ye, W., Heidemann, J., Estrin, D.: An energy-efficient mac protocol for wireless sensor networks. In: Proceedings of the IEEE INFOCOM, vol. 3, pp. 1567–1576 (2002)
19. Ye, W., Heidemann, J., Estrin, D.: Medium access control with coordinated adaptive sleeping for wireless sensor networks. IEEE/ACM Trans. Netw. 12(3), 493–506 (2004)
20. Younis, O., Krunz, M., Ramasubramanian, S.: Node clustering in wireless sensor networks: recent developments and deployment challenges. IEEE Netw. 20(3), 20–25 (2006)
21. Yu, L., Wang, N., Meng, X.: Real-time forest fire detection with wireless sensor networks. In: Proceedings 2005 International Conference on Wireless Communications, Networking and Mobile Computing, 2005, vol. 2, pp. 1214–1217. IEEE (2005)
22. Zou, Q., Zheng, S., Sayed, A.: Cooperative spectrum sensing via sequential detection for cognitive radio networks. In: IEEE 10th Workshop on Signal Processing Advances in Wireless Communications, 2009. SPAWC 2009, pp. 121–125. IEEE (2009)

Network Applications and Tools

Scalability of Passive and Active Solutions for Time-Based Ranging in IEEE 802.11 Networks

Israel Martin-Escalona[✉], Marta Malpartida, Enrica Zola,
and Francisco Barcelo-Arroyo

Universitat Politècnica de Catalunya (UPC), Barcelona, Spain
{imartin,enrica,francisco}@entel.upc.edu

Abstract. Wireless positioning systems have become popular in recent years. Outdoor positioning has been addressed successfully, but location indoors still presents some open issues. One of them is related with the scalability of time-based ranging algorithms. The aim of this study is to develop a simulation framework in order to evaluate the scalability and stability of two time-based ranging positioning algorithms in IEEE 802.11 networks: 2-Way Time of Flight (TOF) and passive TDOA. Details about this simulation model are provided and both algorithms are compared in a proof-of-concept scenario. Results show that Passive TDOA provides a better scalability and more stable measurements than the solutions based on pure 2-Way TOF algorithms.

Keywords: Positioning · Ranging · Scalability · IEEE 802.11

1 Introduction and Goals

The knowledge of their own position is perceived by users as essential information that mobile devices need to provide. This information, which was initially used to enrich already developed services and applications, such as geotagging the pictures users take, has become the core of the new set of services and applications that are to come in the next years, such as augmented reality [1], location-based social networks [2] or smart cities [3].

The widespread inclusion of GPS receivers in mobile phones has boosted the use of location-based services. This technology provides a world-wide coverage and excellent accuracy outdoors. However, the same does not apply to indoor scenarios, where GPS provide low accuracy or simply stops working.

Currently, there is no a counterpart of GPS to be used indoors. The industry and the research community are actively looking for a global technology that allows mobile devices to be globally positioned indoors. Several approaches have been proposed in the last years. Most of them try to take advantage of communication networks already deployed to position the network users as well. This approach simplifies the deployment of location systems and extends their availability. One example of this approach consists of using public land mobile networks (PLMN) to support positioning. Techniques, such as the Observed Time Difference Of Arrival (OTDOA) can be used in LTE networks to

L. Mamatas et al. (Eds.): WWIC 2016, LNCS 9674, pp. 135–146, 2016.
DOI: 10.1007/978-3-319-33936-8_11

get the user's location [4]. Although the accuracy of these solutions are suitable for most of location-based services, those of them designed to run specifically indoors tend to be much more restrictive in terms of accuracy, demanding often a precision around 1 m. Such requirements are hardly satisfied by location systems based on PLMN, since signals used for positioning are often impacted by several radio artifacts: attenuation, blocking, multipath, delay-spread, etc.

Networks local to the user's location are then preferred for positioning purposes. Bluetooth and 802.11 are the technologies that concentrate most of the research on indoor positioning. Bluetooth low energy networks are being used by companies such as Apple [5] and Paypal [6] to provide location systems working indoors. Although Bluetooth-based solutions are promising, they have the drawback of the coverage, requiring usually specific network upgrades to fully support location-based services. On the other hand, communication networks based on IEEE 802.11 are known to be widely deployed, mainly indoors. This fact makes this technology really appealing for location systems. However, location systems using IEEE 802.11 technologies must cope with several issues related with the position accuracy, the latency, the scalability and the integrity of the location system. Solutions based on received signal strength (RSS) are known to be easily implemented in IEEE 802.11 devices, thus providing excellent coverage, but they tend to provide poor accuracy figures [7]. Fingerprinting is a technique usually related with IEEE 802.11 location systems [8]. It consists of a database that stores data vectors related with specific positions. Those vectors typically contain the RSS (sometimes other data) of the set of access points at sight in a given place (x, y, z). When users want to get their own position or a third party request such information, the mobile device computes the vector in real time and delivers that vector to the location server where the database is. Then the reported vector is compared with the data stored in the database and the most likely position according to all these data is returned. Fingerprinting tends to provide excellent accuracy, delay and scalability, but requires setting up the location database before the system is deployed. Furthermore, changes in the environment have a severe impact on the quality of the position, so the database needs to be updated often. Depending on the scenario, this database maintenance may involve a noticeable effort.

Time-based location techniques use the time-of-flight (TOF) to estimate distances to well-known references (i.e. landmarks). Those references are perfectly located so that the only unknown is the position of the mobile user. There are several proposals using this approach, most of them based on the round-trip-time [9] to skip the need for synchronizing all the network devices. This approach is extended in [10] to provide a software-based solution that at the same time improves the accuracy of the regular 2-way time-of-arrival solutions.

Collaborative solutions have been proposed in order to improve the accuracy of time-based solutions [11]. Although the accuracy has been improved, time-based solutions still have an open issue: the scalability. Most of the time-based location systems inject traffic in the network to perform the measurements, which directly impacts the network performance after the traffic increase. The more measurements required, the more likely frames collide and the longer the time to reach a valid computation of the position.

Passive solutions were presented to overcome this issue and boost the scalability of time-based location systems, without a severe degradation of the accuracy of the computed positions.

This work is focused on one of these passive algorithms: the passive TDOA. In [12], the authors presented the benefits of this algorithm and provided a short study on the expected accuracy, showing figures better than those achieved by its active-solution counterpart. However, the scalability benefits, though claimed based on the fact that no extra traffic is injected, were never studied in detail or numerically evaluated. This work is aimed at studying the scalability benefits of the passive TDOA over a regular 2-way TOF solution, both systems working in IEEE 802.11 networks.

The rest of the paper is structured as follows. Section 2 presents the algorithms that are going to be assessed. The simulation tool and the simulated scenario are presented in Sect. 3. The results achieved are shown in Sect. 4, while the main conclusion and the planned future work are drawn in Sect. 5.

2   Passive vs. Active Ranging

Time-based positioning in IEEE 802.11 networks is based on ranging, i.e. it infers the distance between the mobile device that needs to be positioned and several well-located network entities (landmarks or anchors). Those distances feed a multilateration algorithm, which finally fixes the position. Ranging models, i.e. the procedures followed to turn time measurements into distances, tend to require several measurements for a single distance estimation [9]. Only after processing a set of measurements the channel artifacts can be properly filtered and hence their impact on the position accuracy reduced. This approach can be followed as long as only few nodes are being positioning in the network. If there are a large number of nodes requiring their position, positioning traffic tends to flood the radio channel, which yields frames colliding frequently. This increase in the collision rate has a twofold effect. On one hand, the response time of the location system (i.e. the time spent by the system until the requested position is fixed) becomes longer. This fact impacts on the quality-of-service perceived by the user and might have a negative effect on the position accuracy as well, especially when the user is moving. On the other hand, the heavier the location traffic, the lower the available throughput for remaining communications.

Passive ranging solutions try to compute positions by only listening to the radio medium. Thus, they try to take benefit of the regular traffic in the network to infer the position of the user. This kind of solutions are known to favor the scalability, since increasing the amount of nodes requiring their own position does not involve a noticeable increase in the location traffic.

2.1   Assisted Passive TDOA

The Passive TDOA [12] is one of these time-based passive ranging algorithms. This algorithm was designed to complement regular active 2-way TOF systems and enhance their scalability. Accordingly, the passive TDOA algorithm assumes the presence of few nodes in the network running 2-way TOF positioning solutions. The point of the passive TDOA is locating a node using only the information of its active neighbor nodes. The basic procedure followed by Passive TDOA to allow the passive positioning is described in Fig. 1. In the figure, two nodes are represented, one running a 2-way TOF algorithm (i.e. active node) and one running the passive TDOA algorithm (i.e. passive node).

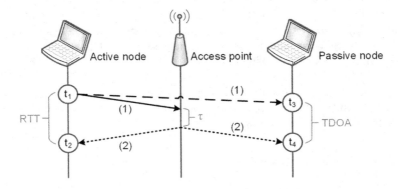

Fig. 1. Estimation of a single TDOA in the passive node

The location process starts when the active node obtains its position by using the 2-Way TOA technique. Meanwhile, the passive node is listening to the radio medium and receiving the messages that the active node exchanges with the access point. Figure 1 illustrates the performance of the algorithm. Whenever the active node wants to estimate the distance to an access point, it sends a message (1) to the access point. This message, because of the diffusion network, is also received in the passive node, which marks the time of arrival before discarding the frame. After a known time τ, the access point sends back a message (2) to the active node, as response to message (1). When this message is received in the active node, the distance between the active node and the passive node can be computed (with an indeterminate error). The message (2), because of the diffusion network is also received in the passive node. Then, a time difference of arrival (TDOA) can be computed in the passive node as $t_4 - t_3$ in Fig. 1.

Repeating this procedure with enough access points (e.g. three in the case of 2D positioning) let the active node to compute its own position using a multilateration algorithm. Finally, this position has to be sent so that the passive node can compute its own position according to the TDOA measurements previously computed.

2.2   Autonomous Passive TDOA

The passive TDOA algorithm is able to estimate both active and passive nodes positions if the measurements are grouped in couples. Accordingly, the measurement procedure . is extended to include two procedures like the one depicted in Fig. 1.

Figure 2 illustrates how the measurements are taken. As shown, the active node is able to compute two RTTs (i.e. RTT_1 and RTT_2) and consequently the passive node collects two TDOAs (i.e. $TDOA_1$ and $TDOA_2$). These TDOAs are observations of the time-distance between two different paths as

$$TDOA = \left(T_a + T_p\right) - \left(T_{ap}\right) \tag{1}$$

where T_a and T_p is the TOF from active and passive nodes to the access point, respectively, and T_{ap} is the TOF between active and passive nodes.

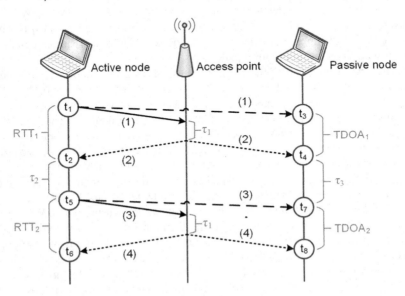

Fig. 2. Joint estimation of TOF and TDOA in the passive node

The point of grouping the measurements in couples is that relating these two TDOAs allows the distance from the active node to the access point to be inferred as

$$RTDOA = \tau_3 = t_7 - t_4 = T_a + \tau_2 + T_{ap} - T_p \tag{2}$$

Accordingly, under the assumption of the measurement-to-measurement delay (τ_2) is known and measurements to enough access points are available (at least 3 for 2D positioning), the passive node is able to compute both the active and the passive node positions, providing a twofold benefit. First, it involves a fully passive solution, minimizing the location traffic in the network (i.e. there is no need for the active node to send its own position). Second, it provides redundancy for active node positions, which can be statistically combined to improve their accuracy.

3   Simulation Tool and Scenarios

Simulation has been used to provide a rich and realistic scenario where to assess the scalability of the algorithm and compare the results with what is expected using regular active 2-way TOF solutions. To achieve this goal, a simulation tool implementing the 802.11 b/g protocol stack and the 2-Way TOF and Passive TDOA algorithms is required. In this simulation, messages showed in Figs. 1 and 2 are implemented over IEEE 802.11 as data frames, while the answers are built using ACK frames.

3.1   Simulation Tool

OMNET++ [13] is the network simulator used to evaluate the scalability of 2-Way TOF and Passive TDOA over IEEE 802.11 networks. The INET framework [14] has been used to provide a full implementation of the IEEE 802.11 protocol stack, including a rich set of radio models and mobility patterns.

Several parts of the code of the INET framework have been modified in order to implement the 2-Way TOF and the Passive TDOA algorithms. In the case of the 2-Way TOF algorithm, two measurements are provided for a single RTT, depending on when the transmission time-marks are taken: (1) in the IEEE 802.11 management layer (RTT-MNGT), i.e. just before the CSMA/CA delay chain begins; and (2) just before sending the data frame to the physical layer (RTT-MAC). The reason to include these two figures for each RTT measurement procedure is to provide thresholds that can match software-based (i.e. only the first measurement is likely to be available) and hardware-based (i.e. the second measurement is likely to be available) implementations. Figure 3 shows the basic flow of the implementation followed to take the time measurements. Whenever a data frame is received in the access point, the location timestamps included in it (if applies) are copied to the ACK frame built as response, as shown in Fig. 4. Finally, the timestamps applied to the received frames are taken once the frame enters in the reception function of the MAC layer, whenever the transmission time is taken, as shown in Fig. 5. As it can be seen, all those figures include the name of the INET files and the methods in these files that have been upgraded to support the 2-way TOF algorithm. In the case of the passive nodes only received frames have to be inspected. Figure 6 shows the basic flow followed in that case.

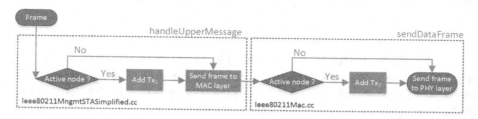

Fig. 3. Flow of the 2-way TOF algorithm (data frames in active nodes)

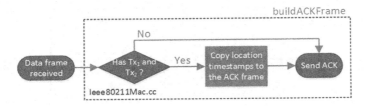

Fig. 4. Flow of the 2-way TOF algorithm (ACK frames in access points)

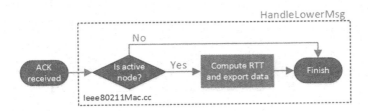

Fig. 5. Flow of the 2-way TOF algorithm (ACK frames in active nodes)

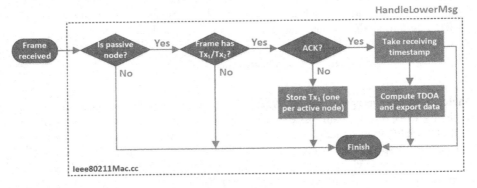

Fig. 6. Flow of the passive TDOA algorithm (passive nodes)

3.2 Simulated Scenario

A basic scenario has been built to provide a preliminary assessment on the scalability of the passive TDOA. It consists of one access point, which is placed at the top-left corner of a square-shaped simulation area, and twenty-six nodes. The nodes form a grid in the simulation area, as shown in Fig. 7. These nodes are static, i.e. they are settled in a position of the square-shaped simulated grid and keep the same position along the whole simulation. Different simulations are run considering from one single active node (i.e. 24 passive nodes) up to 25 active nodes (i.e. no passive nodes). Active nodes take always the first positions, i.e. from 1 up to N in Fig. 7, whilst passive nodes take the remaining positions (i.e. from $N + 1$ up to 25).

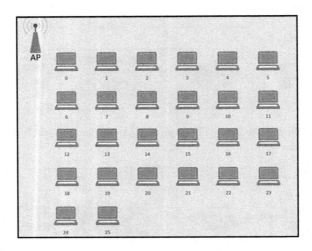

Fig. 7. Layout of the simulated scenario

The IEEE 802.11b standard is used in simulations, although the results can be easily extended to other standards such as 802.11g or n. The lognormal shadowing model [15] has been used to model the radio propagation conditions indoors:

$$PL(dB) = PL(d_0) + 10\alpha log\left(\frac{d}{d_0}\right) + X_\sigma \qquad (3)$$

where PL is the average path loss, $PL(d_0)$ is the path loss at the reference distance d_0 (typically 1 m), α is the path loss exponent and X_σ is a zero-mean Gaussian distributed random variable with standard distribution σ. The parameters α and σ are fixed to 4.02 and 7.36 dB respectively, as reported in [15] for indoor conditions. The transmission power and the sensitivity are set to 3 dBm and 85 dBm respectively and apply to all the nodes in the network, including the access point. The coverage radio of the base station is fixed to 10 m, which yields a 7.07 × 7.07 m square-shaped simulation area. This coverage and density conditions are similar to those present in a Wireless Sensor Network environment, which is one of the target applications of location algorithms. Accordingly, the reduced simulation area was maintained and no other radio parameter was modified.

3.3 Observed Metrics

In order to study and evaluate the performance of 2-way-TOA and Passive TDOA the following metrics are defined:

- Delay. It is the time that active and passive nodes require to obtain a RTT and a TDOA sample, respectively. This time accounts for the delays introduced by the medium access control (MAC) layer, but it does not include other delays such as those associated with the operating system (e.g. multiple-process management).

- Number of collisions. It is the amount of collisions that each node is aware of, once the simulation finishes.

The simulation is run until 2,500 samples for all observed metrics are collected. The simulation time will thus depend on the specific scenario being simulated (e.g. according to the amount of collisions).

4 Performance Assessment

The average amount of collisions are shown in Fig. 8, as an illustration of how loaded is the radio medium. As it is shown and indeed expected, the higher the active nodes, the higher the collision number. The time until a RTT sample is taken (i.e. the RTT delay) depends on the number of times a single frame needs to be transmitted until it is properly received at the access point. Accordingly, the RTT delay is expected to grow with the collision rate (i.e. with the amount of nodes in the network).

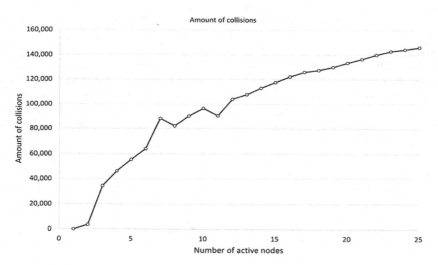

Fig. 8. Average amount of collisions

Figure 9 illustrates the average delay until the node is able to estimate the RTT-related metrics (i.e. RTT-MNGT and RTT-MAC). As expected, the RTT-MNGT delay grows together with the amount of active nodes in the network. The more positioning traffic in the network the more likely the location frames collide. The delay increment can be fitted by means of a linear regression, with a coefficient of determination of 98.96 %. The resulting expression indicates that each active node in the network involves an increment of about 41 ms in the mean delay until an RTT-MNGT sample can be finally taken.

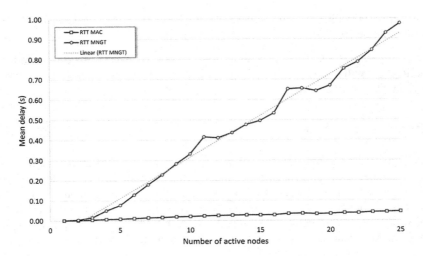

Fig. 9. Mean delay until a new RTT sample is taken

The RTT-MAC delay is not impacted by most of the delays introduced by the CSMA/CA chain, so the delays for this metric are much shorter. In this latter case, each active node involves an increment of less than 2 ms to the RTT-MAC estimation process. It must be noted that the actual RTT delay is expected to be in between of these two set of measurements. Furthermore, the more active nodes, the more error in the time until a new RTT sample is taken, as shown in Fig. 10. Data in this figure shows that, in the

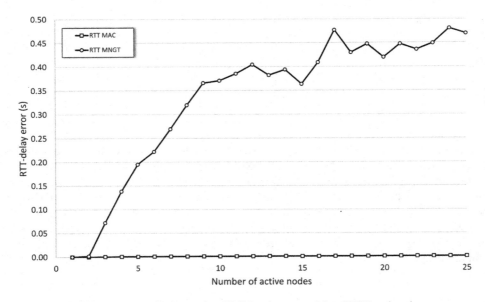

Fig. 10. Confidence interval at 95 % for the mean delay (RTT) estimation

densest scenario (i.e. 25 active nodes), this error can reach up to 50 % of the time required to collect a new RTT sample.

Figure 11 shows the mean time elapsed until TDOA is estimated, using the average and the median estimators. This latter is included to filter some artifacts produced by the way in which active and passive nodes are settled along the simulated scenario. Results demonstrate that passive TDOA technique is much more insensitive to the amount of active nodes in the network, if it is compared with the average delay required by the 2-Way TOA algorithm. Interquartile range (i.e. the difference between the percentiles at 75 % and 25 %) is about $5 \cdot 10^{-14}$. This is because Passive TDOA nodes are able to estimate TDOAs from several active nodes at the same time and hence they can get enough samples before a single active node is able to estimate its own range to the access point.

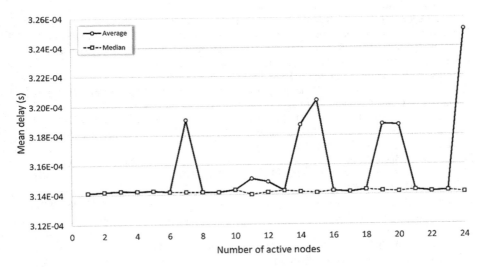

Fig. 11. Mean delay until a new TDOA sample is taken

5 Conclusion and Future Work

This paper presents a preliminary assessment on the scalability of two range time-based solutions for positioning: 2-way TOF and passive TDOA. The INET framework of the OMNeT++ even-driven network simulator has been enhanced to implement those techniques, which have been assessed in a basic scenario implementing a single IEEE 802.11 network with several static nodes. Results indicate that the use of the passive TDOA algorithm can boost the scalability of the active ranging algorithms, providing at the same observation much more stable than those achieved by means of the traditional ranging.

Future work involves a more complete analysis of the scalability under non-static conditions and larger simulation areas and eventually contrasting the results with real measurements achieved by means of an already planned implementation of these techniques on small portable devices such as Raspberry Pi.

Acknowledgments. This work has been partially funded by the ERDF and the Spanish Government through the project TEC2013-48099-C2-1-P.

References

1. Shi, D., Liu, F., Yutian, Q., Ji, Y.: A WLAN-based positioning system for indoor augmented reality services. In: International Conference on Information Science, Electronics and Electrical Engineering, pp. 420–424 (2014)
2. Kunhui, L., Jingjin, W., Zhongnan, Z., Yating, C., Zhentuan, X.: Adaptive location recommendation algorithm based on location-based social networks. In: International Conference on Computer Science and Education, pp. 137–142 (2015)
3. Sahib, U.: M-Governance: smartphone applications for smarter cities—tapping GPS and NFC technologies. In: VinodKumar, T.M. (ed.) E-Governance for Smart Cities. Advances in 21st Century Human Settlements, pp. 245–306. Springer, Singapore (2014)
4. 3GPP: LTE Positioning Protocol. ETSI TS 136.355 V13.0.0 (2016)
5. Apple: iOS: Understanding iBeacon, February 2015. http://support.apple.com/kb/HT6048
6. GSMA: A Guide to Bluetooth Beacons. A white paper by the GSMA (2014)
7. Stella, M., Russo, M., Begusic, D.: Location determination in indoor environment based on RSS fingerprinting and artificial neural network. In: International Conference on Telecommunications, pp. 301–306 (2007)
8. Namiot, D., Sneps-Sneppe, M.: Geofence and network proximity. In: Balandin, S., Andreev, S., Koucheryavy, Y. (eds.) NEW2AN 2013 and ruSMART 2013. LNCS, vol. 8121, pp. 117–127. Springer, Heidelberg (2013)
9. Ciurana, M., Barcelo-Arroyo, F., Izquierdo, F.: A ranging method with IEEE 802.11 data frames for indoor localization. In: Wireless Communications and Networking Conference, pp. 2092–2096 (2007)
10. Hoene, C., Willmann, J.: Four-way TOA and software-based trilateration of IEEE 802.11 devices. In: International Symposium on Personal, Indoor and Mobile Radio Communications, pp. 1–6 (2008)
11. Golden, S.A., Bateman, S.S.: Sensor measurements for Wi-Fi location with emphasis on time-of-arrival ranging. IEEE Trans. Mob. Comput. **6**(10), 1185–1198 (2007)
12. Martin, I., Malpartida, M., Barcelo-Arroyo, F.: Performance evaluation of the passive TDOA algorithm in dark areas. In: Ubiquitous Positioning, Indoor Navigation, and Location Based Service, pp. 1–8 (2012)
13. Vargas, A., et al.: OMNeT++. Discrete event Simulator, March 2016. https://omnetpp.org
14. OMNeT++ Community: INET Framework for OMNeT++, March 2016. https://inet.omnetpp.org
15. Faria, D.B.: Modeling signal attenuation in IEEE 802.11 Wireless LANs, vol. 1. Standford University (2005)

A Collaborative Video Download Application Based on Wi-Fi Direct

Haotian Sha, Argyrios G. Tasiopoulos, Ioannis Psaras$^{(\boxtimes)}$, and George Pavlou

Department of Electronic and Electrical Engineering,
University College London, London, UK
{haotian.sha.14,argyrios.tasiopoulos,i.psaras,g.pavlou}@ucl.ac.uk

Abstract. We developed a collaborative video download application, which allows several users to form a local group via peer-to-peer (P2P) links and collaboratively help one user in the group to download a high quality video. Cellular interface and P2P interface are simultaneously utilised in the application to guarantee quality of experience (QoE) when the cellular connection is disrupted. The application is based on Wi-Fi Direct technology and it exploits the service discovery function of the Wi-Fi Direct framework.

Apart from the implementation itself, we also model collaborative video streaming over the cellular network under periodic cellular disconnections (*e.g.*, the commuters experience poor Internet services when trains travel through tunnels). Our purpose is to exploit the gains of the collaborative download between users in the context of periodic disconnections and limited cellular downlink rate. We simulate several scenarios to find the requirements of the application that guarantee seamless and undisrupted playback.

Keywords: Collaborative download · Wi-Fi Direct · Service discovery · Seamless playback

1 Introduction

People today have growing demand for mobile Internet services and especially video streaming. The applications related to video streaming are increasingly popular over mobile devices, as people want to watch HD video through their mobile devices when they are in cafe or commuting by train. There are, however, several challenges which lower the QoE of video streaming applications.

In underground systems, video streaming is extremely challenging, since the cellular connection is physically disrupted when the trains travel between stations. Often, even when trains are in stations and signal is available, streaming cannot necessarily be supported with acceptable QoE.

In order to deal with the above issues, collaborative video download systems [6–10] based on mobile P2P networks have attracted attention recently. However, these studies focus on downloading through Wi-Fi interface rather than cellular

© IFIP International Federation for Information Processing 2016
Published by Springer International Publishing Switzerland 2016. All Rights Reserved
L. Mamatas et al. (Eds.): WWIC 2016, LNCS 9674, pp. 147–158, 2016.
DOI: 10.1007/978-3-319-33936-8_12

interface. There are also studies, *e.g.*, in [2,3], utilising P2P and cellular links to disseminate content, taking the social ties and geographical proximity into account. They focus, however, on offloading current cellular network rather than video streaming.

In contrast to the above studies, in this paper, we utilise multiple interfaces of mobile devices to improve the QoS of streaming applications in constrained cellular connection environments. We build models to find the requirements of seamless playback in various situations, depending on several parameters, such as the video data rate, the cellular downlink rate and the device-to-device (D2D) data transmission rate.

We implement a collaborative video download application which allows several users who are in the vicinity to form a local group via Wi-Fi Direct and collaboratively help one user in the group download an HD video through the cellular network. The problems above could be effectively solved by *"helper nodes"*, who download content on behalf of the user who wants to watch some video. They then transmit the downloaded content using Wi-Fi Direct. The collaborative download system we design is shown in Fig. 1(a). For the purposes of this study, we do not consider incentives of "helper nodes", but assume that micropayments can complement and incentivise participation.

We choose Wi-Fi Direct for our application since it can transfer data faster and over longer distances compared to Bluetooth. We exploit the service discovery function in Wi-Fi Direct framework, which allows the users (*i.e.*, group members) to identify the user who requires help for video streaming (*i.e.*, group owner) and connect to the group owner to form a many-to-one wireless local network. We assume that an HD video is divided into chunks at the server and each chunk is assigned a unique *identifier*. Once the group of the owner and the helpers is formed, each member is assigned with a number of chunk identifiers to download on behalf of the group owner. We then use the AsyncTask class in java to allow the group owner to simultaneously receive video chunks from multiple group members, which is the key component for achieving seamless playback.

We model the process of video chunk downloading and delivering between users in several different cases, taking into account all the required parameters.

The rest of the paper is organised as follows. In Sect. 2, we describe the implementation of the collaborative video download application on the Android platform. In Sect. 3, we build models for different scenarios to analyse the requirements of seamless playback and the gains of collaborative download. At last, we conclude our findings in Sect. 4, where we also discuss future developments of collaborative download systems.

2   Implementation of Collaborative Video Download Application

The implementation of our application is comprised of four main components: *(i)* establishing local device-to-device (D2D) network, *(ii)* downloading and/or streaming video, *(iii)* video chunk delivery and *(iv)* playing received video chunks.

Establishing Local D2D Network. In Wi-Fi Direct, the service discovery technique allows a device to discover the services published by devices in the vicinity without being connected to a network. The service here is a Bonjour service information object, which has three parameters[1]:

- instanceName (e.g. "MyPrinter").
- serviceType (e.g. "ipp.tcp").
- txtMap, which is a TXT record with key/value pair in a map containing the information of the service.

The DnsSdServiceResponseListener in Wi-Fi Direct framework is utilised to receive the actual service description and connection information. We ask the user who requires help for downloading an HD video (group owner) to publish a service with an instance name of "GroupOwner". The *helper nodes or group members* start the process of discovering a service with the instance name of "GroupOwner" and receive the service description and connection information through DnsSdServiceResponseListener. Once the connection information of group owner is obtained, the helpers connect to the group owner and establish a many-to-one local D2D network.

Streaming/Downloading Video Chunks. An HD video is divided into chunks at the server and each chunk is assigned a unique *identifier*. This can be realised through the *Information-Centric Networking* (ICN) concept (*e.g.*, [1,4,5]). In our application, the group owner streams directly from the source. In the meantime, the group members download the later parts of the video. After downloading, the group members transfer the downloaded content to the group owner.

We utilise the VideoView class in java to implement streaming. AyncTask class in java is utilised to run the downloading process in the background and publish the results in the UI thread.

Video Chunk Delivery. In Wi-Fi Direct, there are "broadcast intents" which inform our application when certain events occur. We instantiate an intent filter and create a new WifiDirectBroadcastReceiver class which extends the BroadcastReceiver class to listen for the intents we are interested in. The application starts different AysncTasks or threads (transferring chunks or receiving chunks) according to the various intents. The logical flowchart is shown in Fig. 1(b).

We use different TCP ports to receive different video chunks. This is to allow the group owner device to receive video chunks from different group members simultaneously. We name the received chunks according to the port numbers which they come from to distinguish different chunks. We use TCP ports with smaller numbers to receive chunks in the former part of the video and TCP ports with bigger numbers to receive chunks in the latter part of the video. This way,

---

[1] Android/sdk/docs/reference/android/net/wifi/p2p/nsd/WifiP2pDnsSdServiceInfo. html.

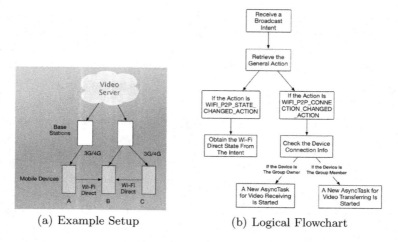

(a) Example Setup   (b) Logical Flowchart

Fig. 1. Overall Setup and Logical Flowchart

we can sort the video chunks according to their names from low to high and play them in order.

Playing Received Video Chunks. When the group owner device has received the video chunks from group members, it needs to play the received chunks seamlessly and in order. VideoView class is a wrapper around the MediaPlayer, which is usually used to play video files on Android platform. In order to achieve seamless playback, we need to sort the received video chunks before the group owner finishes streaming the first few video chunks.

3 Modelling and Evaluation

As is clear from the implementation aspects presented above, the main parameters that affect seamless playback are the *video data rate*, x, the *cellular downlink rate*, y, and the *WiFi-Direct transferring rate*, z. In this Section, we model three separate cases as regards these parameters.

- Scenario 3.1: $z > y > x$, plus periodic disconnections. We first consider the case where the cellular downlink rate is faster than the video data rate. In this case, clearly, the video can be streamed without playback disruptions. For this reason, we add periodic disconnections to emulate public transportation systems, such as underground train networks.
- Scenario 3.2: $z > x > y$. As a second case, we consider the case where the video playback rate is faster than the cellular downlink. This means that playback disruptions will inevitably reduce the perceived QoE as perceived by the end user.

– Scenario 3.3: $z > x > y$, plus periodic disconnections. Finally, we add periodic disconnections to the above case, in order to emulate a more challenging and more realistic case of an underground train network.

We note that in all cases, the WiFi-Direct rate (*i.e.*, the D2D transfer rate) is faster than both the video data playback rate and the cellular rate.

In each of the above cases, we study the relations between the parameters in Table 1 under the requirement of achieving undisrupted playback. The modelling parameters and the related notation is listed in Table 1.

Table 1. Parameters that may affect the video streaming experience of our application.

Parameters we consider	
Video data rate	x (KBps)
Cellular downlink rate	y (KBps)
Wi-Fi Direct transferring rate	z (KBps)
Connection period	C (s)
Disconnection period	D (s)
Number of group members	N
Buffered content in terms of playback time	T_b (s)
Playback duration of a video chunk	T_p (s)
Rounds for the group owner receiving video chunks from the group members	n
Total number of chunks of a video	V
Time for playing video in C	$T_{pc}(s)$
The extra buffered video content	$A(KB)$

3.1 Scenario 3.1: $z > y > x$, Plus Periodic Disconnections

In this case, the group owner can stream more content in connection period C than he can watch, since $y > x$. Therefore, the group owner can play the extra buffered content in the upcoming disconnection period. The group members can utilise the time that the group owner plays the extra buffered content to transfer video chunks to the group owner. The first requirement of seamless playback is that group members transfer the downloaded content to the group owner before the owner's buffered content is played-back. This requirement is shown in inequality (1).

$$\frac{(y-x)C}{x} \geq \frac{Cy}{z} \tag{1}$$

The second requirement of seamless playback is that the video chunks the group owner receives from group members can cover the disconnection period. This case is shown in inequality (2).

$$\frac{CyN}{x} \geq D \tag{2}$$

A special case here is when the cellular downlink rate y is so fast that the extra buffered content could cover the following disconnection period, hence, there is no need for helper users. This subcase is shown in inequality (3).

$$\frac{(y-x)C}{x} \geq D \tag{3}$$

We present 4 evaluation scenarios for this case in Table 2. The purpose is to study how many group members are required in order to realise seamless playback, as well as the relation between transferring rate and video quality.

Table 2. Scenarios for case when $z > y > x$, plus periodic disconnections

Scenario 3.1.1	$x = 350$ KBps, $z = 10$ MBps, $C = 240$ s, $D = 900$ s, and y and N are variables
Scenario 3.1.2	$y = 600$ KBps, $z = 10$ MBps, $C = 240$ s, $D = 900$ s, and N and x are variables
Scenario 3.1.3	$y = 600$ KBps, $C = 240$ s, $D = 900$ s, $N = 5$, and z and x are variables
Scenario 3.1.4	$C = 240$ s, $D = 900$ s, $x = 550$ KBps, $y = 600$ KBps, and z and N are variables

Scenario 3.1.1. According to inequality (1), we find that in order to meet the first requirement of seamless playback the cellular downlink rate should be $y \geq 362.39$ KBps. In turn, according to inequality (3), we find that if $y \geq 1662.5$ KBps there is no need to have helper nodes, as the cellular downlink is so fast that can take the user through the disconnection period and into the next connection period. The relation between y and N is shown in Fig. 2(a).

We can see from Fig. 2(a) that as the cellular rate y increases, less group members are required.

Scenario 3.1.2. The relation between the video data rate x and the minimum number of required helper nodes N is shown in Fig. 2(b).

As expected, we can see from Fig. 2(b) that the relation between x and N is linear. That is, the group owner can improve the quality of the video he receives by adding more group members.

Scenario 3.1.3. Figure 2(c) shows the relation between the WiFi Direct transferring rate and the video data rate under the requirements of seamless playback.

We can see from Fig. 2(c) that as video quality increases, the user requires faster transferring rate between user devices. The gradient of the figure is increasing dramatically when $x \geq 500$ KBps. This means that fast device-to-device transferring rate is necessary if the user wants to watch HD video.

Scenario 3.1.4. Figure 2(d) shows the relation between transferring rate and the required number of group members.

We can see from Fig. 2(d) that increasing transferring rate can reduce the required number of helpers. In this case, the group owner requires only two helpers when the transferring rate is $12,000$ KBps, which is within the range of the WiFi Direct specification.

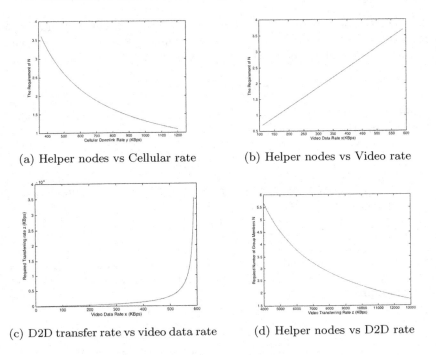

(a) Helper nodes vs Cellular rate   (b) Helper nodes vs Video rate

(c) D2D transfer rate vs video data rate   (d) Helper nodes vs D2D rate

Fig. 2. Scenario 3.1: $z > y > x$, plus periodic disconnections.

Scenario 3.2: $z > x > y$. In this case, the group owner needs to buffer video content in advance of starting the playback, since the cellular rate is smaller than the video playback rate, $y < x$. We therefore, need to guarantee that the buffered video content, T_b, can make up the content that the user cannot stream in T_p secs, that is, in duration equal to the playback time of one chunk. This requirement is shown in inequality (4).

$$yT_b \geq (x - y)T_p \tag{4}$$

We assume that at the point when the group owner starts streaming the first video chunk, each group member has already downloaded one video chunk and is in the process of transferring it to the group owner. After the first round of receiving content from the N helper nodes, the group owner would have N chunks ready for playback. Therefore, the second round of downloading content and transferring it to the group owner is longer than the first. This is because the first round needs to guarantee that video chunks have been downloaded and sent to the group owner before the first chunk finishes, whereas in the second round, the group owner has N chunks to playback before he runs out of buffered content. That said, we assume that each group member can download and transfer r_2 chunks during the second round, and the requirement of r_2 is shown in (5).

$$NT_p \geq \frac{r_2 x T_p}{y} + \frac{r_2 x T_p}{z} \tag{5}$$

The left part of inequality (5) is the playback time of N chunks, and the right part of inequality (5) is the time each group member needs in order to download and transfer r_2 chunks. Inequality (5) can be simplified as follows.

$$r_2 \leq \frac{Nyz}{zx + yx} \tag{6}$$

Similarly, the number of chunks that each group member can download and transfer during the third round, r_3, is shown in inequality (7).

$$r_3 \leq (\frac{Nyz}{xz + xy})^2 \tag{7}$$

Generalising inequalities (6) and (7), we conclude that the number of chunks that each group member can download during the nth round, r_n, is:

$$r_n \leq (\frac{Nyz}{xz + xy})^{n-1} \tag{8}$$

Based on Eq. (8), we find that in order to stream V chunks without disruptions, the group owner needs to complete n rounds of receiving from the helper nodes, according to:

$$V \leq 1 + N(\frac{Nyz}{xz + xy})^0 + N(\frac{Nyz}{xz + xy})^1$$
$$+N(\frac{Nyz}{xz + xy})^2 + \ldots + N(\frac{Nyz}{xz + xy})^{n-1} \tag{9}$$

We present three evaluation scenarios for the case where the video playback rate is faster than the cellular downlink rate. We focus on the number of rounds needed in order for the group owner to receive the video chunks required to achieve undisrupted playback. Note that in this scenario, we assume no physical disruption due to disconnection (Table 3).

Table 3. Scenarios for situation $z > x > y$

Scenario 3.2.1	$x = 450$ KBps, $z = 10$ MBps, $y = 200$ KBps, $V = 50$, and n and N are variables
Scenario 3.2.2	$x = 450$ KBps, $z = 10$ MBps, $y = 200$ KBps, $N = 4$, and V and n are variables
Scenario 3.2.3	$x = 450$ KBps, $y = 200$ KBps, $N = 4$, $V = 50$, and z and n are variables
Scenario 3.2.4	$x = 450$ KBps, $y = 200$ KBps, $z = 10$ MBps, $n = 4$, and N and V are variables

Scenario 3.2.1. The number of helper nodes, N, should be equal or greater than 3 in order to achieve undisrupted playback. The relation between N and n is shown in Fig. 3(a).

The group owner can effectively reduce the receiving rounds by adding more group members, as shown in Fig. 3(a). However, we observe that the group owner does not need to have too many helper nodes. For example, the group owner needs to complete almost the same number of rounds when there are 6 group members and 12 group members.

Scenario 3.2.2. The relation between the total number of video chunks, V, and the number of rounds n is shown in Fig. 3(b).

We can see from Fig. 3(b) that our application is very effective for long videos. For example, a video with 25 chunks and a video with 105 chunks require the same number of rounds. This is because of the fact that the rounds get longer as the video progresses and therefore, more chunks can be downloaded in one round (see Eq. (5) and related discussion).

Scenario 3.2.3. The relation between the WiFi transfer rate z and the required number of rounds n is shown in Fig. 3(c).

We observe from Fig. 3(c) that compared to the number of group members and the size of the video presented before, the WiFi Direct transfer rate has less effect on the number of required rounds. We see that for any transfer speed above $1,500$ KBps, the required number of rounds stays the same and equal to 5. As noted before, this is because, after the first round, the number of chunks downloaded by the helper nodes increases exponentially.

Scenario 3.2.4. The relation between the total number of chunks, V, of the video and the number of group members, N, is shown in Fig. 3(d). As expected, we see from Fig. 3(d) that with more group members the group owner can download longer videos.

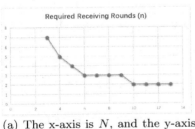

(a) The x-axis is N, and the y-axis is n.

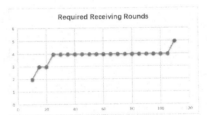

(b) The x-axis is V, and the y-axis is n.

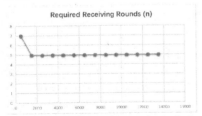

(c) The x-axis is $z(KBps)$, and the y-axis is n.

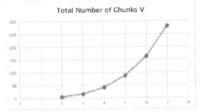

(d) The x-axis is N, and the y-axis is V.

Fig. 3. Results for situation $z > x > y$.

Scenario 3.3: $z > x > y$, Plus Periodic Disconnections. In this last case, we add periodic disconnections into the previous evaluation scenario. Therefore, the user should not only buffer content in advance, T_b, to avoid disruption due to slow downlink rate, but also buffer some extra content A to cover the upcoming disconnection period D. These requirements are shown in (10) and (11).

$$yT_b \geq (x - y)T_{pc} + A \tag{10}$$

$$\frac{A}{x} \geq \frac{yC}{z} \tag{11}$$

We also need to guarantee that the video content received from group members can cover the upcoming disconnection period. This requirement is shown in inequality (12).

$$\frac{NyC}{x} \geq D \tag{12}$$

We present four scenarios to study how much content should the group owner buffer and how long should the connection period be in order to overcome the disconnections and the limited cellular downlink rate. We also study the relation between the WiFi transfer rate and the length of the disconnection period that can be overcome without playback disruptions (Table 4).

Table 4. Scenarios for situation $z > x > y$, plus periodic disconnections

Scenario 3.3.1	$x = 350\,\text{KBps}$, $C = 300\,\text{s}$, $D = 500\,\text{s}$, $N = 4$, $z = 10\,\text{MBps}$, and T_b and y are variables
Scenario 3.3.2	$z = 10\,\text{MBps}$, $x = 350\,\text{KBps}$, $T_{pc} = 200\,\text{s}$, $D = 900\,\text{s}$, $N = 5$, and C and y are variables
Scenario 3.3.3	$x = 350\,\text{KBps}$, $y = 300\,\text{KBps}$, $T_b = 30\,\text{s}$, $C = 150\,\text{s}$, $N = 5$, and z and D are variables
Scenario 3.3.4	$y = 300\,\text{KBps}$, $T_{pc} = 200\,\text{s}$, $N = 5$, $D = 900\,\text{s}$, $z = 2000\,\text{KBps}$, and x and T_b are variables

Scenario 3.3.1. Figure 4(a) shows the relation between the required buffering time T_b and cellular downlink rate y. We see from Fig. 4(a) that as the cellular downlink rate, y, increases, the required buffering time is becoming shorter. The group owner only requires about 10 s for buffering when the cellular downlink rate is 330 KBps.

Scenario 3.3.2. Figure 4(b) shows the relation between cellular downlink rate y and the duration of the connection period C that guarantees undisrupted playback. In Fig. 4(b), we see that as y grows, the required connection period, C, is becoming shorter. Still, however, in order to stream HD video, the connection period needs to be in the order of a couple of minutes.

Scenario 3.3.3. Figure 4(c) shows the relation between the WiFi Direct transfer rate and the length of the disconnection period that the user can overcome without disruptions. We see from Fig. 4(c) that the faster the WiFi Direct rate the longer the disconnection period that the user can tolerate. For example, for WiFi Direct rate equal to 9000 KBps (which is still within the range of the WiFi Direct specification), the user can tolerate up to 1400 s of disconnection.

Scenario 3.3.4. Finally, in Fig. 4(d) we present the relation between video data rate and the amount of content that the user needs to have buffered in terms of playback time. From Fig. 4(d) we see that streaming high quality video requires long buffering time. The user requires about 300 s when watching a video with 600 KBps data rate.

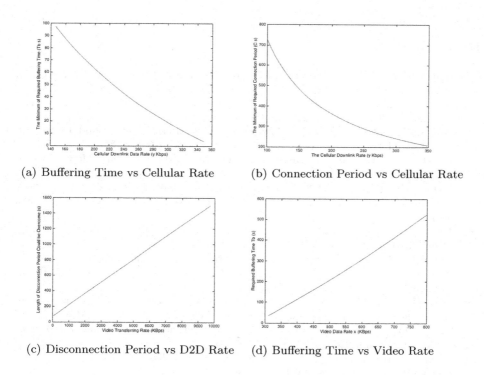

(a) Buffering Time vs Cellular Rate   (b) Connection Period vs Cellular Rate

(c) Disconnection Period vs D2D Rate   (d) Buffering Time vs Video Rate

Fig. 4. Scenario 3.3: $z > y > x$, plus periodic disconnections.

4   Conclusions

We have developed a collaborative video download application based on Wi-Fi Direct to improve the QoE of video streaming when the cellular connection is constrained or physically disrupted. We have built simple models in order to study the requirements of our application to achieve seamless and undisrupted playback. Under the requirement of undisrupted playback, we study the relation between several parameters that affect playback in order to exploit the potential performance gains of our application.

Our work can be considered as a crowd-computing application. As next steps, we plan to develop a third party platform which allows users to exchange resources. For example, helper nodes spend 3G/4G data to help one user (*i.e.*, the group owner) download an HD video. In turn, the user who gets help rewards the helpers with electronic vouchers in return for their services.

Acknowledgements. This work was supported by EU FP7/NICT (GreenICN project) grant no. (EU) 608518/(NICT)167 and H2020 UMOBILE project, grant no. 645124.

References

1. Chai, W., et al.: Curling: content-ubiquitous resolution and delivery infrastructure for next-generation services. IEEE Commun. Mag. **49**, 112–120 (2011)
2. Han, B., et al.: Cellular traffic offloading through opportunistic communications: a case study. In: CHANTS, pp. 31–38. ACM (2010)
3. Ioannidis, S., et al.: Optimal and scalable distribution of content updates over a mobile social network. In: INFOCOM, pp. 1422–1430. IEEE (2009)
4. Kutscher, D., et al.: ICN research challenges. IRTF, IRTF Internet Draft-work in progress 2 (2014)
5. Pavlou, G., Wang, N., Chai, W.K., Psaras, I.: Internet-scale content mediation in information-centric networks. Ann. Telecommun. **68**(3–4), 167–177 (2013). Springer
6. Ramadan, M., et al.: Implementation and evaluation of cooperative video streaming for mobile devices. In: PIMRC, pp. 1–5. IEEE (2008)
7. Seferoglu, H., et al.: Cooperative video streaming on smartphones. In: Allerton Conference on Communication, Control, and Computing, pp. 220–227. IEEE (2011)
8. Stiemerling, M., Kiesel, S.: A system for peer-to-peer video streaming in resource constrained mobile environments. In: U-NET Workshop, pp. 25–30. ACM (2009)
9. Tasiopoulos, A.G., et al.: Mind the gap: modelling video delivery under expected periods of disconnection. In: CHANTS, pp. 13–18. ACM (2014)
10. Tasiopoulos, A.G., et al.: Tube streaming: modelling collaborative media streaming in urban railway networks. In: IFIP Networking (2016)

Human-in-the-loop Connectivity Management in Smartphones

David Nunes[1]([✉]), Jorge Sá Silva[1], Carlos Herrera[2], and Fernando Boavida[1]

[1] Department of Informatics Engineering, University of Coimbra, Coimbra, Portugal
{dsnunes,sasilva,boavida}@dei.uc.pt
[2] Departamento de Electrónica y Telecomunicaciones,
Escuela Politécnica Nacional, Quito, Ecuador
carlos.herrera@epn.edu.ec

Abstract. Cyber-Physical Systems which detect and use human psychological and physiological states as feedback to their control-loop are known as Human-in-the-Loop (HITL). The current understanding of the general requirements and theory behind this new class of systems is, however, still limited. This paper attempts to contribute towards their development by presenting a conceptual model that integrates some of the major ideas spread throughout the literature. In addition, it also discusses how the acquisition of a human's state requires reliable networking. In this respect, an architecture for HITL management of networking configurations is presented. This architecture is implemented in an experimental scenario where a smartphone system attempts to positively impact mood by dynamically adapting privacy settings and networking interfaces to the user's emotions. In this scenario, good hand-off performance is crucial for improving Quality of Experience and reliability. Several experiments regarding emotional classification and mobile handoff are also presented and discussed.

Keywords: Emotion detection · Human-in-the-loop Cyber-Physical Systems · Network management · Smartphones

1 Introduction

Recent years have brought a tremendous evolution in the areas of the Internet of Things (IoT), robotics and wireless sensor networks. It is now possible to develop intelligent Cyber-Physical Systems (CPSs) that easily sense and control our environment. Nevertheless, these technologies are still widely unaware of the human context, which is often considered an external and unpredictable element. Current research indicates that future CPSs will likely strive to become more "human-aware". This is the defining characteristic of "Human-in-the-loop" Cyber-Physical Systems (HiTLCPSs), where the human's emotions and actions are taken into consideration.

© IFIP International Federation for Information Processing 2016
Published by Springer International Publishing Switzerland 2016. All Rights Reserved
L. Mamatas et al. (Eds.): WWIC 2016, LNCS 9674, pp. 159–170, 2016.
DOI: 10.1007/978-3-319-33936-8_13

With this paper, our main goals are to contribute towards a logical and concise organization of HiTLCPS concepts and to provide an innovative HiTLCPS case-study, which achieves emotion-aware smartphone connectivity management, such as the selection of interfaces and privacy levels. In short, this paper's main technical contributions are as follows:

1. An overview of the area of HiTLCPSs, through a general model that organizes its major ideas.
2. A HiTL architecture directed towards smartphone connectivity management.
3. An implementation of our model targeting a mobile application for the improvement of user mood.
4. The results of several experiments that evaluate our system's emotion classification and handoff performance, which have a direct impact on the Quality of Experience (QoE).

Our mobile application, HappyHour, is novel in the way that it is capable of "closing the loop", that is, using an emotion inference result to actuate and provide suggestions that attempt to improve the user's mood. Although there are previous works that attempt to perform emotion inference from smartphones, these are based on analyzing communication history and application usage patterns, instead of environmental and physical information, with the purpose of improving recommendation systems [1] or are primed for data collection, rather than feedback and user interaction [2]. HappyHour also innovates in the way that it is capable of adapting its and the smartphone's functionality to the user's condition, through the dynamic change of privacy settings and networking interfaces. As far as we know, this is the first attempt at using HiTL concepts to optimize networking aspects.

The rest of this paper is organized as follows: Sect. 2 presents a general model for HiTLCPSs; Sect. 3 presents a HiTL model for the management of smartphones connectivity aspects; Sect. 4 presents an implementation of this model targeting a mobile application; Sect. 5 presents an evaluation of our implementation and its handover performance; Sect. 6 summarises the presented ideas and possible future work.

2   Human-in-the-loop Cyber-Physical Systems

Previous research in HiTLCPSs has proposed workstations that detect human distractions to save energy, systems that enable spatial control of the mobile wireless spectrum, semiautonomous wheelchairs controlled through electroencephalography (EEG), wheelchair-mounted robotic arms for disabled people, HiTL drug-delivery pumps and human-aware HVAC systems [3]. Each of these HiTLCPSs provides a tangible example on how the human context can be useful for control-loop decisions [4].

Our previous research [3] has allowed us to gain some insight onto HiTL-CPSs. Thus, we present our own view of the HiTLCPS landscape through a conceptual model, shown in Fig. 1. This model represents, as far as we know, the first attempt at condensing the major processes of HiTLCPS control. Each HiTLCPS requires a **Human-in-the-Loop Intelligence** module, responsible for receiving input from the human sensors and for influencing the control-loop. On a first step, determining a human's state requires the **acquisition of data**, through the use of, for example, IoT devices that act as sensors and acquire data from both the human and the system.

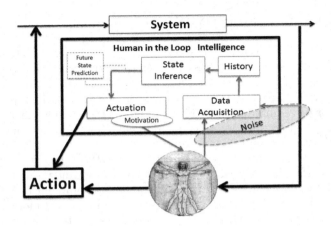

Fig. 1. The Processes of Human-in-the-Loop Control

History is also important for many HiTLCPSs, since humans are creatures of habit and previous data often offers insights that allow more accurate prediction of human context.

State inference techniques, such as advanced mathematical models or machine learning techniques, are usually applied to accurately detect human intents, psychological states and actions.

Actuation in HiTLCPSs can be classified into two major classes. Firstly, there is a direct actuation in the control-loop that results from the feedback provided by the system's current status and the inference of human state. The second class of actuation is related to the actions of humans, since they are far from passive elements and can, themselves, perform tasks.

Noise is a factor that affects the entire system. It is particularly important in data acquisition: for example, HiTLCPSs based on speech or video-captured gestures have to deal with ambient noise and moving background clutter; another example is the acquisition of vital signs, which is prone to interference from physiological functions that have little to do with what needs to be acquired.

In addition, each and every of these processes needs to be **reliable**. The inability to consistently infer a human's state in an accurate manner can have severe consequences on control-loop decisions and compromise the entire system. Additionally, **security and privacy** are equally important to protect industrial

processes, medical data or sensitive personal information from external unautho-
rized exploitation. Networking is a crucial aspect to achieve this reliability and
security, since HiTLCPSs are often large and distributed, with multiple sensing
devices transmitting data between each other and to centralized remote system
controllers.

3   Towards Human-in-the-loop Management of Smartphone Connectivity

As far as we know, no solutions consider the human context in their control-
loop decisions. We believe that this is limiting, in the sense that smartphones
are personal devices that cater for their user preferences. In fact, in the context of HiTLCPSs, the humans' context must be considered, but human attention should not be required. Therefore, automated HiTL management of aspects
such as privacy and network interface handoff can contribute to a more efficient
networking distribution and system usability.

We propose a HiTL architecture directed towards intelligent network management of interfaces and privacy. We refer to it as "Human-in-the-loop over
networks" (HiTLON), of which we are currently developing our own implementation. This HiTLON architecture fits directly in our general model, as shown
in Fig. 2. Our previous "System" box is now represented by a smartphone. The
"data acquisition" is represented by physical, software and resource sensors.
These "sensors" may have very disparate instantiations; for example, **Software
sensors** are usually handled at the application layer and measure non-physical
properties related with applications, such as QoS requirements, communication
history of the user (e.g. number of SMSs, phone call durations), social networking data, among others. The **physical sensors** represent every sensor that is
made available by the smartphone's hardware (e.g. accelerometer, microphone,
camera, GPS, etc.) or even by physically wearable devices (e.g. smartshirts,
smartwatches) that are not an integral part of, but can communicate with, the
smartphone. **System sensors** may implement calls to the system's Kernel to
return current battery level, CPU usage, wireless connection strength or available memory.

Encompassed by the "Human-in-the-loop" control is the state inference. Sensory information is processed here, acquiring context from the raw data. For
example, a state-inference task may be responsible for performing activity classification based on accelerometer data (e.g. standing, walking or running states).

The actuation process (decision-making), is then realized depending on the
state-inference results. The decisions are carried out by **actuation entities**.
Some examples of these entities might be handoff interfaces, security and encryption mechanisms, privacy managers, among others. This way, despite focusing on
privacy and interface management, we intend to present our HiTLON architecture as a general approach for HiTL management of connection characteristics.
In this particular scenario, direct human actuation does not apply, hence, the

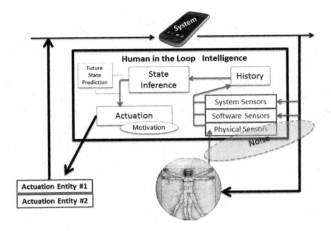

Fig. 2. HiTLON within the processes of Human-in-the-Loop Control

associated connections are not represented. Nevertheless, human motivation is represented by the high-level policies, which materialize the human intent.

The HiTLON concept can be applied to many different scenarios. For example, a health monitoring system may monitor the ECG of a patient to detect arrhythmias, sending this data to a remote doctor's PC. Whenever critical data is detected, the reliability of the network connection could be increased, even at the expense of greater bandwidth or energy requirements which would be lower during normal circumstances.

Another example is a toddler monitoring application where sound or image processing is used to detect patterns of distress. When critical events are triggered, a HiTLON may prioritize connectivity and performance in the parents smartphone to receive a direct video-feed of the child.

Our model also accommodates other types of human-aware management, such as giving higher levels of QoS to messages exchanged with important people (e.g. delivery reports to close friends); sending sensitive and urgent data preferably through encrypted cellular connections to maximize connectivity and security; opportunistically using Bluetooth to save cellular traffic for non-critical and delay-tolerant data; and using multiple interfaces to maximize throughput if the smartphone is currently connected to an energy source.

HiTL control balances the decision between the three main pillars: the application's QoS requirements, the device's current status and the human context, including defined high-level goals and other restrictions (e.g. avoid cellular connection fees).

4   HiTL-over-networks in Mobile BCI

In this section, we will explore a particular application of our HiTLON model targeting a mobile Behavior Change Intervention (BCI) scenario. Traditional BCIs involve therapy sessions where advice and support are provided to induce lifestyle changes that may help people coping with chronic diseases, smoking addiction, diets or even depression. More recently, due to their sensing and processing capabilities smartphones have been used by behavior scientists for more directed interventions [2]. A HiTLON system can play a role in reducing anxiety; when a stressful event is detected, the system may attempt to guarantee the best networking performance in order to avoid further frustrating events. If battery levels are low, HiTLON could choose to preserve battery life instead, so that interventions can be delivered timely. To evaluate these ideas, we developed a mood-oriented BCI case-study over which we developed an implementation of a HiTLON system, based the architecture previously presented in Sect. 3.

4.1 HappyHour App

Common knowledge and scientific research agree that moderate walking exercise and contact with natural environments can provide several cognitive benefits, such as improved memory, attention and mood [5,6]. Other studies suggest that contact with natural environments not only makes people feel better but also makes them behave better, thus having both personal health benefits and broader social benefits [7]. HappyHour is a HiTLCPS based on this premise that takes a BCI approach to positively affect mood [8]. It unobtrusively senses emotions and presents timely walking suggestions when negative moods are inferred.

The system periodically processes data from the smartphone's microphone and accelerometer, a smartshirt's ECG[1] and weather information from a web API[2], feeding it to a neural network[3] in order to infer the user's emotional state. When negative emotional states are detected, the application motivates the user to go for a walk, showing a map with the position of nearby points-of-interest (POI).

The system also periodically collects its users' GPS positioning, microphone sound and acceleration in an anonymous way and aggregates this information in a central server. This allows HappyHour to display the real-time attendance (based on user location) and overall movement (based on average accelerometer data) at each POI through heatmaps with different colors. This information allows users to pick livelier areas (greater attendance and movement) or calmer areas (less attendance and movement), which are more prone to soothing environments. The users' microphone data is processed through a music recognition API[4], allowing the application to display the background music at each POI. In a similar way, HappyHour is also capable of displaying the "general mood" of a certain POI, by aggregating and averaging the individual moods of nearby users. Thus, users are able to select places to visit with the type of environment, mood and music that they feel are best for venting emotional stress.

---

[1] VitalJacket: http://www.vitaljacket.com/.

[2] Open Weather Map: http://openweathermap.org/.

[3] Encog Framework: http://www.heatonresearch.com/encogin.

[4] The Echo Nest: http://the.echonest.com/.

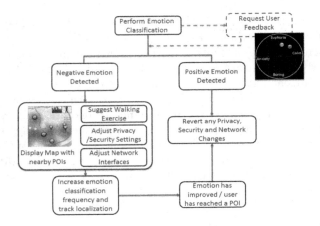

Fig. 3. HappyHour Application Flow

Figure 3 shows HappyHour's application flow. The core of our emotion-awareness lies in HappyHour's machine learning ability to process different forms of sensing. With this work, we do not intend to propose robust methods for emotion detection, but instead, to provide a practical proof-of-concept that shows how emotional information can benefit HiTLCPSs. Thus, in order to determine the best machine learning technique for our application, we studied previous comparisons between the different possibilities. Previous work [9] has scored different classification algorithms in terms of correct classification rate and in terms of central processing unit (CPU) time needed for the classification. The latter is of particular importance for smartphone HiTLCPSs, since these are limited terms of available processing power and energy. This has led us to opt for an artificial neural network as our emotion inference tool, since it offers a reasonable correct classification rate while being one of the least time-consuming techniques.

As previously mentioned, HappyHour's neural-network is fed with different types of data. The relationship between external factors and a person's emotions is still unclear [10]. Nevertheless, we intended to consider at least three general sources of data: environmental clues, vital-signs information and meteorological information [8].

HappyHour also manages network interfaces depending on the human's mood. By default, WiFi is used as the primary networking interface for positive emotions, while cellular communication is used as a backup due to its additional monetary cost. However, if the system detects a negative emotion state, the default network profile defines that both cellular connections and WiFi will be used at the same time, thus providing better QoE. We employ MPTCP [11] in our current implementation to achieve these multipath capabilities over a single TCP connection. Privacy management in HappyHour relates to the automatic sharing of location on a social network[5]. Since some people feel eased by social-

---

[5] In the current prototype, the user can share his location through Facebook.

interaction, the automatic sharing of location among friends may contribute towards positive socialization. Other people may prefer solitude to ease their minds. Thus, through the tailoring of privacy profiles, HappyHour can automatically adapt privacy settings to the current emotional context of the user.

While our current implementation is limited to changes in privacy and network interfaces, we can easily conceive more advanced HiTL mechanisms to control other aspects. For example, the redundancy tradeoff of multiple interfaces could be moderated by the device's battery-level, since completely depleting the battery can result in even greater user frustration. Security measures could also be dynamically adapted depending on the human context, with additional levels of encryption being applied when his/her emotions, position or actions are of sensitive nature.

4.2 Emotion-Aware MPTCP

We believe that it is important to bring this human-awareness to the networking layer. In the particular case of MPTCP, due to the extreme importance of networking in HiTLCPS, HiTL functional parameters should be a part of the protocol's interface with the application layer. These HiTL functional parameters could affect several aspects of the protocol.

MPTCP currently couples the congestion windows of each TCP subflow to achieve fairness at bottlenecks and resource pooling and to push most traffic to uncongested links. We propose that a different congestion controller for MPTCP, could aim at achieving different objectives for quality of service, reliability, and resilience. This congestion controlled resource of pooling/fairness/stability could, instead of focusing exclusively on maximizing throughput through all available paths, consider the possibility of choosing alternative paths base on the human's needs. This choice could be motivated on the monetary cost of links, but could also consider other aspects such as connectivity, range, delay and jitter, since stability can be more important than throughput in HiTLCPSs.

Making effective choices based on the human context requires the network layer to have knowledge of the path "cost" for the human user. This information would be provided by the application layer through an extension of MPTCP's application interface. The application layer can configure send and receive buffer sizes via the sockets API (SO_SNDBUF, SO_RCVBUF). However, it would also be possible for a MPTCP implementation to set a human contextual value for dynamically modifying the send and receive buffers and treating this request as an implicit task of the networking layer. Other possibility is to restore TCP's ability to send "Urgent" data, which is not currently in use by MPTCP [12].

5 Experiments, Simulations and Evaluation

In this section, we will present some experiments and simulations which serve as an evaluation of our HiTL mobile BCI. Firstly, we will focus on the performance and accuracy of our emotion classification. Afterwards, we will discuss the handoffs in our HiTLON implementation.

Table 1. Testing training performance (150 emotions).

Hidden Layers	Epochs
One	100
Two	3000

Table 2. Testing neural network accuracy (41 emotions).

Hidden Layers	Sensitivity	Specificity
One	0,679	0,766
Two	0,720	0,830

5.1 Emotion Classification and Neural-Networks

To test HappyHour's emotion classification, we considered two major requirements: the amount of effort required for training the neural network (which is important in terms of processing power and battery drain) and accuracy of the network. In order to test the training effort, we began by generating simulated emotions. For each type of emotion, we empirically defined a probability value for different ranges of its input components (heart rate, cloudiness, movement, etc.). This method allowed us to generate 150 simulated emotions, that, while not valid for testing accuracy (since they are not derived from actual human beings), are sufficient for testing the training performance. Thus, we counted the number of epochs necessary to successfully train the network for each configuration. The results, shown in Table 1, show that using two hidden layers increases the training effort significantly. Therefore, we also needed to test if using more layers brought any benefits in terms of accuracy. Note that in a typical Artificial Neural Network (ANN) architecture, its neurons are usually grouped in layers; the first layer receives the input, while the last layer transmits the final output. In-between these layers are the hidden layers which allow the ANN to extract higher-order statistics from the data, by providing additional transformations and processing.

In order to assess the impact of the number of layers, we requested a test subject to use our application for a period of a week, during which his sensory data and emotional feedback were recorded for a total of 41 records. We then tested both neural network configurations using this data. Considering that negative emotions are the events of interest, we evaluated performance through two statistical measures known as sensitivity and specificity. In our case sensitivity is the proportion of negative emotions that were correctly identified as such; that is, it measures when our system was capable of detecting that it was necessary to adapt the smartphone's settings. Specificity, on the other hand, measures the proportion of correctly identified positive emotions. A perfect emotional predictor would present the maximum value of 1 for each of these metrics.

The results shown in Table 2 suggest that using a two layer configuration presents considerably better results. After pondering over the results, we decided that, despite being more demanding, a two layer configuration presented a better compromise in terms of training time and accuracy.

5.2   Evaluation of HiTLON Handoff Performance

Our mood-oriented HiTL implementation would not make sense if the hand-offs between different network interfaces introduced even greater connectivity issues. The objective of these experiments was to determine if MPTCP could offer acceptable handoff performance while maintaining the connection flow. This served as preliminary work before trying to further modify the protocol in order to introduce human-awareness components in its congestion control mechanisms and application interface. While our current HappyHour implementation runs on a LG Nexus 5 smartphone with a MPTCP-enabled Android kernel, we performed our experiments on a laptop. This was done to achieve a finer control over the testing conditions. The laptop ran an MPTCP-enabled Linux kernel and was equipped with a WiFi antenna and a 3G USB Dongle. It used these interfaces to connect to a remote host and continuously sent ECG and accelerometer data. The connection was made through a WiFi network supported by a cable Internet backhaul, offering a bandwidth of around 1 Mbps upstream and 18 Mbps downstream, and a 3G network, offering a bandwidth between 0.2 and 0.4 Mbps. To evaluate our default negative emotion scenario, we used both interfaces simultaneously. One interface was disabled mid-test, in order to emulate a disconnection event. Figures 4 and 5 show the throughput of the TCP connection on the remote host. As we can see, a drop on the general throughput is noticeable, but the dropped packets are quickly resent and the connection effortlessly continued through the remaining interface. A second series of tests was performed, where one interface was configured as "backup". Figure 6 shows a typical positive emotional state situation, where WiFi is defined as the primary interface and a 3G cellular connection acts as a backup. As the user goes on with his walking exercise, he eventually loses connection to WiFi hotspots, which have limited range. MPTCP is then responsible for smoothly rerouting traffic through the 3G cellular connection. As the graphic shows, in our experiments the connection to the server took about 4 s to recover.

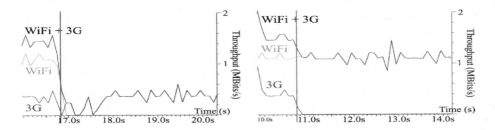

Fig. 4. WiFi being cut off   **Fig. 5.** 3G being cut off

Figure 7 shows another situation where a user has defined a 3G cellular connection as the primary interface in HappyHour's network profile. This would be a configuration used whenever it is important to promote connectivity and avoid

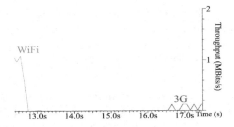

Fig. 6. WiFi as primary interface and 3G acting as backup, with WiFi being cut off

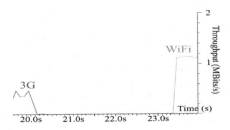

Fig. 7. 3G as primary interface and WiFi acting as backup, with WiFi being cut off

handoffs unless they are absolutely necessary; e.g. the user could be riding a bus or a train, where the connections to WiFi networks can be very transient. WiFi, now being relegated to "backup", recovered the connection in approximately 3 s, which is faster than 3G. This was to be expected, since WiFi has a much greater downlink capacity and its TCP congestion window increases much faster.

6   Conclusion

In this work, we presented an overview on topic of HiTLCPS through a theoretical model of the processes associated with the control-loop. We then approached the problem of managing privacy and networking interfaces in smartphone-based HiTLCPSs. To do so, we devised an architecture for this connectivity management problem. We then applied this architecture to a real-world scenario based on a HiTLCPS for the improvement of mood. For evaluation, we performed some preliminary experiments which indicate that neural-networks might be an adequate machine-learning technique for these scenarios.

During our exposition, we also argued how reliability is an important factor in HiTLCPSs. Thus, another part of our experimental results focused on handoff performance, since intermittent connectivity is a source of frustration with negative impact on the user QoE. The results showed acceptable handoff performance and a definite improvement over "brute-force" handoffs. Thus, MPTCP can be a promising protocol for supporting seamless handoff within our HiTLON architecture.

As future work, we will continue to develop our BCI application and implement some of the concepts that were considered in our model but that have been left out of our test scenario. In particular, we would like to focus on the management of the device's power-consumption based on the human's context.

Acknowledgments. The work presented in this paper was partially financed by Fundação para a Ciência e a Tecnologia, POPH/FSE and by SENESCYT - Secretaría Nacional de Educación Superior, Ciencia, Tecnología e Innovación de Ecuador.

References

1. LiKamWa, R., Liu, Y., Lane, N.D., Zhong, L.: Moodscope: building a mood sensor from smartphone usage patterns. In: Proceeding of the 11th Annual International Conference on Mobile Systems, Applications, and Services, MobiSys 2013, pp. 389–402. ACM, New York (2013)
2. Lathia, N., Pejovic, V., Rachuri, K.K., Mascolo, C., Musolesi, M., Rentfrow, P.J.: Smartphones for large-scale behavior change interventions. IEEE Pervasive Comput. **12**(3), 66–73 (2013)
3. Nunes, D., Zhang, P., Silva, J.S.: A survey on human-in-the-loop applications towards an internet of all. IEEE Commun. Surv. Tutorials **17**(2), 944–965 (2015)
4. Munir, S., Stankovic, J.A., Liang, C.-J.M., Lin, S.: Reducing energy waste for computers by human-in-the-loop control. IEEE Trans. Emerg. Top. Comput. **2**(4), 448–460 (2014)
5. Berman, M.G., Kross, E., Krpan, K.M., Askren, M.K., Burson, A., Deldin, P.J., Kaplan, S., Sherdell, L., Gotlib, I.H., Jonides, J.: Interacting with nature improves cognition and affect for individuals with depression. J. Affect. Disord. **140**(3), 300–305 (2012)
6. Berman, M.G., Jonides, J., Kaplan, S.: The cognitive benefits of interacting with nature. Psychol. Sci. **19**(12), 1207–1212 (2008)
7. Weinstein, N., Przybylski, A.K., Ryan, R.M.: Can nature make us more caring? effects of immersion in nature on intrinsic aspirations and generosity. Pers. Soc. Psychol. Bull. **35**(10), 1315–1329 (2009)
8. Carmona, P., Nunes, D., Raposo, D., Silva, D., Herrera, C., Silva, J.S.: Happy hour - improving mood with an emotionally aware application. In: 15th International Conference on Innovations for Community Services (I4CS) (2015)
9. Guinness, R.: Beyond where to how: a machine learning approach for sensing mobility contexts using smartphone sensors. In: Proceedings of the 2013 International Technical Meeting of The Institute of Navigation (2013)
10. Gunes, H., Pantic, M.: Automatic, dimensional and continuous emotion recognition. Int. J. Synth. Emotions **1**(1), 68–99 (2010)
11. Ford, A., Raiciu, C., Handley, M., Barré, S., Iyengar, J.: Architectural guidelines for multipath TCP development. Internet Engineering Task Force (IETF), Request for Comments 6182, March 2011
12. Scharf, M., Ford, A.: Multipath TCP (MPTCP) application interface considerations. Internet Engineering Task Force (IETF), Request for Comments 6897, March 2013

Hardware MIMO Channel Simulator for Cooperative and Heterogeneous 5G Networks with VLC Signals

Bachir Habib$^{(\boxtimes)}$ and Badih Baz

Department of CS, Faculty of Sciences, USEK, Kaslik, Lebanon
{bachirhabib, badihbaz}@usek.edu.lb

Abstract. This paper presents the design of an 8×8 Multiple-Input Multiple-Output (MIMO) hardware simulator for cooperative time-varying propagation channels (based on relays) using heterogeneous systems (LTE-A and 802.11ac) with Visible Light Communications (VLC) signals. The simulator reproduces a desired radio channel scenario and makes it possible to test "on table" different systems. It uses different impulse responses to cover many types of channels by merging TGn models, 3GPP-LTE models, outdoor-to-indoor measurements results and VLC models. An algorithm is introduced to convert the measured impulse responses from 200 MHz sample frequency to 50 MHz to be compatible with LTE-A signals. A specific architecture of the simulator digital block is presented to characterize 5G scenarios. The architecture is designed on a Xilinx Virtex-VII XC7VX690T Field Programmable Gate Array (FPGA). Its accuracy and FPGA occupation are analyzed.

Keywords: Hardware simulator · FPGA · MIMO · Wireless heterogeneous systems · Cooperative networks

1 Introduction

MIMO techniques [1], cooperative networks and heterogeneous systems [2, 3] became essential in the design of the 5G communication systems. Moreover, VLC technologies [4–7] (LED or laser based), that are under development, show that they could be more than 100 times faster than current Wi-Fi. Therefore, all these technologies have to be considered in the design of any channel simulator platform that makes it possible to predict the received signal for any transmitted signal for a defined environment. With continuing increase of the FPGA capacity, entire baseband simulators can be mapped onto faster FPGAs for more efficient prototyping and testing [8–11].

Several architectures of the digital block of a hardware simulator have been studied [9, 12]. Typically, radio channels are simulated using Finite Impulse Response (FIR) filters [12, 13]. The Fast Fourier Transform (FFT) module with algebraic product can also be used. However, the FFT operates correctly only for signals not exceeding the FFT size. Thus, new frequency architecture avoiding this limitation has been presented and tested in [14]. However, it has been shown [15, 16] that the time domain architecture is better in terms of occupation on FPGA, output error and latency. Thus, in this paper, only the time domain architecture is considered.

© IFIP International Federation for Information Processing 2016
Published by Springer International Publishing Switzerland 2016. All Rights Reserved
L. Mamatas et al. (Eds.): WWIC 2016, LNCS 9674, pp. 171–183, 2016.
DOI: 10.1007/978-3-319-33936-8_14

Impulse responses must be implemented in the simulator to test a desired environment. They can be obtained from standard models, as the TGn 802.11n [17] (for indoor channels) and the LTE models [18] (for outdoor channels), or by using measurements conducted with a MIMO channel sounder realized at IETR [19] to cover outdoor-to-indoor channels. In MIMO context, little experimental results have been obtained regarding time-variations due to several limitations of the channel sounding equipment [19]. However, theoretical models of time-varying channels can be obtained using Rayleigh fading and Kronecker method [20, 21].

The main contributions of the paper are:

- An algorithm is presented to switch between several outdoor environments and make it possible to simulate heterogeneous radio propagation channels.
- An algorithm is used for the measured impulse responses to switch from 200 MHz sampling frequency (f_s) to 50 MHz and make it compatible with LTE-A.
- Two new 5G scenarios are proposed. They consider heterogeneous networks that switch between WLAN and mobile networks. They also consider cooperative networks by using cell phones in the environment as relays.
- Simulation of 5G 8 × 8 MIMO systems using VLC Li-Fi signals is considered.
- The new simulator architecture is implemented on a Virtex VII FPGA. It has better precision compared to [14–16] due to the use of 16 bits DAC/ADC.

The work structure with the contributions is shown in Fig. 1.

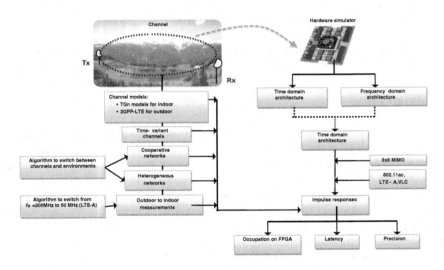

Fig. 1. Work structure. (Color figure online)

The rest of this paper is organized as follows. Section 2 presents the channel characteristics. Section 3 describes the architecture and its hardware implementation. In Sect. 4, the architecture accuracy is analyzed and results are presented. Lastly, Sect. 5 gives concluding remarks and prospects.

2 Channel Characteristics

2.1 Channel Description

Two scenarios are proposed to test the simulator architecture. They cover outdoor, outdoor-to-indoor and indoor environments at different environmental speeds. They consider the movements of a person from an environment to another using:

- LTE-A signal with a sampling frequency (f_s) of 50 MHz, a sampling period (T_s) of 20 ns, a bandwidth (B) of 20 MHz and a central frequency (f_c) of 1.8 GHz.
- 802.11ac signal with f_s = 165 MHz, T_s = 6 ns, B = 80 MHz and f_c = 5 GHz.
- VLC Li-Fi red laser signal for Line-Of-Sight (LOS) communication with a frequency of 472, 440 GHz. It is used especially between base stations.
- VLC Li-Fi red LED signal for LOS and Non-LOS (NLOS) communication with a frequency of 472, 440 GHz. It is used for indoor environments instead of Wi-Fi.

Figure 2 and Table 1 describe the two scenarios in details. In both scenarios, the person driving his vehicle moves from an urban environment to a highway. In this context, another base station is used as a relay. The signal transmitted between the 2 base stations (in LOS) is done using Li-Fi red laser to have fast communication and to surpass the frequency capacity spectrum. On the highway he exits the covered area by the base station. Therefore, the cooperative networks concept is used. Another person's cell phone between the transmitter (Tx) and the receiver (Rx) is used as a relay. It receives the signal, amplify it and retransmit it.

In the first scenario, the person (in red in Fig. 1) walks to his home. When he enters, he will receive an outdoor-to-indoor signal. Therefore, the channel will be simulated using measurements obtained by a campaign realized to retrieve outdoor-to-indoor impulse responses. Later, the system switches to LED Li-Fi once receiving a powerful signal using heterogeneous systems handover techniques [3].

In the second scenario, the person (in black in Fig. 1) switches to 802.11ac signal. This case is considered to simulate heterogeneous systems without VLC signals.

For LOS communications, as in the case of VLC Li-Fi red laser signal, the impulse responses are computed by using the relation $d^{-\gamma}$ between the average received power and the distance to determine the attenuation of the signal, where γ is the path loss exponent and it is equal to 2. The delay of the signal is computed by considering the speed of light as a reference.

The models used are the LTE Extended Vehicular A (EVA), the LTE Extended Typical Urban (ETU), the LTE Extended Pedestrian A (EPA) [18] and the TGn model D, C and B [17]. v is the mean environmental speed, f_{ref} is the refresh frequency between two successive MIMO profiles, t is the duration of movements in the considered environment, d is the traveled distance and $N_p = t \times f_{ref}$ is the number of profiles in each environment. f_d is the Doppler frequency. f_{ref} is chosen greater than $2f_d$ to respect the Nyquist-Shannon sampling theorem.

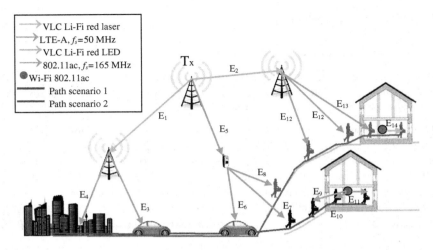

Fig. 2. Proposed scenarios. (Color figure online)

Table 1. Scenarios description.

Scenario/Env.	Model	v (km/h)	f_c (GHz)	f_d (Hz)	f_{ref} (Hz)	t (s)	d (km)	N_p
$1/E_1\ E_3$	Li-Fi laser*ETU	0; 40	472T;1.8	0; 66	0; 150	600	6.6	90,001
$1/E_1\ E_4$	Li-Fi laser*EVA	0; 80	472T;1.8	0; 133	0; 275	600	13.3	165,001
$1/E_5\ E_6$	EPA*EVA	4; 80	1.8; 1.8	18.3; 133	40; 75	300	6.6	94,500
$1/E_5\ E_8$	EPA*EPA	4; 4	1.8; 1.8	18.3; 18.3	40; 40	180	0.2	14,400
$1/E_2\ E_{12}$	Li-Fi laser*EPA	0; 4	472T; 1.8	0; 18.3	0; 40	180	0.2	7,201
$1/E_2\ E_{13}$	Li-Fi laser*measures	0; 2	472T; 1.8	0; 9.1	0; 20	60	0.03	1,201
$1/E_{14}$	Li-Fi LED	1.4	472T	6.5	15	30	0.01	450
$2/E_1\ E_3$	Li-Fi laser*ETU	0; 40	472T; 1.8	0; 66	0; 150	600	6.6	90,001
$2/E_1\ E_4$	Li-Fi laser*EVA	0; 80	472T; 1.8	0; 133	0; 275	600	13.3	165,001
$2/E_5\ E_6$	EPA*EVA	4; 80	1.8; 1.8	18.3; 133	40;275	300	6.6	94,500
$2/E_5\ E_7$	EPA*EPA	4; 4	1.8; 1.8	18.3; 18.3	40; 40	180	0.2	14,400
$2/E_9$	TGn D	4	5	18.3	40	180	0.2	7,200
$2/E_{10}$	TGn C	2	5	9.1	20	60	0.03	1,200
$2/E_{11}$	TGn B	1.4	5	6.5	15	30	0.01	450

2.2   Update Measurements to LTE-A and Environment Switch Algorithms

The measurements, using the MIMO channel sounder, were made with $f_s = 200$ MHz. To use these measurements with LTE-A signals, many steps have to be done. To pass from baseband complex impulse responses to real impulse responses between $[\Delta, B + \Delta]$, the following formula is used where $f_c = \Delta + B/2$:

$$h(t) = h_p(t)\cos(2\pi f_c t) - h_q(t)\sin(2\pi f_c t) \tag{1}$$

The obtained real impulse responses must be limited between 0 and -20 dB to select its significant part. Moreover, to decrease the number of non-null taps of the impulse responses, an algorithm is used which consists of detecting the taps considered as points of change for the sign of the slope of the curve.

Finally, to pass from $f_s = 200$ MHz to 50 MHz, an algorithm is proposed. It consists on replacing each 4 successive taps $(i, i + 1, i + 2, i + 3)$, which have a sampling period $T_s = 5$ ns $(f_s = 200$ MHz), by one tap placed at $i + 1$. Thus, a new sampling period $T_s = 20$ ns $(f_s = 50$ MHz) is obtained. This new tap placed at $i + 1$ is the sum of the linear Relative Powers (RP) of the 4 taps. A normalization algorithm is preceded on the RP to increase the simulator output signals precision. The results are obtained for 8×8 MIMO system. Figure 3 presents the real impulse response on $2048T_s$, the impulse response used by the simulator after discrimination, normalization and limitation between $[0, -20$ dB] of the measured impulse responses with $f_s = 200$ MHz and the impulse responses compatible with LTE-A with $f_s = 50$ MHz, for h_{11}. Moreover, the number of multipliers also decreases. In fact, it is divided by 4 due to the transition from $f_s = 200$ MHz to $f_s = 50$ MHz.

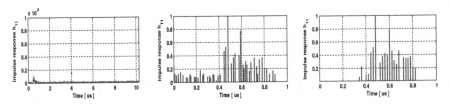

Fig. 3. Data Measured (left), used with $f_s = 200$ MHz (middle), used with $f_s = 50$ MHz (right).

The switch between the environments must be made in continuous mode. Between E_{10} and E_{11} for example, the person speed decelerate from 2 (km/h) to 1.4 (km/h).To pass from the RP of the last tap h_{ij} in E_{10} (RP_1) to the first h_{ij} tap in E_{11} (RP_f), a relation is proposed that varies the RP for each f_{ref}. f_{ref} also changes as in Table 1. It passes from 20 (f_{ref_1}) to 15 Hz (f_{ref_f}). The relations are:

$$RP_i = RP_1 + (i - 1)\frac{RP_f - RP_1}{N - 1}, f_{ref_i} = f_{ref_1} + (i - 1) \times \frac{f_{ref_f} - f_{ref_1}}{N - 1} \tag{2}$$

where i is an integer that varies from 1 to $N \cdot N = 80$, in fact, $80/((20 + 15)/2) = 4.5$ s is the needed time to switch between the impulse responses which is sufficient to pass from $v = 2$ km/h (E_{10}) to $v = 1.4$ km/h (E_{11}). Figure 4 presents the result of the 80 impulse responses (h) while switching between channels.

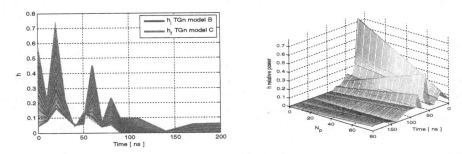

Fig. 4. Switching between TGn model B to TGn model C.

2.3   Channel Real Time Variation Using Rayleigh and Kronecker Method

After computing the impulse responses, this sub-section presents a method to vary the channel. The Rayleigh fading is used of each SISO channel. For 2×2 MIMO fading channel, Kronecker method [21] is considered. It can be characterized by the relative power P_c (resp. P_s) of constant (resp. scattering) channel components corresponding to LOS (resp. NLOS) paths. The ratio P_c/P_s is the Rice K-factor. The same concept is applied to 8×8 MIMO. Assuming that all the elements of the MIMO channel matrix H are Rice distributed, it can be expressed for each tap by:

$$H = \sqrt{P_c} \cdot H_F + \sqrt{P_s} \cdot H_v \text{ with } P_c = P \cdot \frac{K}{K+1}, P_s = P \cdot \frac{1}{K+1} \qquad (3)$$

where H_F and H_V are the constant and the scattered matrices respectively. The total received power is $P = P_c + P_s$. $K = 0$ to obtain Rayleigh fading. For 2 Tx/Rx:

$$H = \sqrt{P} \cdot \begin{bmatrix} X_{11} & X_{12} \\ X_{21} & X_{22} \end{bmatrix} \qquad (4)$$

To correlate the X_{ij} elements, a product-based model is used. This model assumes that the correlation coefficients are independently derived at each end of the link:

$$X = (R_r)^{1/2} \cdot H_{iid} \cdot ((R_t)^{1/2})^T \text{ where } R_t = \begin{bmatrix} 1 & \alpha \\ \alpha^* & 1 \end{bmatrix}, R_r = \begin{bmatrix} 1 & \beta \\ \beta^* & 1 \end{bmatrix} \qquad (5)$$

H_{iid} is a matrix of independent zero means, unit variance, complex Gaussian random variables. R_t and R_r are the Tx/Rx correlation matrices. The correlation coefficients α/β are expressed by $\rho = R_{xx}(D) + j \cdot R_{xy}(D)$, $D = 2\pi d/\lambda$, $d = 0.5\lambda$ the distance between antennas with wavelength λ. The Power Angular Spectrum (*PAS*) matches the Laplacian distribution with σ the standard deviation. Thus:

$$R_{xx}(D) = \int_{-\pi}^{\pi} \cos(D \cdot \sin(\varphi)) \cdot PAS(\varphi) \cdot d\varphi, R_{xy}(D)$$

$$= \int_{-\pi}^{\pi} \sin(D \cdot \sin(\varphi)) \cdot PAS(\varphi) \cdot d\varphi \qquad (6)$$

3 Digital Block Design of the Hardware Simulator

As the development board has 8 Analog-to-Digital Converter ADC (FMC168) and 8 Digital-to-Analog Converter DAC (FMC216), it will be connected to 8 down-conversion and 8 up-conversion RF units. 64 FIR filters are considered to simulate the 8 × 8 MIMO channel. However, as the scenarios contain one relay (intermediate base station or cell phone), the number of FIR filters will be 64*2 = 128 (Fig. 5).

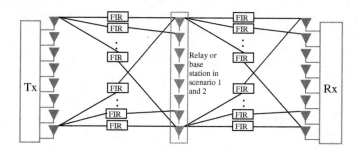

Fig. 5. 8 × 8 MIMO system with relay.

The FIR width and the multipliers number are determined by the taps of each SISO channel. In a scenario, the entire SISO channels have to be considered. To use the limited number of multipliers of the FPGA, a solution is proposed to control the change of delays by connecting each multiplier to the corresponding cells of the shift register and RAM. Thus, the number of multipliers in the FIR filters is equal to the maximum number of taps of all SISO channels. 128 FIR filters, each one with 24 multipliers are considered. Figure 6 presents a FIR filter 250 with 24 multipliers for one SISO channel. We have developed our own FIR filter instead of using Xilinx filter to make it possible to reload the filter coefficients.

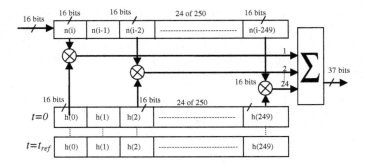

Fig. 6. FIR 250 with 24 multipliers for one SISO channel using h_{11}.

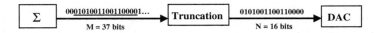

Fig. 7. Sliding window truncation, from 37 to 16 bits.

Due to the use of a 16-bit DAC, the final output must be truncated. The best solution is the sliding window truncation presented in Fig. 7 which uses the 16 most significant bits. The number of bits at the output before the truncation is:

$$n_y = n_h + n_x + n_{MIMO} + n_T \text{ where } n_{MIMO} = \lceil \log_2 N_T \rceil, \ n_T = \lceil \log_2 N_T \rceil \quad (7)$$

where n_y is the number of bits at the output before truncation, n_h is the number of bits at the impulse response, which is equal to 16 bits, $n_x = 16$ is the number of bits of the input signal and N_T is the number of non-null taps of impulse responses.

Figure 8 shows the Xilinx Virtex-VII XC7VX690T [8] used for the implementation of the architecture. The simulations are made with ISE [8] and ModelSim [22]. It also shows the device utilization for 128 FIR filters of 24 multipliers each.

Logic Utilization	Used	Available	Utilization
Logic cells	199,351	693,120	29 %
Occupied Slices	98,457	108,300	91 %
RAM 18Kb blocks	11	2,940	1 %
DSP 25*18	3,072	3,600	86 %

Fig. 8. Virtex-VII FPGA board from Xilinx and FPGA occupation for 128 FIR filters.

The number of DSP multipliers is equal to: 24 taps * 128 FIR filters = 3072. The impulse responses profiles are saved in the RAM memory blocks. The total number of profiles in the scenarios is 745,506. Each profile contains 128 channels each with 24 taps. For each tap the delay in time and the signal power must be known. Therefore, the total number of taps is: 745,506*128*24*2 = 4,580,388,864 taps of 16 bits each = 73,286,221,824 total bits. The capacity of each RAM block is 18 Kb. Thus, the number of blocks needed is: 73,286,221,824/18 K = 4,071,457.

However, the total number of RAM blocks on the FPGA is 2,940. Therefore, another method is used to save the impulse responses. They are saved on the computer and refreshed each f_{ref}. In this way, only 2 profiles are needed to be saved in the RAM blocks of the FPGA. In this case, the total number of taps is: 2*128*24*2 = 12,288 taps of 16 bits = 196608 total bits = 11 RAM blocks < 2,940.

For a MIMO profile, 24 × 128 = 3072 words of 16 bits = 6144 bytes have to be transmitted. Thus, the transfer speed is 6144 × f_{ref} Bps.

4 Results and Analysis

An input Gaussian signal $x(t)$ is considered for all inputs. To obtain a signal that respects the bandwidth, $x(t)$ centered between $[\Delta, \Delta + B]$ is obtained by:

$$x(t) = x_m e^{-\frac{(t-m_x)^2}{2\sigma_x^2}}, \quad 0 \le t \le Wt, \quad \Rightarrow x(t) \to x(t) \cdot \cos\left(2\pi \cdot \left(\frac{B}{2} + \Delta\right) \cdot t\right) \quad (8)$$

In this work, $\sigma_x = 3/\pi B$ is considered. m_x is chosen equal to $20 T_s > 3$ for both 802.11ac and LTE-A signals. Moreover, $\Delta \ll B$ is chosen equal to 2 MHz. The ADC and DAC converters of the development board have a full scale $[-V_m, V_m]$, with $V_m = 1$ V. For the simulations, $x_m = V_m/2$ is considered.

The first theoretic output signals $y_1(t)$ of the 8×8 MIMO channel is computed by:

$$y_1(t) = \underset{E_2\,11}{h}(t) * r_1(t) + \underset{E_2\,21}{h}(t) * r_2(t) + \dots + \underset{E_2\,81}{h}(t) * r_8(t) \quad (9)$$

where

$$r_u(t) = \underset{E_1\,1u}{h}(t) * x_1(t) + \underset{E_1\,2u}{h}(t) * x_2(t) + \dots + \underset{E_1\,8u}{h}(t) * x_8(t) = \sum_{a=1}^{8} \underset{E_1\,au}{h}(t) * x_a(t) \quad (10)$$

Thus

$$y_k(t) = \sum_{b=1}^{8} \underset{E_2\,bk}{h}(t) * \sum_{a=1}^{8} \underset{E_1\,ab}{h}(t) * x_a(t) \text{ with } x * h = \sum_{k=1}^{Nt} h(i_k) \cdot x(t - i_k T_s) \quad (11)$$

The formula of the theoretical $y_k(t)$ becomes:

$$y_k(t) = \sum_{b=1}^{8} \sum_{q=1}^{Nq} \left(\underset{E_2\,bk}{h}(i_q) \cdot \sum_{a=1}^{8} \sum_{p=1}^{Np} \left(\underset{E_1\,ab}{h}(i_p) \cdot x_a(t - (i_q + i_p) T_s) \right) \right) \quad (12)$$

where N_p and N_q are the number of taps of the impulse response and $h(i_n)$ is the RP of the nth path with the delay $i_n T_s$.

In order to determine the accuracy, a comparison is made between the theoretical/Xilinx output signals. Figure 9 presents a snapshot of the Xilinx output signal using Brutal (BT) and Sliding (ST) Truncations, with the theoretical signal, the relative error and the SNR for $y_I(t)$ using measured outdoor-to-indoor data (left) and 3GPP-LTE model ETU (right) with and $x_{LTE}(t)$ at the input. Figure 10 presents a snapshot of the result for $y_I(t)$ using TGn model B (left) with $x_{WLAN}(t)$ and VLC LED Li-Fi (right).

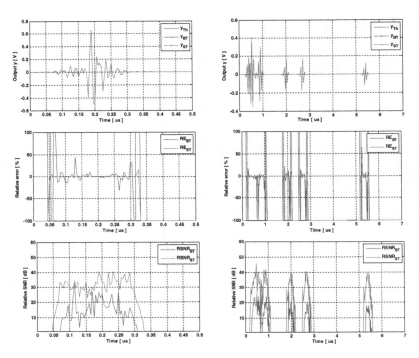

Fig. 9. Snapshot results for y_I using measured outdoor-to-indoor data (left) and 3GPP-LTE model ETU (right).

The relative error and SNR are computed by:

$$RE_k(i) = \frac{y_{qk}(i) - y_k(i)}{y_k(i)} \times 100, \; SNR_k(i) = 20\log_{10}\left|\frac{y_k(i)}{y_{qk}(i) - y_k(i)}\right| \; [dB] \qquad (13)$$

where y_{qk} is the vectors containing the samples of the Xilinx output signals.
The global relative error and global SNR are computed by:

$$RE_{Gk} = \frac{\|y_{qk} - y_k\|}{\|y_k\|} \times 100, \; SNR_{Gk} = 20\log_{10}\frac{\|y_k\|}{\|y_{qk} - y_k\|} \; [dB] \qquad (14)$$

Figure 11 presents the Global SNR variation in time for all profiles of $y_1(t)$ and $y_2(t)$ of four different environments of the scenarios. For the ETU environment only 1,000 profiles of 90,000 are presented.

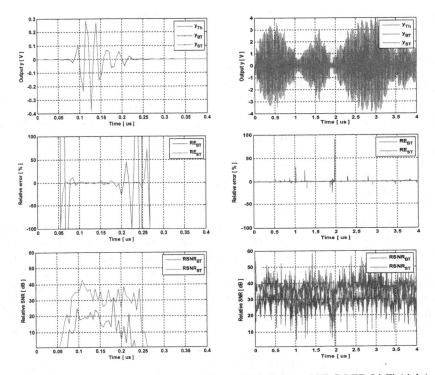

Fig. 10. Snapshot results for y_1 using TGn model B (left) and VLC LED Li-Fi (right).

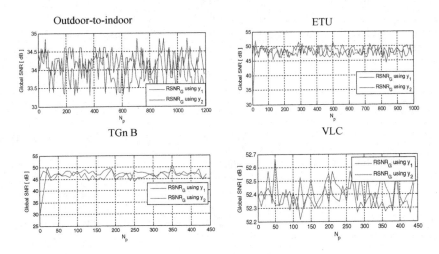

Fig. 11. Global SNR variation in time for y_1 and y_2.

Table 2 shows the average total global SNR for different environments. The results are given with BT and ST.

Table 2. Global SNR (dB) for different environments of the scenarios.

	Outdoor-to-indoor	ETU	TGn model B	VLC LED
BT	34.32	49.15	47.12	52.38
ST	61.77	72.68	73.38	75.31

The table shows the benefit of a ST in the case of using real input signals that respects the band $[\Delta, \Delta + B]$. The previous figures of the relative errors show that the ST provides low variations (around zero %) for the relative error where the output signal is high. However, the BT presents high variations.

5 Conclusion

In this paper, tests have been made for scenario models that switch between different environments to simulate heterogeneous propagation environments and cooperative networks. Moreover, VLC signals are used. An algorithm has been proposed to switch between the environments in a continuous manner and another algorithm is introduced to convert the measured impulse responses from 200 MHz sample frequency to 50 MHz to be compatible with LTE-A signals. In order to simulate a time-varying channel, Rayleigh fading method is used to vary the relative power of the taps of the channel impulse response. The architecture of the 8×8 MIMO simulator has been implemented on FPGA Virtex VII and analyzed.

This work can be completed by developing RF cards for the new standards and for heterogeneous systems. The hardware simulator realized considers the variation of the channel on small scale. Thus, variation on large scale must be considered. For the future cooperative communication systems, the Tx/Rx are in motion, the V2V concept has to be considered. Finally, the Tx/Rx distance has to be considered and simulation must be made not just for scenario models but also for real scenarios.

References

1. Behbahani, S., Merched, R., El tawil, A.: Optimizations of a MIMO relay network. IEEE Trans. Sig. Process. **56**(10), 5062–5073 (2008)
2. Agyapong, P.K., Iwamura, M., Staehle, D., Kiess, W., Benjebbour, A.: Design Considerations for a 5G Network Architecture. IEEE Commun Mag. **52**, 65–75 (2014)
3. LTE Advanced: Heterogeneous Networks. Qualcomm Incorporated, January 2011
4. Cossu, G., Khalid, A.M., Choudhury, P., Corsini, R., Presi, M., Ciaramella, E.: VLC-signals distribution over GI-POF for in-home wireless networks. In: International Workshop on Optical Wireless Communications (IWOW), 22 October 2012, pp. 1–3 (2012)

5. Kim, Y., Shin, Y., Yoo, M.: VLC-TDOA using sinusoidal pilot signal. In: International Conference on IT Convergence and Security (ICITCS), 16–18 December 2013, pp. 1–3 (2013)
6. Yu, Z., Redfern, A.J., Zhou, G.T.: Using delta-sigma modulators in visible light OFDM systems. In: IEEE Wireless and Optical Communication Conference (WOCC 2014), May 2014, Newark, NJ (2014)
7. Arnon, S.: Visible Light Communication. Cambridge University Press, Cambridge (2015)
8. Xilinx: FPGA, CPLD and EPP solutions. www.xilinx.com
9. Murphy, P., Lou, F., Sabharwal, A., Frantz, P.: An FPGA based rapid prototyping platform for MIMO systems. In: Asilomar Conference on Signals, Systems and Computers, ACSSC, 9–12 November 2003, vol. 1, pp. 900–904 (2003)
10. Wireless Channel Emulator. Spirent Communications (2006)
11. Baseband Fading Simulator ABFS: Reduced costs through baseband simulation. Rohde & Schwarz (1999)
12. Fouladi Fard, S., Ali Mohammad, A., Cockburn, B., Schlegel, C.: A single FPGA filter-based multipath fading emulator. In: Globecom, Honolulu, November 2009 (2009)
13. Eslami, H., Tran, S.V., Eltawil, A.M.: Design and implementation of a scalable channel emulator for wideband MIMO systems. IEEE Trans. Veh. Technol. 58(9), 4698–4708 (2009)
14. Habib, B., Zaharia, G., El Zein, G.: MIMO hardware simulator: new digital block design in frequency domain for streaming signals. J. Wirel. Netw. Commun. 2(4), 55–65 (2012)
15. Habib, B., Zaharia, G., El Zein, G.: MIMO hardware simulator: digital block design for 802.11ac applications with TGn channel model test. In: IEEE VTC Spring, Yokohama, Japan, May 2012 (2012)
16. Habib, B., Zaharia, G., El Zein, G.: Digital block design of MIMO hardware simulator for LTE applications. In: ICC, Ottawa, Canada (2012)
17. Erceg, V., Shumacher, L., Kyritsi, P., et al.: TGn channel models. In: IEEE 802.11-03/940r4, 10 May 2004
18. Agilent Technologies: Advanced design system – LTE channel model - R4-070872 3GPP TR 36.803 v0.3.0 (2008)
19. Farhat, H., Cosquer, R., Grunfelder, G., Le Coq, L., El Zein, G.: A dual band MIMO channel sounder at 2.2 and 3.5 GHz. In: IMTC, Victoria, BC, Canada, May 2008 (2008)
20. Almers, P., Bonek, E., et al.: Survery of channel and radio propagation models for wireless MIMO systems. EURASIP J. Wirel. Commun. Netw. 2007, 1–19 (2007). Article ID 19070
21. Schumacher, L., Pedersen, K.I., Mogensen, P.E.: From antenna spacing to theoretical capacities – guidelines for simulating MIMO systems. In: PIMRC Conference, September 2002, vol. 2, pp. 587–592 (2002)
22. ModelSim - Advanced Simulation and Debugging. http://model.com

Network Protocols

Improving Spatial Indexing and Searching for Location-Based DNS Queries

Daniel Moscoviter[1]([⊠]), Mozhdeh Gholibeigi[1], Bernd Meijerink[1],
Ruben Kooijman[2], Paul Krijger[2], and Geert Heijenk[1]

[1] University of Twente, Enschede, The Netherlands
d.moscoviter@student.utwente.nl,
{m.gholibeigi,bernd.meijerink,geert.heijenk}@utwente.nl
[2] Simacan B.V., Amersfoort, The Netherlands
{ruben.kooijman,paul.krijger}@simacan.com

Abstract. In the domain of vehicular networking, it is of significant relevance to be able to address vehicles based on their geographical position rather than the network address. The integration of geocasting (i.e. the dissemination of messages to all nodes within a specific geographical region) into the existing addressing scheme of the Internet is challenging, due to its logical hierarchy. One solution to Internet-based geographical addressing is eDNS, an extension to the DNS protocol. It adds support for querying geographical locations as a supplement to logical domain names. In this work, eDNS is extended with nearest neighbor resolution support, and further, a prototype server is developed that uses bounding box propagation between servers for delegation. Our experiments confirm that distributing location records over multiple servers improves performance.

Keywords: Geocasting · Vehicular networks · DNS · eDNS

1 Introduction

The concept of Intelligent Transportation Systems (ITS) is an emerging area of research [11]. The main objective of such systems is to use vehicular communication to develop novel applications for increasing safety, traffic management, Internet access, or other valuable services. Aside from the opportunities for delivering many novel applications, a significant amount of research has focused on ITS because of the technological difficulties that are involved. Mainly, vehicular networks have to deal with highly dynamic network topologies of vehicles, their high speed, limited communication ranges, and real-time constraints of potential applications. We can differentiate between two different types of communication in vehicular networks: Vehicle-to-Vehicle (V2V) and Vehicle-to-Infrastructure (V2I) communication. In the former type, data packets are exchanged between vehicles using vehicular communication technologies without involvement of an infrastructure. The latter type extends the vehicular ad hoc networks (VANETs) with a fixed infrastructure (e.g., Roadside Units (RSUs)).

L. Mamatas et al. (Eds.): WWIC 2016, LNCS 9674, pp. 187–198, 2016.
DOI: 10.1007/978-3-319-33936-8_15

Vehicles in ITS will typically be equipped with localization technologies. This allows vehicles to be addressed based on their geographical positions rather than the network address (i.e. targeting a certain area, not a certain vehicle), utilizing domain-specific forwarding strategies [1]. Messages can be sent to any single node within a target region (geoanycast), or to all nodes within a target region (geocast). Geocasting in particular enables a large number of new applications. Warning about dangerous road conditions, assisting in speed management, and delivery of infotainment are examples of use cases that geocasting can facilitate.

Geocasting requires a routing protocol that delivers messages to the intended targets. It is a challenge to integrate geographically-scoped broadcasting into the existing addressing scheme of the Internet, as IP-based addressing does not support geographical routing. Though solutions to this problem have been proposed, there are bottlenecks and the concept is an open research issue. For instance, GPS-based addressing and routing [9,10] requires a specialized infrastructure; use of a geographical IPv6 prefix format [8] relies on a standardized allocation of IPv6 addresses; and GeoNet [4,12] has Internet-wide scalability limitations [6].

One solution that was proposed to tackle these shortcomings is the Extended DNS (eDNS) [5,6]. It is based on the Internet Domain Name System (DNS) protocol, and extends it to support geographical addressing. While DNS already supports storing locations using location (LOC) resource records, the novelty of eDNS is that the locations can be used as a primary key to return Internet Protocol (IP) addresses that are associated with geographical regions. The appeal of this method is that it does not require specialized hardware or software, nor protocol modifications. Only modification of existing DNS implementations is required, as described later in this document. Support for more efficient indexing, as well as delegation was added at a later stage [17]. However, opportunities for improvement remain. For example, we can consider use cases where one would be interested in entities close to a certain point, rather than entities within a region. More possible improvements can be identified, and will be discussed further in this paper.

As mentioned earlier, the concept of integrating geocasting into the existing infrastructure of the Internet is an important research issue in the field of ITS research. Because of the aforementioned shortcomings in several proposed solutions, this paper focuses on the eDNS protocol as a solution for the problem of addressing all entities within a geographical area. In our work, we have improved and evaluated the eDNS protocol in several ways. This has resulted in the following main contributions.

- We have designed and implemented nearest neighbor resolution by introducing a new DNS resource record containing a location's distance to a queried area.
- We have designed and implemented the propagation of bounding boxes to parent DNS name servers, upon receiving location updates via the Dynamic DNS (DynDNS) protocol.
- We have evaluated the performance of our eDNS implementation in terms of throughput and latency for various input parameters.

The remainder of this paper is structured as follows. We review related work on eDNS in Sect. 2. Then, we discuss our approach to improve eDNS in Sect. 3. Section 4 shows the performance evaluation of our developed prototype. Finally, we draw conclusions and discuss future work in Sect. 5.

2   Background and Related Work

Given the importance of geographical location based addressing in the domain of vehicular networking, various research activities have been carried out over the recent years. In this section we refer to some research relevant to our work.

Fioreze and Heijenk [5] propose the extension of DNS such that clients can resolve IP addresses based on geographical coordinates, rather than domain names. The proposal relies on the existing LOC record specification. The novelty of the proposal is that LOC records are allowed to be used as the primary key for DNS queries, in addition to the methods of using hostnames or IP addresses. The eDNS proposal has various strengths. For one, it is based on the existing DNS architecture, which has proven its high scalability, being used as the addressing scheme in the Internet. Secondly, it does not require specialized hardware or software, or modification of existing protocols.

In [6], a prototype implementation is described based on Name Server Daemon (NSD)[1]. The prototype follows the suggestions made in the proposal by adding support for the use of LOC records as the primary key. Geographical queries have the following format, based on the format of the LOC record: `('dLat mLat sLat 'N'|'S' dLon mLon sLon 'E'|'W' alt['m'] size['m']')'.domain`. The geographical query format is hybrid, in the sense that logical domain names can be mixed with a geographical location. The geographical part is used on the lowest level. Thanks to this property, top-level domains are not required to support the geographical format. The document also describes a delegation strategy.

Westra [17] extended eDNS based on the previously mentioned implementation. The extended prototype is based on R*-trees [2] as an efficient spatial data indexing and searching method. R*-trees are a variant of R-trees, which are dynamic, hierarchical data indexing structures. To reduce network traffic for delegation, [17] introduces the bounding box (BND) record type which defines the bounding rectangle of child servers, preventing blind delegation of a location request if it falls outside of the known coverage of the child server. Compatibility with existing DNS implementations is preserved. The query format was extended to provide a higher precision.

Previous iterations of eDNS have mainly focused on storing location of nodes that have a fixed location, such as RSUs. In [13], Van Leeuwen extends eDNS with functionality to dynamically manage locations. In the work, it is assumed that a central server exists that tracks dynamics of the environment. Functionality is added to the modified NSD server that retrieves records from this server,

---

[1] https://www.nlnetlabs.nl/projects/nsd/.

rewrites its own zone file, rebuilds the database, and reloads. However, this method does not work if no central server with locations exists.

3   The Approach

The problem of finding nearby nodes in tree data structures is known as k-nearest neighbor (kNN) resolution in the literature, where k is the number of closest results. This can be used to find the nearest RSU that has at least a certain number of vehicles in its coverage range. These vehicles may potentially forward information to the target geocast area in multiple hops. A client could request nearest neighbor resolution in an eDNS query by appending a parameter ('nn='nn) to the geographical coordinates. The authoritative name server parses this parameter and performs an algorithm to find nearby neighbors, ordered by distance, rather than finding overlapping LOC records.

Nearest neighbor resolution becomes more complicated when delegation is to be considered. Although it is possible for a name server to ask each subdomain about its nearest neighbors, it is not doable to combine results from multiple sources and selecting the nearest neighbors from that set, without knowing the individual distances. One possible solution would be to have the authoritative server request the actual LOC records from the subdomain, in addition to the record type originally requested. The authoritative server could then parse these records, apply its own distance calculations, and compare these results to the distances of its own LOC records. Another solution is to have the authoritative servers for the subdomains report the distances for its results. Every unique record name would require its distance to be reported. There is no standardized way to transfer such a distance value, so we propose the use of a new volatile record for every unique result name, the distance (DST) record. These records are not added to the persistent zone storage of the authoritative server, but instead only generated temporarily for inclusion in the query answer. Its definition is an implementation of the TXT record: `'v=dst1'` distance. The distance is a decimal value in meters. Because each authoritative server already knows the distances of the requested shape to its own LOC records after doing the local nearest neighbor resolution, no additional computation is required. The parent authoritative server uses these temporary records to order the other result records, and trim the number of records to the requested number. Because DST records are essentially metadata, they are returned in the 'additional' section of DNS query answers. This is comparable to how the OPT pseudo-resource record (RR) is returned for the Extension mechanisms for DNS (EDNS(0)) protocol [3,15].

One considerable drawback of the first proposed solution is that it increases the computational burden on the non-leaf authoritative servers, as they would have to perform additional distance calculations. These distance calculations are wasteful, because they were already performed by the subdomains to return the initial nearest neighboring records set. After considering this imposed computational overhead, we chose to implement the second proposed solution in the prototype.

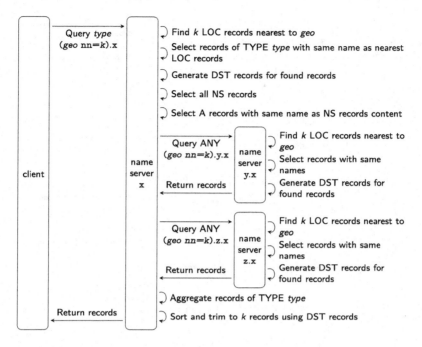

Fig. 1. eDNS nearest-neighbor resolution with delegation.

A visualization of the processing done for nearest neighbor resolution in a delegated deployment is shown in Fig. 1 for name server x with two subdomains. Note that unlike the process for diameter-based delegation, no overlap with BND records is checked, because all subdomains have to be queried regardless of the result. Requests are sent to subdomains for ANY records, rather than the type requested by the client, as we want to receive DST records in addition to the requested type. It is argued by some that ANY queries should be deprecated to prevent their use in amplification attacks [7], which attempt to overload a victim's bandwidth capacity. DNS ANY queries are well-suited to this attack type, because the response size of a request is significantly larger than the request itself. We therefore note that the subdomain requests can alternatively be performed using two separate queries for the *type* and TXT (the base type of DST) records. Assuming x and each of its s subdomains have at least k LOC records, the total number of records of the requested type that are known by x, will be $(1 + s) \times k$. They are typically not included in the records returned to the client, but are used to sort the resource record set (RRset) by distance and trim them to k records. These are returned to the client. If less than, or exactly k records of the requested type are known, all these records are returned.

The problem of managing dynamic nodes, such as vehicles, has been discussed in [13]. The author added support for dynamic nodes by implementing a process in the name server software that periodically reads an updated text file with a list of nodes, rewrites its zone file, rebuilds the internal database, and reloads the server. It is noted that an alternative approach to this problem is to use the DynDNS Update protocol [16], but this protocol was not supported by the version of the name server software that was used.

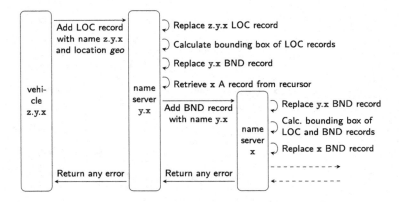

Fig. 2. eDNS location updating.

We implement dynamicity for vehicles using DynDNS Updates by making use of a DNS name server that supports the DynDNS protocol. A layer of complexity is added when the problem of dynamicity is combined with delegation. An eDNS server needs to know the bounding box coverages of its child servers. If locations in the child servers change, the known bounding boxes may need to be updated as well. The process is visualized in Fig. 2. A similar process involves the deletion of a LOC record. Rather than inserting a new record, only an old entry is removed. Nothing changes from the perspective of x, as deletion can also result in the need to send an updated bounding box to the parent server. Finally, one edge case of deletion exists. If the last LOC record in a specific domain is deleted, there is no valid bounding box to be created. The related BND record needs to be removed, both in y.x and its parent name server x. The latter should therefore be removed with a new DNS Update deletion message.

4   Evaluation and Numerical Results

This section highlights the results of evaluating the implemented functionalities with various configurations and settings to get insight into system behavior in terms of throughput and latency. The evaluation is performed with sets of real historic vehicle location data to simulate the realistic use case of tracking vehicles in an eDNS system.

The prototype is deployed to clusters on Amazon Web Services for reliable performance testing. A PostgreSQL database instance is launched for each server instance, and all database instances are extended with PostGIS functionality.

The server instances are of the type *m3.medium*. Experiments that attempt to replicate or compare to our results should therefore be run on instances with equivalent computing performance.

4.1   Test Setups

Given the focus of our work, it is important to evaluate the performance of the system by querying nodes within a specified geographical region; querying nodes with the smallest distance to a specified geographical region; and updating nodes with dynamic locations. Location data is needed to evaluate these perspectives. We have used a historic data set of real vehicle location data. We represent such a location with a LOC record, as well as an A record with a fictional IP address of the vehicle.

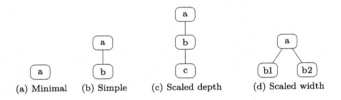

(a) Minimal   (b) Simple   (c) Scaled depth   (d) Scaled width

Fig. 3. Evaluation server setups.

We test the influence of server setups by configuring multiple name space tree setups. Various testing setups are visualized in Fig. 3. The setups provide a variety in terms of tree width and depth. Query performance is tested by querying the top node in the name space tree. The LOC records are divided over the edge nodes. The allocation of records to the edge nodes is close to optimal, in the sense that each edge node is responsible for its own geographical region. This causes the bounding boxes of the edge nodes to have no overlap. The performance of location updates is tested by sending DynDNS updates to one or more of the available edge nodes and measuring the performance. Various input parameters of the setup can influence system performance.

4.2   Performance Metrics

The performance of the system is quantified in terms of throughput and latency as the two most relevant performance indicators of the introduced system. For our use case, the throughput determines how many vehicles the system is able to keep track of, in terms of the number of queries and also the number of location record updates the system can handle within one second. The latency influences the responsiveness of the system, and how up-to-date the stored locations are. This metric specifies the time interval between issuing queries and receiving the corresponding reply back. Throughput has a strong inverse correlation to latency. Therefore, we only show throughput in the figures.

All DNS query and update operations are performed with a reasonable time-out of 1 s. If no result is received before this timeout expires, the operation is considered to have failed, and will not contribute to the overall throughput.

In our testing setup, each eDNS server connects to a database backend on another server. The latency between these servers can be measured to determine its influence on the other results. The `ping` command was used from an Elastic Compute Cloud (EC2) instance to determine the communication delay between two servers in the same availability zone. Executing consecutive `ping` requests showed that latency between servers in the same availability zone lies within the range [0.634,0.648] ms with $\alpha = 0.01$.

For the sake of simplicity, we assume that the result data is normally distributed. This allows us to compute confidence intervals for the data points. All results are displayed with a 95 % confidence interval ($\alpha = 0.05$). Note that some graphs contain confidence intervals that are too small to be visible.

4.3   Numerical Results

In order to get reliable results for throughput of the system, it is necessary to have reasonable packet arrival rate, such that the system does not wait for packets to arrive. On the other hand, the system should also not be overloaded to the point where it is unable to reduce its internal buffer or respond within time-out limits. To prevent the system from idling, it is necessary to send multiple packets simultaneously. Initial tests have been performed to evaluate the performance with different numbers of simultaneous packets. This is implemented as a thread pool, with each packet being sent in its own thread (a 'worker'). As expected, employing more workers generally results in higher throughput, although with significant diminishing returns. For every tested configuration, throughput converges to a certain rate where at least one non-buffer related performance bottleneck emerged, such as limited processor power. Even though higher number of workers do not negatively affect throughput performance, we saw that using an arbitrarily large number of workers is not reasonable because of latency. Latency appears to consistently increase when a larger number of workers is used. This happens because the server has to divide its resources over all incoming requests, resulting in longer processing times for each request. Based on these results, we do not consider there to be an optimal number of workers, as even for specific configurations it is a trade-off between throughput and latency. We have opted to perform the rest of the evaluation with 8 concurrent workers. With that number of workers, the majority of the potential performance increase from concurrency has been achieved under most testing configurations while having lower latencies than any higher number of workers.

We now evaluate the performance of both querying and updating of locations.

Querying. Throughput and latency have been evaluated for every combination of setup, LOC record count and diameter. The LOC record count represents the number of LOC records present in the system. This can be evaluated with a varying number of LOC RR inserted in the eDNS servers. We have taken subsets of various sizes from the previously mentioned data set to evaluate the influence of the amount of LOC records in the databases. Three subsets containing 100, 1000 and 10000 locations were created. Since each of the locations represents a vehicle, the diameter of the corresponding LOC record should be small. We have chosen the default LOC diameter of 1 m as the diameter for each record. Multiple setups are tested, and records are added to one or more edge nodes based on their geographical position. Each edge node is allocated roughly the same number of LOC records. Upon receiving a DynDNS update message that inserts or removes a LOC or BND resource record, the BND record of the node itself will need to be renewed. The total number of LOC and BND servers can therefore influence the performance as they increase the number of spatial database operations that need to be performed.

The query location diameter represents the size of the queried circular area, specified via a diameter. It can be tested on the same data set by querying various area sizes. For this, we can consider querying areas with diameter sizes as low as 1 m up to 500 km. The larger sizes in this range would encompass our entire data set. The query locations originate from the same data set as the locations described earlier, but represent a different subset. They do share the same characteristics of being more likely to refer to a location on a highway.

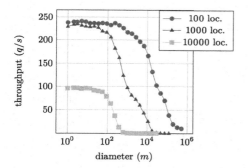

Fig. 4. Querying throughput (setup (a)).

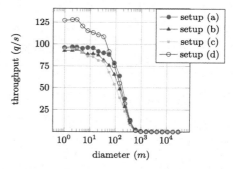

Fig. 5. Querying throughput (10000 locations).

The throughput of the system with setup (a) is shown in Fig. 4. One may note that both the query diameter and data set size have a significant influence on the results. Given that a throughput of around 240 queries per second is achieved for both the data set of 100 and 1000 locations with low diameter sizes, we can conclude that the performance is not limited by spatial computations at this point. Rather, it is likely that network performance or packet handling overhead are responsible for the bottleneck. Additionally, the graph shows that for large diameter sizes and large data set sizes, the throughput approaches 0. This indicates that within the timeout limit, the system is not able to return a result with a large amount of matching locations. The performance for queries applied to the data set of 100 locations also appear to converge, but to a different value. This can be explained by the fact that queries with diameter sizes larger than roughly 200 km already encompass most of the location points in the data set, so increasing the diameter further will not increase the number of results.

Equivalent comparisons have been made for other setups, but graphs for these are omitted because they show the same pattern of larger data set sizes resulting in slower queries. Instead, we consider the performance of identical data set sizes between different setups. With data sets of 10000 locations, shown in Fig. 5, performance of setup (c) rises above that of the other setups for small diameters. This is likely the result of the system being able to divide its spatial computations over the two edge nodes. At a diameter of around 100 m, throughput becomes lower than setup (a)'s before converging to the same value.

The same comparison between setups for nearest neighbor queries is shown in Fig. 6. The query nearest neighbor count represents the number of requested nearby results. It can be tested with simple integers. The same location data set as described for the query location diameter is used. Results roughly follow the patterns discovered in the evaluation for diameter-based queries. Queries on a system with this number of locations tend to perform better on setup (d)'s load distribution, up to a point where the portion of packets that does not fit within the specified timeout window becomes large enough that setup (a)'s single server is able to more reliably provide a result.

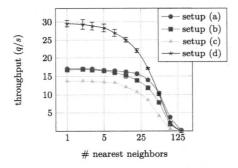

Fig. 6. Querying throughput (nearest neighbors, 10000 locations).

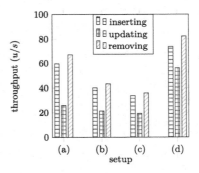

Fig. 7. Updating throughput (10000 locations).

Updating. We have evaluated three aspects of the dynamic location functionality: insertion, updating and removal. The insertion operation involves adding an A record with an IP address, as well as an entity's initial location in a LOC record. For updating a location, we assume that an entity's IP address has not changed. The updating operation therefore involves removing an old LOC record and replacing it with one containing a new location. The removal operation removes both the last know location in the form of a LOC record, but also the associated A record. The three different aspects therefore each involve two database operations. The aspects are evaluated as follows for a data set with x locations. For each location, a DNS Update message is sent that inserts both a fictional IP address and a location. Then, all x locations are updated with individual DNS Update messages that remove the old LOC record and insert the new one. Finally, x DNS Update messages are sent that remove all entities. As with the query evaluation, all operations are executed with 8 concurrent workers to increase utilization. Storage of locations is also distributed over different edge nodes depending on geographical coordinates, as described in Sect. 4.1.

In Fig. 7, we show the performance of the three mentioned operations when executed on different setups and using the 10000 locations data set. As expected, introducing more depth to the server tree results in a higher latency, because each parent server needs to be updated with the renewed bounding boxes of its direct child servers. Setup (d) shows that the system scales well in width. Dividing LOC records over multiple servers appears to increase performance, even if it includes the extra operation of updating the parent server compared to setup (a). Updating locations is more expensive than the insertion and removal operations. At least part of this discrepancy can be explained by observing that the updating operation is always performed on a system that contains all x locations in a data set. The insertion and removal operations work on a system with 0 to x entities, depending on how many entities have already been inserted or removed.

5   Conclusions and Future Work

In this paper we introduced two main improvements to the eDNS protocol. To solve the problem of finding nearby results, we have described an approach for nearest neighbor resolution functionality. This can be used when vehicles need to be addressed via RSUs, but RSUs provide incomplete coverage of an area.

After previous works have shown that updating individual entities with new locations is possible, we have also added the concept of dynamicity in eDNS using the standardized DynDNS method. This allows us to track the locations of vehicles in LOC resource records by keeping coverage information synchronized over servers in the system.

Performance has been evaluated for queries and updates. The performance is shown to be strongly dependent on server setup, as well as input parameters. The test results show that in most of the evaluated scenarios, horizontal scaling of server setups frequently influences the performance positively, while vertical scaling always influences the performance negatively. Distributing LOC records over multiple servers allows the system to perform its calculations faster, potentially improving both throughput and latency.

In future work, focus can be placed on improving compatibility of the eDNS protocol with the existing DNS protocol. This includes changing the query format to only include characters that are allowed by default, as well as making use of the OPT pseudo resource record for communication of distances between servers. Additionally, the scaling of the protocol may be evaluated more extensively.

Acknowledgments. This paper is a result of research performed for a Master thesis [14]. The authors would like to thank the support provided by OVSoftware B.V. and Simacan B.V.

References

1. Baldessari, R., Bödekker, B., Deegener, M., Festag, A., Franz, W., Kellum, C.C., Kosch, T., Kovacs, A., Lenardi, M., Menig, C., et al.: Car 2 car communication consortium manifesto. Technical report, CAR 2 CAR Communication Consortium (2007)
2. Beckmann, N., Kriegel, H.P., Schneider, R., Seeger, B.: The R*-tree: an efficient and robust access method for points and rectangles, vol. 19. ACM (1990)
3. Damas, J., Graff, M., Vixie, P.: Extension mechanisms for DNS (EDNS(0)). STD 75, RFC Editor, April 2013
4. Ernst, T.: Final geonet architecture design, January 2010
5. Fioreze, T., Heijenk, G.: Extending DNS to support geocasting towards vanets: a proposal. In: Vehicular Networking Conference (VNC), pp. 271–277. IEEE (2010)
6. Fioreze, T., Heijenk, G.: Extending the domain name system (DNS) to provide geographical addressing towards vehicular ad-hoc networks (VANETs). In: Vehicular Networking Conference (VNC), pp. 70–77. IEEE (2011)
7. Gudmundsson, O., Majkowski, M.: Deprecating the DNS any meta-query type, March 2015
8. Hain, T.: An ipv6 geographic global unicast address format. Internet-Draft draft-hain-ipv6-geo-addr-02, IETF Secretariat, July 2010
9. Imieliński, T., Navas, J.C.: Gps-based addressing and routing. RFC 2009, RFC Editor, November 1996
10. Imieliński, T., Navas, J.C.: Gps-based geographic addressing, routing, and resource discovery. Commun. ACM **42**(4), 86–92 (1999)
11. Karagiannis, G., Altintas, O., Ekici, E., Heijenk, G., Jarupan, B., Lin, K., Weil, T.: Vehicular networking: a survey and tutorial on requirements, architectures, challenges, standards and solutions. Commun. Surv. Tutorials IEEE **13**(4), 584–616 (2011)
12. Kovacs, A.: Final geonet specification, January 2010
13. van Leeuwen, J.: Dynamicity Management in Domain Name System Resource Records. University of Twente, Bachelorreferaat (2014)
14. Moscoviter, D.: Improving spatial indexing and searching for location-based DNS queries. Master's thesis, University of Twente (2016)
15. Vixie, P.: Extension mechanisms for DNS (EDNS0). RFC 2671, RFC Editor, August 1999
16. Vixie, P., Thomson, S., Yakov, R., Bound, J.: Dynamic updates in the domain name system (DNS update). RFC 2136, RFC Editor, April 1997
17. Westra, M.: Extending the Domain Name System with geographically scoped queries. Master's thesis, University of Twente (2013)

QoS Multi-tree Based Routing Protocol for Inter-mesh Infrastructure Communications

Hajer Bargaoui[1]([⊠]), Nader Mbarek[1], Olivier Togni[1], and Mounir Frikha[2]

[1] LE2I Laboratory, University of Burgundy, Dijon, France
{Hajer.Bargaoui,Nader.Mbarek,
Olivier.Togni}@u-bourgogne.fr
[2] MEDIATRON Laboratory,
High School of Communication of Tunis (SUP'COM), Tunis, Tunisia
m.frikha@supcom.rnu.tn

Abstract. Quality of service (QoS) in wireless mesh networks (WMN) is an active area of research, which is driven by the increasing demand for real-time and multimedia applications, such as VoIP (Voice over IP) and VoD (Video on Demand). In this paper, we propose a QoS multi-tree based routing protocol for wireless mesh environments, named Inter-Mesh Infrastructure Proactive Routing (IMPR). It is a proactive multi-tree routing protocol enabling QoS guarantee for communications from/towards the Internet network through the Mesh Gateway (MG) of the mesh infrastructure. We describe and analyze the simulation results of different scenarios conducted on the network simulator ns-3 to demonstrate the effectiveness of our IMPR routing protocol in forwarding real-time applications with QoS guarantee.

Keywords: Wireless mesh network · Qos routing · Multi-tree routing · IMPR · Performance evaluation

1 Introduction

Popularity of WMNs in Internet access layer has been growing in the recent years. They are self-organizing and self-configuring multi-hop wireless networks, which are similar to ad hoc networks [1, 2]. However, a wireless ad hoc network is generally considered as a decentralized network that does not have any infrastructure. A main difference is that WMNs can support the multi-hop communications, but also be connected to the infrastructure networks through portal mesh points.

Forwarding real-time and streaming applications, such as VoIP and VoD, is a major challenge for wireless mesh networks due to radio channels limitations. Different routing protocols were proposed to ensure the discovery of a route with satisfying QoS parameters. However, forwarding different kinds of flows using a single route may cause the perturbation of multimedia flows by non-QoS constrained ones. Thus, the challenging issue we address in this paper is how to forward flows depending on their requested service level (QoS) towards/from the Internet gateway in a WMN.

© IFIP International Federation for Information Processing 2016
Published by Springer International Publishing Switzerland 2016. All Rights Reserved
L. Mamatas et al. (Eds.): WWIC 2016, LNCS 9674, pp. 199–211, 2016.
DOI: 10.1007/978-3-319-33936-8_16

As a solution, we propose a QoS multi-tree based routing protocol (IMPR) for inter-mesh infrastructure communications, jointly with an adapted clustering algorithm to reduce efficiently the network's load within a wireless mesh infrastructure. IMPR is a proactive multi-tree routing protocol that provides QoS guarantee for communications from/towards the Internet network through the Mesh Gateway of the infrastructure. The proposed protocol defines three different service classes depending on the applications' QoS requirements. A different routing tree would forward each service class.

In the other hand, in order to ensure QoS for communications within the wireless mesh infrastructure, the IMPR protocol operates jointly with a second QoS based routing sub-protocol. It is a reactive routing protocol proposed to ensure QoS guarantee for intra-infrastructure communications. Moreover, in order to reduce the overhead and the routing table size at each node, we proposed a one-hop clustering algorithm, which divides the topology of the infrastructure into a set of groups called clusters. A node named Cluster-Head (CH) coordinates each cluster. The inter-clusters communications are maintained thanks to Cluster-Gateway nodes (C-Gw), used to ensure connectivity between two Cluster-Heads in direct vision and the Distributed-Gateway nodes (D-Gw), used to ensure communications between two disjoint clusters. More details about the reactive QoS based routing protocol and the clustering algorithm have been published in [3].

In this paper, we aim to present the design details of our proposed IMPR routing protocol as well as the discussions of the different simulation results. The remainder of this paper is organized as follows. In Sect. 2, we present some related works. Then, we define in Sect. 3, the novel proactive QoS multi-tree based routing protocol IMPR and we introduce in Sect. 4 the performance evaluation and the results analysis. Finally, Sect. 5 concludes the paper.

2   Related Work

Given the particular topology of WMNs, characterized by the existence of a gateway node to ensure communications with the external networks, a tree based routing protocol was considered as a solution to handle this type of communication. The default routing protocol of the IEEE 802.11s standard, i.e. Hybrid Wireless Mesh Protocol (HWMP), defines a tree based path selection algorithm for inter-infrastructure communications [4], using the portal mesh gateway as a root. It is a proactive distance vector routing protocol, using a radio aware metric. HWMP is based on a periodic broadcast of proactive control messages to announce the existence of the root. Each node records and updates the metric to the root and forwards the received control message. Then, it chooses the best parent node and replies with a route reply message to the root. However, this approach does not consider the applications' QoS requirements in the tree construction process. In the research work [5], the authors propose a solution to reduce the number of routing packets sent to build the tree based topology. They define a new address space based on the link state and propose an initial route establishment method with greedy forwarding by using addresses as positional information. Other research works address the bottleneck problem at the root node by defining multiple gateway nodes in a WMN. Tree-Based with Multi-Gateway

Association (TBMGA) routing protocol [6] efficiently balance the load among the different Internet gateways in the wireless mesh network, by creating a tree from each gateway. In the same manner, Optimized Tree based Routing (OTR) [7] lightens the load on the root node by changing it in order to join another routing tree when its corresponding gateway node gets congested. Madhusudan et al. [8] propose also a new routing protocol as a solution to bottleneck issues at the root node. Their proposed protocol, named Decentralized Hybrid Wireless Mesh Protocol (DHWMP), is an enhancement of the HWMP routing protocol in order to provide a different root for each different transmission between a source and a destination node.

The previous mentioned tree based routing algorithms mainly focused on the bottleneck issues at the root node whereas the routes establishment for QoS-constrained applications was not fully investigated by those works. In this context, some reactive routing protocols were proposed to ensure QoS guarantee for real-time and multimedia traffic within a wireless mesh infrastructure. Wireless Mesh Routing (WMR) [9] is a QoS based routing solution for wireless mesh LAN networks. It provides QoS guarantees in terms of minimum bandwidth and maximum end-to-end delay. Kon et al. [10] improve the WMR protocol by proposing a novel end-to-end packet delay estimation mechanism thanks to a stability-aware routing policy. The delay estimation is based on packets named DUMMY-RREP, which have the same size, priority and data rate as real data traffic. However, these proposed approaches do not take into account traffic heterogeneity within a WMN. Enabling QoS verification while using a single path for different traffic types may create congestion or overloading in this path. The research conducted in [11] attempts to address this limitation to some extent, in order to enhance the video quality over IEEE 802.11e WMN, by proposing a cross-layer approach combined with the use of ETX metric. Depending on the priorities and dropping probability specified by the application layer for a specific traffic, the network layer chooses different routing metrics. A multiple metric routing protocol has been proposed in [12], by using an active network architecture to provide QoS within WMNs. Their proposed routing protocol, named active AODV, adapts the AODV routing protocol to use five routing metrics, namely the hop count, ETX metric, ETT metric, Available Bandwidth metric and Expected Interference (EI) metric.

Most of the research works that we have presented, do not consider QoS requirements of traffic belonging to different service classes. Thus, to guarantee various QoS parameters for heterogeneous traffic types, it is important to use multiple good quality paths with appropriate routing metrics. In this context, we propose the IMPR routing protocol, which provides mesh nodes with QoS based routing capability enabling a service level guarantee for communications toward external networks, by differentiating the traffic into three different service classes.

3   IMPR: Inter-mesh Infrastructure Proactive Routing

Inter-infrastructure Mesh Proactive Routing (IMPR) is a proactive multi-tree based routing protocol, designed to ensure communications towards external networks, especially Internet network, for WMNs. IMPR deploys a multi-path routing concept over each mesh node to ensure the construction of three partially node-disjoint routing trees; with a common root (i.e. Mesh Gateway), over a WMN. The routing trees construction process is based on the exchange of three different control messages, namely the Root Announcement (RANN) message, the Path Request (PREQ) message and the Path Relay (PREP) message. Thus, to reduce the overhead of the network, IMPR is used only over the different cluster-head and cluster gateways nodes. The cluster members would not participate to the trees construction process.

In fact, this multi-tree construction process of IMPR routing protocol is defined to provide QoS guarantees for real-time and multimedia applications, in a wireless mesh network. Each routing tree is set to forward a specific type of traffic. Therefore, we differentiate three service classes, namely interactive real-time applications class, Streaming applications class and Best Effort class. The first class is more sensitive to delay and jitter variations. The Streaming applications class is more sensitive to jitter variation while the third one is a non QoS-constrained traffic class. In brief, IMPR routing protocol allows the construction of three QoS partially node-disjoint trees with a common root: the Real Time tree, the Streaming tree, and the Best Effort tree.

In the following, we detail the operation of our IMPR routing protocol. Indeed, it is mainly executed according to two phases: the routes caching phase and the routing trees construction phase.

3.1   Routes Caching Phase

During this phase, each mesh node participating to the trees construction process, stores as much as possible routes towards the root node, by receiving a Root Announcement (RANN) message. In fact, the root node broadcasts periodically a RANN message (Table 1) to its neighboring mesh nodes to announce its presence. Only the CH and the Gw nodes consider this message. So, all the CM nodes reject it. Then, in order to keep an overall QoS value of the path, the RANN message introduces a QoS Metric field. It includes three QoS parameters, namely the bandwidth, the delay and the jitter.

Table 1. RANN message

Root IP address	Path	QoS Metric

When receiving a RANN message, each intermediate node stores the Path parameter in its route cache and updates it by adding its address. Furthermore, it modifies the QoS Metric and forwards the updated RANN message to its multicast group formed by the CHs, the Gws, and the root. In order to keep as many routes as possible, duplicated RANN messages are not rejected. Instead, to avoid an infinite loop of a message, each node verifies first if its address already exists in the Path field or not. Besides, each node keeps the entire path received through the RANN message in its route cache in order to be able to verify later the disjunction of two paths.

3.2 Routing Trees Construction Phase

Each node waits for a certain time Ts, enabling a maximum of paths local storage, before starting the routing trees construction phase. Once the timer expires, each node starts the selection of a potential Real Time Tree path from its route cache, according to our proposed routes selection algorithm (Routes Selection Algorithm). Then, this route is validated as one of the tree branches by an exchange of PREQ and PREP messages with the root node. In fact, this exchange of control messages between the mesh node and the root is used to ensure that each intermediate node of a path is using the same path toward the root, so that each node has no more than a single branch toward the root for a specific routing tree. Once a PREP message is received from the root, the node validates the path for the actual under construction routing tree, removes it from its route cache and starts the construction process of the next routing tree in the same way.

A Finite State Machine (FSM) diagram in Fig. 1 illustrates this process. We distinguish four different states to describe a mesh node behavior at the routing trees construction phase:

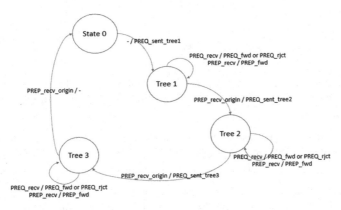

Fig. 1. FSM diagram of IMPR routing trees construction phase

- "State 0": it is the initial state where a node has already in cache the maximum of paths towards the root node.
- State "Tree 1": the node is participating in the construction of the first tree, i.e. the Real Time Tree. By executing the routes selection algorithm of IMPR (Algorithm 1), the node selects a path and sends a PREQ message to the root. In the same time, it forwards or reject the other control messages received from the other node, depending on the corresponding condition (Flowchart in Fig. 2).
- State "Tree 2": by receiving a PREP message from the root for the first routing tree, the node validates the first tree path and changes to state "Tree 2" to start the construction of the second routing tree, i.e. Streaming Tree.

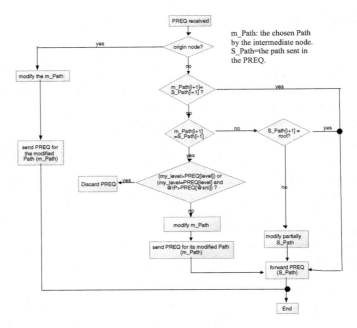

Fig. 2. Flowchart of PREQ process

- State "Tree 3": similarly, once the mesh node validates a path for the second routing tree, it changes its state to start the selection of a path to the third routing tree, i.e. Best Effort Tree.

In the following, we present the proposed algorithm for routes selection corresponding to different QoS routing trees. Then, we define the Path request and the Path reply process designed to validate each chosen path for each routing tree.

Routes Selection Algorithm. The routes selection algorithm (Algorithm 1) is proposed to provide each mesh node with the capability of selecting a potential path for each QoS routing tree, satisfying the requirements of three specified service classes. For the first path corresponding to the Real Time Tree, we select the best in terms of delay and jitter while optimizing the bandwidth parameter. For the Streaming Tree, we choose not only a partially disjoint path from the selected first tree path to reduce congestion issues, but also a path with low values of jitter. Lastly, from the remaining paths, we choose for the Best Effort Tree, the best in terms of disjunction over the other paths.

In case none of the stored paths satisfies the required QoS parameters, we introduce a weight parameter (W) for each path. It combines the different required QoS parameters with the disjunction parameter in order to allow the selection of the best path in terms of QoS guarantee while optimizing disjunction.

We specify in Algorithm 1 these concepts enabling the selection of routes for the different QoS routing trees. Besides, we present in Table 2 the notations used in the IMPR routes selection algorithm.

Algorithm 1 : IMPR Routes Selection Algorithm

1: If tree = 1 then
2: $A = \{P\}_{(D<Dmax\ and\ J<Jmax)}$
3:   If $A \neq \emptyset$ then
4: $p_1 = min_{HC} \{max_{Bw} (A)\}$
5:   Else
6: $B = \{P\}_{(D<Dmax)}$
7:   If $B \neq \emptyset$ then
8:   //Calculate W for each path in B
9: $W = w_1*rank\_D (Bw) + w_3*rank\_A (J)$
10: $p_1 = min_W (B)$
11:   Else
12:   //Calculate W for each path in P
13: $W = w_1*rank\_D(Bw) + w_2*rank\_A(D) + w_3*rank\_A(J)$
14: $p_1 = min_W (P)$
15:   End If
16:   End If
17: End If
18: // Once the origin node receives a PREP from the root -> tree = tree+1
19: If tree = 2 then
20: $P = P\backslash\{p_1\}$
21: $A = \{P\}_{(J<Jmax)}$
22:   If $A \neq \emptyset$ then
23:   //Calculate W for each path in A
24: $W = w_1*rank\_D(Bw) + w_4*rank\_A(Disj)$
25: $p_2 = min_W (A)$
26:   Else
27:   //Calculate W for each path in P
28: $W = w_1*rank\_D (Bw) + w_3*rank\_A (J) + w_4*rank\_A (Disj)$
29: $p_2 = min_W (P)$
30:   End If
31: End If
32: // Once the origin node receives a PREP from the root -> tree = tree+1
33: If tree = 3 then
34: $P = P\backslash\{p_2\}$
35: $p_3 = min_{HC} \{min_{Disj} (P)\}$
36: End If

Path Request Process. By executing the route selection algorithm, a node selects a path for its ith routing tree and sends a PREQ message (Table 3), to the root node for validation. Each intermediate node compares its chosen path for its ith routing tree to the path carried by the PREQ message. If the intermediate node is already the origin of the PREQ message, it modifies its chosen path in order to eliminate the corresponding loop and sends a new PREQ message with the modified path. Otherwise, if the next hop in the two paths is different, the node either modifies its entire path or updates the path in the PREQ message, depending on the corresponding conditions. The Flowchart in Fig. 2 presents the different cases that an intermediate node may encounter, mainly based on the use of the level parameter, which represents the level of a node in the first routing tree, namely the Real Time Tree.

Path Reply Process. For each received PREQ message, the root node replies to the origin mesh node with a PREP message (Table 5), after updating its routing table.

Table 2. Notations used in the Algorithm 1

Notation	Description
tree	The routing tree being constructed; initialization tree = 1
P	Set of the stored paths in the cache of a node
p_i	Path selected for the ith tree
W	The weight of a path
Bw; w_1	Bandwidth; its coefficient in the weight (W) calculating
D; w_2	Delay; its coefficient in the weight (W) calculating
J; w_3	Jitter; its coefficient in the weight (W) calculating
Disj; w_4	Number of common nodes between paths; its coefficient
HC	Number of hops in the path towards the root
rank_D/A (X)	Function that returns the rank of a path in a set of paths sorted in **D**escending/ **A**scending order according to the parameter X.

Table 3. PREQ message

Src IP address	Dest IP address	Path	ID-Path	Level[a]

[a]Level: the level of the source node in the Real Time Tree

Table 4. IMPR routing table

Dest IP address	Next hop	ID-path

Table 5. PREP message

Dest IP address	Path	ID-path

When an intermediate node receives a PREP message, it updates the Path field by adding its IP address and forwards it to next hop towards the destination.

By receiving the PREP message, the destination node updates its routing table (Table 4) and its chosen path for the routing tree if it is different from the Path field in the PREP message. Then, it removes it from its route cache before starting the construction of the next routing tree.

4 Performance Evaluation and Results

4.1 Simulation Environment

To evaluate the performance of our IMPR routing protocol, we have developed our source code using the network simulator ns-3 environment [13]. Then, we have conducted some simulation scenarios to evaluate its performance and to compare it to the IEEE 802.11s default routing protocol HWMP, in a wireless mesh environment.

In fact, HWMP routing algorithm defines also a tree-based sub-protocol for inter-mesh infrastructure communications [4].

The simulation environment consists of up to 30 stationary mesh nodes arranged in a grid topology. Simulation time is 200 s. Two different traffic models are used according to the elaborated scenarios. The first one is a generic Constant Bit Rate (CBR) traffic used in scenario 1 to evaluate our routing protocol performance in terms of overhead and convergence (Sect. 4.2). The second one simulates a VoIP traffic used in scenario 2 (Sect. 4.3) to evaluate real time traffic performance in terms of delay and jitter when using our protocol compared to HWMP. Each scenario is simulated ten times and an average value is considered for the performance analysis. Table 6 shows the used simulation parameters.

Table 6. Simulation parameters

Simulation parameters	Value
Routing protocols	IMPR & HWMP
Simulation time	200 s
Nodes 'number	6 to 30 nodes
Mobility model	GridPositionAllocator/static
Traffic model	CBR (UDP)/VoIP (UDP)
Packet size	512 bytes/160 bytes
Data rate	512 kbps/64 kbps

4.2 Scenario 1: Routing Protocol Performance Evaluation

We evaluate our routing protocol performance in terms of routing overhead and tree(s) construction convergence. To this end, we perform different simulations, by varying the number of nodes within a wireless mesh infrastructure, while considering a CBR traffic. This traffic is modeled with 512-byte data packets and a data rate of 512 kbps.

Figure 3a shows the global routing overhead of IMPR and HWMP routing protocols. We observe a close variation of the routing overhead between the two protocols. In fact, to ensure the routing tree construction, HWMP protocol is based on the exchange of PREQ and PREP messages. The root broadcasts a PREQ message to announce its existence and each mesh node replies with a PREP message. However, IMPR routing protocol uses three different control messages, i.e. RANN, PREQ and PREP messages, to enable the construction of three partially node-disjoint trees with a common root. Despite the different control messages and the construction of three trees (unlike HWMP with only one tree), IMPR routing overhead remains acceptable, thanks to the adapted clustering algorithm, since the broadcast is limited to the multicast group formed by the CH and the cluster gateway nodes.

Figure 3b illustrates the variation of the routing Tree(s) Construction Time (TCT) according to the size of the mesh topology. For both protocols, the TCT parameter increases with the number of nodes since more delay is needed to reach all the nodes in the mesh infrastructure. HWMP protocol presents better TCT variation than our IMPR protocol. This is explained by the fact that HWMP protocol is based

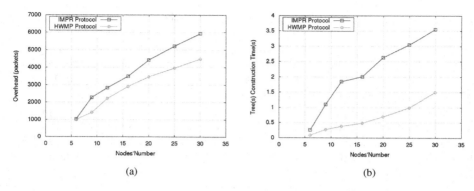

Fig. 3. IMPR vs HWMP (a) Overhead (b) Tree(s) Construction convergence

only on one routing tree, when IMPR offers three different QoS based routing trees at the end of the trees construction phase, to offer better QoS guarantee for real-time and streaming applications.

4.3 Scenario 2: Traffic Performance Evaluation

To demonstrate the effectiveness of our routing protocol in forwarding real-time applications with QoS guarantee, we evaluate the corresponding QoS parameters by generating a VoIP traffic towards an external network. We evaluate the VoIP real-time application in terms of average end-to-end delay and average jitter parameters, since such application is very sensitive to these QoS parameters.

To simulate a voice conversation, we used a traffic pattern corresponding to the G711 encoder, which produces 50 packets per second with 160 bytes of payload each. Then, we have introduced a noise over some links to simulate network perturbation. Besides, different source nodes are installed in the network, to simulate a more realistic scenario. The simulations are conducted to compare the IMPR routing protocol and the HWMP protocol usage by varying the mesh infrastructure size.

The obtained results concerning the end-to-end delay and jitter QoS parameters for a VoIP application are shown in Fig. 4. We observe a considerable difference concerning the variation of the delay and jitter parameters for the VoIP traffic while using HWMP and IMPR protocols. The corresponding values while using HWMP are almost twice the QoS values while using IMPR protocol. Thus, our IMPR protocol offers better guarantee in terms of QoS than HWMP protocol for real-time applications.

Actually, HWMP protocol offers a single tree for different service classes. Forwarding a real-time traffic may be perturbed by a Best Effort traffic generated by another node. On the other hand, IMPR protocol offers three partially disjoint QoS based routing trees to be used depending on the type of the application to forward in order to satisfy the requested QoS parameters.

Thus, to demonstrate the effectiveness of the IMPR QoS multi-tree approach, we conduct a different simulation scenario, enabling three different service classes' flows generation between the root node and a mesh node. In this scenario, we simulate a

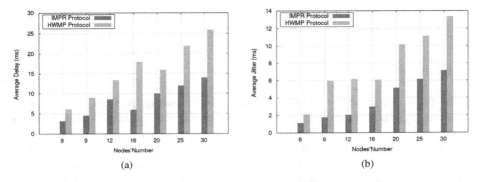

Fig. 4. VoIP traffic (a) Delay evaluation (b) Jitter evaluation

5 × 5 grid network topology consisting of 24 mesh nodes and a root node, in order to evaluate the performance of IMPR and HWMP protocols.

In the considered simulation scenario, the first flow (i.e. Flow 1) starts at Time = 10 s. Flow 1 has a rate of 64 kbps and a payload of 160 bytes, corresponding to a VoIP traffic (first service class). At Time = 50 s, the source node starts generating a CBR UDP flow (Flow 2) with a rate of 512 kbps and a payload of 1000 bytes, simulating a streaming type traffic. As a Best Effort traffic, a third flow (Flow 3) begins at Time = 80 s with a rate of 1 Mbps and a payload of 1460 bytes.

We present in Fig. 5, the delay evaluation for each traffic flow while using, respectively, HWMP and IMPR as routing protocols in a WMN. We observe that the delay while using the HWMP protocol increases for Flow 1 (Time = 50 s) and Flow 2 (Time = 80 s) when the source node generates an additional flow. Indeed, we notice that the delay of the first flow get larger with the start of the second traffic flow, which could result in a QoS degradation for the VoIP real-time application simulated by Flow 1.

Nevertheless, we note a stable and a better delay, comparing to HWMP, while considering the different types of flows in the simulation scenario using the IMPR protocol. Actually, the HWMP protocol uses a single route to forward the three

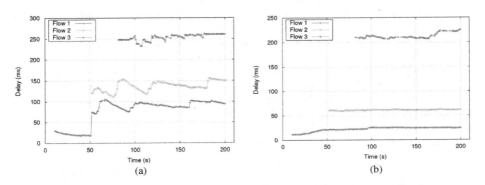

Fig. 5. Delay evaluation for different flows (a) using HWMP (b) using IMPR

different flows, whereas the IMPR protocol uses a specific QoS routing tree for each traffic flow, reducing the inter-flows perturbation.

5 Conclusion

In this paper, we presented our QoS multi-tree based routing protocol jointly with a clustering algorithm, to ensure better performance for inter-mesh infrastructure communications, regarding the amount of traffic oriented to the Internet network. We compared the performance of our IMPR routing protocol to the HWMP protocol in terms of routing overhead and tree establishment convergence and showed that we obtain better results while using our routing protocol to guarantee the average end-to-end delay and jitter for real-time application such as VoIP in a wireless mesh environment.

As ongoing work, we are conducting simulations to compare IMPR routing protocol to other proactive QoS based routing protocols for wireless mesh networks.

Acknowledgment. This work has been funded by the regional Council of Burgundy, France.

References

1. Akyildiz, I.F., Wang, X., Wang, W.: Wireless mesh networks: a survey. Comput. Netw. **47**(4), 445–487 (2005)
2. Akyildiz, I.F., Wang, X.: A survey on wireless mesh networks. IEEE Commun. Mag. **43**(9), S23–S30 (2005)
3. Bargaoui, H., Mbarek, N., Togni, O., Frikha, M.: Hybrid QoS based routing for IEEE 802.16j mesh infrastructure. Presented at the AICT 2014, The Tenth Advanced International Conference on Telecommunications, pp. 110–118 (2014)
4. IEEE Standard for Information Technology–Telecommunications and information exchange between systems–Local and metropolitan area networks–Specific requirements Part 11: Wireless LAN Medium Access Control (MAC) and Physical Layer (PHY) specifications Amendment 10: Mesh Networking, pp. 1–372 (2011)
5. Ueda, K., Baba, K.: Proposal of an initial route establishment method in wireless mesh networks. In: Ninth Annual International Symposium on Applications and the Internet, SAINT 2009, pp. 173–176 (2009)
6. Maurina, S., Riggio, R., Rasheed, T., Granelli, F.: On tree-based routing in multi-gateway association based wireless mesh networks. In: 2009 IEEE 20th International Symposium on Personal, Indoor and Mobile Radio Communications, pp. 1542–1546 (2009)
7. Wenjiang, M., Jianfeng, M., Zhuo, M., Youliang, T.: Tree-based proactive routing protocol for wireless mesh network. China Commun. **9**(1), 25–33 (2012)
8. Madhusudan, S., Song-Gon, L., HoonJae, L.: Non-root-based hybrid wireless mesh protocol for wireless mesh networks. Int. J. Smart Home **7**(2), 71–84 (2013)
9. Xue, Q., Ganz, A.: QoS routing for mesh-based wireless LANs. Int. J. Wirel. Inf. Netw. **9**(3), 179–190 (2002)
10. Kone, V., Das, S., Zhao, B.Y., Zheng, H.: QUORUM: quality of service in wireless mesh networks. Mob. Netw. Appl. **12**(5), 358–369 (2007)

11. Malgi, M.A., Gaikwad, G.N.: A study on QoS enhancement of MPEG-4 video transmission over wireless mesh network. In: 2015 International Conference on Pervasive Computing (ICPC), pp. 1–5 (2015)

12. Yun, J., Han, J., Seong, G., Cho, W., Seo, J., Khan, M., Kim, B., Park, G., Han, K.: Self-organized multi-metric routing for QoS in wireless mesh networks. In: 2014 International Conference on Information Networking (ICOIN), pp. 160–163 (2014)

13. ns-3. http://www.nsnam.org/. Accessed 22 Feb 2016

A Variable-Length Network Encoding Protocol for Big Genomic Data

Mohammed Aledhari[1], Mohamed S. Hefeida[2], and Fahad Saeed[1(✉)]

[1] Western Michigan University, Kalamazoo, MI 49008, USA
{mohammed.aledhari,fahad.saeed}@wmich.edu
[2] American University of the Middle East, Eqaila, Kuwait

Abstract. Modern genomic studies utilize high-throughput instruments which can produce data at an astonishing rate. These big genomic datasets produced using next generation sequencing (NGS) machines can easily reach peta-scale level creating storage, analytic and transmission problems for large-scale system biology studies. Traditional networking protocols are oblivious to the data that is being transmitted and are designed for general purpose data transfer. In this paper we present a novel data-aware network transfer protocol to efficiently transfer big genomic data. Our protocol exploits the limited alphabet of DNA nucleotide and is developed over the hypertext transfer protocol (HTTP) framework. Our results show that proposed technique improves transmission up to 84 times when compared to normal HTTP encoding schemes. We also show that the performance of the resultant protocol (called VTTP) using a single machine is comparable to BitTorrent protocol used on 10 machines.

Keywords: Network protocol · Big Data · Genomics · HTTP

1 Introduction

Next generation sequencing (NGS) machines, such as the Illumina HiSeq2500 can generate up to 1TB of data per run and the data grows exponentially for large systems biology studies [21]. More often than not, these large genomic data sets have to be shared with fellow scientists or with cloud services for data analysis. The usual practice is to transfer the data using a networking protocol such as HTTP or FTP. Traditional networking protocols are oblivious to the data that is being transmitted and are designed for general purpose data transfer. Consequently, transfer takes exceedingly long time when large data sets are involved. Previous methods to improve transmission has focused on using FTP/HTTP protocols and multiple machines to increase throughput [14]. However, those solutions are inefficient in terms of hardware and do not exploit the additional data redundancy of DNA sequences for efficient transmission.

This paper introduces a data-aware variable-length text transfer protocol (VTTP) that is able to efficiently handle big genomic datasets. We assert that if

© IFIP International Federation for Information Processing 2016
Published by Springer International Publishing Switzerland 2016. All Rights Reserved
L. Mamatas et al. (Eds.): WWIC 2016, LNCS 9674, pp. 212–224, 2016.
DOI: 10.1007/978-3-319-33936-8_17

the scope of the data is known a priori (such as genomic data) then networking protocols should be able to take advantage of this information for better efficiency. The key idea of VTTP is utilizing variable length codewords for DNA nucleotides in content-encode of HTTP to maximize network resources usage [8]. Our proposed transfer technique decreases the size of the data that needs to be transmitted via assigning shortest possible codewords for repeated symbols; hence shortening the transfer time. The proposed VTTP does not require any extra hardware resources and is shown to be much faster than other competing techniques and protocols.

1.1 Paper Contribution

Creating the proposed content encoding mechanism relies on assigning variable-length binary codewords for the genomic symbols based on the frequency of the nucleotides in the dataset. The VTTP dynamically switches between the traditional charsets for symbols that do not belong to the genomic charset (A, G, C, T) and to our efficient encoding for DNA nucleotides. Lengths of genomic charset codewords is static variable-length in range of 1–3 bits long. We have implemented our encoding technique on top of HTTP for its universality and flexibility on various platforms. We are not aware of any other data-aware protocols that exploits redundancy in genomic data for efficient transmission. This VTTP is an improvement over our earlier work that used fixed-length codewords for genomic symbols i.e. 2-bit long for each character [3].

1.2 Paper Organization

The goal of this paper is design and implementation of a data-aware transfer protocol called VTTP. We implement VTTP by modifying the HTTP content encoding approach to transfer a big genomic dataset. We compare our results with traditional HTTP, FTP and BitTorrent like transfer protocols to transfer large genomic data sets.

The paper is organized as follows: Sect. 2 presents a short background of this work. Section 3 provides a summary of the related works that are used as a baseline for our implementation. Section 4 discusses the overall architecture of the proposed protocol and model description and formulation. Experimental results of the baseline and the proposed content encoding approaches are presented in Sect. 5. HTTP behaviors using the 2 mentioned encoding schemes are discussed in Sect. 5. Finally, we discuss future work and our conclusions in Sect. 6.

2 Background

2.1 Networking

There are two conceptual models for network transfer protocols in the network literature called open system interconnection (OSI) model [25] (7 layers) and the transmission control protocol/ Internet protocol (TCP/IP), or defense advanced research projects agency (DARPA) model (4 layers) [22]. A simple scenario to transfer data between a server and client starts by generating data via an application layer to next (transport) layer using different protocols such as HTTP [8] and FTP [18]. Transport layer establishes a connection between the server and client through 2 main protocols that are transmission control protocol (TCP) [17] and user datagram protocol (UDP) [15]. Transport layer protocols pass data packets to the Internet layer that accomplish many functions. The protocols accomplish these functions such as packet routing using Internet protocol (IP) that put packets on network mediums such as WI-FI in the network interface layer. The normal HTTP is data-oblivious and hence cannot take advantage of redundant data or data with a limited global set. HTTP currently utilizes a fixed length binary encoding that converts each incoming symbol into fixed 8-bits even when the data can be encoded in fewer bits [13]. HTTP transfers data via locating data sources and encoding, after which it compresses and transfer data over network medium. This paper introduces a new content encoding scheme for the HTTP using a variable-length binary encoding that converts genomic symbols into fewer bits and makes it an efficient approach for big genomic data called VTTP.

2.2 HTTP Compression Algorithms

Data compression converts a certain input file into a smaller file size with compressed (low-redundancy) data. There are two main types of data compression: lossy and lossless. Lossless compression used by HTTP protocol are: compress [19], deflate [6], and gzip [7]. Compress is a file compression program that was originally developed under UNIX environment and uses LZW algorithm [24]. Deflate algorithm combines 2 other algorithms: Huffman coding [11] and Lempel-Ziv (LZ-77) [26] algorithms. GZIP is an open source compression technique that relies on LZ-77 algorithm. LZ-77 algorithm works by replacing repeated occurrences of symbols with their references that indicate length and location of that string which occurred before and can be presented in the tuple (offset, length, symbol). The basic performance metric for compression algorithms is a compression ratio, which refers to the ratio of the original to the compressed data size [20] as shown in the Eq. 1:

$$Compression\ ratio = \frac{compressed(output)data}{uncompressed(input)data} \tag{1}$$

For example, an 0.3 ratio means that the data occupies 30 % of its original size after compression (positive compression). Whereas, a 1.2 ratio means that the output file size (after compression) is larger than the original file (negative compression). There are 2 important factors that impact the compression ratio: symbol *occurrences* and alphabet *scope*. We will use a GZIP as a baseline of compression technique for this implementation because it is a standard, fast and universal and is used by most of today's browsers.

2.3 Binary Encoding Schemes

In general, binary representations can be divided into 2 categories: *fixed* length binary encoding (FLBE) and *variable* length binary encoding (VLBE). The next subsections summarize these binary representations and highlights the pros and cons of each.

Fixed Length Binary Encoding. The FLBE scheme, also called singular encoding, converts the alphabet symbols into a fixed number of output bits such as in ASCII code 8 bits long for each codeword [12]. For instance, an alphabet of 3 symbols *a, b, c* needs 2-bit fixed length codes for each symbol such as c(a) = 00, c(b) = 01, c(c) = 10 codewords, where *c* refers to coding. Based on the previous example, codeword length can be formatted by LogN-bit for N symbols alphabet. The main advantage of this scheme is both the client and server have prior knowledge of each symbol codeword length and is simple to implement. The disadvantage is that more number of bits are needed than are actually required, wasting precious bandwidth resources.

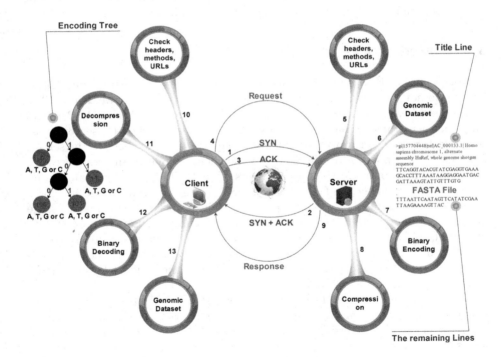

Fig. 1. Client-Server model for the HTTP protocol including our proposed encoding scheme. Also, FASTA file format that consists of 2 main parts: title and data lines.

Variable Length Binary Encoding. A VLBE sometimes called uniquely decodable and non-singular code that converts n alphabet symbols λ_n into variable-length codewords, such as $\lambda_i \neq \lambda_j$ for all i and j symbols [10]. For example, the alphabet of 3 symbols i.e. a, b, c, can be encoded (E) in 3 unique variable-length codewords, such that $E(a) = 0$, $E(b) = 11$, $E(c) = 100$. The variable length encoding assigns short codes to more symbol repetitions and long codes to less frequent repetitions similar to Huffman coding. Also, VLBE codes the alphabet symbols in a way that assures that each codeword is unique for a given data as an above example. The major advantage of the VLBE is saving space (or bit that needs to be transferred) that positively reflect on the transfer time if employed for data transportation. VLBE has the disadvantage of creating random encoding tables when data needs to be transferred in real-time which makes its implementation rather cumbersome and need extra processing by both the client and the server. However, we show the VTTP, which is based on VLBE, is much more efficient for transmission of genomic datasets and is shown to be 84 times faster than regular HTTP even with extra computational costs associated with VLBE. Binary tree structure is used in this implementation to simplify a binary encoding/decoding table representation [16]. By convention, the left child is labeled 0 and the right child is labeled 1 as shown in Fig. 1.

3   Related Works

Protocols such as HTTP and FTP are techniques for general purpose data transfer and do not modify their behavior with the contents of the data. The HTTP, is a request/response protocol located in the first layer of the TCP/IP model (application), transfers data among web applications i.e. client(s)-server [9] as shown in Fig. 1. HTTP works via sending a request from the client to the server, followed by a response from the server to the client. Requests and responses are represented in a simple ASCII format (8 bits). The HTTP request contains many elements: a method such as GET, PUT, POST, etc. and a uniform resource locator (URL). Also, HTTP request/response contains information such as message headers, and compression algorithm (content encoding) along with needed data by the client. The server handles the request, then responds according to the specified method. After that, the server sends a response to the client, including the status code indicating whether the request succeeded, along with the reason(s), if any.

FTP is an application layer protocol of the TCP/IP that transfers files between 2 machines only i.e. client-server. FTP works via sending a request from the client to the server along with a valid username and password. FTP needs two connection lines: one for commands called control connection and another one to transfer data itself called data connection. In FTP, data compression occurs during the transfer phase using a deflate compression algorithm via MODE Z command [4]. We implement our encoding method on top of HTTP due to its versatility, friendly interface, its usage in one-to-many/many-to-many modes and security properties of HTTP that are absent in FTP [23].

4   Proposed Model of HTTP Content Encoding

In this section, we illustrate our implementation of VTTP that utilizes VLBE for content encoding. Model formulations are also discussed for different possible scenarios of symbol repetitions to compare our proposed encoding to the current method used in HTTP encoding:

4.1   Model Description

This subsection presents our implementation of HTTP that relies on VLBE content encoding to transfer big genomic datasets. This model assigns short variable codewords for genomic symbols. The fact that a genomic alphabet consists of only 4 symbols A, G, C, T makes it an ideal candidate for VLBE encoding and can be represented in less than 8-bits. We can encode the genomic dataset symbols in 4 unique decipherable codewords i.e. [0, 11, 100, 101] or simply [0, 3, 4, 5] as shown in Figs. 1 and 2. HTTP in most browsers, starts when client searches for specific data, the HTTP client side initiates a connection with the server that contains the required data. The connection between the client and the server establishes a 3-way handshake using the TCP/IP protocol. After establishing the connection, the client sends a request for certain dataset(s) to the server that checks the header(s), the method(s), and the resource address(es). The server retrieves the required data and starts to convert file symbols to binary form using a VLBE and passes it to a compression technique (GZIP in this implementation). FASTA file for a single sequence is described by a title line followed by one or more data lines. The title line begins with a right angle bracket followed by a label. The label ends with the first white space character. The data lines begin right after the title line and contain the sequence characters in order as shown in Fig. 1. At this point we read the first line of the FASTA file [5] using ASCII character set and the remaining lines are read using VTTP. The server starts encoding using the VLBE character set, compresses via GZIP and transfers the data (response) through network medium. The compressed data is received by the client along with header(s) and method(s) to store it. Client starts decompress the received data using GZIP to obtain the binary form.

We utilize a binary tree as a structure to represent our VLBE because it is faster to search, avoids duplicate values, and easy to decode at a receiver side. Assuming we have a file of 18 symbols with different symbol repetitions: a_1 appears in a frequency rate of 61 %, a_2 has a repetition rate of 17 %, and 11 % for both a_3 and a_4 as shown in Fig. 2. In this example, the file has redundancy and VLBE works by assigning a variety of bit lengths reaching 1 bit per symbol (bps). There are 3 possible code lengths for the symbol a_1 in this example as appears in Fig. 2. As can be seen it still produces better results in contrast to the FLBE. Therefore, encoding 18 symbols in 29 bits yields an average of 1.6 bits/symbol in VLBE as compared to 144 bits in current HTTP encoding. The 3 VLBE possibilities of this example show 3 different code lengths 29, 37 and 47-bit long. However, VLBE still assigns short codes for the whole string in contrast to FLBE for the real-time applications i.e. data transfer.

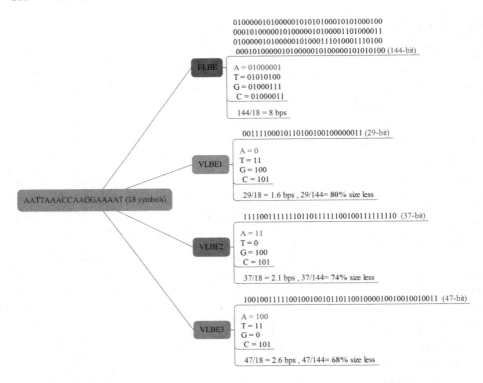

Fig. 2. Example of the HTTP content encoding schemes for a string of 18 symbols with variety of repetitions. 3 possible codes for the genomic symbols [A, T, G and C].

We designed variable codes in Fig. 2 in a way that makes it easy to decode using a prefix property (unambiguously). This property assigns a unique binary codeword for each single alphabet symbols to make decode operation easy in a client side. The variable length binary encoding has been used for static applications but transferring dynamic decoding trees has not been investigated.

Although the proposed VLBE does not guarantee minimal codewords for the data since the frequency of the data is not calculated (which is a compute intensive process for big data). However, it is expected that the proposed strategy will transfer data much more rapidly as compared to traditional HTTP protocol. For the current implementation, a 1-bit codeword length for a genomic symbol that has the highest occurrence (based on a local sample) and a 2-bit codeword length for a symbol with next largest repetition and 3-bit codeword length for the remaining two symbols. The pseudocode for our protocol can be seen in Algorithm 1.

4.2   Problem Formulation

Our analysis starts from the fact that in practical cases, the transfer time of data fluctuates due to several reasons such as bandwidth and message loss. The data

Algorithm 1. VLBE-based HTTP

```
 1: procedure ENCODING
 2:     if !inputStream.hasGenomicFileheader then
 3:         STOP (IS NOT Genomic File)
 4:     else
 5:         Encode the whole first line using a traditionalChar
 6:     end if
 7:     VLBE.writeGenomicSymbolsEncoder(outputStream)
 8:     while !inputStream.EOF do
 9:         if inputStream.GetChar() ∈ {A, T, G, C} then
10:             genomicChar ← inputStream.GetChar()
11:             code ← VLBE.encode(genomicChar)
12:         else
13:             traditionalChar ← inputStream.GetChar()
14:             code ← VLBE.encode(traditionalChar)
15:         end if
16:         oneByteStore.store(code)
17:         if oneByteStore.ISFull() then
18:             outputStream.write(oneByteStore)
19:             oneByteStore.empty()
20:         end if
21:     end while
22:     if !oneByteStore.ISEmpty() then
23:         outputStream.write(oneByteStore)
24:         outputStream.write(NumOfExtraBits)
25:     end if
26: end procedure
```

transfer throughput (Th) measured by the minimum time needed (t) to transfer certain data amount (N) from the sender to the receiver. In order to minimize transfer time, we need to either maximize the bandwidth (which costs more) or minimize data size (which will reduce overall resources and time) and is being pursued in this work. The transfer throughput can be formalized as follows:

$$Th = \frac{N}{t} \tag{2}$$

A higher Th means better protocol throughput via transferring large data amount in less time. Consequently, the protocol throughput increases when a bit per symbol (bps) is reduced as much as possible. For example, transferring N string symbols in B bits indicate efficiency of the encoding scheme as shown in:

$$bps = \frac{B}{N} \tag{3}$$

Here the minimum bps is better and hence shows a more time-efficient performance as compared to the original 8-bit transfers. The VLBE scheme utilizes all unused space in each single byte, which reduces the transfer time by decreasing data size in the next phases (compression, transfer, decompression, decoding to plain text). To simplify our model, lets assume we have an A alphabet as $\{a_1, a_2, a_3, ..., a_n\}$ that consists of n symbols, for the genomic dataset, $A \in \{A, T, G, C\}$(nucleotides). Codeword can be represented in $C(A) \in \{0,11,100,101\}$. The *time* complexity for encoding a string of N symbols using the HTTP fixed encoding is $O(N)$ and the *space* complexity S can be calculated in:

$$S_{http} = \sum_{i=1}^{n} a_i * 8 \tag{4}$$

The space complexity of our proposed encoding scheme can be formulated in:

$$S_{vlbe}(A) = \sum_{i=1}^{n} a_i * codeword_{length} \tag{5}$$

VTTP has a time complexity of $O(N/P)$, where P depends on the connection bandwidth and *bps*. Also, we can divide and formulate our model costs (C) into the following equations:

$$C_{total} = C_{computation} + C_{communication} \tag{6}$$

$$C_{computation} = O\left(C_{header\ check} + C_{encoding} + C_{compression} \right) \tag{7}$$

$$C_{communication} = O\left(C_{3\ way\ handshake} + C_{bandwidth} \right) \tag{8}$$

The Eqs. (6–8) show that the computational of VTTP consumes an extra time to encode symbols since it switches between two charsets during reading the file. However, it takes much less time in next steps shortening the transfer time many times.

5   Experimental Results

In this section we discuss FTP and HTTP behaviors using both the current (fixed) and the proposed (variable) length encoding schemes for a variety of genomic datasets. The examined datasets that are FASTA format files were downloaded through two sources: National Center for Biotechnology Information (NCBI) [1] and University of California Santa Cruz (UCSC) [2] websites as shown in a Table 1.

5.1   Experimental Setup

This paper compares the proposed VTTP with FTP, HTTP and BitTorrent-like transfers. Several datasets size up to 430 GB of FASTA files have been fed to these implementations to validate our approach. The experiments were performed on machines that have specifications shown in Table 2.

Table 1. Experimental datasets

IDs	Source	Size (KB)	Renamed
pataa	NCBI	563,318	1
refGeneexonNuc	UCSC	639,183	2
envnr	NCBI	1,952,531	3
hg38	UCSC	11,135,899	4
patnt	NCBI	14,807,918	5
gss	NCBI	30,526,525	6
estothers	NCBI	43,632,488	7
humangenomic	NCBI	45,323,884	8
othergenomic	NCBI	346,387,292	9

Table 2. Experimental setup

Specifications	Details
Processor	2.4 GHz Intel Core i7
Memory	8 GB 1600 MHz DDR3
Graphics	Intel HD Graphics 4000 1024 MB
Operating system	Windows 8.1 Pro
Download	87 Mb/s
Upload	40 Mb/s
Programming Language	C# .Net
Protocols	FTP, HTTP, BitTorrent and VTTP
Dataset sizes	550 MB – 340 GB

5.2 Results

Our experimental results as shown in Figs. 3 and 4, Tables 3 and 4 and compared with FTP and HTTP. As can be seen VLBE decrease the size of the data that needs to be transferred sharply and the corresponding decrease in the transfer time also decreases rapidly. As can be seen in the Tables 3 and 4; 1.20×10^5 millisecond (ms) are required to transfer 550 MB dataset using the traditional HTTP encoding, 3.82×10^4 ms via the FTP whereas 3.25×10^3 ms to transfer the same file via the HTTP-VLBE. This rate of transfer is about 37 times faster than HTTP-FLBE and about 12 times faster than FTP. Also, the 30 GB dataset was transferred in 7.20×10^6 ms using the HTTP, 6.31×10^6 ms by FTP whereas it only took 3.39×10^5 ms to transfer the file using VLBE. This is about 21 times faster than HTTP and 18 times faster than FTP. We show results for up to 340 GB. The average decrease in the size of the data sets as compared to HTTP and FTP is around 15 times. The corresponding decrease in the running time is 33 times faster as compared to HTTP and 16 times faster as compared to FTP over all data sets.

In order to compare the results of the proposed approach with that of existing BitTorrent protocol we implemented the latter approach as well. The results are shown in Fig. 4 for a 1 GB FASTA file that was downloaded from the NCBI website (Homo_sapiens.GRCH38.dna_sm_toplevel). Only 1 machine (server) is used to transfer the same file using VLBE while n machines are used to transfer file

Table 3. Size reduction of VTTP

Dataset	HTTP (KB)	FTP (KB)	VLBE (KB)
1	5.63 + 05	5.63 + 05	1.75 + 04
2	6.39 + 05	6.39 + 05	8.85 + 04
3	1.95 + 06	1.95 + 06	7.04 + 04
4	1.11 + 07	1.11 + 07	7.95 + 05
5	1.48 + 07	1.48 + 07	2.98 + 06
6	3.05 + 07	3.05 + 07	6.42 + 06
7	4.36 + 07	4.36 + 07	8.79 + 06
8	4.53 + 07	4.53 + 07	1.10 + 07
9	3.46 + 08	3.46 + 08	8.32 + 07

Table 4. Time acceleration of VTTP

Dataset	HTTP (ms)	FTP (ms)	VLBE (ms)
1	1.20 + 05	3.82 + 04	3.25 + 03
2	1.22 + 05	5.88 + 04	6.26 + 03
3	4.20 + 05	1.41 + 05	4.97 + 03
4	2.52 + 06	1.14 + 06	4.54 + 04
5	3.60 + 06	2.77 + 06	1.82 + 05
6	7.20 + 06	6.31 + 06	3.39 + 05
7	1.08 + 07	8.62 + 06	4.65 + 05
8	1.80 + 07	1.04 + 07	6.97 + 05
9	7.98 + 07	3.24 + 07	5.39 + 06

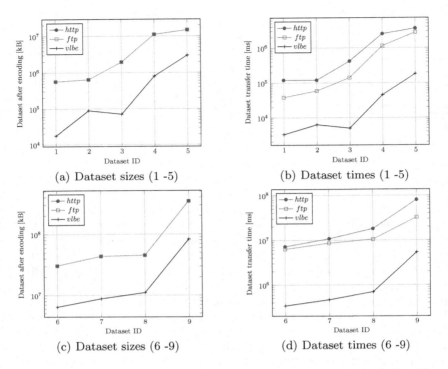

Fig. 3. Dataset transfer time and size comparisons for 9 genomic datasets $(1-9)$ over FTP, HTTP using both content-encoding FLBE and VLBE.

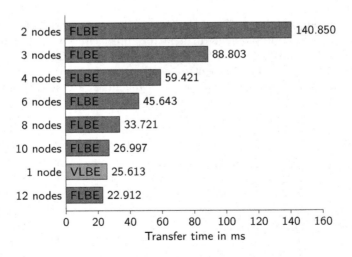

Fig. 4. Transfer time of 1 G FASTA dataset using (1) VLBE-based machine and up to (12) FLBE-based machines work in parallel.

utilizing HTTP over BitTorrent protocol. As expected, with increasing number of machines the time to transfer decrease sharply over BitTorrent. It can also be observed that the transfer time required for 1 GB of genomic file using our proposed protocol (VTTP) with using only 1 machine is approx. equivalent to 10 machines used in parallel using BitTorrent protocols. This is due to massive reduction in size due to our encoding strategy. The results are presented for 1 GB file only and the performance of VTTP is expected to increase with increasing size of the data due to increase in redundancy. Also note that employing VTTP for multiple machines will massively decrease the time needed to transfer a file of a give size.

6 Conclusion

This paper presents design and implementation of a data-aware variable-length text transfer protocol (VTTP) that works on top of HTTP. Our protocol exploits the fact that genomic data is limited in its alphabet and is largely redundant. This allow us to design a variable length encoding scheme which decreases the size of the genomic data that needs to transferred over the network significantly. Consequently, enormous reduction in the time is also observed as compared to traditional HTTP and FTP protocols. Our results also show that using the proposed encoding scheme the resulting protocol using a single machine is better than 10 machines that use traditional HTTP protocol to transfer genomic data.

Acknowledgment. This work was supported in part by the grant NSF CCF-1464268.

References

1. (02 2016). http://www.ncbi.nlm.nih.gov
2. (02 2016). http://www.ucsc.edu
3. Aledhari, M., Saeed, F.: Design and implementation of network transfer protocol for big genomic data. In: IEEE 4th International Congress on Big Data (BigData Congress 2015), June 2015
4. Bhushan, A.: File transfer protocol. The Internet Engineering Task Force (1972)
5. Chenna, R., Sugawara, H., Koike, T., Lopez, R., Gibson, T.J., Higgins, D.G., Thompson, J.D.: Multiple sequence alignment with the clustal series of programs. Nucleic Acids Res. **31**(13), 3497–3500 (2003)
6. Deutsch, L.P.: Deflate compressed data format specification version 1.3. The Internet Engineering Task Force (1996)
7. Deutsch, P.: Gzip file format specification version 4.3. The Internet Engineering Task Force (1996)
8. Fielding, R., Gettys, J., Mogul, J., Frystyk, H., Masinter, L., Leach, P., Berners-Lee, T.: Hypertext transfer protocol – http/1.1 (1999)
9. Forouzan, B.A.: TCP/IP Protocol Suite. McGraw-Hill, Inc., New York (2002)
10. Gilbert, E.N., Moore, E.F.: Variable-length binary encodings. Bell Syst. Tech. J. **38**(4), 933–967 (1959)

11. Huffman, D.: A method for the construction of minimum-redundancy codes. Proc. IRE **40**(9), 1098–1101 (1952)
12. Krakauer, L.J., Baxter, L.: Method of fixed-length binary encoding and decoding and apparatus for same (1989)
13. Mogul, J.C., Douglis, F., Feldmann, A., Krishnamurthy, B.: Potential benefits of delta encoding and data compression for http. SIGCOMM Comput. Commun. Rev. **27**(4), 181–194 (1997). http://doi.acm.org/10.1145/263109.263162
14. Néron, B., Ménager, H., Maufrais, C., Joly, N., Maupetit, J., Letort, S., Carrere, S., Tuffery, P., Letondal, C.: Mobyle: a new full web bioinformatics framework. Bioinformatics **25**(22), 3005–3011 (2009). http://www.ncbi.nlm.nih.gov/pmc/articles/PMC2773253/
15. Postel, J.: User datagram protocol. RFC 768, August 1980
16. Pajarola, R.: Fast prefix code processing. In: Proceedings of the International Conference on Information Technology: Coding and Computing [Computers and Communications], ITCC 2003, pp. 206–211. IEEE (2003)
17. Postel, J.: Transmission control protocol. The Internet Engineering Task Force (1981)
18. Postel, J., Reynolds, J.: File transfer protocol. The Internet Engineering Task Force (1985)
19. Rathore, Y., Ahirwar, M.K., Pandey, R.: A brief study of data compression algorithms. Int. J. Comput. Sci. Inf. Secur. **11**(10), 86 (2013)
20. Sayood, K.: Introduction to data compression. Newnes (2012)
21. Singh, E.: Sap hana platform for healthcare: Bringing the world closer to real-time personalized medicine, October 2013
22. Stevens, W.R.: TCP/IP Illustrated (vol. 1): The Protocols. Addison-Wesley Longman Publishing Co., Inc., Boston (1993)
23. Touch, J., Heidemann, J., Obraczka, K.: Analysis of http performance. ISI Research report ISI/RR-98-463, (original report dated August 1996), USC/Information Sciences Institute (1998)
24. Welch, T.A.: A technique for high-performance data compression. Computer **6**(17), 8–19 (1984)
25. Zimmermann, H.: OSI reference model—the ISO model of architecture for open systems interconnection. Innovations in Internetworking, pp. 2–9. Artech House Inc., Norwood (1988) http://dl.acm.org/citation.cfm?id=59309.59310
26. Ziv, J., Lempel, A.: A universal algorithm for sequential data compression. IEEE Trans. Inf. Theory **23**(3), 337–343 (1977)

Network Modeling

On the Evolution of Complex Network Topology Under Network Churn

Vasileios Karyotis$^{(\boxtimes)}$, Eleni Stai, and Symeon Papavassiliou

Institute of Communication and Computer Systems (ICCS)/NTUA,
Iroon Polytechniou 9, 15780 Athens, Greece
{vassilis,estai}@netmode.ntua.gr, papavass@mail.ntua.gr

Abstract. The future Internet is becoming more diverse, incorporating heterogeneous access networks. The latter are characterized by numerous devices that join/leave the network dynamically, creating intense churn patterns. New approaches to analyze and quantify churn-induced network evolution are required. In this paper, we address such need by introducing a new analysis framework that maps network evolution into trajectories in multi-dimensional vector spaces. Each network instance is characterized by a feature vector, indicating network properties of interest. To demonstrate the potentials of this approach, we exemplify and study the effect of edge churn on various complex topologies, frequently emerging in various communications environments. We investigate via simulation the impact of network evolution, by quantifying its effect on key network analysis metrics, such as the clustering coefficient and the plethora of centrality metrics, employed at large for analyzing topologies and designing applications. The proposed framework aspires to establish more holistic and efficient complex network control.

Keywords: Network evolution · Complex networks · Social network analysis metrics · Future Internet · Edge churn

1 Introduction

Future networks are expected to be highly heterogeneous, consisting of different complex topologies with diverse characteristics and behaviors. For example, 5G is expected to consist of a wired-wireless broadband core, while assuming wireless heterogeneous access networks at the periphery, characterized by numerous simple devices, e.g., Internet of Things (IoT) [1], fog networks [2], etc. Due to pushing cloud services towards the access network [2] and a multitude of factors, such as operational environment, user trends and device heterogeneity, it is anticipated that the on/off behavior (churn) of network nodes and corresponding communication links between them will become critical for the feasibility and scaling of future resource allocation/optimization mechanisms, signalling, etc.

© IFIP International Federation for Information Processing 2016
Published by Springer International Publishing Switzerland 2016. All Rights Reserved
L. Mamatas et al. (Eds.): WWIC 2016, LNCS 9674, pp. 227–240, 2016.
DOI: 10.1007/978-3-319-33936-8_18

For this reason, network evolution as a consequence of network churn[1], will be one of the key dynamic processes that will impact and possibly determine the success of future network design/planning efforts. Network design and optimization will need to take into account the anticipated churn rates in order to provide services at low cost and with predictable resource demands.

The impact of network churn on network structure, management and application services has been more or less neglected in the literature. Only a few scattered works have addressed it under targeted settings. The authors in [4] have focused on sensor network churn induced by energy depletion, addressing it via a queuing framework. Churn of users in online social networks, i.e., how users enter-leave the system have been studied in [5,6]. In [3] a mechanism for network robustness against node churn in single-hop wireless networks was developed, while [7] addressed the impact of node churn on malware spreading under random attacks. The scope of our work is broader, aiming at extending the study of churn-induced network evolution to arbitrary complex networks and eventually to more general churn mechanisms.

More specifically, in this paper, we first introduce a general analysis framework for evolving networks, and then use it to study the impact of churn on various complex network topologies that emerge as components in current and future networks. The proposed framework maps topology evolution into multi-dimensional vector trajectories and quantifies the similarity of different topologies. We analyze the impact of evolution on random, scale-free and small-world topologies via various graph metrics typically employed for social/complex network analysis, i.e., average values of node degree, path length, clustering coefficient and centrality measures, thus obtaining a clearer picture of the impact anticipated by network churn. The latter is considered in the form of random edge (link) churn and various types of preferential edge churn, namely churn based on degree, closeness and betweenness centrality metrics. We analyze the impact of churn on each topology and compare their evolution cumulatively, thus obtaining useful knowledge for efficient network design and planning.

The rest of this paper is structured as follows. Section 2 summarizes related work and background on complex networks, analysis metrics and churn, and explains the contribution of this paper. Section 3 introduces the proposed network evolution analysis framework, while Sect. 4 describes the considered edge churn processes. Section 5 provides extensive simulation results on synthetic complex network topologies analyzing the impact of churn on their evolution. Finally, Sect. 6 concludes the paper and provides directions for future research.

2   Network Evolution and Complex Network Analysis Metrics

2.1   Network Evolution and Churn

Networks in general, and computer networks in particular, are characterized by various forms of topological and operational evolution [8]. For instance, different

---

[1] Network churn is the process where users enter and leave a network modifying its topology in terms of nodes and/or links [3].

traffic patterns emerge as networks grow, or as user habits change over time. Network evolution can involve variations of nodes/users, or most frequently connection links (edge) variations. With respect to the latter, the authors in [9] proposed a continuum model for dynamic wireless networks, assuming that communications links change in a continuous fashion. They formulated network evolution through differential equations and obtained the long-term behavior of the average node degree. The work in [10] studied the evolution of real networks, implicitly focusing on power-law (scale-free) topologies, with respect to the metrics of the average path length, network diameter and node degree. The evolution was analyzed under the regime of network growth, which is realistic for commercial communications networks. In [11,12] network evolution models for wireless multihop networks were considered, and especially, a methodology for adding features typical of social networks (small-world characteristics, etc.) into multihop networks via network churn evolution mechanisms was proposed.

Compared to the above works addressing various facets of network evolution, our work attempts a more holistic consideration. More specifically, in contrast to [9], we consider more network analysis metrics and various complex network topologies for random and preferential edge churn. Like [10], we focus on the impact of churn on complex topologies that emerge at various capacities in real networks, but in a broader setting where more topologies and analysis metrics are considered. Finally, compared to [11,12], this paper focuses on studying how diverse topology transformations impact the network properties, rather than imposing specific churn-based network evolution as in [11,12]. In essense, this work aspires to pave the way for a more general topology control framework, by enabling controlled network evolution towards desired topologies, for arbitrary initial complex topologies and several analysis metrics, as each application setting specifies.

2.2   Complex and Social Network Analysis Metrics

Various metrics have been employed for complex and social network analysis. The most significant ones have been the node degree and the associated degree distribution, the average path length, the clustering coefficient (CC) and the variants of centrality measures [12,13]. Some of these metrics refer to network nodes independently, others to the overall network, and some to both. Thus, the CC and centrality can be defined for individual nodes and also computed as network averages. Node degrees refer to individual nodes, but the node degree distribution uniquely characterizes a specific type of network topology. The average path length is a network wide metric, as well.

The clustering coefficient is a measure of the degree to which nodes in a graph tend to cluster together. For a network node, the local CC is given by the number of links between the nodes within its neighborhood divided by the number of links that could possibly exist among them [12]. Centrality is a measure of node importance in a network. Since the latter is subjective in many application settings, there exist various centrality metrics, e.g., degree centrality (a normalized version of node degree), closeness centrality, betweenness centrality, eigenvector centrality, etc., [12]. In this paper we focus on degree, betweenness and closeness centrality metrics, but other variations/definitions of centrality can be used in a similar fashion. Node betweenness centrality is defined as a normalized sum of the percentages of the number of shortest paths between each pair of vertices that pass through that node. Various approaches have been employed for computing efficiently such type of centrality, including variants of its definition [14]. Node closeness centrality is typically defined as the normalized reciprocal of the sum of distances of a node from all other nodes in the network.

3 Analyzing Network Evolution with Network Feature Vector

Network topologies are typically represented as graphs bearing structural features, characteristic of the interactions among nodes/users. In this section, we introduce a framework for tracking and analyzing network evolution, based on the observation of graph properties and other metrics of interest.

For that, we define the notion of network feature vector. Assume a set of m parameters of interest of a network graph, each of which is denoted as $g_i, 1 \leq i \leq m$. The number m of available/employed network metrics can be arbitrary but finite, and mainly depends on the application setting and the objectives of network evolution analysis. For instance, the metrics mentioned in Sect. 2.2 are sufficient for an overall study of network evolution or node importance, while additional features are required for the study of resource allocation.

In the general case, the metrics can be split into node-oriented and edge-oriented. The first are characteristic of node properties, e.g., node centrality or node clustering coefficient. The second are characteristic of edge properties, e.g., edge weight distribution or average weight of the links, etc. Thus, the set of parameters employed can be split in two subsets, one with node-related features $\{g_i^{(n)}, 1 \leq i \leq m_1\}$ and a second with edge-related metrics $\{g_i^{(e)}, 1 \leq i \leq m_2\}$, $m_1 + m_2 = m$.

With this in mind we can define the *network feature vector*, consisting of all the employed network metrics:

$$\mathbf{g} = [\underbrace{g_1^{(n)} \; g_2^{(n)} \; \cdots \; g_{m_1}^{(n)}}_{\text{node-related features}} \, | \, \underbrace{g_1^{(e)} \; g_2^{(e)} \; \cdots \; g_{m_2}^{(e)}}_{\text{edge-related features}}]^T \qquad (1)$$

If the topology varies with time, at least some of the features will be time-varying and a time-dependence can be considered. In this paper, we will demonstrate the framework with a small number of parameters and we will not maintain the aforementioned distinction of features to node-related and edge-related. Thus, we will employ a more compact form of the feature vector $\mathbf{g}(t) = [g_1(t) \; g_2(t) \; \cdots \; g_m(t)]^T$. Also, for simplicity and without loss of generality, we will drop the time variable whenever the time-dependence is clear.

Through the feature vector $\mathbf{g}$, a specific network topology with its properties is mapped to a vector (point) in a metric space. As the topology evolves, so does the point in the metric space and the direction of the associated position vector $\mathbf{g}(t)$, i.e., the angle coordinates and measure of $\mathbf{g}(t)$ evolve in time. The dimension of the metric space, denoted as network feature space, depends on the number of network properties considered, so that different network feature spaces correspond to studying different properties of network evolution.

The time-varying feature vector can be used to assess the similarity of different topologies, namely quantify how "close" the final topology is to the initial, after a series of modifications. It can be also used to assess the similarity of different types of topologies. Since by the above mapping a topology snapshot corresponds to a point in space, various distance or similarity metrics can be employed to quantify the distance/similarity between topologies. In the special case that each component (metric) of the feature vector is independent of the rest, the network feature vector can be cast as a probability density function, and thus, in addition to distance/similarity, entropy-like measures can be employed as well [15]. With respect to the metrics employed in this work, and since the relation among them has not been absolutely clarified, we will employ only distance and similarity metrics.

Distance metrics are more adequate to quantify the "magnitude" of network evolution, corresponding to the magnitude change of the network feature vector. On the other hand, inner product metrics (e.g., cosine metric) depict the "direction" of change (e.g., if a network changes character drastically or to a lesser degree) corresponding to the directional change of the network feature vector.

In this paper, and in order to demonstrate the potentials of the topology evolution framework and the role of distance/similarity metrics, we will show one simple representative metric from each category. Specifically, we will employ the Euclidean distance and cosine metrics, to quantify the magnitude and direction of change, respectively, between two topology instances, $\mathbf{g}(t_1)$ and $\mathbf{g}(t_2)$:

$$d_e = \sqrt{\sum_{i=1}^{m} |g_i(t_1) - g_i(t_2)|^2} \tag{2}$$

$$s_c = \frac{\sum_{i=1}^{m} g_i(t_1)g_i(t_2)}{\sqrt{\sum_{i=1}^{m} g_i^2(t_1)}\sqrt{\sum_{i=1}^{m} g_i^2(t_2)}} \tag{3}$$

It should be noted that $\mathbf{g}(t)$ corresponds to the instance of a topology at time t, as explained above. $\mathbf{g}(t')$ denotes another instance, namely the evolution of the topology up to time $t' > t$. Furthermore, it is noted that since the Euclidean distance is a special case of the Minkowski distance family [15] and the cosine similarity a special case of the inner product family of similarities [15], the results provided are indicative of the trends one would obtain by any other member of the Minkowski and inner product families, apart from some scaling factors.

Another important observation refers to the dimension of the network feature space. It should be stressed that this is defined by the number of metrics employed in the feature vector definition and not the number of nodes in the network. The dimension of the feature vector (not its values) is independent from the size and order of the network graph.

One of the most fascinating potentials of the introduced network feature vector is the control capability over topology evolution. As explained above, different instances in time of an evolving topology correspond to a trajectory of a vector in a metric space. By properly defining a cost function of the form $J = h(\mathbf{g}(t_f), t_f) + \int_{t_0}^{t_f} k(\mathbf{g}(t), \mathbf{u}(t), t) dt$, where $[t_0, t_f]$ is the observation time interval, $h(\cdot), k(\cdot)$ properly defined continuous functions and $\mathbf{u}(t)$ a control function related to the real mechanics of network evolution that determines the evolution of the topology through the system of equation $\dot{\mathbf{g}}(t) = \mathbf{a}(\mathbf{g}(t), \mathbf{u}(t), t)$, where $\mathbf{a}(\cdot)$ determines the relation of the network feature vector with each control, one can potentially develop an optimal control problem on $\mathbf{g}(t)$ and exploit the constraints and controls for optimally balancing trade-offs relevant to network evolution and the benefit-cost relations of network processes emerging. The type of cost J, controls $\mathbf{u}(t)$ and relation between network feature vector-controls $\mathbf{a}(\cdot)$, are application/network dependent and define the type of control problem emerging. They also determine the required solution methodology to be employed.

In the following, we demonstrate the impact of edge churn on network topology, by exploiting the capabilities of the framework described above to quantify and provide intuition on the similarity between instances of an evolving topology and of different networks among them.

4 Network Churn and Network Evolution

In this work, we will focus on edge churn for relational complex networks, i.e., variation of links between nodes. In the latter, any link can be added or deleted (no constraint on link formation). Examples of such networks with edge churn are peer-to-peer and online social network, where users enter/leave the network arbitrarily and form relational links arbitrarily with other users. This would not be the case in lattice and random geometric networks, where spatial constraints would apply for the links that could be added/deleted. However, even in these cases, network evolution could be analyzed similarly. We restrict ourselves to relational graphs only in order to directly compare the results between them and focus on the churn effect, rather than take into account evolutionary features induced by the type of analyzed network.

We consider a generic edge churn mechanism and several variations of it, as described in the forthcoming subsection. Edge churn is a combined effect in complex networks, including environmental aspects (wireless access cases), user behavior (turning on/off devices), service patterns (connectionless, service-oriented, etc.). A general trend discovered in [10] is that of network "densification", i.e., edges are added with higher rate than edges deleted. Thus, we will also consider a slightly higher edge addition than deletion rate, reducing also in this way the probability of rendering the network topology disconnected. Furthermore, by considering the churn-based constructive nature of many complex networks, such as the ones included in this work (especially the scale-free and small-world ones), we further study the effect of edge churn mechanisms on their structure, thus obtaining clearer picture of its impact on their evolution, while exemplifying the proposed framework.

Edge churn is performed successively in multiple steps, in a constructive process [12]. We assume that at each step, only one of the sub-processes takes place, as described below:

- **Edge Addition:** With probability p, $0 \leq p \leq 1$, we add one new link to a selected pair of nodes that are not currently linked.
- **Edge Deletion:** With probability r, $0 \leq r \leq 1$, we delete one selected edge from an already connected node pair.
- **No Action:** With probability $1-p-r$, neither edge addition, nor edge deletion are performed.

Note that it should hold $p + r \leq 1$, i.e., the vector $[p \; r \; 1 - p - r]$ is a probability distribution over the above processes.

The selection mechanism for which edges to add/delete determines diverse edge churn types. We consider random edge churn (RC) that corresponds to selecting randomly and uniformly which edge to add/delete, as well as which process to perform. We also consider preferential edge churn, which selects nodes and edges for edge churn preferentially with respect to a selected feature (i.e., centrality metric). We consider three types of preferential edge churn. In the first, new edges are preferentially attached to nodes with high degree centrality and deleted from nodes with low degree centrality. The second and the third variants are similar, but instead of degree centrality, we use betweenness and closeness centrality correspondingly. Also, we examine the inverse of these edge churn types, i.e., the inverse of the first type corresponds to adding new edges preferentially to nodes with low degree centrality and deleting edges from nodes with high degree. The reason of applying such preferential attachment (PA) edge churn mechanisms is to study how network evolution based on a particular network feature (part of the network feature vector) impacts the other features and the behavior/structure of each network as a whole. It is also in line with network churn processes as the ones described above in peer-to-peer or online social networks, and IoT networks within the fog computing paradigm.

5   Numerical Evaluation

In this section, we exemplify the application of the proposed framework via numerical results obtained by simulating RC and PA edge churn in various complex networks. Initially, we explain the models for the complex networks employed and then present and analyze the obtained results.

5.1   Relational Complex Networks

We consider three different types of relational graphs, random graphs (RG), scale-free (SF) and small-world (SW). The simplest model of RG is the Gilbert $\mathcal{G}(N, p)$, where every possible edge occurs independently with probability

$0 < p < 1$. This is a model extensively used for peer-to-peer networks and other spontaneously forming networks. We consider the Erdős-Rényi (ER) model, $\mathcal{G}(N, E)$, where a graph is chosen uniformly at random from the collection of all graphs which have N nodes and E edges. If $pN^2 \to \infty$, then $\mathcal{G}(N, p)$ behaves fairly similarly to $\mathcal{G}(N, E)$ with $E = \binom{N}{2}p$, as N increases [12,13]. We choose E in the range of $\frac{N \log(N)}{2} < E < \frac{N(N-1)}{2}$. The lower bound ensures a connected topology, while the upper $\frac{N(N-1)}{2}$ signifies a massively dense network, i.e., a completely connected graph.

Scale-free (SF) is a type of network whose degree distribution follows a power-law. The fraction $P(k)$ of nodes having k connections to other nodes scales as $P(k) \sim k^{-\gamma}$, where $2 < \gamma < 3$ [12,13]. Many real-world networks such as the WWW and the router network of the Internet belong in this category. We consider the Barabasi-Albert (BA) model of scale-free networks, which generates random scale-free networks using the preferential attachment mechanism. If a network begins with an initially connected and d-regular network of m_0 nodes ($d < m_0$) and new nodes are added to the network one at a time, each new node will connect to $m \leq m_0$ existing nodes with a probability that is proportional to the degree of the latter. Such probability p_i that the new node connects to the existing node i is $p_i = \frac{k_i}{\sum_j k_j}$, where k_i is the degree of node i and the sum is over all pre-existing nodes j. Heavily linked nodes (hubs) tend to quickly accumulate even more links and usually have high betweenness and closeness centrality values.

Small-world (SW) is defined as a network where the typical distance L between two randomly chosen nodes grows proportionally to the logarithm of the number of nodes N, i.e., $L \propto \log N$ [12,13] and the clustering coefficient is high. Practically, nodes are linked with a small number of local neighbors. However, the average distance between nodes remains small, i.e., nodes are virtually close to each other. We consider the Watts-Strogatz (WS) model of SW. It starts from a regular lattice of degree d and randomly rewires each edge with a probability g_p, connecting nodes that are otherwise far apart with shortcuts. The initial lattice ensures high clustering coefficient, while a suitable number of shortcuts can further reduce the average path length. For comparison purposes, one should consider that RGs exhibit a small average shortest path length (varying typically as the logarithm of the number of nodes) along with small clustering. Examples include some types of smartgrids, telephone networks, etc.

5.2   Case Study of the Application of the Proposed Framework: Impact of Edge Churn on Complex Networks

In this subsection we investigate via simulations the impact of edge churn on complex network evolution. We performed them in MATLAB, averaging over 50 topologies for each considered scenario. The feature vector consists of the following features, in this order: average degree centrality (normalized average node degree), average path length, average clustering coefficient, average betweenness centrality, average closeness centrality, where averaging is performed for all network nodes. We consider $N = 100$ nodes for all topologies, $E = 2000$ edges for ER-RGs, initial d-regular lattice with $d = 10$ for BA-SF and initial lattice with $d = 10$ and a rewire probability $g_p = 0.25$ for WS-SW networks. Edge addition takes place with probability 0.60, and edge deletion with probability 0.40.

Impact of Edge Churn on Each Type of Network. In this subsection, we study how the use of the introduced network feature vector can aid at tracking and visualization of the evolution of several types of networks when random and preferential edge churn takes place. The results are shown in Figs. 1, 2 and 3, where edge churn takes place in an initial RG, SF and SW topology correspondingly. For visualization purposes, we divide the set of features in two subsets one including the degree, clustering coefficient and average path length and the other all the centrality metrics (degree, betweenness and closeness). The subfigure (a) of each figure corresponds to the first subset and the subfigure (b) to the second. The vectors with only a graph type indication in the legend correspond to the features' values in the initial topology, while the vectors having also an edge churn mechanism indication in the legend correspond to the final topology after the application of the edge churn.

From Fig. 1, we observe that an RG is not significantly affected by edge churn, either PA-based or random, as it is intuitively expected. The final vectors remain very close to the initial ones for RG for all types of churn. The churn type (e.g., random, preferential) does not seem to affect the final vector, which differs from the initial one mainly due to the increase of the average node degree, as an outcome of network densification. This behavior is intuitively expected for RGs, since due to the random nature of the initial network, even preferential additions/deletions eventually behave similarly to random ones. Given the rest of random connections, the ones added/deleted do not alter considerably the initial structure of the RG.

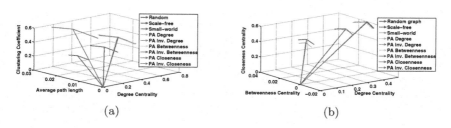

| (a) | (b) |

Fig. 1. Illustration of the proposed framework when edge churn with diverse attachment types is applied to an initial random graph.

From Fig. 2, we observe that an evolved SF network under all types of edge churn examined, eventually moves closer to an RG, as the node degree increases due to network densification (nodes with low degree in the initial SF structure also obtain edges) and so does the clustering coefficient. Note that the SF topology has the lowest clustering coefficient compared to the RG and SW ones. The final topologies under PA edge churn based on degree and betweenness centrality distinguish themselves among the rest by staying closer to the initial SF topology, while the second also moves closer to the SW topology, as shown more clearly in Fig. 2(a).

For an initial SW topology under edge churn (Fig. 3), we can make similar observations as in Fig. 2, as the network feature vector moves towards the one corresponding to an RG. However, the final topology under preferential edge churn based on betweenness centrality distinguishes itself among the rest by staying closer to the SW feature vector. Thus, such illustrations of the network evolution reveal important observations for maintaining a non-random network structure, e.g., for SF and SW. For the first, in order to maintain a completely non-random structure, node degree and betweenness centrality should be prevented from changing significantly. For the SW network only betweenness centrality should be prevented from drastic modification.

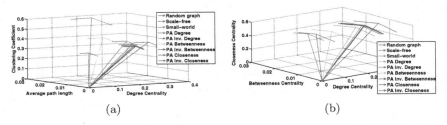

(a)   (b)

Fig. 2. Illustration of the proposed framework when edge churn with diverse attachment types is applied to an initial scale-free graph.

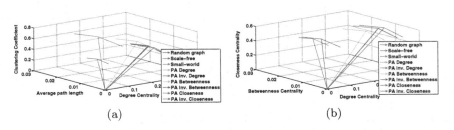

(a)   (b)

Fig. 3. Illustration of the proposed framework when edge churn with diverse attachment types is applied to an initial small-world graph.

Comparative Analysis of Churn Types on Complex Relational Topologies. In this subsection, we compare the evolved complex topologies with the initial ones, in terms of the distance and similarity metrics. In the following table pairs, the left-hand corresponds to the (Euclidean) distance metric between the pure topologies (not evolved) indicated in each row and the final topologies derived by the initial topologies indicated in columns. The right-hand table corresponds to the (cosine) similarity metric. As an example, the entry in row 1 and column 1 of Table 1 corresponds to the distance between the feature vector of a pure RG (row) and the feature vector of an evolved RG topology (column) under RC. The observations follow the lines of the ones made in Sect. 5.2.

Tables 1 and 2 present the distance and similarity of the evolved topologies for random edge churn compared to the initial ones. Similarly, table pairs: Tables 3–4, 5–6, 7–8, present the distance and similarity of the evolved topologies compared to the initial ones for the PA edge churn based on degree, closeness and betweenness centralities, respectively.

For random edge churn, the most important observations are that it has almost no impact on RG topologies, lesser (and small) impact on SF and noteworthy impact on SW (which move closer to RG topologies). This is expected since random edge modification are not expected to affect an already random network. However, they are expected to have some effect on a SW, where the few shortcuts may be modified and thus affect its structure.

A similar but modified trend is emerging in preferential based edge churn. Evolved RGs are not affected notably by any type of preferential edge churn and always remain close enough to the features of the initial random graph. Evolved SFs and SWs after PA edge churn based on degree and closenness centralities become almost RGs as their distance to a pure RG network decreases and their similarity increases. This is counter-intuitive for SF graphs when considering PA edge churn based on degree centrality, however edges are added and deleted probabilistically, although preferentially, while the characterization of the network is now more holistic based on a set of features and not on specific features. Notably SF modified via PA edge churn based on betweenness centrality maintains its pure graph's properties as shown in Tables 7 and 8 and also observed in the previous subsection. The same observation is true for the evolved SW graph although to a lesser degree. Note that more specific observations targeted to the extent of change of each topology can be made by comparing the absolute values of the distances.

Another general observation is that with respect to distance, SF-SW networks are relatively close and RG is farther away from them in the 5-dimensional network feature space considered. This is also expected since several features of SW networks are also present in SF graphs [12,13], which is also illustrated in the plots of the previous subsection. All the above observations can be exploited for advanced network design and optimization. By taking into account the anticipated network changes due to edge churn, network planning will be more realistic, and more accurate optimization can be achieved.

Table 1. Distance comparison for random churn.

Pure \ Fin.	RG	SF	SW
RG	0.1195	0.2333	0.1643
SF	0.3936	0.1068	0.1389
SW	0.4133	0.4602	0.4262

Table 2. Similarity comparison for random churn.

Pure \ Fin.	RG	SF	SW
RG	0.9979	0.9816	0.9923
SF	0.9541	0.9875	0.9855
SW	0.9013	0.8378	0.8618

Table 3. Distance comparison for preferential churn (degree-based).

Pure \ Fin.	RG	SF	SW
RG	0.1882	0.0997	0.0581
SF	0.4593	0.2055	0.2752
SW	0.4353	0.3251	0.3424

Table 4. Similarity comparison for preferential churn (degree-based).

Pure \ Fin.	RG	SF	SW
RG	0.9954	0.9945	0.9977
SF	0.9466	0.9837	0.9728
SW	0.9067	0.9225	0.9183

Table 5. Distance comparison for preferential churn (closeness-based).

Pure \ Fin.	RG	SF	SW
RG	0.1881	0.0767	0.0521
SF	0.4599	0.2041	0.2733
SW	0.4377	0.3734	0.3475

Table 6. Similarity comparison for preferential churn (closeness-based).

Pure \ Fin.	RG	SF	SW
RG	0.9955	0.9983	0.9981
SF	0.9463	0.9811	0.9728
SW	0.9055	0.8967	0.8967

Table 7. Distance comparison for preferential churn (betweenness-based).

Pure \ Fin.	RG	SF	SW
RG	0.1873	0.2130	0.1875
SF	0.4567	0.1833	0.3261
SW	0.4292	0.2468	0.2372

Table 8. Similarity comparison for preferential churn (betweenness-based).

Pure \ Fin.	RG	SF	SW
RG	0.9953	0.9699	0.9783
SF	0.9474	0.9840	0.9647
SW	0.9094	0.9566	0.9646

6   Conclusions

In this work, we demonstrated a framework for quantifying network evolution and similarity based on the mapping of a set of network parameters on points of a vector space. It allows to track network evolution by observing the trajectory of the network feature vector, which can include different graph features, and thus accommodate various applications. Consequently, it is a very flexible, yet descriptive framework for analysis and study of network evolution. In this work, we further demonstrated the potentials of the proposed framework by analyzing edge churn for various complex networks of relational type, namely random, scale-free and small-world. The outcomes are in accordance with observed trends and can be used for advanced network design/optimization.

In the future, we plan to demonstrate the full spectrum of potentials by extending the proposed framework to a topology control one. By proper definition of a cost function, optimal control theory can be used to drive the network feature vector to desired values, thus allowing modifying one type of network to another based on feasible trade-offs and precise specifications.

Acknowledgment. E. Stai gratefully acknowledges the Foundation for Education and European Culture (IPEP) for financial support.

References

1. Al-Fuqaha, A., Guizani, M., Mohammadi, M., Aledhari, M., Ayyash, M.: Internet of things: a survey on enabling technologies, protocols, and applications. IEEE Commun. Surv. Tutorials **17**(4), 2347–2376 (2015)
2. Bonomi, F., Milito, R., Zhu, J., Addepalli, S.: Fog computing and its role in the internet of things. In: Proceedings of 1st Workshop on Mobile Cloud Computing (MMC), pp. 13–16 (2012)
3. Holzer, S., Pinkolet, Y.A., Smula, J., Wattenhofer, R.: Monitoring churn in wireless networks. Elsevier J. Theo. Comput. Sci. **453**, 29–43 (2012)
4. Kar, K., Krishnamurthy, A., Jaggi, N.: Dynamic node activation in networks of rechargeable sensors. In: Proceedings of 24th Annual Joint Conference of IEEE Computer and Communications Societies (INFOCOM), vol. 3, pp. 1997–2007 (2003)
5. Stutzbach, D., Rejaie, R.: Understanding churn in peer-to-peer networks. In: Proceedings of 6th ACM SIGCOMM Conference on Internet Measurement (IMC), pp. 189–202 (2006)
6. Karnstedt, M., Hennessy, T., Chan, J., Basuchowdhuri, P., Hayes, C., Strufe, T.: Churn in social networks. In: Furht, B. (ed.) Handbook of Social Network Technologies and Applications, pp. 185–220. Springer, Heidelberg (2010)
7. Karyotis, V., Papavassiliou, S.: Macroscopic malware propagation dynamics for complex networks with churn. IEEE Commun. Lett. **19**(4), 577–580 (2015)
8. Dorogovtsev, S.N., Mendes, J.F.F.: Evolution of Networks: From Biological Nets to the Internet and WWW. Oxford University Press, Oxford (2013)
9. Papavassiliou, S., Zhu, J.: A continuum theory based approach to the modeling of dynamic wireless sensor networks. IEEE Commun. Lett. **9**(4), 337–339 (2005)
10. Leskovec, J., Kleinberg, J., Faloutsos, C.: Graphs over time: densification laws, shrinking diameters and possible explanations. In: Proceedings of the ACM SIGKDD (2005)
11. Stai, E., Karyotis, V., Papavassiliou, S.: Topology enhancements in wireless multihop networks: a top-down approach. IEEE Trans. Parallel Distrib. Syst. **23**(7), 1344–1357 (2012)
12. Karyotis, V., Stai, E., Papavassiliou, S.: Evolutionary Dynamics of Complex Communications Networks. CRC Press, New York (2013)

13. Newman, M.E.J.: The structure and function of complex networks. SIAM Rev. **45**, 167–256 (2003)
14. Brandes, U.: On variants of shortest-path betweenness centrality and their generic computation. Soc. Netw. **30**(2), 136–145 (2008)
15. Cha, S.-H.: Comprehensive survey on distance/similarity measures between probability density functions. Int. J. Math. Models Meth. App. Sci. **1**(4), 300–307 (2007)

A Reputation-Based Coalition Game to Prevent Smart Insider Jamming Attacks in MANETs

Taiwo Oyedare[(✉)], Ashraf Al Sharah, and Sachin Shetty

Department of Electrical and Computer Engineering,
Tennessee State University, Nashville, TN 37209, USA
{toyedare,aalshara,sshetty}@tnstate.edu

Abstract. Mobile Adhoc Networks (MANET) are susceptible to jamming attacks which can inhibit data transmissions. There has been considerable work done in the detection of external jamming attacks. However, detection of insider jamming attack in MANET has not received enough attention. The presence of an insider node that has constantly monitored the network and is privy to the network secrets can acquire sufficient information to cause irreparable damage. In this paper we propose a framework for a novel reputation-based coalition game between multiple players in a MANET to prevent internal attacks caused by an erstwhile legitimate node. A grand coalition is formed which will make a strategic security defense decision by depending on the stored transmission rate and reputation for each individual node in the coalition. Our results show that the simulation of the reputation-based coalition game would help improve the network's defense strategy while also reducing false positives that results from the incorrect classification of unfortunate legitimate nodes as insider jammers.

Keywords: Coalition · Reputation · Insider jamming · Transmission rate

1 Introduction

Mobile Ad-hoc Network (MANET) is a group of self-organized, infrastructure-less mobile nodes that relies on interdependence and cooperation of all nodes to carry out critical network functions. MANETs are vulnerable to jamming attacks due to the shared nature of the wireless medium. There are two main categories of jamming attacks: external jamming and insider jamming[1]. External jamming attacks are launched by foreign devices that are not privy to network secrets such as the network's cryptographic credentials and the transmission capabilities of individual nodes the network [1]. These types of attacks are relatively easier

---

[1] Insider jamming is also known as internal jamming.

© IFIP International Federation for Information Processing 2016
Published by Springer International Publishing Switzerland 2016. All Rights Reserved
L. Mamatas et al. (Eds.): WWIC 2016, LNCS 9674, pp. 241–253, 2016.
DOI: 10.1007/978-3-319-33936-8_19

to counter through some cryptography based techniques, some spread spectrum methodology[2], Antenna Polarization and directional transmission methods [3].

Smart insider jamming attacks on the other hand are much more sophisticated in nature because they are launched from a compromised node.[3] The attacker exploits the knowledge of network secrets to deceptively target critical network functions. In order to effectively prevent the smart insider jamming attack, we adopt a reputation mechanism to detect the presence of smart jammer nodes when they are passively eavesdropping and collecting information about the network prior to launching the jamming attack. A lower reputation threshold is set such that the jammer would not be able to successfully jam the network without being detected by its neighbors. In this paper, we propose a reputation-based coalition game to prevent an attack that could be posed by an erstwhile legitimate node. Game theoretic based approaches for mitigating attack can be seen in the works of [4] where a coalition game with cooperative transmission was implemented as a cure for the curse of boundary nodes in selfish packet-forwarding. Alibi-based protocol [5] and self-healing protocol [6] have been used to either detect or recover from a jamming attack. Our reputation-based coalition game differs from the aforementioned approaches by (1) Designing a coalition formation algorithm, (2) Maintaining the coalition via a reputation mechanism, (3) Identifying the insider jammer based on reputation score, and (4) Excluding the attacker from the coalition by rerouting transmission path and randomly modifying communication channel. The game is fully distributed and does not rely on any trusted central entity to operate at optimal performance.

The remainder of this paper is organized as follows. Section 2 we present relevant works that are closely related to our model; in Sect. 3 we present the network and jammer model; Sect. 4 contains the proposed defense model and in Sect. 5 we show our simulation results and finally in Sect. 6 we conclude the work and highlight prospective future work.

2   Related Work

Researchers have devoted great efforts on security in MANET. In [7] and [8], the authors used watchdog/pathrater and collaborative reputation (CORE) mechanisms respectively to prevent to mitigate node misbehavior in MANETs. Other works have used non-cooperative games to model security scenarios as well as the corresponding defense strategies to such attacks [9]. Most of these works focused on two player games where all legitimate nodes are modelled as a single node and attacker nodes are also modeled as a single node as well; this is only valid for centralized networks, whereas MANETs are self-organized networks.

Some researchers have also used coalition game to ensure security in MANETs. Li et al. [6] designed a self-healing wireless networks under insider

---

[2] Spread spectrum techniques include Frequency-Hopping Spread Spectrum (FHSS) and Direct Sequence Spread Spectrum (DSSS) [2].

[3] Smart insider jammers are capable of passively scanning the network and then launching an attack based on the information gotten.

jamming attacks. The concept of a pairwise key mentioned in their design shows that the design works best in a centralized system and not a self-organized system like MANETs. Some other works have only focused on node selfishness and not on intentional malicious acts or jamming attacks. Zhu et al. [4] used coalition game in which boundary nodes used cooperative transmission to help backbone nodes in the middle of the network and in return the backbone nodes would be willing to forward the boundary nodes' packets.

Our approach is unique in that (1) we refrain from treating the nodes in a collective manner, instead we consider them as individual node by defining a security characteristic function for the coalition formation (2) we use reputation mechanism to prevent false positives (3) we kept a history of the nodes' transmission rates (4) we successfully identify the insider jammer and excluded it from the coalition.

3   Network and Jammer Model

3.1   Network Model

Our network model involves a characteristic function and a coalition formation model. This model is similar to related efforts [10–13]. It departs from the related efforts in the usage of accumulative feedback adaptation transmission rate (AFAT) [14] in the coalition formation; use of maximum transmission rate in security characteristic function; and the necessary conditions needed for the grand coalition formation.

Coation Formation Model. According to [11], a coalition game is an ordered pair $\langle N, v \rangle$ where $N = (1, .., n)$ is the set of players[4] and v is the characteristic function.[5] By convention, $v(\phi) = 0$, where ϕ denotes the empty set [11].

The coalition formation process starts with nodes forming small disjoint coalition with neighboring nodes in their range of transmission and then gradually grows until the grand coalition is formed with the testimony of intersecting nodes. Such an intersecting node will serve as the referee for a new node that seeks to join the coalition. Our coalition formation process depends on the transmission rate table that has been stored according to the previous work done by [14].

In [14], we proposed an accumulative feedback adaptation transmission rate (AFAT). AFAT is a decentralized approach to ensure the communication of transmission rates between neighboring nodes in a network. The knowledge of neighbor's transmission rates helps a node to adjust its own rate accordingly. In other words, AFAT provides the maximum transmission rates for the nodes in order to meet the specific application bandwidth requirements. According to AFAT, the transmission rates of the nodes is adjusted based on the history of

---

[4] Any subset of N is called a coalition, and the set involving all players is called the grand coalition.

[5] The characteristic function $v: 2^N \rightarrow R$ assigns any coalition $C \subseteq N$ a real number $v(C)$, which is called the worth of coalition C.

neighbors' transmission rates. A list of the transmission rates has been built into the transmission rate table and is updated during every time instant.

The final outcome of the coalition formation process is to form a stable grand coalition which comprises of all nodes in the network. The intersecting nodes would be very key to the formation of the grand coalition because they belong to the smaller coalitions that would be merged into a single coalition.

There are N nodes in the network, for any coalition, $C \epsilon 2^N$ [6] As mentioned previously, many literature [11,12] have made use of the characteristic function in modeling a coalition game. This function helps to calculate the payoff of individual nodes such that they can see their joining the coalition as a rational decision since rationality is a key assumption in game theory.[7]

A node has neighbors in its transmission range that can testify about its cooperation based on the transmission rate table updated at every time-slot. This testimony means that these neighboring node can give a firsthand information about the node when queried. Let $|G_i|$ be the set of neighboring nodes in the transmission range of node i, therefore, at time slot t, the support rate for a node i in a coalition C, is:

$$S_t(C) = |G_i| - 1 \tag{1}$$

The transmission rate, $T_t(C)$, of coalition C at time, t, is another important parameter in the characteristic function, Li et al. [12] on the other hand made use of the overlapping distance. The nodes' sharing of their transmission rate is very key to their admittance into the small coalition. In other to form a coalition with any node, there is a need to know the maximum available transmission rate. The maximum transmission rate ensures that the nodes match with the best nodes in terms of transmission rate before settling for the next best option as seen in the coalition formation algorithm. The maximum transmission rate in a coalition C is given by:

$$D_t(C) = max\{T_t(C)\} \tag{2}$$

According to [12] the maximal admitting probability is given by:

$$A_t(C) = max_{j\epsilon C}\{\frac{\sum_{i\epsilon C} P_{ij}}{|C|} | C = \{i | i\epsilon C, i \neq j, P_{ij} \neq 0\}\} \tag{3}$$

Incorporating these three parameters we can write the characteristic function by weighing each parameter. The characteristic function proposed is then;

$$v_t(C) = \begin{cases} 0, & \text{if } |C| = 1 \\ \alpha S_t(C) + \beta A_t(C) + \gamma D_t(C), & \text{if } |C| \geq 1 \end{cases} \tag{4}$$

---

[6] The number of nodes in C is $|C|$.

[7] The security characteristic function's key parameters, support rate, maximum transmission rate and maximal admitting probability, captures the node mobility in the MANET, a property not included in [11,12]. The support rate is the neighbors in the node's transmission range. The maximum transmission rate in the coalition is provided by AFAT while the maximal admitting probability or cooperation probability is unchanged.

Table 1. A summary of notations provided for reference

Notation	Definition
N	Number of nodes in the network
C	Coalition of nodes
$G(i)$	Nodes in the transmission range of node i
$v_t(C)$	Security characteristic function for coalition C
$v(N)$	Payoff of the grand coalition
$S_t(C)$	Support rate for the coalition C
$T_t(C)$	Transmission rate of coalition C
$P_{i,j}$	Probability of cooperation of node i with node j
$A_t(C)$	Maximal admitting probability for coalition C
$x_t(i)$	Payoff share of node i
$R_{i,j}$	Reputation value of node i by node j
$R_{i,j}^*$	Previous reputation value of node i by node j
$R_{i,k}$	Reputation value of node i by node k
$v_{i,j}(y)$	Factor responsible for increasing reputation value
$k_{i,j}(m)$	Factor responsible for reducing reputation value
q_L, q_N, q_U	Lower, neutral and upper threshold value respectively
T_f, b_f	Tolerance factor of the network and broadcast factor
σ, λ	Rate of increase and decrease of reputation value respectively

These weight parameters α, β and γ can be used to provide variability for the characteristic function of the nodes. Due to the mobility factor in our model, it is important to keep track of the neighbors of any node at a given time, α helps to weigh the support rate parameter which is responsible for the number of neighbors of a node. Our assumption is that the nodes are slow-moving and there cannot be a rapid change of neighbors. β provides a weight value for the maximal admitting probability. The value assigned to β depends on the size of the coalition, if the coalition size is very big (say about 100 nodes), then it could be important to make it bigger than the other parameters. The transmission rate is affected by two major factors: propagation environment and the degree of congestion. Depending on these two factors, we could assign a weight value for the maximum transmission rate using γ. The weights would have an impact on the coalition as a whole. It is important for these weights to add up to 1 in order to allow prioritization based on the topology of the network. Because of the nature of our network, we will give the highest weight to the maximum transmission rate parameter.

$$\alpha + \beta + \gamma = 1 \tag{5}$$

New nodes are accepted into the grand coalition based on the testimony from intersecting nodes in the smaller coalition. Nodes take some time to gain a good reputation within the small coalition before it can be accepted into the grand coalition. There is a possibility that a new node might fail to enter into the grand coalition if it is out of range from the intersecting node when the smaller coalition is merged into a grand coalition. This merging process continues while there are intersecting nodes to testify about the new nodes which ensures that the grand coalition will continue to grow, thereby providing more robust security. Algorithm 1 shows the coalition formation process. The coalition formation is a dynamic process and no matter the location of a node in the network, it still has neighbors that can testify about it. From the coalition formation algorithm we can see that at each round of formation, every coalition looks to find a partner. The grand coalition is eventually formed only when two conditions are met: presence of an intersecting node to aid the merging and if $v(N)$ is atleast greater than the individual payoff of any disjoint smaller coalition.

There are no fixed number of neighbors for a particular node because of the mobile nature of the wireless environment. From our proposed model the size of the grand coalition could be any size of three nodes and above. For rationality sake it is important to show the individual payoff of the nodes so that they would have a basis for joining a coalition. The individual payoff share is also found in [15]. For any node $i \, \epsilon \, C, \mid C \mid > 1$, the individual payoff[8] share is defined in Eq. 6

$$x_t(i) = \frac{1}{|C|}(\alpha S_t(C) + \beta A_t(C) + \gamma D_t(C)) \tag{6}$$

Based on the characteristic function used, we will be making use of the core. The core states that the sum of total payoff of all members of the coalition must be greater than the value of that single payoff of any individual node [11,15]. Hence looking at Eqs. 4 and 6, we should be able to conclude that:

$$\sum_{i\epsilon C} x_t(i) \geq v_t(C) \tag{7}$$

The game only has a core if it satisfies the concept of core of the coalition game [11].

Network Assumptions. We assume N mobile nodes with A attackers, where A is less than $N/2$.[9] Below are the assumptions under which we present our work:

- All players (or nodes) are rational (i.e. they would always choose the strategy that benefits them the most).
- The network model does not adopt a hierarchical organization, such as, leader-follower or centralized organization.
- The goal of the game is to form a stable grand coalition where any node that is unable to join this grand coalition would be designated as a malicious node.

---

[8] Payoff computation is calculated using any of core, shapley value, or nucleolus.
[9] The number of attackers should not exceed the number of legitimate nodes.

Algorithm 1. Algorithm for Coalition Formation

1: *Start* for all nodes, N
2: Begin the 1st round of formation
3: Pick a node with the highest $v_t(C)$
4: Broadcast forming option to the neighboring nodes in the network
5: **if** $v_t(C)$ is beyond threshold and ≥ 2 nodes match **then**
6:    Form a small coalition
7: **else**
8:    Do not pick any node
9: **end if**
10: Update transmission rate table in AFAT [14] with the rate of newest members
11: Begin the 2nd round
12: Pick a node with the highest security value, $v_t(C)$
13: **if** the first option has been matched successfully **then**
14:    Pick the next best option available
15: **else**
16:    Broadcast the forming option to the neighbors again
17: **end if**
18: **if** there is an intersecting node- nodes that belongs to more than one small coalition **then**
19:    Merge the small coalitions
20: **else**
21:    Re-broadcast forming option again to the network
22: **end if**
23: **if** $v(N) \geq$ payoff from any disjoint set of smaller coalition **then**
24:    Form a grand coalition
25: **else**
26:    Repeat step 11
27: **end if**

- The nodes are moving slowly because fast movement brings about a frequent change in the node's neighbors which may affect the reputation of the nodes adversely.
- A node's continuous membership in the grand coalition is dependent on its reputation value.

3.2 Jammer Model

The jammer type modeled in this section is a smart insider jammer who only launches its attack after collecting enough information to cause huge network disruptions. The jammer's goal is to launch a successful attack rather than building a very high reputation, however, it has to wait until it crosses the lower reputation threshold value, q_L before attempting to jam the network. The potential jammer is first a member of a smaller coalition where it earns a good reputation from its neighboring nodes. The attack is a combination of both subtle and palpable attacks as explained in [16]. The attacker passively scans the network as an eavesdropper while also sharing its transmission rate with all the neighbors in its range of transmission in the coalition. After a certain time, at which the attacker has gathered enough information about its neighbors and what channel they are transmitting on, the attacker stops sharing its own transmission rate because it needs enough power to jam the channel on which the best transmission rate is used.

The jammer would launch its attack when it knows that such an attack is feasible. By feasible, we mean that the jammer has the required jamming power, the chance of being detected is low and it has specific information about the channel on which the best transmission rate is used. The jammer would launch its palpable attack by intentionally sending a high-powered interference signal to that channel, thereby attempting to disrupt communication. The principal aim of jamming a selected channel is to disable the functionality of that channel. The complexity of the jamming can be seen in the fact the movement of the jammers may hinder the detection capability of the coalition. In Fig. 1, the jammers are part of two smaller coalitions which merged to become a grand coalition. The node marked yellow is the intersecting node for smaller coalitions.

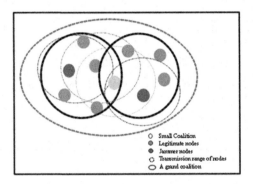

Fig. 1. A Coalition of ten (10) nodes with two (2) jammers

4 Proposed Defense Model

4.1 Maintaining the Coalition Through Reputation

We present a maintenance algorithm that employs the node reputation to track all the history of each node's cooperation as they broadcast their transmission rate. Reputation is simply defined as the goodness of a node as observed by other neighbors in its transmission range or the coalition in general.[10] Specifically, we adapt the mechanism used for modeling increase and decrease of reputation values. The reputation of a node is maintained by nodes in the same transmission

---

[10] The maintenance algorithm was inspired by the work done by [17].

range as itself. Each node updates the reputation table every time slot.[11] When a node broadcasts it's transmission rate, it receives an increment and if it fails the opposite happens. A new node that joins the network can be assigned a neutral reputation q_N. All reputations would be valid for a time period, T_v. There is an upper threshold, q_U and a lower threshold q_L, where $q_L < q_N < q_U$.

Reputation can be increased at the rate of σ and decreased at the rate of λ, where $\sigma, \lambda < 1$ and are both real numbers. For this algorithm, the two parameters are set equal to each other in order to ensure fairness. If these parameters are not made equal, for example when σ is larger than λ, there is the tendency for a node to quickly attain the maximum reputation value in a very short time and then lack the enthusiasm to continue sharing its transmission rate as it should be doing in order for network activity to continue. Also decreasing at a high rate also results in an undeserved punishment for any node in an unpleasant network location due to the mobility of the system.

Algorithm 2 shows the monitoring process and how the reputation is either increased or decreased depending on the node's behavior. m is the number of observations made by node j about node i's refusal to share its transmission rate. T_f is the tolerance of the network i.e. m per reputation value before reducing reputation of a node. y is the number of observations made by node j when node i shares its transmission range in the time period b_f. b_f is the broadcast factor of the network [17]. This algorithm makes use of only firsthand information as the support rate and the intersecting node is enough to cater for the need for a secondhand information.

4.2 Jammer's Exclusion from the Coalition

The jammer prevention algorithm aims to reduce the number of false positives. False positive occurs when a legitimate node is been classified as a jammer when it fails to share its transmission rate at a particular time-slot due to been out of range, which is typical of MANET. Nodes that belong to the coalition have a monitor for observations and reputation records for first-hand information about the degree of cooperation of their neighbors as regards sharing their transmission rates. The coalition excludes the jammer by Algorithm 3.

For our setup, an excluded node will not be granted re-entry. Algorithm 3 provides the needed self-dependency and self-organization in MANET.

5   Simulation and Results

We evaluate the performance of the reputation-based coalition game by conducting simulations in NS2. We compare the performance of the reputation-based coalition game with non-reputation based mechanism. The non-reputation based scheme is gotten when we remove the reputation mechanism in our coalition

---

[11] A time slot is defined as a period of time during which one transmission rate is shared.

Algorithm 2. Coalition Maintenance through Reputation

1: Assign values for σ and λ
2: *Start* for all nodes
3: Node i checks its transmission rate table to assign reputation value for neighbor j.
4: **if** j shares its transmission rate **then**
5:    compute reputation value according to:
6:

$$v_{i,j}(y) = y/R_{i,j} \qquad (8)$$

7: **else**
8:    Set $v_{i,j}(y) = 0$ if $y/R_{i,j} \leq b_f$
9: **end if**
10: **if** j refuses to share its transmission rate **then**
11:    compute reputation value according to
12:

$$k_{i,j}(m) = m/R_{i,j} \qquad (9)$$

13: **else**
14:    Set $k_{i,j}(m) = 0$ if $m/R_{i,j} \leq T_f$
15: **end if**
16: Node i updates node j's reputation value according to:
17:

$$R_{i,j} = R_{i,j}^* + \sigma * (v_{i,j}(y)) - \lambda * (k_{i,j}(m)) \qquad (10)$$

18: Store this reputation value in its reputation table
19: Share reputation table with neighbors at every time-slot.
20: **return** $R_{i,j}$
21: All nodes continue to update their reputation table.

---

maintenance. The evaluation is based on four metrics: the detection accuracy, detection delay, the percentage of false positives and the detection time of the insider jammer.

5.1   Simulation Setup

Table 2 shows a list of the simulation parameters. Twenty percent of the nodes in the network are classified as the insider jammers.

5.2   Results

In Fig. 2, we compare the detection accuracy of the reputation-based scheme with a non reputation-based scheme. The non-reputation based scheme only detects the insider jammer half of the time, our reputation-based scheme, however, performs better with increasing coalition size. In our simulation results, the scheme achieves the maximum accuracy with a coalition of 80 nodes. Detection accuracy is of utmost importance because it is the most important factor that helps to reduce the number of false positives and false negatives.

Algorithm 3. Jammer Exclusion from the Coalition

1: Node i checks node j' reputation value after update.
2: Node j is tolerated until its reputation falls below q_L
3: Classify misbehaving nodes according to:

$$\begin{cases} jammer, & \text{if } R_{i,j} < q_L \\ regular, & \text{if } R_{i,j} \geq q_L \end{cases} \tag{11}$$

4: **if** $R_{i,j}$ is below q_L **then**
5:     Node i sends an alarm message
6:     All nodes change their channel of transmission
7:     Accused node's payoff reduces due to bad testimony
8:     Node j attempts to jam the communication channel that has the best transmission rate.
9:     Jammer records little or no success because of the proactive step taken by the coalition.
10:     Neighbors of node j, blacklist him and exclude him from their small coalition.
11:     Nodes with reputation greater than q_L regroup again.
12: **else**
13:     No alarm is sent and nodes continue their transmission
14: **end if**
15: Nodes with $R_{i,j}$ greater than q_L are retained
16: Continue transmission

Figure 3 illustrates the time taken by the coalition to detect the insider jammer. The support rate has an impact on the number of neighboring nodes which in turn affects the detection time. For the result shown in Fig. 3, the number of attackers is exactly twenty percent of the size of the coalition. The time taken to detect insider jammer reduces significantly with increasing number of nodes in the network.

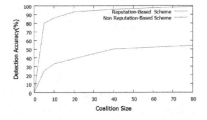

Fig. 2. Detection accuracy

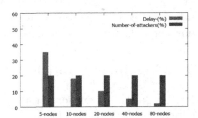

Fig. 3. Detection delay

Figure 4 compares false positives for the reputation-based model and the non reputation-based model. False positives are easily detected with our reputation-based mechanism because the rate of increase (σ) and decrease (λ) of reputation

Table 2. Parameters for simulation

Parameter	Level
Area	2300 x 1300
Speed	$15m/s$
Radio range	250m
Simulation time	130s
Number of mobile nodes	5, 10, 20, 40 and 80 nodes
Network interface & Channel type	Wireless
Transmission rate	1-11 Mbps
Percentage of jammer	20 percent
Thresholds, q_U & q_L	0.975 & 0.70 respectively

value is equal resulting in fewer instances of errors in detecting insider jammers. As observed in Fig. 4, the 80 node coalition has the least false positive percentage.

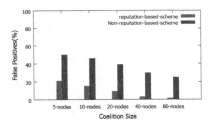

Fig. 4. False positives

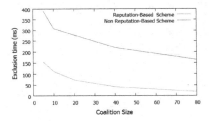

Fig. 5. Jammer exclusion time

Figure 5 illustrates the time it takes to exclude the insider jammer from the grand coalition after detection. As the size of the coalition increases, the time taken to exclude insider jammers decreases because the jammer's neighboring nodes quickly raises an alarm when the reputation values fall below q_L.

6   Conclusion and Future Work

In this paper, we presented a reputation-based coalition game to detect insider threats in MANET. The key components of the game include algorithms for coalition formation, coalition maintenance and jammer exclusion and security characteristic function for admitting nodes into a coalition. Simulation results demonstrate the effectiveness of our reputation-based coalition game to detect insider jammers in a MANET. Specifically, the results demonstrate few false positives and small detection delay. In the future, we would like to investigate a case of a cooperative attacks that could occur when the excluded nodes form a coalition with the aim of jamming communication in the MANET.

Acknowledgment. This work is supported by Office of the Assistant Secretary of Defense for Research and Engineering agreement FAB750-15-2-0120, NSF CNS-1405681, and DHS 2014-ST-062-000059.

References

1. Mpitziopoulos, A., Gavalas, D., Konstantopoulos, C., Pantziou, G.: A survey on jamming attacks and countermeasures in WSNs. Commun. Surv. Tutorials, IEEE **11**(4), 42–56 (2009)
2. Pickholtz, R.L., Schilling, D.L., Milstein, L.B.: Theory of spread-spectrum communications-a tutorial. IEEE Trans. Commun. **30**(5), 855–884 (1982)
3. Stutzman, W.L., Thiele, G.A.: Antenna Theory and Design. John Wiley & Sons, New York (2012)
4. Han, Z., Poor, H.V.: Coalition games with cooperative transmission: A cure for the curse of boundary nodes in selfish packet-forwarding wireless networks. IEEE Trans. Commun. **57**(1), 203–213 (2009)
5. Nguyen, H., Pongthawornkamol, T., Nahrstedt, K.: ALIBI: A novel approach for detecting insider-based jamming attacks in wireless networks. In: MILCOM Conference, pp. 855–884 (2009)
6. Li, L., Zhu, S., Torrieri, D., Jajodia, S.: Self-healing wireless networks under insider jamming attacks. IEEE Conf. CNS IEEE **2014**, 220–228 (2014)
7. Marti, S., Giuli, T.J., Lai, K., Baker, M.: Mitigating routing misbehavior in mobile ad hoc networks. In: Proceedings of the 6th Annual International Conference on Mobile Computing and Networking, pp. 255–265. ACM (2000)
8. Michiardi, P., Molva, R.: Core: A collaborative reputation mechanism to enforce node cooperation in mobile ad hoc networks. In: Advanced Communications and Multimedia Security, pp. 107–121. Springer, Heidelberg (2002)
9. Michiardi, P., Molva, R.: A game theoretical approach to evaluate cooperation enforcement mechanisms in mobile ad hoc networks. In: WiOpt 2003: Modeling and Optimization in Mobile, Ad Hoc and Wireless Networks, p. 4 (2003)
10. Peleteiro, A., Burguillo, J.C., Arcos, J.L., Rodriguez-Aguilar, J.A.: Fostering cooperation through dynamic coalition formation and partner switching. ACM (TAAS) **9**(1), 1 (2014)
11. Ferguson, T.: Game Theory (2nd/ed). Mathematics Department, UCLA 2014 (2014)
12. Li, X.: Achieving Secure and Cooperative Wireless Networks with Trust Modeling and Game Theory (2009)
13. Gale, D., Shapley, L.S.: College admissions and the stability of marriage. Am. Math. Monthly **69**(1), 9–15 (1962)
14. Al-Sharah, A., Shetty, S.: Accumulative feedback adaptation transmission rate in mobile ad-hoc networks. In: 2015 IEMCON, pp. 1–5. IEEE (2015)
15. Saad, W., Han, Z., Debbah, M., Hjørungnes, A.: A distributed coalition formation framework for fair user cooperation in wireless networks. IEEE Trans. Wirel. Commun. **8**(9), 4580–4593 (2009)
16. Liao, X., Hao, D., Sakurai, K.: Classification on attacks in wireless ad hoc networks: A game theoretic view. In: 7th International Conference on NCM, 2011, pp. 144–149. IEEE (2011)
17. Balasubratuanian, A., Ghosh, J.: A reputation based scheme for stimulating cooperation in MANETs. In: Proceedings of the 19th International Teletraffic Congress (2005)

A Goodness Based Vertical Handoff Algorithm for Heterogeneous Networks

Shankar K. Ghosh and Sasthi C. Ghosh$^{(\boxtimes)}$

Advanced Computing and Microelectronics Unit,
Indian Statistical Institute, Kolkata 700108, India
shankar.it46@gmail.com,
sasthi@isical.ac.in

Abstract. While moving across heterogeneous networks with strict rate requirement, the possibility of getting the required rate from the target network, depends on the QoS-awareness of the network selection strategy of the concerned vertical handoff (VHO) algorithm. Inclusion of MAC layer scheduling information in the design of different VHO algorithms has previously been very limited though it is important as both user and system performance depend on it. In this paper, we introduce the notion of *goodness* of an access network and based on it propose a goodness based VHO (GVHO) algorithm. The notion of goodness explicitly considers the MAC layer scheduling along with current load and interference of the candidate networks. The GVHO algorithm accounts the goodness values of the candidate networks to select the target network. Simulation results confirm that GVHO algorithm improves both user and system performance compared to RSS and SINR based VHO algorithms.

Keywords: Vertical handoff algorithm · Heterogeneous networks · MAC scheduling · Throughput maximization · QoS

1 Introduction

The modern communication system consists of different types of wireless access networks such as wireless local area networks (WLAN) and 3G cellular networks. The WLAN provides a high data rate with a lower cost over a small coverage area, whereas, cellular networks provides a relatively lower data rate with a relatively higher cost while providing a greater coverage compared to WLAN. Till date, there exists no single radio access technology which can simultaneously provide high data rate, lower cost and high mobility [1]. The next generation (4G) wireless system therefore, focuses on the convergence of existing radio access technologies so that a mobile user, having a multi-mode terminal can access *ubiquitous* and *always the best connected* services while roaming across the heterogeneous networks [1,2].

© IFIP International Federation for Information Processing 2016
Published by Springer International Publishing Switzerland 2016. All Rights Reserved
L. Mamatas et al. (Eds.): WWIC 2016, LNCS 9674, pp. 254–267, 2016.
DOI: 10.1007/978-3-319-33936-8_20

Due to the complementary characteristics, integration of 3G cellular networks and WLAN has received much attention from research communities [3]. In 3GPP, an integrated architecture for the 3G cellular network and WLAN has been developed [1,4] and its interconnection specifications have been standardized in 3GPP2 [5]. In this integrated network, a mobile terminal (MT) may perform vertical handoff (VHO) [1] while roaming across the networks. During the handover, an MT uses its network selection strategy (NSS) to select the target network from a set of candidate networks. To get the best connected service, an MT has to rely on the quality of services (QoS) awareness of the network selection strategy of the concerned VHO algorithm. The network selection strategy of a VHO algorithm, therefore plays a crucial role in supporting seamless mobility and guaranteeing the QoS. Consequently, the upper layer application performances are also limited by the choice of the target network. As a result, designing a QoS-aware VHO algorithm is still a challenging problem to the research communities.

To address the above problem, a number of VHO algorithms have been proposed. A detailed survey of the VHO algorithms can be found in [2]. In most of these works, either RSS [6–8] or SINR [9–11] have been used as the fundamental decision indicator. In RSS based approaches, an MT mostly selects the access network having minimum Euclidean distance as the target network. This leads to non-uniform load distribution causing serious degradation of user and system performance. To overcome these drawbacks, SINR based VHO algorithms have been proposed. The SINR based approaches improve both user and system performance as the SINR measurements in wideband code division multiple access (WCDMA) system implicitly considers the network load along with the interference level of the received signal [12]. From the measured value of SINR, an MT can compute the theoretical maximum limit of achievable data rate from a particular access network using shannon's capacity formula. In practice, however much lower rates are achieved [13]. It is to be noted that, the actual physical rate perceived by an MT depends not only on the network load and interference level of the received signal, but also on the medium access control (MAC) layer scheduling algorithm run by the corresponding access network. For example, the effective throughput obtained by an MT from WLAN depends on its MAC scheduling mechanism such as random pooling access and proportional fair access [14]. In random polling access, the individual throughput obtained by all the MTs served by a common access point (AP) is equal. Whereas, in proportional fair access, the obtained throughput by an MT is proportional to the physical rate at which the MT is associated with the concerned AP. In WCDMA systems such as universal mobile telecommunication system (UMTS), an MT can get its requested service if the received energy per bit compared to the spectral noise density is sufficient to get the particular requested service [12].

Since, providing the requested rate to an MT having strict rate requirement (e.g., VoIP, Vconf, clinical applications) is one of the major goals of next generation wireless system, design of any VHO algorithm must consider the availability of the requested rate to the user in addition to the overall system performance. To the best of the authors knowledge, till date there exists no VHO algorithm which accounts the MAC layer scheduling details as a decision attribute to select the optimum target network. In this paper, our contributions are threefold:

- We first introduce the notion of *goodness* for an access network. We consider that, at any time while roaming across the 3G-WLAN heterogeneous network with strict rate requirement, an user can stay in one of the two states namely *good state* and *bad state*. The user is considered to be in good state if it gets the requested physical rate from the system and in bad state otherwise. The goodness of an access network is defined as the estimated time an user will get it's requested rate from that particular access network. The notion of goodness explicitly considers the MAC layer scheduling information along with the current load and interference of an access network.
- We propose a goodness based vertical handoff (GVHO) algorithm based on the notion of goodness of access networks. The GVHO algorithm accounts the goodness values of different candidate networks to select the optimum one.
- The performance of GVHO algorithm have been compared with a RSS based VHO algorithm [6] and a multicriteria adaptive SINR based VHO algorithm (MASVH) [9]. It has been shown by simulation results that GVHO algorithm improves both user and system performance compared to the considered RSS and SINR based VHO algorithms.

The rest of the paper is organized as follows. Related works are presented in Sect. 2. Section 3 presents the notion of goodness for access networks. Section 4 presents the proposed VHO algorithm. Section 5 presents results and discussion. Finally, Sect. 6 concludes the paper.

2   Related Works

In most of the previous studies, either RSS or SINR has been considered as the fundamental decision metric in the design of VHO algorithms [6–11]. In RSS based VHO algorithms [6–8], RSS acts as the fundamental decision parameter along with other factors such as available bandwidth, monetary cost and user preference to select the target network from the candidate networks. In [6], a VHO algorithm is proposed based on a cost function which considers traffic load, RSS and variations of RSS (VRSS). The RSS based VHO algorithms proposed in [7,8], uses fuzzy control theory for selecting the target network. Since RSS based algorithms do not consider network load and current interference level of the candidate networks, SINR based VHO algorithms have been proposed to improve the system performance [9–11]. The algorithms proposed in [9,10] consider the combined effect of SINR, user required bandwidth, user traffic cost and utilization from participating access networks to make the handoff decision. In [11], a service adaptive multicriteria vertical handoff (SAMVHO) algorithm has been proposed to improve the performance from system's perspective. The SAMVHO algorithm considers the weighted average of different decision attributes such as SINR, bandwidth utilization, packet loss rate to determine the target network.

Consideration of MAC scheduling, although having a decisive role in both user and system performance, have been very limited previously in the design of VHO algorithms. In this work, we have proposed a goodness based VHO algorithm (GVHO) which explicitly considers MAC scheduling mechanism of the candidate networks for selecting the target network. It has been shown that GVHO algorithm outperforms the considered RSS based [6] and SINR based [9] VHO algorithm.

3   Notion of Goodness for an Access Network

The actual physical rate perceived by an user while roaming across the 3G-WLAN heterogeneous network explicitly depends on the MAC scheduling algorithm run by the corresponding base station (BS) or access point (AP). In WLAN the throughput perceived by an MT from an AP depends on the physical rate at which the MT is associated with the AP and the total number of users associated with that AP. In 3G WCDMA system such as UMTS, an MT can get its requested service if the received energy per bit compared to the spectral noise density is sufficient to get that particular requested service [12]. In this work, we consider only downlink traffic as they require higher bandwidth than that of uplink traffic [10]. We assume that an user while roaming across the 3G-WLAN heterogeneous network with strict rate requirement may be in one of the two states: *good state* or *bad state*. The user is in good state if it gets the requested rate from the system, otherwise, it is in bad state. To judge the serving capacity of the candidate networks, we introduce the notion of goodness for both AP and BS which represents the estimated time of getting the requested rate by an user from the concerned AP or BS.

3.1   Goodness of an AP with Respect to an User

We define the goodness of AP i with respect to user j as the estimated period of time user j will get its requested rate R_j^{req} from AP i. The estimation period is a time varying quantity as it depends on dynamic factors such as user mobility and network traffic load. Clearly, user j will be in good state while associated with AP i at time t if the following is satisfied:

$$r_{ij}(t) \geq R_j^{req} \qquad (1)$$

where $r_{ij}(t)$ is the effective throughput perceived by user j from AP i at time t. Assuming that APs are running proportional fair access [14] as the MAC scheduling, $r_{ij}(t)$ can be expressed as:

$$r_{ij}(t) = \frac{b_{ij}(t)}{u_i(t) + 1} \qquad (2)$$

where

– $u_i(t)$ denotes the total number of users associated with AP i at time t, and

– $b_{ij}(t)$ denotes the physical bit rate at which user j is associated with AP i at time t. Here $b_{ij}(t) \in \mathcal{C}$, a finite data rate set. This rate set $\mathcal{C}$ depends on the type of network under consideration. As an example, $\mathcal{C} = \{1, 2, 5.5, 11\}$ for IEEE 802.11b network [14].

It is to be noted that, during 3G to WLAN handovers, the information regarding scheduling and load $u_i(t)$ can be obtained from AP i by overloading the service set identifier (SSID) field of 802.11 beacon frame with necessary details [15]. The physical bit rate $b_{ij}(t)$ at which user j can associate with AP i can be derived from the received signal strength indicator (RSSI) values [16]. Accordingly, $r_{ij}(t)$ can be estimated from Eq. (2).

Now, the time average value of the effective throughput, $\overline{r_{ij}}(t)$, can be calculated using the moving average method [2,17] as follows:

$$\overline{r_{ij}}(t) = \frac{1}{\omega} \sum_{x=0}^{\omega-1} r_{ij}(t-x) \tag{3}$$

where ω is the slope estimator window size and can be estimated depending on the user velocity as described in [17]. The rate of change of $r_{ij}(t)$, $S_{ij}(t)$, can be computed as:

$$S_{ij}(t) = \frac{F_{ij}(t) - L_{ij}(t)}{\omega \times T_b} \tag{4}$$

where $F_{ij}(t)$ and $L_{ij}(t)$ are the average RSS measurements performed at user j as received from AP i in first half and last half of the slope estimator window ω. Here $F_{ij}(t)$ and $L_{ij}(t)$ can be measured as:

$$F_{ij}(t) = \frac{2}{\omega} \sum_{x=0}^{\frac{\omega}{2}-1} \overline{r_{ij}}(t - \omega + 1 + x) \text{ and} \tag{5}$$

$$L_{ij}(t) = \frac{2}{\omega} \sum_{x=\frac{\omega}{2}}^{\omega} \overline{r_{ij}}(t - \omega + 1 + x). \tag{6}$$

Here T_b denotes the sampling interval of $r_{ij}(t)$. Using Eqs. (3) and (4), the goodness of AP i with respect to user j at time t, $A_i^j(t)$, can be defined as:

$$A_i^j(t) = \frac{\overline{r_{ij}}(t) - R_j^{req}}{S_{ij}(t)} \tag{7}$$

3.2   Goodness of a BS with Respect to an User

The goodness of BS i with respect to user j is defined as the estimated period of time user j will get its requested rate R_j^{req} from BS i. Similar to AP, goodness of a BS is also a time varying quantity. Now, user j will get the requested rate from BS i if, in addition to adequate pilot power, sufficient traffic channel power is allocated by BS i to user j. More specifically, user j will be in good state with BS i at time t if the following is satisfied [12]:

$$\delta_{ij}(t) \geq \left(\frac{E_b}{N_0}\right)_{R_j^{req}} \tag{8}$$

where

- $\delta_{ij}(t)$ is the energy per bit relative to spectral noise density $\left(\frac{E_b}{N_0}\right)$ as received at user j from BS i at time instant t.
- $\left(\frac{E_b}{N_0}\right)_{R_j^{req}}$ is the target threshold of $\left(\frac{E_b}{N_0}\right)$ to get R_j^{req}.

Here, $\delta_{ij}(t)$ can be computed as [12]:

$$\delta_{ij}(t) = \frac{W}{R_j^{req}} \times \frac{p_{ij}(t)}{N_0 + (1-\alpha)\eta_{ij}(t) + \sum_{x \neq i} \eta_{xj}(t)} \tag{9}$$

where

- $p_{ij}(t)$ is the traffic channel power received by user j from BS i at time instant t,
- $\eta_{xj}(t)$ is the total interference received at user j from BS x at time instant t,
- α is the orthogonality factor and N_0 is the thermal noise,
- W is the CDMA chip rate.

The target threshold $\left(\frac{E_b}{N_0}\right)_{R_j^{req}}$ can be computed as [13]:

$$\left(\frac{E_b}{N_0}\right)_{R_j^{req}} = \frac{W_{BS}}{R_j^{req}} \times \left(2^{\frac{R_j^{req}}{W_{BS}}} - 1\right) \tag{10}$$

where W_{BS} is the carrier bandwidth of WCDMA. Now, the time average value of $\delta_{ij}(t)$, $\overline{\delta_{ij}}(t)$, can be calculated using the moving average method [2] as follows:

$$\overline{\delta_{ij}}(t) = \frac{1}{\omega'} \sum_{x=0}^{\omega'-1} \delta_{ij}(t-x) \tag{11}$$

where ω' is the slope estimator window size and can be estimated as described in [17]. The rate of change of $\delta_{ij}(t)$, $S'_{ij}(t)$, is given by:

$$S'_{ij}(t) = \frac{F'_{ij}(t) - L'_{ij}(t)}{\omega' \times T'_b} \tag{12}$$

where $F'_{ij}(t)$ and $L'_{ij}(t)$ are the average RSS measurements at user j as received from BS i in first half and last half of the slope estimator window ω'. Here $F'_{ij}(t)$

and $L'_{ij}(t)$ can be measured as:

$$F'_{ij}(t) = \frac{2}{\omega'} \sum_{x=0}^{\frac{\omega'}{2}-1} \overline{\delta_{ij}}(t - \omega' + 1 + x) \text{ and} \tag{13}$$

$$L'_{ij}(t) = \frac{2}{\omega'} \sum_{x=\frac{\omega'}{2}}^{\omega'} \overline{\delta_{ij}}(t - \omega' + 1 + x) \tag{14}$$

Here T'_b denote the sampling interval of $\delta_{ij}(t)$. Using Eqs. (10), (11) and (12), the goodness of BS i with respect to user j at t, $B_i^j(t)$, can be defined as:

$$B_i^j(t) = \frac{\left(\overline{\delta_{ij}}(t) - \left(\frac{E_b}{N_0}\right)_{R_j^{req}}\right)}{S'_{ij}(t)} \tag{15}$$

4 The Proposed Goodness Based Vertical Handoff Algorithm

Our proposed goodness based vertical handoff (GVHO) algorithm consists of three phases namely network discovery, best network determination and target network selection. In network discovery phase, user j periodically determines the set of candidate networks. In the next phase, the best network is determined from the set of candidate networks based on their goodness values. In target network selection phase, user j decides whether the active sessions should be continued with the current network or be switched to the target network.

4.1 Network Discovery

The network discovery phase of GVHO is based on the RSS measurements. Suppose the set of candidate networks N^j for user j found after the network discovery phase include y_j APs and z_j BSs. We represent N^j as:

$$N^j = [\text{AP } 1, \text{AP } 2, \ldots, \text{AP } y_j \, ; \, \text{BS } 1, \text{BS } 2, \ldots \text{BS } z_j]$$

4.2 Best Network Determination

The goodness values of the set of candidate networks N^j for user j at time t can be expressed as:

$$\Omega^{N^j}(t) = [A_1^j(t), A_2^j(t), \ldots A_{y_j}^j(t) \, ; \, B_1^j(t), B_2^j(t), \ldots B_{z_j}^j(t)]$$

where $A_i^j(t)$ and $B_{i'}^j(t)$ are the goodness values of AP i $(1 \leq i \leq y_j)$ and BS i' $(1 \leq i' \leq z_j)$ with respect to user j at time t as computed using Eqs. (7) and (15) respectively. The best network $N_{best}^j(t)$ for user j at time t is the AP or BS whose goodness value is maximum among the candidate networks. That is:

$$N_{best}^j(t) = \begin{cases} \text{AP } i, & \text{if Maximum}(\Omega^{N^j}(t)) = A_i^j(t) \\ \text{BS } i', & \text{if Maximum}(\Omega^{N^j}(t)) = B_{i'}^j(t) \end{cases}$$

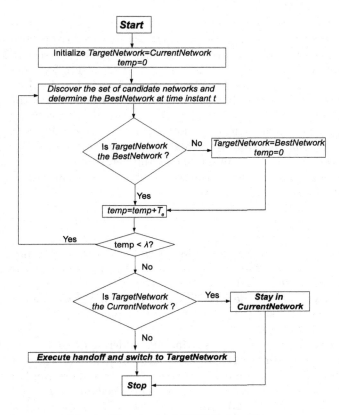

Fig. 1. Flowchart of GVHO algorithm

4.3   Target Network Selection

The target network selection algorithm finds the best network at every time interval T_e. A network is selected as the target network if it is continuously the best for larger than λ time. The active sessions are then switched to the target network. Note that λ is a predefined threshold used here to avoid the ping-pong effect. The proposed GVHO algorithm in the form of a flowchart is presented in Fig. 1.

5   Results and Discussions

5.1   Performance Evaluation Metrics

We have considered the user and system throughput as the metrics for evaluating the performance of different VHO algorithms. *User throughput* measures the mean data rate perceived by an user while roaming across the heterogeneous network. *System throughput* measures the absolute amount of data communicated by the users per unit time. Note that user throughput measures the performance from user's perspective while, system throughput measures the performance from system's perspective. According to our considered application scenario the users have strict rate requirement. So, it is important to measure how long an user is in good state, i.e., getting its requested rate and what fraction of users are in good state. Clearly, these can not be captured by user and system throughput as they are concerned only about the absolute amount of data communicated per unit time. To capture this effect, we introduce two other metrics namely *user goodness* and *system goodness*. We define *user goodness* as the expected time an user is in good state while roaming across the heterogeneous network. *System goodness* is defined as the ratio of mean number of users in good state to the total number of users in the system.

5.2 Simulation Setup

To evaluate the performances of different VHO algorithms, we have used the simulation environment similar to that of [9]. In our simulation environment 7 BSs and 13 APs are placed in a 4000×4000 m^2 area where APs are placed at the boundary points of the BSs. The BSs are assumed to provide ubiquitous coverage. We have considered all kind of overlapping: BS $\leftrightarrow$ BS, AP $\leftrightarrow$ AP, and AP $\leftrightarrow$ BS. The BS coverage radius is set to 1200 m [9]. The physical rate obtained by the users from their respective serving APs is derived based on their received signal strength indicator (RSSI) values as described in [16]. Users are assumed to be uniformly distributed and moving according to smooth random way point mobility model [19] with velocity v km/hr and acceleration f m/s^2 where $v \in \{0, 20, 60\}$ and $f \in \{0, 10, 20\}$. An user accelerates or decelerates depending on its current and target velocity. The slope estimator windows ω and ω' has been estimated depending on the velocity of the user as described in [17]. The sampling intervals T_b and T_b' have been set to 0.01 s [17]. We have assumed the log linear path loss model with shadow fading as [18]: $RSS = P_T - L - 10nlog(d) + f(\mu, \sigma)$ dBm where P_T denotes the transmitted power, L is the constant path loss, n is the path loss exponent and $f(\mu, \sigma)$ represents shadow fading modeled as a Gaussian variable with zero mean and standard deviation σ ranging from 6 to 12 dB. The maximum transmitting power of BS and AP are set to 43 and 20 dBm respectively [9]. The different parameter values considered in our simulation are depicted in Table 1.

5.3 Simulation Results

Figures 2 and 3 depicts the effect of total number of users on user goodness and system goodness respectively. Here all users are assumed to have a typical data rate request for video traffic (384 Kbps). Total number of users in the system varies from 100 to 700 with a step of 100 users.

Figure 2 shows that GVHO significantly improves user goodness compared to MASVH (9–17 % approximately) and RSS based VHO (21–28 % approximately). The underlying impetus of this phenomenon is the better QoS-awareness of GVHO

Table 1. Parameter settings

Parameter	Value	Parameter	Value
W_{BS} [9]	5 MHz	T_e	0.01 s
n [18]	2	λ	0.1 s
σ [18]	7 dB	W [12]	3840000 Kbps
α [12]	0.5	N_0 [9]	−99 dB

compared to MASVH and RSS based approach. It is to be noted that, the user goodness depends on the user perceived throughput, which in turn depends on the interference, user density and the MAC scheduling. In RSS based approaches, the users always select the nearest BS or AP, which may lead to choose a highly loaded target network causing serious degradation of user throughput. Increasing traffic load in WCDMA system causes degradation of user throughput due to self interference. User perceived throughput in WLAN decreases with increasing load as depicted in Eq. (2). On contrast, the MASVH approach considers the current interference level while selecting the target network. The SINR measurements in WCDMA system implicitly considers the network load [12]. As a result, user perceived throughput increases compared to RSS based approach. Although MASVH increases the user mean throughput, it can not guarantee whether an user will get its requested data rate from the target network. From the measured SINR values, an user can determine the theoretical maximum limit of achievable data rate from a channel. Practically, however much lower rate are achieved [13]. A user in WCDMA system can get its requested service if the received energy per bit compared to the spectral noise density $\left(\frac{E_b}{N_0}\right)$ is sufficient to get that particular requested service [12]. Clearly, MASVH algorithm do not consider this MAC layer details. The proposed GVHO algorithm while selecting the target network considers goodness of the participating access networks which accounts MAC scheduling information in addition to the current load and interference level. As a result, the selected target network in GVHO is more reliable to provide the requested data rate.

Figure 3 depicts the effect of total number of users on system goodness. Simulation results show that GVHO significantly improves the system goodness compared to MASVH (1–20 % approximately) and RSS based approach (2–24 % approximately). System goodness depends on total number of users associated with the system, which in tern depends on load balancing among different access networks. System goodness in MASVH is better than RSS as MASVH leads to a fairer load distribution among different access networks in comparison to RSS. Since MASVH is cost aware, this is effectively a WLAN-first strategy under moderate traffic load. It is important to note that, unlike BS, in case of AP, nothing can be predicted regarding the user density from the received SINR. As a result, load under APs quickly reach the maximum limit of allowable traffic load as depicted in Eq. (2) and all subsequent calls are dropped. Being equipped with the scheduling details,

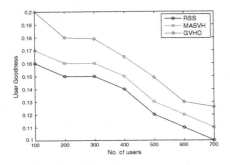
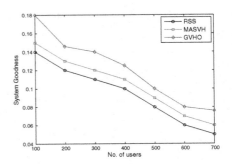
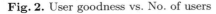

Fig. 2. User goodness vs. No. of users

Fig. 3. System goodness vs. No. of users

GVHO can have better insight regarding achievable data rate in APs. In WCDMA system, whether an user will be able to associate with a particular BS depends on the power availability in the corresponding BS, which can not be estimated only from the received SINR values. The power availability can be closely estimated from $\left(\frac{E_b}{N_0}\right)$ values which the notion of goodness explicitly considers. As a result, GVHO outperforms the SINR based MASVH approach.

Figures 4, 5, 6 and 7 shows the effect of requested data rate on different performance evaluation metric. We vary the requested data rates from 64 to 640 Kbps with a step of 64 Kbps. Total number of users are kept fixed to 300.

Figure 4 depicts the effect of requested data rate on user goodness. The results show that GVHO outperforms MASVH (8–12 % approximately) and RSS based approach (11–14 % approximately) because of its better Qos-awareness as explained earlier. As the requirement for system resources increases with increasing data rate, the user goodness decreases while increasing the requested data rate. The user goodness degrades drastically as soon as the requested rate become more than 384 Kbps (approximately). The differences among different VHOs become narrower as the data rate request increases beyond 384 Kbps. This intuitively suggests that for the considered number of user (300), the system reaches the saturation point when the data rate request per user is 384 Kbps.

Figure 5 depicts the effect of requested data rate on system goodness. Here also GVHO have been found to outperform MASVH (3–7 % approximately) and RSS based approach (10–15 % approximately). It may be noted that system goodness decreases with increasing user requested data rate. This is because, the maximum number of users that can be associated with an AP in good state decreases with increasing the requested data rate as depicted in Eq. (2). On the other hand, the power requirement for an user to stay in good state with a BS increases exponentially with the requested data rate as depicted in Eq. (10).

Figures 6 and 7 depict the effect of requested data rate on user mean throughput and system throughput. It can be seen that GVHO outperforms MASVH (performance gain is 2–7 % approximately for user throughput and 1–15 % approximately for system throughput) and RSS based approach (5–25 % approximately

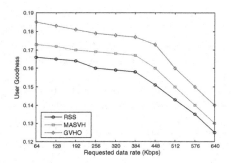

Fig. 4. User goodness vs. requested rate

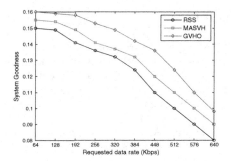

Fig. 5. System goodness vs. requested rate

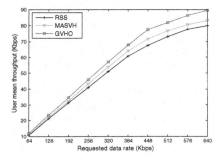

Fig. 6. User mean throughput vs. requested rate

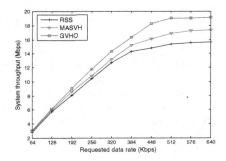

Fig. 7. System throughput vs. requested rate

for user mean throughput and 2–25 % approximately for system throughput). The reason behind is the advanced Qos-awareness of GVHO as described earlier.

6 Conclusions

We have introduced the notion of goodness for access networks and based on it proposed a goodness based vertical handoff (GVHO) algorithm which explicitly considers the MAC scheduling information along with the current load and interference. We have compared the performance of GVHO with an SINR based and a RSS based approach from the existing literature. It has been shown that GVHO significantly improves both user and system performances compared to the considered SINR and RSS based approaches.

Acknowledgment. Mr. Shankar K. Ghosh would like to thank CSIR for providing Junior Research Fellowship (File No: 09/093(0162)/2015-EMR-I) for pursuing Ph.D works.

References

1. Wang, H., Laurension, D.I., Hillston, J.: A general performance evaluation framework for network selection strategies in 3G-WLAN interworking networks. IEEE Trans. Mob. Comput. **12**(5), 868–884 (2013)
2. Yan, X., Ahmet, Y., Narayanan, S.: A survey of vertical handover decision algorithms in fourth generation heterogenous wireless networks. Comput. Netw. **54**, 1848–1863 (2010)
3. Zaharan, A.H., Liang, B., Saleh, A.: Mobility modeling and performance evaluation of heterogeneous wireless networks. IEEE Trans. Mob. Comput. **7**(8), 1041–1056 (2008)
4. 3GPP systems to wireless local area network (WLAN) interworking; system description, Technical report TS23.234 v7.70, 3GPP, June 2008
5. 3rd generation partnership project 2 (3GPP2). http://www.3gpp2.org/
6. Shen, W., Zeng, Q.A.: A novel decision strategy of vertical handoff in overlay wireless networks. In: Proceedings of the 5th IEEE International Symposium on Network Computing and applications (IEEE NCA 2006) (2006)
7. He, Q.: A fuzzy logic based vertical handoff decision algorithm between WWAN and WLAN. In: Proceedings of the International Conference on in Networking and digital society (ICNDS), vol. 2, pp. 561–564 (2010)
8. Kunarak, S., Suleesathira, R.: Predictive RSS with fuzzy logic based vertical handoff algorithm in heterogeneous wireless networks. In: Proceedings of the International Symposium on Communications and Information Technologies (ISCIT), pp. 1235–1240 (2010)
9. Yang, K., Gondal, I., Qiu, B.: Multidimensional adaptive SINR based vertical handoff for heterogenous wireless networks. IEEE Commun. Lett. **12**(6), 438–440 (2008)
10. Yang, K., Gondal, I., Dooley, L.S.: Combined SINR based vertical handoff algorithm for next generation heterogenous wireless networks. In: proceedings of the IEEE GLOBECOM (2007)
11. Chen, J., Wei, Z., Wang, Y., Sang, L., Tang, D.: A service-adaptive multi-criteria vertical handoff algorithm in heterogeneous wireless networks. In: Proceedings of the 23rd International symposium on Personal, Indoor and Mobile Radio Communications (PIMRC) (2012)
12. Ghosh, S.C., Whitaker, R.M., Allen, S.M., Hurley, S.: Dynamic data resolution to improve the tractability of UMTS network planning. Ann. Oper. Res. **201**, 197–227 (2012)
13. Stallings, W.: Data and Computer Communications, 8th edn. Prentice Hall, New York (2005)
14. Kumar, A., Kumar, V.: Optimal association of stations and APs in an IEEE 802.11 WLAN. In: Proceedings of the National Communications Conference (NCC), January 2005
15. Chandra, R., Padhye, J., Ravindranath, L., Wolman, A.: Beacon-stuffing: Wi-Fi without associations. In: Proceedings of the 8th IEEE workshop Mobile Computing Systems and Applications, Tucson, Arizona, 26–27 February (2007)
16. Gong, D., Yang, Y.: On-line AP association algorithms for 802.11n WLANs with heterogeneous clients. IEEE Trans. Comput. **63**(11), 2772–2786 (2014)
17. Zahran, A.H., Liang, B., Saleh, A.: Signal threshold adaptation for vertical handoff in heterogeneous wireless networks. Mob. Netw. Appl. **11**, 625–640 (2006)

18. Zaharan, A.H., Liang, B.: Performance evaluation framework for vertical handoff algorithms in heterogenous networks. In: Proceedings of the IEEE ICC (2005)
19. Stevens-Navarro, E., Wang, V.: Smooth is better than sharp: A random mobility model for simulation of wireless networks. In: Proceedings of the ACM MSWiM (2001)

Wireless Sensor Networks

Routing-Aware Time Slot Allocation Heuristics in Contention-Free Sensor Networks

Lemia Louail[✉] and Violeta Felea

Femto-ST Institute, University of Bourgogne-Franche-Comté, Besançon, France
{lemia.louail,violeta.felea}@femto-st.fr

Abstract. Traditionally, in Wireless Sensor Networks, protocols are designed independently in the layered protocol stack, and metrics involved in several layers can be affected. Communication latency is one metric example, impacted by both the routing protocol in the network layer and the MAC protocol in the data link layer. Better performances can be obtained using cross-layer approaches.

In this paper, we address latency optimizations for communications in sensor networks, based on cross-layer decisions. More particularly, we propose new time slot scheduling methods correlated to routing decisions. Slot allocation for nodes follows particular routing tree traversals, trying to reduce the gap between the slot of a child and that of its parent.

Simulations show that latency performance of our contributions improves similar cross-layer approaches from 33 % up to 54 %. Duty cycle of obtained schedules are also improved from 7 % up to 11 %.

Keywords: Wireless sensor networks · Cross-layer approaches · Contention-free time slot scheduling · Routing protocol

1 Introduction

Wireless Sensor networks (WSN) are an innovating technology used nowadays in many domains (healthcare, military, environment monitoring, etc.). Sensor nodes are deployed in an area to collect information and to relay it to the Base Station (also called Sink) through multi-hop communications. To handle communications in this kind of network, the five layered protocol stack is used [1]. In this stack, the Network layer is responsible for finding paths between sensors and the sink through the routing protocol, and the Data Link layer is responsible for organizing communications to avoid interference and collisions through the MAC protocol. Each of these layers aims to optimize specific metrics as latency or energy consumption.

Generally, designing MAC and Routing protocols separately in the traditional protocol stack gives good performance in terms of metrics related to the Data Link layer or the Network layer, but they are not optimized to improve the overall network performance. For example, when the MAC protocol is trying to minimize the latency by designing a schedule for communications, the routing

© IFIP International Federation for Information Processing 2016
Published by Springer International Publishing Switzerland 2016. All Rights Reserved
L. Mamatas et al. (Eds.): WWIC 2016, LNCS 9674, pp. 271–283, 2016.
DOI: 10.1007/978-3-319-33936-8_21

protocol can counteract its decisions by adopting a path with a high latency. That is why the two protocols need to communicate with each other to overcome this counteraction.

Recently, cross-layer approaches [2,3] were adopted, in which two or more layers communicate with each other to achieve better performances. Cross-layer design addressed here concerns protocols, and not transversal information as energy or mobility (as used in cross planes, which are the power management plane, the mobility management plane and the task management plane). For example, the cross-layer design we are interested in concerns situations where the MAC protocol can use information coming from the Routing protocol to design better schedules.

In this context, we propose new TDMA scheduling methods to minimize the latency of communications. The cross-layer aspect is the use of routing information in order to allocate communication time slots for nodes. The routing protocol is supposed to be tree-based. Our main contribution proposes different routing tree traversals to allocate communication time slots in order to reduce communication latency. Each scheduling approach was evaluated with different routing trees to prove the good results of our contribution.

Moreover, an improvement of an existing cross-layer approach, CoLaNet [5], is proposed. The latter constructs a TDMA schedule based on vertex-coloring solutions. To make comparison with our TDMA schedules fair, we include routing tree information in coloring decisions in order to reduce communications latency.

In the next section we present some related works in cross-layering then we present our main contribution in Sect. 3. In Sect. 4 is presented the configuration of simulations and in Sect. 5, the performance evaluation of our approaches compared with the state of the art. Finally, we conclude with the advantages of our contributions.

2   State of the Art

Each layer of the sensor network protocol stack is responsible of particular functionalities. For example, the Data Link layer schedules communications between nodes through the MAC protocol and the Network layer finds a path between a sender and a receiver through the routing protocol.

There are two types of MAC protocols. The first type is the collision free protocols (TDMA-like) in which the communications are organized according to a schedule, such that one-hop communications do not generate collisions. The second type is the collision based protocols (CSMA-like) in which no schedule is defined and carrier sense techniques are used to avoid collisions.

In this paper we are interested in the first type, more specifically in TDMA (Time Division Multiple Access) scheduling in which each node has a slot to send information to its neighborhood. The other slots are used to either receive information from the neighborhood or to go to sleep mode. The most important advantage of the TDMA is that it ensures that there will be no collision caused either by the one-hop neighborhood or induced by the hidden terminal problem during communications and the latency is easily controlled. Moreover, in sleep mode, radio is turned off so energy can be conserved.

Traditionally, this kind of protocol is designed without using any information from the routing protocol [4]. Therefore, resulting schedules could be inadequate in terms of latency because of the path chosen by the routing protocol. Cross-layer approaches are the solution to correlate decisions taken in different layers. We assume that routing information integrated into TDMA-based schedules decisions can improve latency. We use tree-based routing protocols in this work.

CoLaNet [5] is a cross-layer protocol that uses the characteristics of the routing tree to construct a collision-free MAC schedule. Its main idea is to formulate the MAC issue as a vertex-coloring problem. By solving this problem, CoLaNet is able to determine the schedule of each sensor node using an approximation algorithm. CoLaNet is the only TDMA-based cross-layer protocol found in literature, that is why we consider it as a comparison reference.

First, as a routing tree, CoLaNet constructs the MinDegree tree in which the sink is the root, the neighbor of the sink are its children and then each node chooses the node with the fewest children nodes as its parent.

Second, CoLaNet applies the vertex-coloring algorithm in [6] to establish the schedule as follows:

- CoLaNet finds the node with the maximum degree in the routing tree.
- A color is given to this node. In this process, CoLaNet ensures that none of its one-hop or two-hop neighbor in the graph has this color and this to avoid collisions. If not, a new color is generated and is given to the node.
- CoLaNet continues to color vertices that have an already colored neighbor. If two or more vertices have a colored neighbor, no order is applied on them, they are taken randomly one by one.
- When all nodes have a color, the colors are transformed into a schedule where the number of colors represents the length of the schedule, and each color represents a slot. The slot used for transmission is the number of the color assigned to the node. Slots used for reception can be computed based on the color of the neighboring nodes and on the network graph.

The goal of CoLaNet is to provide an allocation of communication slots, for every node, with no collisions. CoLaNet does not generate minimum schedule length, as their goal is not to propose a better approximation algorithm for solving the vertex-coloring problem (the minimum vertex coloring problem is often intractable).

3   Slots Allocation Based on Routing Tree Traversals

3.1   Motivation

While CoLaNet aims to define a transmission schedule of each sensor node to avoid collisions, it neglects completely the aspect of latency. We noticed that the max-degree node, with which the vertex-coloring begins, can be located anywhere in the routing tree which is not the best way to start the slot allocation in the schedule. That is why, in this part, we propose a different method to allocate slots than the vertex-coloring algorithm. Three different ways of routing tree traversal are proposed. They all start with the leaves of the routing tree rather than with the node of maximum degree. We first present our general slot allocation method used for all scheduling techniques.

3.2   Slot Allocation Method

The initial schedule length is the maximum node degree incremented (the node with the maximum degree needs a slot for each neighbor to receive information and one slot for itself for the transmission). The initial schedule length is the minimal value but may be increased, during the allocation algorithm, if no free slot is available because of possible collisions in 2-hop neighborhood communications.

This technique is based on the identification of a free slot for a node. A slot is considered free for a node if none of its one-hop or two-hop neighbor has been allocated in the slot (this ensures that the TDMA schedule is collision free). Considering the routing tree, we suggest the slots allocation to be done as follows.

– Case 1: If the current node is a leaf (in the routing tree), it is given the first free slot starting from the beginning of the schedule.
– Case 2: If the current node is not a leaf, it is given the first free slot starting from the last slot of its children and doing a circular search (look for a free slot up to the last slot of the schedule and possibly, restart from the first slot of the schedule, up to the last slot of the children, if no free slot is found in the first search).
– In both cases (1 and 2), if no free slot is found, a new slot is added at the end of the schedule and it is allocated to the current node.

Case 1 gives to leaves of the routing tree more chances to be scheduled earlier and Case 2 makes internal nodes to be scheduled after all of their children in a circular way.

The schedule for a node contains one slot to send information to its neighborhood and the other slots are used to either receive information from the neighbor or to go to sleep mode. The Slot Allocation Method allows to define the sending slot of each node. The other slots can be deduced by exchanging messages with the neighborhood because the sending slot of a node is a receiving slot for all its one-hop neighbor.

3.3   Tree Traversals

Using the Slot Allocation Method, we propose 3 approaches to allocate slots starting from the leaves of the routing tree. The idea is that starting from the bottom of the routing tree allows nodes that are far from the sink and being, therefore, on longer routes, to have earlier slots.

An example of a network composed of 8 sensor nodes with its MinDegree routing tree is given in Fig. 1 (node 1 is considered to be the sink node). This example will be used to illustrate the scheduling methods we propose.

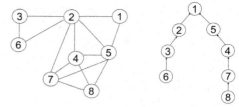

Fig. 1. A sensor network graph with its MinDegree routing tree

Rand-LO (Random Leaves Ordering). The Rand-LO allocation begins by scheduling leaves of the routing tree in a random order, then it continues to schedule nodes while ascending the routing tree:

1- Leaves of the routing tree are selected randomly and each one of them is allocated in the schedule using the previous Slot Allocation Method.
2- Parents of the already allocated nodes are selected and are considered for allocation in the same order as their children. According to this order, each parent is allocated in the schedule using the Slot Allocation Method (see Subsect. 3.2).
3- Repeat step 2 while ascending the tree until all nodes are allocated in the schedule.

The traversal order of the routing tree in Fig. 1, given by the Rand-LO allocation algorithm, is the following: 6 - 8 - 3 - 7 - 2 - 4 - 1 - 5.

Using the Slot Allocation Method, the schedule is constructed as follows:

- Initial schedule length = maximum node degree + 1 = 6 (degree of node 2) + 1 = 7.
- node 6: is a leaf, so it takes the first slot.
- node 8: is a leaf, try to allocate it in the first slot. node 6 and node 8 are not one-hop or two-hop neighbors and thus they can use the same slot. Therefore, node 8 takes the first slot.
- node 3: is parent of node 6, start allocation from slot 2. Slot 2 is free for node 3, so node 3 takes slot 2.
- node 7: is parent of node 8, start allocation from slot 2. Slot 2 is taken by node 3. Node 3 and node 7 are two-hop neighbors, they can not use the same slot. Next slot is free for Node 7, so node 7 takes slot 3.

This procedure continues until all nodes are allocated in the schedule.

The resulting schedule is presented in Fig. 2. Every line i gives the slot allocation for node i as a vector. The jth element of the vector for node i, $sched_j$, contains the node concerned by the communication of node i during the slot j. When $i = sched_j$, the slot j is used by the current node i to transmit. Otherwise, when no value is defined, the node does not communicate. When $i \neq sched_j$, the slot j is a slot used by node i to receive information from node $sched_j$. For example, in Fig. 2, node 2 uses the 4th slot to transmit information and receives in the next slot (5th) information from node 4.

The latency is computed in number of slots, considering the first slot $sched_1$ of the initial sending node as the first time to send.

For example, when node 6 needs to transmit information (using the routing tree in Fig. 1), its latency is of 4 slots (no waiting slots before starting communication, as node 6 has the first slot to transmit, 1 slot for node 6 to transmit, no waiting slots before node 3 transmits, 1 slot for node 3 to transmit, 1 waiting slot for node 2 before transmission and 1 slot for node 2 to transmit). This schedule generates an average latency of 5.714.

nodes	slots						
1			2			1	5
2	6	3	7	2	4	1	5
3	6	3		2			
4	8		7	2	4		5
5	8		7	2	4	1	5
6	6	3		2			
7	8		7	2	4		5
8	8		7		4		5

Fig. 2. TDMA schedule for the sensor network in Fig. 1 using Rand-LO

Depth-LO (Depth Leaves Ordering). The idea is to improve the previous method (Rand-LO) by giving leaves that are far from the sink the privilege to be scheduled earlier than the other leaves:

1- Leaves of the routing tree are selected and sorted by their depth in the routing tree, i.e. the leaf with the highest depth is processed first.
2- According to the appropriate order, each leaf is allocated in the schedule using the Slot Allocation Method.
3- Parents of the already allocated nodes are selected and are processed in the same order as their children.
4- According to this order, parents of the already scheduled children are allocated in the schedule using the Slot Allocation Method.
5- Repeat step 3 while ascending the routing tree until all nodes are allocated in the schedule.

According to the Depth-LO algorithm, the traversal of the routing tree in Fig. 1 is done in this order: 8 - 6 - 7 - 3 - 4 - 2 - 5 - 1. The resulting schedule is presented in Fig. 3 which gives an average latency of 5.571 that is lower than the latency obtained with Rand-LO.

nodes	slots						
1				2	5	1	
2	6	7	3	4	2	5	1
3	6		3		2		
4	8	7		4	2	5	
5	8	7		4	2	5	1
6	6		3		2		
7	8	7		4	2	5	
8	8	7		4		5	

Fig. 3. TDMA schedule for the sensor network in Fig. 1 using Depth-LO

Depth-ReLO (Depth Remaining Leaves Ordering). In Depth-ReLO, nodes on long paths in the routing tree are privileged and scheduled earlier than other nodes:

1- The leaf with the highest depth in the tree is allocated in the schedule using the Slot Allocation Method.
2- This leaf is deleted from the tree.
3- If the tree is not empty go to step 1, otherwise the scheduling is done.

According to the Depth-ReLO algorithm, the traversal of the routing tree in Fig. 1 is done in this order: 8 - 6 - 7 - 4 - 3 - 5 - 2 - 1. The resulting schedule is presented in Fig. 4 which gives an average latency of 5.428 that is lower than the latency obtained by Rand-LO and Depth-LO.

slots →

nodes							
1				5	2	1	
2	6	7	4	3	5	2	1
3	6			3		2	
4	8	7	4		5	2	
5	8	7	4		5	2	1
6	6			3		2	
7	8	7	4		5	2	
8	8	7	4		5		

Fig. 4. TDMA schedule for the sensor network in Fig. 1 using Depth-ReLO

4   Simulations Configuration

In this section, we present the configuration parameters used in the simulations. We used a Java-based library called JUNG [8] which allows modeling, analysis and visualization of networks as graphs.

We generated 5000 random networks using $n = 100$ nodes, each node having a communication range $r = 25$ m. Nodes were deployed in a square area of size a^2. The connectivity model used is UDG (Unit Disk Graph [7]), in which two nodes are considered neighbor if they are within each other's communication range (r). Based on this model, the density of the generated networks is: $\delta = \pi * r^2 * n/a^2$. The deployment area size was changed to obtain different densities $\delta \in [4, 20]$.

CoLaNet is based on the MinDegree tree which is not the best routing tree in terms of number of hops or energy consumption. That is why, in addition to the MinDegree tree, we evaluated the performance of our contributions using: the Geographic tree (each node chooses as its parent the closest neighbor to the sink, in terms of distance) and the Hop Count tree (each node chooses as its parent the closest neighbor to the sink, in terms of number of hops).

Due to lack of space, we only present the results obtained with the MinDegree tree, to make comparison feasible with CoLaNet. Experiments with the other routing trees give similar results.

We note that, similarly to LEACH cited in [1], an initialization phase is used before the scheduling process. In this phase, the sink processes the routing protocol using the positions of the nodes. After this phase, the sink computes the TDMA and broadcasts the routes and the TDMA in the network.

4.1   Evaluated Metrics

Average latency: The average latency was computed as the average of all total communication latencies from each node to the sink. This latency is the number of slots before the source node transmits (the reference slot being the first slot), and for every node in the routing path, except for the sink, one slot for transmission and the number of slots before its parent can transmit.

Average normalized latency: The average normalized latency is computed as the average of per link latencies for all the nodes in the network. The latency per link for a node is computed as the total latency for the node divided by the number of hops in the routing path for the node to the sink.

Schedule length: The schedule length is computed as the number of slots of the obtained schedule.

Duty cycle: The duty cycle is computed as the ratio of the active period (estimated by the number of slots used either in transmission or in reception) to the total period (the schedule length). A lower duty cycle results in a lower energy consumption [9].

4.2   Improved-CoLaNet (I-CoLaNet)

As already explained, CoLaNet does not consider latency when defining the transmission schedule. Continuing to color all its neighbor in the tree does not reflect the direction of the communications in the routing tree. Whereas, our objective is latency optimization. This difference in objectives makes us propose I-CoLaNet, an improved version of CoLaNet in which an order is given to nodes during the vertex-coloring, in order to improve communication latencies, simultaneously for all sensor nodes.

As in CoLaNet, I-CoLaNet uses the MinDegree tree as a routing tree and a similar vertex-coloring algorithm. The idea of I-CoLaNet is the following:

1- Color the max-degree node in the routing tree.
2- Continue with coloring recursively each node that has an already colored parent node in the tree.
3- Restart with step 1, without considering the colored nodes, until all nodes have a color.
4- Transform the obtained coloring into a schedule for each node.

In this coloring solution, nodes are colored according to the parent-child relation and the data flow direction given by the routing tree. Therefore, the communication slot of children are generally close to the communication slot of their parents, thus reducing communication latencies.

5   Performance Evaluation

This section presents the evaluation of the performances of Rand-LO, Depth-LO, Depth-ReLO and I-CoLaNet obtained by simulations.

First, the performance of I-CoLanet in terms of latency and schedule length was compared with that of CoLaNet and with that of Random TDMA. Random TDMA is a basic protocol (which is not cross-layered) where slots are given to nodes randomly (no specific order is defined) while ensuring that communications are collision free. The computed metrics represent averages of the results for the 5000 randomly generated networks.

As shown in Fig. 5, CoLanet and I-CoLaNet have better average latency than Random TDMA, because they use information coming from the routing tree in the TDMA schedule. These results show that cross-layer protocols have better performance than traditional layered protocols. Moreover, as I-CoLaNet aims to

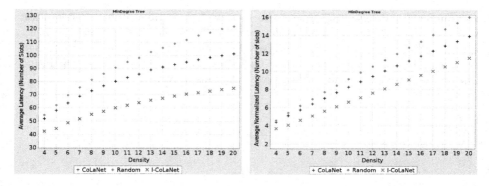

Fig. 5. Average Latency depending on δ

Fig. 6. Average Normalized Latency depending on δ

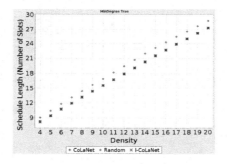

Fig. 7. Schedule Length depending on δ

respect the aspects of parent-children relation and direction in the routing tree, its average latency is better than that of CoLaNet.

Similar to the average latency results, Fig. 6 shows that I-CoLaNet has a better average normalized latency because it gives an importance to the order of communication between a parent and its children in the routing tree. This aspect is not dealt with in CoLaNet, that is why its average normalized latency is close to that of Random TDMA where no routing order is respected.

The CoLaNet allocation algorithm is based on an approximation solution for the vertex-coloring problem. Therefore, the obtained schedule length (corresponding to the number of colors) is not optimal. Figure 7 shows that I-CoLaNet has the same schedule length as CoLaNet which gives the same energy consumption. That is because I-CoLaNet and CoLaNet are based on similar vertex-coloring algorithms. Also, both CoLaNet and I-CoLaNet have lower schedule length than the schedule length of Random TDMA, thanks to the vertex-coloring algorithm. Moreover, I-CoLaNet has better performance than CoLaNet because it does not just reduce the length of the schedule, but it also searches optimized allocation for the latency metric. The parent-children relation and the communication direction given by the routing tree is taken into consideration while coloring the nodes. This helps reducing both the average and the average normalized latencies. Since I-CoLaNet has better performances (in terms of latencies) than Random TDMA and CoLaNet, we will compare the scheduling approaches based on three routing tree traversals only with I-CoLaNet.

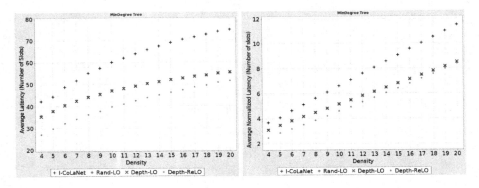

Fig. 8. Average Latency (left side) and Average Normalized Latency (right side)

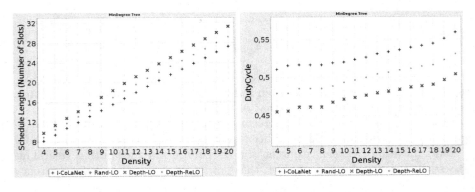

Fig. 9. Schedule Length (left side) and Duty Cycle (right side)

As shown in the left side of Fig. 8, it is clear that starting slot allocation with the leaves of the routing tree gives better average latency results than starting with the max-degree node. Starting with the leaves of the tree gives the chance to nodes that are far from the sink to be scheduled first. In Depth-LO, we order leaves by their depth in the routing tree, to give the farthest nodes from the sink the privilege to be scheduled first. This gives the same average latency for MinDegree tree because this tree has few routes and is not balanced (routes with different lengths), so the order does not have great impact. Moreover, eliminating already scheduled nodes from the routing tree before moving to the next step of the allocation (as in Depth-ReLO) allows to give more importance to long routes so their nodes can be given earlier slots, which improves the average latency.

The right side of Fig. 8 shows results of average normalized latency when varying the network density. Giving earlier slots to deep leaves and privileging the nodes of long routes, as in Depth-LO and Depth-ReLO, reduces even more the gap between the slots of a node and its parent in the routing tree and gives better average normalized latency. The difference between Depth-LO and Depth-ReLO is that the first one privileges one node of each route, while the second one privileges more nodes of the same route (if the route is long) thanks to the elimination. That is why Depth-ReLO has the best average normalized latency.

As shown in the left side of Fig. 9, I-CoLaNet has the fewest number of slots. Our traversal-based allocation methods generate schedules with one or two slots longer than the schedules of I-CoLaNet. Nevertheless, longer schedules of our approaches are counteracted by better transmission latencies.

The right side of Fig. 9 shows that our approaches have lower duty cycle and thus a smaller energy consumption. Rand-LO and Depth-LO have the best duty cycle thanks to their schedule length. Depth-ReLO comes in second place in terms of duty cycle because its schedule length is smaller than the first ones. Unlike I-CoLaNet, which reduces the schedule length with the vertex-coloring algorithm but most of the slots are active (either in transmission or in reception) and this increments the duty cycle and therefore, the energy consumption. We remind that nodes can turn off their radio during the inactive slots.

All the previous results are averages and do not reflect data individually. We analyze the extent of variability of the obtained values in relation to the correspondent mean, on the basis of the coefficient of variation (Relative Standard Deviation). It is expressed in percentage as $\frac{\sigma}{\mu}$ where σ is the standard deviation and μ is the mean. We remind that the size of the analyzed population is 5000. Table 1 shows the intervals of the coefficient of variation, irrespective of density, for all the three metrics, depending on the analyzed allocation methods. All the obtained coefficients of variation are inferior to 11.5 % which proves that the absolute values are not very scattered.

Table 1. Intervals of the coefficient of variation irrespective of density

	Latency	Normalized latency	Schedule length
Random	[8.9 ; 11.2] %	[5.8 ; 7.2] %	[3.1 ; 5.2] %
CoLaNet	[8.8 ; 9.5] %	[5.5 ; 7.6] %	[3.6 ; 4.8] %
I-CoLaNet	[7.4 ; 8.3] %	[6.6 ; 8.5] %	[3.6 ; 5.0] %
Rand-LO	[10.2 ; 11.5] %	[7.4 ; 9.2] %	[3.6 ; 5.4] %
Depth-LO	[9.4 ; 11.5] %	[7.4 ; 9.0] %	[3.6 ; 4.6] %
Depth-ReLO	[10.3 ; 11.0] %	[7.6 ; 9.8] %	[3.3 ; 5.9] %

Synthesis of simulations. CoLaNet is a cross-layer MAC protocol in which the scheduling is constructed applying a vertex-coloring algorithm on the MinDegree routing tree. It is not oriented to optimize the latencies of communications.

I-CoLaNet is also based on the vertex-coloring algorithm but respecting the parent-child order; it reduces the latency by 19 % compared with CoLaNet.

The main goal of the Slot Allocation Method used in our scheduling approaches is to reduce the gap between the slot of a child and the slot of its parent in the routing tree. Therefore, when considering communications on routing paths, latency is reduced. Compared with CoLaNet, Rand-LO improves latency by 33 %, Depth-LO improves it by 35 % and Depth-ReLO by 54 %. Even though all our approaches generate longer schedule lengths than I-CoLaNet, duty-cycle is improved of 7 % for Depth-ReLO and of 11 % for Rand-LO and Depth-LO. Better duty-cycle helps minimizing energy consumption in collision-free MAC protocols because inactive nodes may be switched to sleep mode.

6   Conclusion and Future Work

This paper presents new scheduling methods to reduce latency of communications simultaneously for all nodes of the sensor network, based on the routing information. We present a different slot allocation method associated with several traversals of the routing tree, beginning with its leaves, that are Rand-LO, Depth-LO and Depth-ReLO. Results of simulations show that these techniques have better performance than the state of the art and improve latency up to 54 %. Even if the obtained schedules are longer than the schedules of CoLaNet by 1 or 2 slots on average, the duty cycle is improved up to 11 % which results in less energy consumption. These results show the importance of the traversal of the routing tree in the slot scheduling method and reveal the need to study more extensively the effect of nodes enumeration of the network's graph on the slot allocation method.

References

1. Akyildiz, I.F., Su, W., Sankarasubramaniam, Y., Cayirci, E.: Wireless sensor networks: a survey. Comput. Netw. **38**, 393–422 (2002)
2. Mendes, L.D.P., Rodrigues, J.J.P.C.: A survey on cross-layer solutions for wireless sensor networks. J. Netw. Comput. Appl. **34**(2), 523–534 (2011)
3. Melodia, T., Vuran, M.C., Pompili, D.: The state of the art in cross-layer design for wireless sensor networks. In: Cesana, M., Fratta, L. (eds.) Euro-NGI 2005. LNCS, vol. 3883, pp. 78–92. Springer, Heidelberg (2006)
4. Brzozowski, M., Salomon, H., Langendoerfer, P.: Support for a long lifetime and short end-to-end delays with TDMA protocols in sensor networks. Int. J. Distrib. Sens. Netw. **2012**, 29 (2012). Hindawi Publishing Corporation
5. Cheng-Fu, C., Kwang-Ting, C.: CoLaNet: a cross-layer design of energy-efficient wireless sensor networks. In: IEEE Systems Communications, pp. 364–369 (2005)
6. Pemmaraju, S., Skiena, S.: Computational Discrete Mathematics: Combinatorics and Graph Theory with Mathematica. Cambridge University Press, New York (2003)

7. Schmid, S., Wattenhofer, R.: Algorithmic models for sensor networks. In: 14th WPDRTS, pp. 450–459 (2006)
8. O'Madadhain, J., Fisher, D., Smyth, P., White, S., Boey, Y.: Analysis and visualization of network data using JUNG. J. Stat. Softw. **10**(2), 1–35 (2005)
9. Shuguo, Z., Ye-Qiong, S., Zhi, W., Zhibo, W.: Queue-mac: a queue-length aware hybrid csma/tdma mac protocol for providing dynamic adaptation to traffic and duty-cycle variation in wireless sensor networks. In: 9th IEEE WFCS, pp. 105–114 (2012)

System Design and Analysis of UAV-Assisted BLE Wireless Sensor Systems

Mikhail Komarov[1,2(✉)] and Dmitri Moltchanov[2]

[1] Faculty of Business and Management, School of Business Informatics,
National Research University Higher School of Economics, Moscow, Russia
`mkomarov@hse.ru`
[2] Department of Communications Engineering, Tampere University of Technology,
Tampere, Finland
{`mikhail.komarov,dmitri.moltchanov`}`@tut.fi`

Abstract. Inefficiency of wireless sensor networks (WSN) in terms of the network lifetime is one of the major reasons preventing their widespread use. To alleviate this problem different data collection approaches have been proposed. One of the promising techniques is to use unmanned aerial vehicle (UAV). In spite of several papers advocating this approach, there have been no system designs and associated performance evaluation proposed to date. In this paper, we address this issue by proposing a new WSN design, where UAV serves as a sink while Bluetooth low energy (BLE) is used as a communication technology. We analyze the proposed design in terms of the network lifetime and area coverage comparing it with routed WSNs. Our results reveal that the lifetime of the proposed design is approximately two orders of magnitude longer than that of the routed WSNs. Using the tools of integral geometry we show that the density of nodes to cover a certain area is approximately two times more for routed WSNs compared to our design.

Keywords: Sensor networks · BLE · UAV · System design · Performance

1 Introduction

A wireless sensor network is defined as a collection of devices capable of sensing environmental parameters, connected in a network and collectively delivering the collected data to a certain location. As a result of more than a decade of investigations, the challenges and requirements of modern WSNs are well understood [1,13]. There are already a number of complete solutions available on the market. At the same time, in spite of significant market push from the vendors WSNs are still not widely deployed. One of the major reasons is inefficiency of such systems in terms of the network lifetime.

© IFIP International Federation for Information Processing 2016
Published by Springer International Publishing Switzerland 2016. All Rights Reserved
L. Mamatas et al. (Eds.): WWIC 2016, LNCS 9674, pp. 284–296, 2016.
DOI: 10.1007/978-3-319-33936-8_22

Uneven energy consumption is one of the reasons for short WSN lifetimes. The root cause of this phenomenon is networking of nodes. In practical deployments there are only few locations, where sinks can be positioned. In this case there is always a set of nodes that are more involved in packets routing and forwarding. Since the lifetime of a network is defined as the time till there is no path to the sink we see that uneven energy consumption places severe constraints on lifetime. Over the last decade researchers addressed this problem identifying a number of feasible solutions such as multi-path routing, clusterization, data aggregation, in-network data processing, etc. However, none of those are general enough to be applicable to any arbitrary deployment [3]. On top of this, the routed principle of WSNs adds to this problem. Indeed, networking mechanisms such as neighbor discovery, connectivity and topology maintenance, routing and packet forwarding require substantial amount of energy [2,4].

One way to avoid unequal energy consumption is to get rid of networking. Mobile sinks may allow to achieve this goal. To avoid human involvement the collection of data must be completely automatic. The obvious choice would be to use unmanned aerial vehicles (UAV), particularly, quadrocopters, also known as drones. UAVs are a new technology at the "rapid improvement" phase of the S-curve of technology development cycle. As improvements are made, drones are becoming more agile, autonomous, power efficient and safe. The idea of using UAVs for data collection in WSNs is not new. Particularly, the authors in [12] advocated the use of UAV to interconnect sparse WSN clusters. The use of UAV as a mobile WSN node for emergency applications has been suggested in [8]. The authors in [11] proposed to use UAV for charging and deploying WSN nodes. Nevertheless, to date, no detailed investigations of such solutions and/or their comparison with conventional routed WSN designs have been performed.

We propose a new UAV-assisted solution for data collection in WSNs. We optimize performance of single hop communications between a sensor node and UAV in terms of optimal altitude and flying speed. We also compare lifetimes, coverage and required density of nodes of our solution with those of routed WSN designs. Using the tools of integral geometry and random graphs theory we show that (i) the lifetime of our design is 10–18 times longer compared to routed WSNs operating using the same BLE technology, (ii) the required density of nodes for environment monitoring is approximately two times smaller even when sensing range coincides with the communications range. These two properties make UAV-assisted WSN design an attractive option for many applications including smart agriculture, forest fire monitoring, etc.

The rest of the article is organized as follows. Section 2 provides state-of-the-art in UAV and short-range wireless communications backing up the choice of drones and BLE for our design. System parameters are optimized in Sect. 3. We analytically compare performance of routed WSN solution and the proposed one in terms of network lifetime, coverage and connectivity in Sect. 4. Conclusions are drawn in the last section.

2   Technological Choices

2.1   Communication Technology

There are several options to consider as a candidate wireless technology for single hop wireless sensor systems. The comparison of these technologies is shown in Table 1, where PPC stands for peak power consumption, PPB refers to power-per-bit. In this paper we advocate the use of recently standardized BLE. BLE is an evolution of Bluetooth for state transmission systems, i.e. sensor data. Table 2 summarizes the most important improvements introduced in BLE compared to Bluetooth. Modifications affected the critical features including physical layer modulation, communications protocols, application interface and security. One important improvement is the use of Gaussian Frequency Shift Keying with larger modulation index, $0.45 - 0.55$ instead of $0.25 - 0.35$ in Bluetooth. Recall, that the modulation index in GFSK affects the wideness of the signal spectrum. This allowed to increase the communications range of the BLE technology while using the same amount of emitted power. Further, significant changes has been introduced to the communication protocol limiting almost all basic parameters. Targeting state applications the maximum packet size was reduced to 27 bytes while the acknowledgement packet size was reduced from 100 bytes to 12 bytes. The authentication in BLE is performed for each packet favoring single packet transactions. Encryption is performed using AES-128. Of special importance is the reduction in the connection establishment time allowing to perform it in just 3 ms and completing the transfer of one packet in less than a second. Recalling compatibility with Bluetooth, these features make BLE an excellent choice for power-constrained single-hop wireless sensor systems.

Table 1. Comparison of low power communications technologies.

Metric	PPBμW/bit	Range, m	Rate, Mbps	Delay, ms	PPC, mA
Bluetooth	0.05	30	2.1	20	100
BLE	0.153	50	0.3	3–6	12.5
ANT+	0.71	30	0.002	<1	17
ZigBee	185	100	0.1	20	40
Wi-Fi	0.005	150	6	1.5	50
Nike+	2.48	10	0.0003	1000	12.3

2.2   UAV Technology

Over the last decade the UAV technology has advanced beyond the domain of military sponsored projects. Civilian applications are becoming more and more common. A whole new class of drones has evolved over the last decade – the Micro Air Vehicles (MAV). It encompasses a whole range of miniature, flying vehicles that have been around for a while now. Recently, multi-rotor UAVs, also referred to as drones, have attracted significant attention. These devices use three or more vertically aligned engines and movement is achieved by creating a difference in thrust on motors on the opposite sides of the frame resulting the UAV tilting and creating sideways acceleration. The thrust regulation needs to be very precise and cannot be done without a microcontroller. To perform basic operations, the microcontroller needs sensors including gyroscope and accelerometer.

Table 2. Comparison of Bluetooth and BLE.

Parameter	Bluetooth	BLE
Channels	79	40
Modulation/index	GFKP/0.35	GFSK/0.55
Tolerable pathloss	90 dB	95 dB
Range	30 m	50 m
ACK length	100 B	12 B
Max packet size	1021 B	27 B
CRC length	2 B	3 B
Encryption	Safer+	AES-128
Authentication	Once	Every packet
Connection states	Inquiry/Page/Connected	Advertizing
Connection time	20 ms	3 ms

The first drones were built around Arduino platform, so they already had a surplus of processing power and are compatible with many more sensors than just the essentials. Achieving autonomous flight was just a matter of adding additional sensors and programming the software to use them. This trend still continues today and, as the sensors grow in numbers, so does the processing power needed to make effective use of them. As of today, widely available drones use dedicated Flight Management Units (FMUs) that come with all the basic sensors integrated on one board and a further support for the most common sensor buses like CAN or I2C.

A commercial UAV include systems for precise navigation, collision protection, home landing and programmable flying route. With maximum flying speed of 15 m/s (54 km/h) and time of 30 − 90 m an UAV can fly up to 79.2 km in a single run. Assuming that an UAV carries a BLE device with communication range of 50 − 100 m, flies in zig-zag way to scan sensors on monitored area, the coverage area of a single flight is 5.5 − 16.0 km².

2.3   System Design Overview

The system design is illustrated in Fig. 1. Instead of keeping sink node stationary and gathering data by multi-hop routing, we make it mobile and apply BLE technology to further reduce power consumption of nodes. There are multiple advantageous features of using UAVs for data collection. First, flexibility of

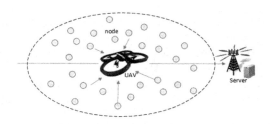

Fig. 1. Proposed WSN data collection mechanism.

movement allows to freely optimize trajectories collecting data from the whole network or only from a part of it. Secondly, the movement speed is high allowing to cover the large areas of interest. Taking into account the recent progress in UAVs, the flight navigation could be made completely automatic using GPS. In this mode, an UAV can be configured to follow a predetermined route to collect sensors' data then come back to a ground station to transfer data and recharge battery. A group of UAVs can be used in combination with a ground station or adjacent stations to collect sensors' data in one sensing area or in different ones.

The proposed WSN system is based on single-hop data transmission approach where a UAV carries a sink node, BLE master, and fly over the monitored area to collect data from deployed sensor nodes, BLE slaves. Sensor and sink nodes communicate with each other using BLE. Sink node continuously scan for BLE slave nodes to establish connections and exchange data. After data collection, UAV comes back to ground station. The system does not require time synchronization between UAV flying time and BLE slave wake up pattern.

3   System Design

3.1   Device Discovery Time

To exchange data BLE device have to discover its neighbors. It starts with entering the advertising state and then proceeding with connection state. In advertising state the sensor node sends advertising packets over three designated channels (37, 38, and 39). The scanner scans these channels continuously. The role of the scanner is performed by the UAV. When scanner discovers an advertiser, it sends a connection request packet to establish connection. Once replied, both devices enter the connection mode. While connected, advertiser becomes slave and scanner is designated as master.

The advertising interval, T_A, consists of a static interval $T_{A,0}$ and a random part ρ, where ρ is uniformly distributed between 0 and 10 ms, $T_{A,0}$ is chosen in between 20 ms and 10 s. There are two time intervals defined for the scanner, scanning interval T_S, chosen in between 20 ms and 10 s, and the scanning event time d_s chosen in between 0 and T_S. The channel interval corresponds to the time to send 38 bytes of advertizing packet and equals to 446 μs. The interval between sending advertizing packets within a single adverstizing event is $d_{ch} = 150$ μs.

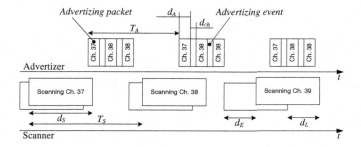

Fig. 2. Time diagram of advertising/scanning phase in BLE.

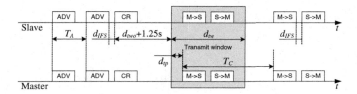

Fig. 3. Time diagram of connection phase in BLE.

Let T_{dis} be the discovery time. Analyzing Fig. 2 we see that the discovery is successfull if $d_A < T_{dis} < T_A + d_A$ implying that the upper bound on the discovery time is $10.24 + 0.01 + 0.000446 \approx 10.25$ s while the minimum is exactly the time to transmit 38 bytes of data, 446 μs.

3.2   Connection Time

Having received an advertising packet, the scanner sends a connection request packet after waiting for distributed interframe spacing time (DIFS, d_{IFS}). This packet contains two parameters, *transmitWindowOffset*, d_{two}, and *transmitWindow*, d_{tw}. According to our assumptions all the data can be transmitted in just one packet. Figure 3 illustrates the connection phase between master and slave.

Denoting the connection time by T_{con} we see that

$$T_{con} = d_{IFS} + 1.25\text{ms} + d_{two} + d_{tw}, \tag{1}$$

where $d_{IFS} = 150\,\mu s$, $0 < d_{two} < T_C$, 1.25 ms $< d_{tw} < 10$ ms, T_C is the connection interval which could be tuned between 7.5 ms and 4 s. Thus, we see that connection time is bounded by

$$d_{IFS} + 1.25\text{ ms} \approx 1.4\text{ ms} < T_{con} < 4.0114\text{ s}. \approx d_{two} + 1.25\text{ s} + d_{tw}. \tag{2}$$

In the proposed system, an UAV scans for advertising packets continuously while the BLE module of a sensor node enter advertising state after each wake up. The bounds on the time to transfer data, $T = T_{dis} + T_{con}$, is

$$446\,\mu s + 1.4\text{ ms} \approx 2\text{ ms} < T < 14.262\text{ s} = 10.250446\text{ s} + 4.0114\text{ s}. \tag{3}$$

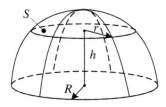

Fig. 4. An illustration of the UAV flying over a BLE sensor node.

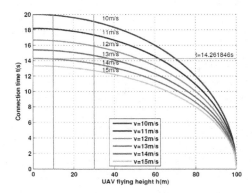

Fig. 5. UAV altitude and transaction time for different UAV speeds.

implying that remaining in the coverage of a sensor node for at least 14 s will guarantee exchange of data.

3.3   Optimal UAV Altitude and Speed

Consider a sensor node positioned on the ground and UAV flying over. Assume that the radio of a sensor node is omnidirectional forming a half-sphere around the node's position as shown in Fig. 4. The typical speed of UAV varies in the range of $30 - 45$ km/h, $10 - 15$ m/s. BLE range, R, is assumed to be upper bounded by 100 m. According to the previous section the connection time is upper bounded by approximately 14 s. We assume that when UAV crosses the half-sphere shown in Fig. 4 it goes through the center of the cutting plane to increase its chances to establish connection and collect the data from the sensor.

Analyzing Fig. 4, we see that the maximum altitude of UAV is given by

$$h = \sqrt{R^2 - (vT_T/2)^2}, \tag{4}$$

where $T_T = T_{dis} + T_{con}$ is the transaction time, v is the speed of UAV.

Keeping UAV flying speed low, UAV may have enough time to exchange data with sensor node but the coverage range of UAV decreases. To increase UAV velocity, we need to decrease the altitude. The dependencies between UAV altitude, speed and connection time is shown in Fig. 5.

3.4 Transmission Power Requirements

The commercial BLE chipsets (CC2541, CC2540, [5]) are produced with programmable output power that could be adjusted over a wide range. Relying on the estimated UAV flying parameters the task is to determine the minimum transmission power needed to establish connection and exchange the data [9].

Since the proposed system is applied for monitoring flat area with line-of-sight between UAV and sensor node, the free space path loss propagation model can be applied. Using Friis equation in the form

$$P_{Rx} = P_{Tx} + G_T + G_R - 20\log_{10}(d) - 20\log_{10}(f) + 147.55, \tag{5}$$

we derive P_{Tx}, where P_{Rx} is the minimum power at the receiver set to $-90\,\mathrm{dBm}$, P_{Tx} is the transmission power we are looking for, $G_T = G_R = 6\,\mathrm{dBi}$ are antenna gains at the transmitter and receiver, respectively, d is transmission range in kilometers and $f = 2.4\,\mathrm{GHz}$ is the operating frequency.

Figure 6 shows the relation between the required transmission power and transaction time when UAV altitude varies between 10 m and 20 m. The transmission power in the proposed WSN design is extremely low ranging from $-224.946\,\mathrm{dBm}$ to $-207.702\,\mathrm{dBm}$.

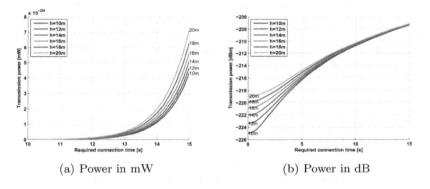

(a) Power in mW (b) Power in dB

Fig. 6. The required transmission power for different transaction times.

4 Performance Analysis and Comparison

4.1 Network Lifetime

In the proposed design all the nodes spend equal amount of power. Consider the power required to perform a single transaction. The power consumption of the radio states of advertising and connection events is provided in [5]. Based on these data, the power consumption for advertising and connection events are

$$P_A = \frac{U \sum_i I_i t_i}{\sum_i t_i} = 32.759, \qquad P_C = \frac{U \sum_i I_i t_i}{\sum_i t_i} = 24.762, \tag{6}$$

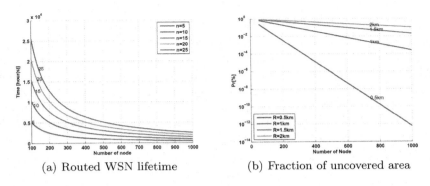

(a) Routed WSN lifetime   (b) Fraction of uncovered area

Fig. 7. Performance comparison of the proposed and conventional designs.

leading to the overall consumption per transaction $P = 57.521\,\text{mW}$, that is, $19.173\,\text{mA}$ in $6.92\,\text{ms}$. Assuming that sensor nodes typically use a coin-cell CR2032 battery with capacity 225mAh, a single node can work continuously during $20.605\,\text{h}$. If we set the device to wake up periodically in each $10\,\text{s}$, it can last for approximately 2020 days or around 5.53 years.

Consider now a lifetime of a routed WSN. Nodes are assumed to be connected forming a network and all the data are routed to the sinks. Thus, sink nodes will be the first to run out of power. The lifetime of sink nodes depends on the number of nodes in a network, M, the number of sink nodes, n, and the data collection interval, d_t. The lifetime of a routed WSN can be approximated as

$$T_f = \frac{T_c}{T_d} d_t = \frac{T_C N d_t}{t_C M}. \tag{7}$$

Assume that the routed WSN use BLE with the data exchange event consuming $24.762\,\text{mW}$. The lifetime of a routed WSN is shown in Fig. 7(a). Observe that the maximum lifetime of a routed WSN with the same communication technology ($n = 25$, $M = 100$, $d_t = 10\,\text{s}$) is approximately $2552\,\text{h}$ (106 days) which is 18 times smaller than $48482\,\text{h}$ (2020 days) for the proposed design.

4.2   Network Coverage

Consider the number of nodes needed to cover a monitored area in the proposed system. The analysis relies upon the results of [7] and is based on integral geometry approach involving, particularly, the notion of kinematic density.

Let $A_0(F_0, L_0)$ be the monitored area with perimeter L_0 and area F_0. Assume N sensors are distributed according to $K(A_0)$ distribution over A_0. Each sensor has a sensing area $A_i(F_i, L_i)$, $i = 1, 2, \ldots, N$, where L_i and F_i are the perimeter and area, respectively. We are interested in the following metrics: (i) the fraction of area of A_0 that is not covered, and (ii) the probability that a randomly selected point of A_0 is covered by at least k, $k \geq 1$ sensors. Assuming that A_0 and A_i are convex, the fraction of area A_0 that is not covered by any sensors when N sensors are randomly and uniformly deployed is given by [7]

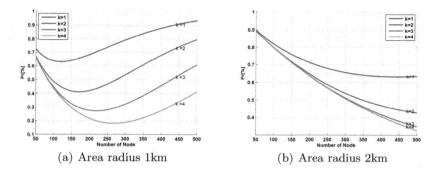

(a) Area radius 1km   (b) Area radius 2km

Fig. 8. Probability of an arbitrary point covered by at least k sensors.

$$Fr(S = 0) = \prod_{i=1}^{N} \frac{2\pi F_0 + L_0 L_i}{2\pi(F_0 + F_i) + L_0 L_i}.$$ (8)

The probability that a point is covered by at least k, $k \geq 1$ sensors is [7]

$$Pr\{S \geq k\} = 1 - \sum_{h=0}^{k-1} \frac{\sum_i^{C_h^N} (\prod_{j=1}^{N}(2\pi F_{T_{i,j}}) \prod_{z=1}^{N-h} \Theta(i,z))}{\prod_{r=1}^{N}(2\pi(F_0 + F_r) + L_0 L_r)},$$ (9)

where, $\Theta(i, z) = 2\pi F_0 + L_0 L_{G_{i,z}}$, $T_{i,j}$ is a matrix whose each row i is a k-permutation of $[1, 2 \ldots, N]$, $G_{i,z}$ is a matrix whose each row i contains the elements of $[1, 2, \ldots, N]$ that do not appear in the ith row of $T_{i,z}$. The notation C_h^N denotes binomial coefficient.

The fraction of uncovered area as a function of the number of uniformly deployed nodes is shown in Fig. 7(b). The sensing radius of nodes are assumed to be $100\,m$ while the monitoring area radii are $0.5, 1, 1, 5, 2\,km$. The fraction of uncovered area decreases exponentially when the number of nodes increases. Using these data one can estimate the number of nodes required to cover a certain area such that only a given small fraction on area is unmonitored.

Figure 8 illustrates the probability that an arbitrary point of an area is covered by at least k sensors as a function of the number of nodes for different area radii. The redundancy added attempting to cover the largest possible fraction is significant. For example, recalling that for area radius of $1\,km$ 365 nodes cover $95\,\%$ of area, we see that this amount of nodes results in non-negligible probability of having two and more nodes covering an arbitrary point of an area. This is a usual price to pay for simplicity of stochastic deployment.

4.3 Connectivity

In routed WSN nodes have to be connected. This may require denser deployment than that needed to ensure a coverage only. Here, we evaluate the nodes density required to ensure k connectivity and compare it to that dictated by the coverage.

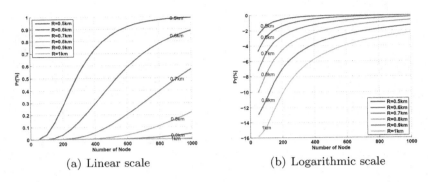

(a) Linear scale   (b) Logarithmic scale

Fig. 9. Probability of 1-connectivity.

We approach the connectivity problem using the results of random graph theory. In his seminal paper [10], M. Penrose addressed the question of the distribution of longest edge in a random geometric graph and k-connectivity of these graphs, respectively. Assuming uniform distribution of nodes over the monitored area and knowing the communications range of a node the former result immediately gives the probability that the network is disconnected while the latter one provides quantities such as the probability of exactly or at least k paths between two randomly chosen nodes.

Let R be the radius of a circular area, d be the communication range of a sensor, n be number of nodes and k be the number of neighbors of arbitrary node. The probability that an arbitrary node has at least k neighbors is [10]

$$Q_{n,k}(d) = 2\pi \int_0^C rf(r)(1 - \sum_{i=0}^{k-1} C_i^{n-1} p(r,d)^i (1 - p(r,d)^{n-1-i}))dr, \qquad (10)$$

where $f(r)$ is the density of node location, see [6].

The probability that a network with n nodes is k-connected is [10]

$$C_{n,k}(d) \approx [Q_{n,k}(d)]^n. \qquad (11)$$

Figure 9 shows the probability that the network is connected (1-connected) as a function of the number of deployed nodes for different radius of an area in both linear and log scales. A routed WSN requires much more nodes than the proposed design and the reason is the need for connectivity of the system. Recall that for the proposed WSN design, for an area radius of 1 km and sensing radius of 100 m, the number of nodes ensuring 95 % coverage is 365. For routed WSN with nodes having communication range of 100 m, to keep the network connected with 0.95 probability, we need to deploy more than 1000 of nodes. Deploying 365 nodes randomly, the probability of connected network is $6.4E - 7$.

5   Conclusions

We proposed and evaluated a new UAV-assisted WSN design. It is based on BLE wireless technology for single-hop communications and UAVs for collection of data. The proposed system allows to enforce even energy consumption in WSNs, improves the network lifetime and is still completely automatic in terms of data collection. Based on the modern BLE and UAV specifications, we developed a single-hop sensor-UAV interaction model estimating the optimal altitude and flying speed of UAV for the worst case BLE transaction time as well as the energy required to establish reliable communications.

We analyzed the performance of the proposed design in terms of the lifetime and coverage properties. We also compared these metrics to those of conventional routed WSN design revealing that (i) the proposed system provides 10 to 18 times longer lifetimes compared to conventional WSN and (ii) the density of nodes required to ensure coverage is approximately two times smaller compared to routed WSNs even when sensing region of nodes coincides with their communications range. These properties make the proposal an attractive option for monitoring environmental parameters in large open areas.

References

1. Akyildiz, I., Kasimoglu, I.: Wireless sensor and actor networks: research challenges. Ad Hoc Netw. **2**, 351–367 (2004)
2. Andreev, S., Gonchukov, P., Himayat, N., Koucheryavy, Y., Turlikov, A.: Energy efficient communications for future broadband cellular networks. Comp. Comm. **35**(14), 1662–1671 (2012)
3. Andreev, S., Koucheryavy, Y., Himayat, N., Gonchukov, P., Turlikov, A.: Active-mode power optimization in ofdma-based wireless networks. In: Proceedings of GLOBECOM, pp. 799–803 (2010)
4. Horneber, J., Hergenroder, A.: A survey on testbeds and experimentation environments for wireless sensor networks. IEEE Comm. Surv. Tutor. **16**(4), 1820–1838 (2014)
5. Kamath, S., Lindh, J.: Measuring bluetooth low energy power consumption. Application Note, Texas Instruments (2012)
6. Lassila, P., Hyytia, E., Koskinen, H.: Connectivity properties of random waypoint mobility model for ad hoc networks. In: Al Agha, K., Guérin Lassous, I., Pujolle, G. (eds.) Challenges in Ad Hoc Networking. IFIP AICT, vol. 197, pp. 159–168. Springer, Boston (2006)
7. Lazos, L., Poovendran, R.: Stochastic coverage in heterogeneous sensor networks. ACM Trans. Sensor Netw. **2**(3), 325–358 (2006)
8. Leng, J.: Using a UAV to effectively prolong wireless sensor network lifetime with wireless power transfer. Ph.D. dissertation, University of Nebraska (2014)
9. Moltchanov, D., Koucheryavy, Y., Harju, J.: Simple, accurate and computationally efficient wireless channel modeling algorithm. In: Braun, T., Carle, G., Koucheryavy, Y., Tsaoussidis, V. (eds.) WWIC 2005. LNCS, vol. 3510, pp. 234–245. Springer, Heidelberg (2005)
10. Penrose, M.: The longest edge of the random minimal spanning tree. Ann. Appl. Prob. **7**(2), 340–361 (1997)
11. Tuna, G., Mumcu, T.V., Gulez, K., Gungor, V.C., Erturk, H.: Unmanned aerial vehicle-aided wireless sensor network deployment system for post-disaster monitoring. In: Huang, D.-S., Gupta, P., Zhang, X., Premaratne, P. (eds.) ICIC 2012. CCIS, vol. 304, pp. 298–305. Springer, Heidelberg (2012)

12. Valente, J., Sanz, D., Barrientos, A., Cerro, J., Ribeiro, A., Rossi, C.: Anair-ground wireless sensor network for crop monitoring. Sensors **11**(6), 6088–6108 (2011)
13. Vinel, A., Vishnevsky, V., Koucheryavy, Y.: A simple analytical model for the periodic broadcasting in vehicular ad-hoc networks. In: Proceedings of GLOBECOM, pp. 1–5 (2008)

Implementing a Broadcast Storm Attack on a Mission-Critical Wireless Sensor Network

Irina Krivtsova[1], Ilya Lebedev[1], Mikhail Sukhoparov[1], Nurzhan Bazhayev[1],
Igor Zikratov[1], Aleksandr Ometov[2]([✉]), Sergey Andreev[2], Pavel Masek[3],
Radek Fujdiak[3], and Jiri Hosek[3]

[1] Saint Petersburg National Research University of Information Technologies,
Mechanics and Optics (ITMO University), St. Petersburg, Russia
[2] Tampere University of Technology, Korkeakoulunkatu 10,
33720 Tampere, Finland
aleksandr.ometov@tut.fi
[3] Brno University of Technology, Technicka 3082/12, Brno, Czech Republic

Abstract. In this work, we emphasize the practical importance of
mission-critical wireless sensor networks (WSNs) for structural health
monitoring of industrial constructions. Due to its isolated and ad hoc
nature, this type of WSN deployments is susceptible to a variety of malicious attacks that may disrupt the underlying crucial systems. Along
these lines, we review and implement one such attack, named a broadcast
storm, where an attacker is attempting to flood the network by sending
numerous broadcast packets. Accordingly, we assemble a live prototype
of said scenario with real-world WSN equipment, as well as measure the
key operational parameters of the WSN under attack, including packet
transmission delays and the corresponding loss ratios. We further develop
a simple supportive mathematical model based on widely-adopted methods of queuing theory. It allows for accurate performance assessment as
well as for predicting the expected system performance, which has been
verified with statistical methods.

Keywords: Information security · Ad hoc networks · Multi-agent systems · Vulnerability · Device availability · Prototyping

1 Introduction and Background

The evolution of wireless sensor networks supports increasingly novel and sophisticated applications across various fields [1]. Modern wireless sensor networks
(WSNs) find their use in diverse environments, starting with the marine [2]
and vehicular [3] through the forestry [4], and towards the growing industrial
Smart Cities [5,6]. Generally, the main advantage and the limitation of the WSNs
is in their ad hoc nature, which makes them easy to deploy but difficult to manage. Most of the practical WSN deployments are utilizing wireless relaying to the
remote control center, which brings a variety of potential vulnerabilities to be
exploited.

© IFIP International Federation for Information Processing 2016
Published by Springer International Publishing Switzerland 2016. All Rights Reserved
L. Mamatas et al. (Eds.): WWIC 2016, LNCS 9674, pp. 297–308, 2016.
DOI: 10.1007/978-3-319-33936-8_23

Arguably, the most demanding areas of the WSN research may be shaped by urban and environmental applications [7]. In this work, we focus on a representative urban WSN application for industrial sensing – *structural health monitoring* [8]. This concept allows to maintain the appropriate condition of engineering structures by deploying sensors in the essential parts of buildings and other constructions, i.e. bridges, tunnels, skyscrapers, etc. The main purpose of such a WSN is to notify the control center about any significant change of the monitored object due to earthquakes, disasters, explosions, or other accidents. A secondary function is to provide continuous health monitoring. As a characteristic example, we may consider the Golden Gate Bridge in San Francisco Bay (shown in Fig. 1), where a similar network was deployed 10 years ago [9].

Clearly, a bridge of any kind is an object of national importance and therefore the serving WSN should be protected from the malicious attackers. However, due to the lack of relevant standardization activities, different manufacturing companies are utilizing a variety of dissimilar security solutions across their deployments, thus making them easier to attack. The use of wireless ad hoc sensor networks for critical applications poses novel information security challenges [10,11], such as: channel sniffing [12]; packet spoofing [13]; physical access to the device [14]; non-standardized communications protocols [15], and many others. We face the fact that development, deployment, and management of such a network is limiting the chance to use conventional information security solutions [16–18].

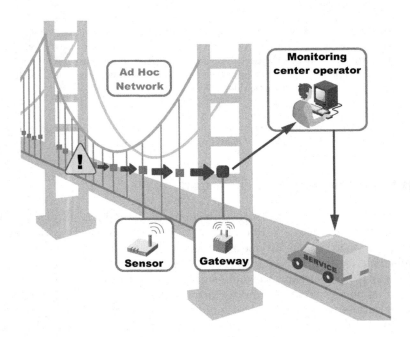

Fig. 1. Example ad hoc WSN deployment for structural health monitoring

In this work, we focus on one of the most threatening attacks on mission-critical WSNs – the broadcast storm [19]. Broadcasting in any ad hoc network is an elementary operation required for the core system functionality. However, intentional broadcasting by flooding may introduce uncontrollable redundancy, contention, and collisions that would lead to a so-called broadcast storm problem.

The rest of this work is organized as follows. Section 2 introduces the proposed system model for considering a broadcast attack in the network of interest. Further, in Sect. 3 we prototype the corresponding ad hoc WSN deployment and attack it by following said approach. In Sect. 4, we propose a simple analytical model validating our proposed framework. Finally, the conclusions are drawn in the last section.

2   Considered WSN System Model

In this work, we consider a system hosting a number of autonomous wireless nodes equipped with a set of measuring modules (sensors), and thus the challenges of efficient data transmission and processing are brought into focus [20]. On the other hand, ad hoc WSNs of this type are susceptible to possible attacks by implosion, blind flooding and, finally, broadcast storm [21–23].

Focusing primarily on the most challenging broadcast storm concept, the multicast control messages in a mission-critical WSN may become the main vehicles of this attack. Therefore, a high number of such packets is affecting the QoS for each transmitting node, which results in shorter battery life and lower reliability. The main configuration flaws that may enable such an attack are listed in what follows:

1. No limitations on the packet time-to-live parameter;
2. A possibility to transmit a broadcast packet from any unknown address in the network;
3. A device that could continuously generate packets.

Our research indicates that the easiest and cheapest way for an attacker to affect the operation of the ad hoc network in question is to generate harmful messages, when already residing *inside* the network. This may cause not only a partial denial-of-service effect for one particular node, but also provoke a fault of the entire wireless network [24]. Another factor affecting the system operation with substantial impact is a lack of continuous management and support, i.e. the network is assumed to be a standalone instance without continuous monitoring exercised. Some of the devices may become disabled due to natural factors, and may not be replaced immediately. However, there should always remain a crucial number of the operational devices available to deliver an alarm message. Summarizing all of the above, in this paper we focus on the problem of probabilistic device availability estimation in cases of a broadcast storm attack.

The most common implementation of said attack may be described as a significant increase in the intensity of broadcast requests in the target WSN or flooding by the attacker device, as it is presented in Fig. 2. As each transceiver node has to rebroadcast the messages, it leads to the difficulties in serving them over the reliable time. Basically, this scenario would appear when the incoming buffer of the device is full and/or the wireless channel is congested [25], and thus the denial-of-service attack is successful [26].

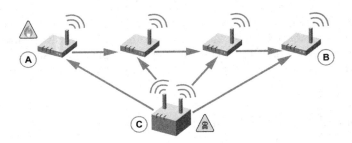

Fig. 2. Implementing the broadcast storm attack in an ad hoc WSN

In our target scenario, we employ the widely used WSN technology, IEEE 802.15.4 (ZigBee) [27], under the broadcast storm conditions. The WSN nodes equipped with such a radio module are typically small autonomous devices with limited computational power [28]. They are operating under a predefined configuration and utilize a constant set of vendor-specific signaling messages.

3   Prototyping a Broadcast Storm Attack

In order to verify the feasibility of our above discussion, we have conducted a set of experimental tests utilizing ZigBee-equipped Telegesis ETRX357 devices [29]. The prototype structure is given in Fig. 2 and the actual deployment example is presented in Fig. 3. Here, the traffic is transmitted from the device A to the device B via the relying node. USB-dongle C is utilized as the attacker device, generating broadcast messages.

The main goal of our installation is to obtain the probabilistic packet loss values. We assume a high-density industrial WSN deployment, where each node may receive data not only from its immediate neighbor, but also from the attacker device, thus escalating the effects of the broadcast storm. Node B as the destination device analyzes the amount of received meaningful data as well as the share of unclassified (attacker's) packets. The key setup parameters and the corresponding notation are given in Table 1.

Further, we analyze the impact produced by the attacker on the packet transmission delay, and the respective results are presented in Fig. 4(a) and (b). For our test scenario, we utilize two Telegesis command types (i) AT+N and (ii) AT+SN:00 [30]. The first command has as its main purpose to request the node's surrounding network information. The second command AT+SN is generally used to force a particular device to scan the network and "00" causes each

Fig. 3. Photo of the practical test deployment

Table 1. Main setup parameters

Parameter	Description	Practical value
λ_p	Packet arrival rate	120 packets per second
λ_{sh}	Attacker's packet arrival rate	1–15 packets per second
μ	Packet service rate	180 packets per second
n	Buffer size	10 packets
k	Number of relaying nodes	1, 2, 3
n	Packet size	15 kb
T	System throughput	250 kbps

attacked node to search across the entire network for neighbors. As we learn from the test results, by increasing the packet arrival rate one might cause a dramatic surge in the delay for up to 2 times by only introducing 14 additional broadcast messages in our network. Importantly, this extra packet delay has a direct impact on the energy consumption values due to increased packet retransmission cost after a collision in the wireless channel.

We emphasize the fact that prototyping of a large-scale real-world WSN is difficult to implement in the laboratory environment due to the space limitations and thus we decided to support our test deployment with a simple analytical model that can validate and predict the ad hoc WSN behavior under broadcast storm conditions.

4   Supportive Analytical Modeling of Our Prototype

By employing simple methods of the queuing theory in our model [31], we first assume that the packet loss probability is not affected by the attacker. We further

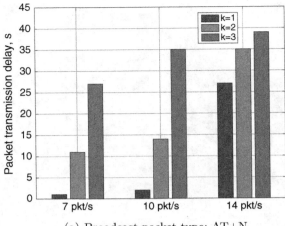

(a) Broadcast packet type: AT+N

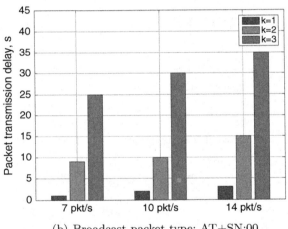

(b) Broadcast packet type: AT+SN:00

Fig. 4. Data transmission delay based on attacker's packet arrival rate (prototype)

consider that the packet generation intensity on the end-device is given as a Poisson process and that the packet service interval is distributed exponentially [32]. We verify this hypothesis at the end of this work. Hence, in the single-relay WSN case the packet loss probability may be calculated as

$$P_l = \rho^n \frac{1 - \rho}{1 - \rho^{n+1}}, \quad \rho = \frac{\lambda}{\mu},$$

(1)

where λ is the packet arrival rate, μ is the packet service rate, and n is a node's buffer size.

Further, for the multi-relay case we modify Eq. (1) accordingly

$$P_l^k = 1 - (\rho^n \frac{1-\rho}{1-\rho^{n+1}})^k, \tag{2}$$

where k is the number of relaying hops.

The majority of the analytical frameworks available today do not take into account the attacker [33–36] that can initiate an attack by generating the broadcast messages with higher arrival rate.

Every broadcast packet is served by each attacked WSN node and then forwarded to the following hop. Clearly, the number of nodes under attack could be significantly increased if the attacker would modify the radio equipment to utilize transmission at higher power.

Further, using Eqs. (1) and (2), we evaluate the packet loss probability for a network affected by the broadcast storm attack as follows

$$\begin{cases} P_l^{k=1} = 1 - \left(1 - \left(\frac{\lambda_p + \lambda_{sh}}{\mu}\right)^n \frac{1 - \left(\frac{\lambda_p + \lambda_{sh}}{\mu}\right)}{1 - \left(\frac{\lambda_p + \lambda_{sh}}{\mu}\right)^{n+1}}\right), k = 1 \\ \\ P_l^{k\geq 2} = P_l^{k=1} \prod_{k=2}^{m} \left(1 - \left(\frac{\lambda_p + k\lambda_{sh}}{\mu}\right)^n \frac{1 - \left(\frac{\lambda_p + k\lambda_{sh}}{\mu}\right)}{1 - \left(\frac{\lambda_p + k\lambda_{sh}}{\mu}\right)^{n+1}}\right), k \geq 2 \end{cases} \tag{3}$$

where λ_{sh} is the attacker packet arrival rate.

In order to quantitatively characterize the proposed prototype, we first study the impact of the system parameters on the packet loss rates. To this end, Fig. 5(a) shows the influence of the attacker's packet generation rate on the WSN packet loss at a fixed WSN node data generation rate. Clearly, by increasing the number of affected relaying nodes system saturation is achieved faster. This is due to the broadcast message distribution, which has repetitive nature.

In our second scenario presented in Fig. 5(b), we fix the attacker's packet generation rate and vary that of the WSN node. As we observe in the plots, the ad hoc network is providing a certain level of QoS even in the situation when the node's packet generation rate is higher than the service rate.

Our third scenario depicted in Fig. 6 corresponds to a situation, when both node's and attacker's packet generation rates are fixed and only the service rate is varied. Accordingly, for each number of relaying nodes we can find the corresponding lowest service rate to guarantee the minimal reachable packet loss for a particular attacker's packet generation rate.

Furthermore, our simple analytical model is able to probabilistically predict the likely ad hoc WSN conditions taking into account the effects of the broadcast storm attack that alters the underlying packet generation rate.

Finally, we compare the analytical and prototype packet loss performance based on the key system parameters given in Table 1. By focusing on the obtained prototype-driven results and those delivered by our analytical prediction, as summarized in Fig. 7, it can be concluded that the analytical and the experimental values agree within acceptable bounds.

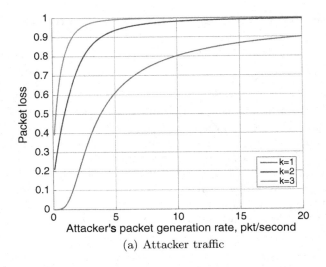

(a) Attacker traffic

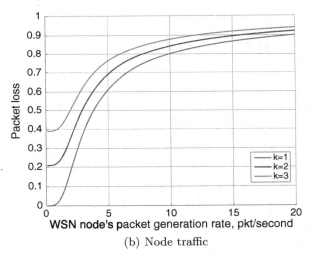

(b) Node traffic

Fig. 5. Impact of packet generation rate on packet loss rate

To confirm the obtained results, we have additionally verified our prototype-based and analytical data using Pearson's chi-squared test [37] with $\alpha = 0.05$ by executing a set of 100 independent trials. Therefore, it could be concluded that the resulting difference between the compared distributions of the packet loss values in a realistic WSN under the broadcast storm conditions is statistically insignificant. Thereby, our initial assumption on the Poission packet arrival distribution and the exponential service time distribution are practical.

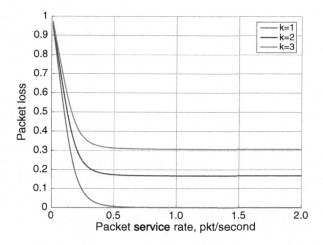

Fig. 6. Impact of packet service rate on the system packet loss rate under broadcast storm attack $\lambda_p = \lambda_{sh}$

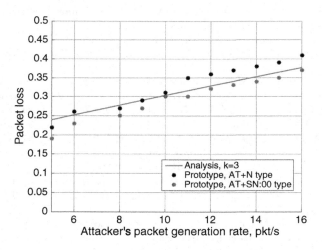

Fig. 7. Analytical results agreeing with our experimental setup

5   Conclusions

This paper developed a model and the respective practical prototype of a broadcast storm attack, which may disrupt the desired reliable operation of a mission-critical WSN deployment. To this end, we collected the packet loss probabilities together with the packet transmission delays produced with our testbed, and compared some of those against the corresponding values provided with our simple queuing theoretic model. The obtained results not only evidence the feasibility of this convenient custom-made approximation for predicting the operational parameters of a real-world WSN under attack, but also help identify conditions that become threatening for the intended operation of the industrial monitoring system under consideration.

References

1. Iyengar, S.S., Brooks, R.R.: Distributed Sensor Networks: Sensor Networking and Applications. CRC Press, Boca Raton (2012)
2. Hendee, J., Gramer, L., Heron, S., Jankulak, M., Amornthammarong, N., Shoemaker, M., Burgess, T., Fajans, J., Bainbridge, S., Skirving, W.: Wireless architectures for coral reef environmental monitoring. In: Proceedings of the 12th International Coral Reef Symposium, Cairns, Australia (2012)
3. Vinel, A., Vishnevsky, V., Koucheryavy, Y.: A simple analytical model for the periodic broadcasting in vehicular ad-hoc networks. In: Proceedings of the GLOBECOM Workshops, pp. 1–5. IEEE (2008)
4. Aslan, Y.E., Korpeoglu, I., Ulusoy, Ö.: A framework for use of wireless sensor networks in forest fire detection and monitoring. Comput. Environ. Urban Syst. **36**(6), 614–625 (2012)
5. Dohler, M., Vilajosana, I., Vilajosana, X., LLosa, J.: Smart cities: An action plan. In: Proceedings of the Barcelona Smart Cities Congress (2011)
6. Andreev, S., Gonchukov, P., Himayat, N., Koucheryavy, Y., Turlikov, A.: Energy efficient communications for future broadband cellular networks. Comput. Commun. **35**(14), 1662–1671 (2012)
7. Rashid, B., Rehmani, M.H.: Applications of wireless sensor networks for urban areas: a survey. J. Netw. Comput. Appl. **60**, 192–219 (2016). Elsevier
8. Kim, S., Pakzad, S., Culler, D., Demmel, J., Fenves, G., Glaser, S., Turon, M.: Health monitoring of civil infrastructures using wireless sensor networks. In: Proceedings of the 6th International Symposium on Information Processing in Sensor Networks (IPSN), pp. 254–263. IEEE (2007)
9. Pakzad, S.N., Kim, S., Fenves, G.L., Glaser, S.D., Culler, D.E., Demmel, J.W.: Multi-purpose wireless accelerometers for civil infrastructure monitoring. In: Proceedings of the 5th International Workshop on Structural Health Monitoring (IWSHM) (2005)
10. Kumar, P., Ylianttila, M., Gurtov, A., Lee, S.-G., Lee, H.-J.: An efficient and adaptive mutual authentication framework for heterogeneous wireless sensor network-based applications. Sensors **14**(2), 2732–2755 (2014)
11. Sridhar, P., Sheikh-Bahaei, S., Xia, S., Jamshidi, M.: Multi-agent simulation using discrete event and soft-computing methodologies. In: Proceedings of the International Conference on Systems, Man and Cybernetics, vol. 2, pp. 1711–1716. IEEE (2003)
12. Wright, J.: Killerbee: practical ZigBee exploitation framework. In: Proceedings of the 11th ToorCon Conference, San Diego (2009)
13. Chen, Y., Xu, W., Trappe, W., Zhang, Y.: Detecting and localizing wireless spoofing attacks. In: Securing Emerging Wireless Systems, pp. 1–18. Springer, New York (2009)
14. Patwari, N., Hero III, A.O., Perkins, M., Correal, N.S., O'dea, R.J.: Relative location estimation in wireless sensor networks. IEEE Trans. Signal Process. **51**(8), 2137–2148 (2003)

15. Hosek, J., Masek, P., Kovac, D., Ries, M., Kropfl, F.: Universal smart energy communication platform. In: Proceedings of the International Conference on Intelligent Green Building and Smart Grid (IGBSG), pp. 1–4. IEEE (2014)
16. Conti, M., Giordano, S.: Mobile ad hoc networking: milestones, challenges, and new research directions. IEEE Commun. Mag. **52**(1), 85–96 (2014)
17. Page, J., Zaslavsky, A., Indrawan, M.: Countering security vulnerabilities using a shared security buddy model schema in mobile agent communities. In: Proceedings of the First International Workshop on Safety and Security in Multi-Agent Systems (SASEMAS 2004), pp. 85–101 (2004)
18. Zikratov, I.A., Lebedev, I.S., Gurtov, A.V.: Trust and reputation mechanisms for multi-agent robotic systems. In: Balandin, S., Andreev, S., Koucheryavy, Y. (eds.) NEW2AN/ruSMART 2014. LNCS, vol. 8638, pp. 106–120. Springer, Heidelberg (2014)
19. Tseng, Y.-C., Ni, S.-Y., Shih, E.-Y.: Adaptive approaches to relieving broadcast storms in a wireless multihop mobile ad hoc network. IEEE Trans. Comput. **52**(5), 545–557 (2003)
20. Wyglinski, A.M., Huang, X., Padir, T., Lai, L., Eisenbarth, T.R., Venkatasubramanian, K.: Security of autonomous systems employing embedded computing and sensors. Micro, IEEE **33**(1), 80–86 (2013)
21. Lipman, J., Liu, H., Stojmenovic, I.: "Broadcast in ad hoc networks," in Guide to wireless ad hoc networks, pp. 121–150, Springer, (2009)
22. Hu, Y.-C., Perrig, A., Johnson, D.B.: Rushing attacks and defense in wireless ad hoc network routing protocols. In: Proceedings of the 2nd ACM Workshop on Wireless Security, pp. 30–40. ACM (2003)
23. Tseng, Y.-C., Ni, S.-Y., Chen, Y.-S., Sheu, J.-P.: The broadcast storm problem in a mobile ad hoc network. Wireless Netw. **8**(2–3), 153–167 (2002)
24. Korzun, D.G., Nikolaevskiy, I., Gurtov, A.: Service intelligence support for medical sensor networks in personalized mobile health systems. In: Balandin, S., Andreev, S., Koucheryavy, Y. (eds.) NEW2AN/ruSMART 2015. LNCS, vol. 9247, pp. 116–127. Springer, Heidelberg (2015)
25. Kelly IV., C., Ekanayake, V., Manohar, R.: SNAP: A sensor-network asynchronous processor. In: Proceedings of the 9th International Symposium on Asynchronous Circuits and Systems, pp. 24–33. IEEE (2003)
26. Denko, M.K.: Detection and prevention of denial of service (dos) attacks in mobile ad hoc networks using reputation-based incentive scheme. J. Systemics, Cybern. Inf. **3**(4), 1–9 (2005)
27. Xu, S., Man, Y., He, H., Zhao, L., Zheng, Y., Wang, T.: A security personnel information collection system based on ZigBee wireless ad-hoc network. In: Proceedings of the International Conference on Computer and Communications (ICCC), pp. 410–414. IEEE (2015)
28. Andreev, S., Koucheryavy, Y., Himayat, N., Gonchukov, P., Turlikov, A.: Active-mode power optimization in OFDMA-based wireless networks. In: Proceedings of the GLOBECOM Workshops, pp. 799–803. IEEE (2010)
29. Telegesis, The ETRX357-DVK development kit is an ideal starting point for development and evaluation of the ETRX357 2.4 GHz ZigBee modules, February 2016. http://www.telegesis.com/products/etrx3-based-products/etrx3-zigbee-development-kit/
30. Telegesis, ETRX2 and ETRX3 Series ZigBee Modules AT-Command Dictionary, December 2014. http://www.telegesis.com/download/document-centre/etrx3_technical_manuals/TG-ETRXn-R308-Commands.pdf

31. Bisnik, N., Abouzeid, A.A.: Queuing network models for delay analysis of multihop wireless ad hoc networks. Ad Hoc Netw. **7**(1), 79–97 (2009)
32. Andreev, S., Galinina, O., Koucheryavy, Y.: Energy-efficient client relay scheme for machine-to-machine communication. In: Proceedings of the Global Telecommunications Conference (GLOBECOM 2011), pp. 1–5. IEEE (2011)
33. Zhao, J., Govindan, R., Estrin, D.: Computing aggregates for monitoring wireless sensor networks. In: Proceedings of the First International Workshop on Sensor Network Protocols and Applications, pp. 139–148. IEEE (2003)
34. Ni, Y., Ye, X., Ko, J.: Monitoring-based fatigue reliability assessment of steel bridges: analytical model and application. J. Struct. Eng. **136**(12), 1563–1573 (2010)
35. Moltchanov, D., Koucheryavy, Y., Harju, J.: Simple, accurate and computationally efficient wireless channel modeling algorithm. In: Braun, T., Carle, G., Koucheryavy, Y., Tsaoussidis, V. (eds.) WWIC 2005. LNCS, vol. 3510, pp. 234–245. Springer, Heidelberg (2005)
36. Li, Z., Chan, T.H., Ko, J.M.: Fatigue analysis and life prediction of bridges with structural health monitoring data–part i: methodology and strategy. Int. J. Fatigue **23**(1), 45–53 (2001)
37. Pearson, K.: X. on the criterion that a given system of deviations from the probable in the case of a correlated system of variables is such that it can be reasonably supposed to have arisen from random sampling. London, Edinb., Dublin Philos. Mag. J. Sci. **50**(302), 157–175 (1900)

Critical Sensor Density for Event-Driven Data-Gathering in Delay and Lifetime Constrained WSN

Debanjan Sadhukhan$^{(\boxtimes)}$ and Seela Veerabhadreswara Rao

Department of Computer Science, Indian Institute of Technology,
Guwahati 781039, India
{debanjan,svrao}@iitg.ernet.in

Abstract. In rare-event detection wireless sensor network (WSN) applications maximizing lifetime and minimizing end-to-end delay (e-delay) are important factors in designing a cost-efficient network, which can be achieved using asynchronous sleep/wake (s/w) scheduling techniques and anycasting data-forwarding strategies, respectively. In this paper, we address the problem of finding an optimal cost WSN that satisfies given delay constraint and lifetime requirement, assuming random uniform deployment of nodes in a circular-shaped Field-of-Interest (FoI) and estimate the maximum of minimum expected e-delay in an anycasting forwarding technique for a given sensor density. We use this analysis to find the critical expected sensor density that satisfies given e-delay constraint, and lifetime requirement. We also validate our analysis.

Keywords: Wireless networks · Sensor density · Event-driven application

1 Introduction

In rare event driven data gathering applications like, intrusion detection, tsunami detection, forest-fire detection, and many more, nodes remain idle for most of the time until an event occurs. Extending lifetime while maintaining delay and coverage constraints, are the most essential quality of service parameters. In WSN, energy consumption is reduced using s/w scheduling techniques where the communication device is switched off when no event is detected in the vicinity. Nodes exchange synchronization messages in synchronous s/w scheduling protocols. Whereas, in asynchronous s/w scheduling technique sensor nodes wake up independently without any s/w synchronization. In the rare event detection scenario, asynchronous s/w scheduling techniques conserve more energy compared to synchronous s/w scheduling because of additional energy required in synchronization.

© IFIP International Federation for Information Processing 2016
Published by Springer International Publishing Switzerland 2016. All Rights Reserved
L. Mamatas et al. (Eds.): WWIC 2016, LNCS 9674, pp. 309–320, 2016.
DOI: 10.1007/978-3-319-33936-8_24

Several asynchronous s/w scheduling techniques are proposed in the literature. Generally, e-delay and lifetime depend on wake up rate of sensor nodes. With higher wake up rate, nodes consume more energy with reduced e-delay, and vice versa. Although there are other factors like queuing delay and clock skew that affects overall e-delay of the network, but wake up rate is the most dominating. Hence, in this paper we consider wake up rate as the governing factor of e-delay and lifetime The lifetime is the time duration of the first node depletes its energy completely in the network.

In anycasting strategy, packet is forwarded to the first node that wakes up within a set of candidate nodes. Since each node maintains a set of forwarding nodes, compared to a single forwarding node in traditional approaches, anycasting strategy decreases expected waiting time significantly, which in turn decreases e-delay [1].

In anycasting forwarding strategy, density also govern e-delay and lifetime. With increasing density, e-delay may decrease for a given wake up rate. In contrary, for a given e-delay, increasing density may result in increasing overall lifetime of the network. In order to increase network lifetime, for a given e-delay constraint, one can decrease the wake up rate by increasing the density. But, increasing density increases the overall cost of the network. Hence, we address the problem: *what is the critical sensor density that satisfies given delay constraint and lifetime requirement, when nodes follow anycasting forwarding strategy?* We use a stochastic approach to estimate expected e-delay for a given sensor density and use this analysis to find the critical sensor density that satisfies given requirements.

The next section reviews the significant contributions in the literature. Section 3 derives stochastic analysis to estimate expected e-delay for given sensor density and Sect. 4 uses this analysis to estimate critical sensor density. We validate our analysis using ns2 simulation in the fifth section and the final section points to the future work direction.

2   Related Work

Anycasting strategy first applied to wireless networks by Awerbuch et al. in [3]. In [4], the authors used the shortest path anycasting tree to route a data-packet. In [5,6] the authors proposed heuristic anycasting protocols that exploit geographical distance to the sink in order to minimize e-delay. In [7–9], the authors used hop-count information to minimize delay along the routing path. Whereas in [10], the authors used both hop-count and power consumption metrics to reduce the overall cost of forwarding a data-packet from a source to the sink.

In anycasting based forwarding strategy if the number of nodes in a forwarding set increases, expected one hop delay decreases. Adding more nodes to the forwarding set may increase expected e-delay, especially when the newly added nodes have larger expected e-delay. Hence, nodes must be added to the forwarding set according to their expected e-delay. Based on this observation, Kim et al. proposed an anycasting forwarding technique, in which neighboring nodes are added to the forwarding set only when they collectively minimize overall expected e-delay [1]. But packets may follow a longer route to the base station. In order to minimize this effect, the same authors developed a delay optimal any-casting scheme [2], where nodes do not immediately forward the packet, instead they wait for some time and then opportunistically forward only when expected delay involves for waiting is more.

Motivation: For given strict delay constraint, the lifetime is proportional to the density of the network. If the number of nodes in forwarding set increases with increasing density, the wake up rate decreases in order to maintain given delay constraint. This in-turn increases the lifetime of the sensor nodes. Hence with given delay, coverage, and lifetime constraint, the density of the overall FoI can be adjusted according to the requirements. Although, the analysis provided in [1,2] calculates expected lifetime of a node, with periodic wake up rate, but not directly applicable for satisfying the expected lifetime constraint. For given delay, coverage and lifetime requirements, deployment density over the FoI must be minimized to reduce the overall cost of sensor network. The proposed any-casting forwarding techniques [1,2,5–9] in the literature are unable to provide any analysis for expected lifetime varying sensor density.

3   Expected E-Delay

We use a stochastic approach to calculate expected e-delay of a randomly chosen sensor i, located at a distance dis_i from the base-station in a circular shaped FoI. The nodes that can directly communicate with the base-station, can forward the data-packet immediately, since the base-station is awake all the time. In general, if the distance of a node from the base-station increases, the number of hops required to send a data-packet also increases, which in-turn increases e-delay. The maximum e-delay is nothing but the end-to-end delay of the node located at the farthest point from base-station.

3.1   Expected E-Delay for a Fixed Size Forwarding Set

We assume random uniform deployment of nodes in a cir-cular-shaped Field-of-Interest (FoI). We also assume that a sensor located at a point c, can only communicate per-fectly within a circular region of radius C centered at c,

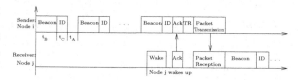

Fig. 1. Example of packet forwarding protocol

which is denoted by $A(c, C)$. We follow the forwarding strategy given in [1,2]. Before sending a packet, a node sends a beacon signal, followed by an ID signal, and listens for acknowledgment. If any node hears the beacon (followed by ID), it sends acknowledgment only if it belongs to the forwarding set, else go to sleep and wakes up after $\frac{1}{w}$, where w denotes the asynchronous periodic wake up rate (as shown in Fig. 1, redrawn from [1]). Hence, the probability of any node in the forwarding set wakes up at h^{th} beacon signal is defined as $p_w = \frac{t_I}{1/w}$, if $h < \frac{1/w}{t_I}$, else 1, where $t_I = t_A + t_B + t_C$ [1]. Moreover, $h_{max} = \frac{1/w}{t_I}$ denotes the total number of beacons.

Let $\{i_1, i_2, ..., i_k\}$ be the forwarding set of node i. Let W be the event that denotes the set of forwarding nodes wake up during their respective beacon intervals. The probability of the event W, denoted by $P(W)$, is $(p_w)^k$. Let X be the event denotes no node wakes up during the first $h - 1$ beacons, j nodes wake up during the hth beacon, and remaining $k - j$ nodes wake up during the last $h_{max} - h$ beacons. The probability of X, $P(X)$, is given by,

$$P(X) = ^k C_j (h_{max} - h)^{k-j} (p_w)^k, \qquad (1)$$

since there are ^kC_j different possible sets of nodes that can wake up during h^{th} beacon and remaining $(k - j)$ nodes wake up during the remaining $(h_{max} - h)$ beacons in $(h_{max} - h)^{k-j}$ different ways. Let W_h denotes the event that the packet is forwarded after h beacon intervals so that no node wakes-up during first $(h - 1)$ beacons and at least one node wakes up during h^{th} beacon and remaining nodes wake up during remaining $(h_{max} - h)$ beacons. Hence, the probability of the packet is forwarded after h^{th} beacon is,

$$P(W_h) = \sum_{j=1}^{k} {}^k C_j (h_{max} - h)^{k-j} (p_w)^k. \qquad (2)$$

Hence expected one hop delay is given by

$$d_{k,w} = \sum_{h=1}^{\lfloor \frac{1/w}{t_I} \rfloor} P(W_h) * h + t_D, \qquad (3)$$

where, t_D denotes the transmission delay. The expected e-delay of a node i is the sum of the expected one hop delay and the expected e-delay of the nodes in its forwarding set. Since, every node in forwarding set has equal asynchronous periodic wake up rate w, the probability of the packet is forwarded to any node is $\frac{1}{k}$, and the expected e-delay of its forwarding set nodes is $\sum_{j=1}^{k} \frac{1}{k} * D_{i_j,k,w}$, for $1 \leq j \leq k$, where $D_{i_j,k,w}$, denotes the respective expected e-delay of node i_j. Hence, follows the lemma.

Lemma 1. *Let $\{i_1, i_2, ..., i_k\}$ be the forwarding set of node i. If $D_{i_j,k,w}$, denotes the respective expected e-delay of node i_j, for $1 \leq j \leq k$, then expected e-delay of node i, such that $(i \neq j)$, is given by $D_{i,k,w} = d_{k,w} + \sum_{j=1}^{k} \frac{1}{k} * D_{i_j,k,w}$, where*

$$d_{k,w} = \sum_{h=1}^{\lfloor \frac{1/w}{t_I} \rfloor} P(W_{h,k}) * h + t_D.$$

3.2   Estimation of E-Delay of a Circular-Shaped FoI

Note that the overall e-delay decreases if neighboring nodes with less e-delay are given priority for including in the forwarding set [1]. Increasing the number of nodes in the forwarding set decreases expected one-hop delay but may increase expected e-delay of its forwarding set nodes. Hence in order to reduce expected e-delay for a node i, only neighboring nodes which collectively minimizes overall expected e-delay, are included in its forwarding set. Note that when density remains constant, with increasing distance from the base station may increase the overall e-delay but not decreases it. Hence, a linear search within the neighboring nodes, with higher priority for the nodes closer to the base-station, efficiently selects the forwarding set which minimizes overall expected e-delay. Expected e-delay of a given FoI is the expected e-delay of the farthest node from the base-station.

E-delay of the nodes are estimated in the increasing order of
their distance from the base-station.
We estimate e-delay of the nodes
closer to the base-station first, and
use the results to estimate the e-
delay of their neighbors which are
away from the base-station. Since
the base-station is always awake,
the e-delay of the nodes within
the communication range of the
base-station is equal to transmission delay, t_D. We denote this *direct
communication circle* by C_D.

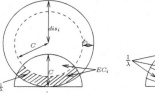

(a) Only one node
is expected in the
shaded region.

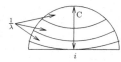

(b) EC_i is divided
into equal area sec-
toral annuli.

Fig. 2. Example of our analysis

In order to estimate maximum expected e-delay, we divide the FoI into rings using concentric circles centered at base-station, and estimate the expected e-delay for a randomly chosen node in each ring. First we estimate the expected e-delay of a randomly chosen node within the first ring using the e-delay of nodes within the direct communication range of the base-station. Assuming base-station is positioned at b_p, we estimate the minimum expected e-delay of a randomly chosen node i within the circular annulus $CA(b_p, C, C + \delta_1)$, such that the neighboring nodes closer to base-station belongs to C_D. The circular annulus $CA(b_p, R_i, R_j)$ between two concentric circles, centered at b_p with radii R_i, R_j, such that $R_j > R_i$, is defined as the area between their boundaries. In order to estimate δ_1, we first define the effective forwarding region of communication.

For a node i at a distance dis_i from the base station, the effective forwarding region of communication EC_i is the intersection of the open circular area with radius dis_i centered at the base-station and communication region of node i, as shown in Fig. 2(a). The following lemma quantifies the effective forwarding region of communication which can be verified using simple geometry.

Lemma 2. *Area of the effective forwarding region of communication of node
i at a distance dis_i from the base station with communication range C such*

that $dis_i > C$, is $\|EC_i\| = \cos^{-1}\left(\frac{C}{2dis_i}\right)C^2 + \cos^{-1}\left(1 - \frac{C^2}{2dis_i}\right)dis_i^2 - dis_i\sqrt{C^2 - \frac{C^2}{2dis_i}}$.

Let δ_1 denotes the maximum width of the circular annulus $CA(b_p, C, C+\delta_1)$, such that the effective forwarding region of communication EC_i is expected to contain only neighbors which are in the direct communication range of the base-station. In order to estimate the expected value of δ_1, we use the following lemma which estimates the intersection of a circle and the effective forwarding region of communication of a random node, and can be proved using simple geometry.

Lemma 3. *Consider a node i at a distance dis_i from the base station, with communication range C. The intersection of a circle centered at base-station (b_p) with radius $R_j = dis_i - \delta, 0 < \delta \leq C$, and the effective forwarding region of communication of node i, can be given as $CI(dis_i, \delta) = \cos^{-1}\left(\frac{c^2 - \delta^2 + 2dis_i\delta}{2dis_iC}\right) * C^2 - \frac{c^2 - \delta^2 + 2dis_i\delta}{2dis_i}\sqrt{C^2 - \frac{c^2 - \delta^2 + 2dis_i\delta}{2dis_i}} + \cos^{-1}\left[\left(dis_i - \frac{c^2 - \delta^2 + 2dis_i\delta}{2dis_i}\right)\Big/(dis_i - \delta)\right] * C^2 - \left[\left(dis_i - \frac{c^2 - \delta^2 + 2dis_i\delta}{2dis_i}\right)\Big/(dis_i - \delta)\right] * \sqrt{C^2 - \frac{c^2 - \delta^2 + 2dis_i\delta}{2dis_i}}$.*

Since the effective forwarding region of communication contains only neighbors that are in the direct communication range of the base-station, the expected number of nodes in the shaded region in Fig. 2(a) of a node i is one, which is node i itself. Moreover, the expected area of the shaded region in Fig. 2(a) is $\frac{1}{\lambda}$, where λ denotes the node density. The expected maximum value of δ_1 can be found by solving the following equation.

$$EC_i - CI(dis_i, \delta_1) = \frac{1}{\lambda}. \tag{4}$$

We assume that Eq. 4 can be solved in constant time because it is a single variable equation. In the following lemma we estimate the minimum expected e-delay of a node belongs to $CA(b_p, C, C+\delta_1)$.

Lemma 4. *The expected minimum e-delay of a randomly chosen node i within the circular annulus $CA(b_p, C, C+\delta_1)$ such that the effective forwarding region of communication, EC_i is expected to contain only neighbors which can directly communicate with base-station, is $D_{i,k,w} = \sum_{h=1}^{\lfloor \frac{1/w}{t_I} \rfloor} p_{h,k,w} * h + t_D$, where $k = EC_i * \lambda - 1$ and λ denotes the density.*

Proof. Since $C < dis_j \leq C + \delta_1$ and the effective forwarding region of communication EC_i is expected to contain only neighbors which can directly communicate with the base-station, then the expected number of sensors belong to this area is $\|EC_i\| * \lambda - 1$. Since these nodes have minimum e-delay t_D, the overall e-delay of node i decreases if more nodes are included in its forwarding set. Hence, the minimum expected e-delay of node i is,

$$D_{i,k,w} = \sum_{h=1}^{\left\lfloor \frac{1/w}{t_I} \right\rfloor} p_{h,k,w} * h + t_D, \tag{5}$$

where $k = ||EC_i|| * \lambda - 1$.

We gradually increase the distance from the base-station in steps of γ, and estimate the minimum expected e-delay. We calculate the expected e-delay of a random node i at a distance $C + \delta_1 + m\gamma$ for $m \in N$, using the estimated expected e-delay of the nodes which are within the distance $C + \delta_1 + (m - 1)\gamma$ from the base-station.

We divide the effective forwarding region of communication EC_i, into several sectoral annuli such that every sectoral annulus is expected to contain only one node, as shown in Fig. 2(b), for $1 \leq j \leq k$, where $k = ||EC_i|| * \lambda - 1$. The jth sectoral annulus $SA_{i,j}(\beta_{i_{j1}}, \beta_{i_{j2}})$ of node i, between two concentric circles, centered at b_p with radii $\beta_{i_{j1}}, \beta_{i_{j2}}$, such that $\beta_{i_{j1}} > \beta_{i_{j2}}$, is defined as the intersection of the area between their boundaries and EC_i.

Let i_1 denotes the closest sectoral annulus to the base-station. $\beta_{i_{11}}$ is equal to $dis_i - C$. $\beta_{i_{12}}$ can be found by solving the following equation.

$$CI(dis_i, \beta_{i_{12}} - (dis_i - C)) = \frac{1}{\lambda}. \tag{6}$$

Note that $\beta_{i_{21}} = \beta_{i_{12}}$. Moreover, $\beta_{i_{j1}} = \beta_{i_{(j-1)2}}$, for $2 \leq j \leq k$. For an arbitrary i_j, $\beta_{i_{j2}}$ can be calculated by solving the following equation.

$$CI(dis_i, \beta_{i_{j2}} - \beta_{i_{j1}}) = \frac{1}{\lambda}, \tag{7}$$

for $1 \leq j \leq k$. We assume the Eqs. 6 and 7 can be solved in constant time because these are single variable equations.

We first estimate the expected minimum e-delay of a random node within j^{th} sectoral annulus, for $1 \leq j \leq k$, and use these to estimate expected minimum e-delay of a random node i.

Consider a random sectoral annulus $SA_{i,j}(\beta_{i_{j1}}, \beta_{i_{j2}})$. Assume m_{i_1} be the largest integer such that $C + \delta_1 + m_{i_1}\gamma \leq \beta_{i_{j1}}$ and m_{i_2} be the smallest integer such that $C + \delta_1 + m_{i_2}\gamma \geq \beta_{i_{j2}}$. In order to calculate the expected e-delay of a random node belongs to $SA_{i,j}(\beta_{i_{j1}}, \beta_{i_{j2}})$, we use the expected e-delay of nodes at distances $C + \delta_1 + (m_{i_1} + 1)\gamma, C + \delta_1 + (m_{i_1} + 2)\gamma, ..., C + \delta_1 + m_{i_2}\gamma$. The node can belong to any one of the areas induced by the intersection between $SA_{i,j}(\beta_{i_{j1}}, \beta_{i_{j2}})$ and the ring formed by the circular annuli $CA(b_p, C + \delta_1 + t\gamma, C + \delta_1 + (t + 1)\gamma)$, where $m_{i_1} \leq t \leq (m_{i_2} - 1)$. In fact, estimated minimum expected e-delay of a random node belongs to $SA_{i,j}(\beta_{i_{j1}}, \beta_{i_{j2}})$ is proportional to the area induced by the intersection between $SA_{i,j}(\beta_{i_{j1}}, \beta_{i_{j2}})$ and the ring formed by the corresponding circular annuli.

Area induced by $SA_{i,j}(C + \delta_1 + m_{i_1}\gamma, C + \delta_1 + (m_{i_1} + 1)\gamma)$ is $CI(dis_i, dis_i - (C + \delta_1 + (m_{i_1} + 1)\gamma)) - \frac{1}{\lambda}(k - j)$. Moreover, the area induced by $SA_{i,j}(C + \delta_1 + t\gamma, C + \delta_1 + (t + 1)\gamma)$ for $m_{i_1} < t \le (m_{i_2} - 1)$ is,

$$\|SA_{i,j}(C + \delta_1 + t\gamma, C + \delta_1 + (t + 1)\gamma)\| = CI(dis_i, dis_i - (C + \delta_1 + t\gamma))$$

$$- \sum_{s=1}^{t-1} \|SA_{i,j}(C + \delta_1 + s\gamma, C + \delta_1 + (s + 1)\gamma)\| - \frac{1}{\lambda}(k - j).$$

The probability of node i_j belongs to $SA_{i,j}(C + \delta_1 + t\gamma, C + \delta_1 + (t + 1)\gamma)$ is $\|SA_{i,j}(C + \delta_1 + t\gamma, C + \delta_1 + (t + 1)\gamma)\|\lambda$. Let $D_{i_j,t\gamma}$ denotes the minimum expected e-delay of a random node within $SA_{i,j}(C + \delta_1 + t\gamma, C + \delta_1 + (t + 1)\gamma)$. Hence, an upper bound for the expected e-delay D_{i_j} of node i_j, is

$$\sum_{t=m_{i_1}}^{(m_{i_2}-1)} \|SA_{i,j}(C + \delta_1 + t\gamma, C + \delta_1 + (t + 1)\gamma)\|\lambda D_{i_j,t\gamma}.$$

We use expected e-delay D_{i_j} of a random node belongs to i_j^{th} sectoral annulus, to find the minimum expected e-delay of node i at a distance $dis_i = C + \delta_1 + m\gamma$. Consider a randomly chosen node i at a distance $dis_i = C + \delta_1 + m\gamma$ from the base-station. We divide the effective forwarding region of communication EC_i, into $EC_i * \lambda - 1$ sectoral annuli such that every sectoral annulus is expected to contain only one node. Assuming D_{i_j} denotes the estimated minimum expected e-delay for a randomly selected node within circular annulus i_j, for $1 \le j \le (EC_i * \lambda - 1)$, which is calculated as shown earlier using the minimum expected e-delay of nodes at distances $C + \delta_1 + \gamma, C + \delta_1 + 2\gamma, ..., C + \delta_1 + (m-1)\gamma$. A linear search over the nodes at every sectoral annulus, with higher priority given to nodes closer to the base-station effectively selects k' required number of nodes in the forwarding set, that minimizes overall e-delay [1]. Hence, minimum expected e-delay of node i is upper bounded by,

$$D_{i,k',w} = d_{k',w} + \sum_{j=1}^{k'} \frac{1}{k'} * D_{i_j}, \qquad (8)$$

where $d_{k',w} = \sum_{h=1}^{\left\lfloor \frac{1/w}{t_I} \right\rfloor} P(W_{h,k'}) * h + t_D$. Hence, follows the theorem.

Theorem 1. *Assume D_{i_j} denotes the estimated minimum expected e-delay for a randomly selected node within circular annulus $SA_{i,j}(\beta_{i_{j1}}, \beta_{i_{j2}})$ of node i at distance $dis_i = C + \delta_1 + m\gamma$ from the base station, for $1 \le j \le (EC_i * \lambda - 1)$. Let k' nodes are included in the forwarding set. An upper bound on minimum expected e-delay of node i is $D_{i,k',w} = d_{k',w} + \sum_{j=1}^{k'} \frac{1}{k'} * D_{i_j}$, where $d_{k',w} = \sum_{h=1}^{\left\lfloor \frac{1/w}{t_I} \right\rfloor} P(W_{h,k'}) * h + t_D$.*

In order to estimate the maximum of minimum e-delay in the FoI, we gradually increase the distance (such that $dis_i > \delta_1$) of a random node i from the base-station, by small γ, and estimate the minimum expected e-delay of a node at this distance. We keep on increasing dis_i till we reach the farthest point which is at a distance equal to the radius of FoI.

In the next section, we use this analysis to find the critical sensor density required to satisfy the given e-delay constraint and lifetime requirement.

4   Critical Sensor Density

Assume sensor nodes are deployed with the initial energy Q and consume average energy E during a wake up interval, the energy required for wake up. Average wake up rate w of a node can be given as $\frac{Q}{LE}$, where L is required lifetime constraint. The expected e-delay D_e of the FoI can be found using the analysis given in the previous section, for a given density. If the maximum of minimum expected e-delay D_e in FoI is greater than the delay constraint D, it is necessary to increase the density. The minimum sensor density λ_m is defined as the density required to satisfy the coverage requirement, which can be found using the methods described in [11]. In order to find the critical sensor density λ_c required to satisfy given delay D and lifetime constraint L, we formulate the problem as follows.

$$\min_{\lambda_c}\{||A|| * \lambda_c * C\} \quad subject \ to$$
$$D_e \leq D, \lambda_m \leq \lambda_c, \ and \ D_e, L, \lambda_c > 0,$$

where C denotes the cost of any sensor.

In order to find an upper bound λ_u for the critical sensor density that satisfies given delay constraint D and lifetime requirement L, we exponentially increase the density λ from λ_m and find λ_u that satisfies the delay constraint using Sect. 3.2, with the average wake up rate $w = \frac{Q}{LE}$. Next we use binary search between λ_u and $\frac{\lambda_u}{2}$ to find the critical sensor density λ_c that minimizes the overall deployment cost.

5   Validation

In order to verify the estimation of the maximum of minimum expected e-delay and the critical sensor density for given delay and lifetime constraints, we evaluate numerically the methods described in Sects. 3.2 and 4, and compare these with that obtained in a ns2 simulation.

We deploy sensor nodes with 200 m communication range, using uniform distribution in a circular shaped FoI of radius 1000 m. For simplicity we place the base-station at the center of the FoI. We set data-rate to be 19.2 kbps. We also set respectively transmission and receiving/idle power as 19.5 mW and 13.0 mW. The data and beacon/control packet length is set to 8 byte and 3 byte, respectively. The sensor nodes follow anycasting forwarding strategy [1].

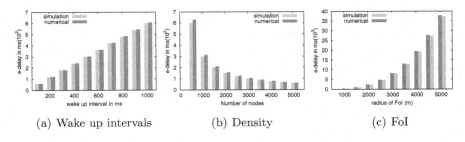

(a) Wake up intervals   (b) Density   (c) FoI

Fig. 3. Validating the estimated expected e-delay

5.1 Validating Estimated Expected E-Delay

In this section we validate the estimated maximum of minimum expected e-delay obtained from numerical evaluation given in Sect. 3.2 and compare it with simulation results. In order to calculate the maximum of minimum e-delay in each experiment, we select the farthest node from the base-station and calculate its average e-delay by simulating 100 events originating at this node. We repeat the experiment for 100 times by changing the seed of uniform deployment. The average of maximum e-delay of the simulation results along with the numerical estimations are shown in Fig. 3. Our numerical estimation are close to the simulation results for various scenarios.

Impact of wake up interval: The average maximum e-delay for different wake up intervals are shown in Fig. 3(a), for 1000 nodes. As wake up interval increases, average maximum e-delay also increases. This is because, if wake up interval increases, expected one-hop delay increases, which in-turn increases e-delay. It can also be noted that the estimation results are always higher than the simulation results.

Impact of density: In order to show the effectiveness of our approach at different densities, we varied the number of nodes deployed. For a fixed wake up interval 500 ms results are shown in Fig. 3(b). Note that, increasing the number of nodes in the given FoI, decreases expected one hop delay, which in turn decreases expected e-delay. The percentage of over estimation on maximum expected e-delay is almost same for different densities.

Impact of FoI: The average maximum e-delay for different areas of FoI are shown in Fig. 3(c), for a wake up interval 500 ms. As radius of circular shaped FoI increases with fixed density, e-delay also increases rapidly. This is because, if the radius of FoI increases, maximum number of hops from the farthest node increases as well, which in turn increases e-delay. Moreover, it can also be noted that the estimation results are always higher than the simulation results.

5.2 Validating Critical Sensor Density

In this section we validate the estimated critical sensor density λ_c, for given delay and lifetime constraints, obtained from numerical evaluation given in Sect. 4 and compare it with simulation results. We gradually increase the sensor density and find the critical sensor density that satisfies given delay constraint and lifetime requirement using simulation. Our numerical estimation is close to the simulation results for various scenarios.

Impact of E-delay: We compare the numerically estimated critical sensor density with that of simulation, for different delay constraint and fixed wake up interval 500 ms(refer Fig. 4(a)). As given e-delay constraint increases, critical sensor density decreases. This is because, increasing critical sensor density decreases expected one hop delay, which in turn decreases expected e-delay.

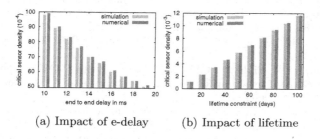

(a) Impact of e-delay   (b) Impact of lifetime

Fig. 4. Validating critical sensor

Impact of lifetime: Critical sensor densities for different lifetime requirements are shown in Fig. 4(b), for a fixed delay constraint as 10 ms. When lifetime requirement increases, the critical sensor density also increases. This is because, increasing lifetime decrease wake up interval, which in turn decreases expected one-hop and e-delay. In order to maintain the given delay constraint, the critical sensor density needs to be increased.

6   Conclusion and Future Work

In this work we estimated the maximum expected e-delay for circular shaped FoI with given density and used this analysis to find the critical sensor density that satisfies given delay constraint and lifetime requirement. Similar analysis can be extended to estimate the critical sensor density for a convex-shaped FoI. In a convex-shaped FoI, for a node i, the actual effective forwarding area of communication is nothing but the intersection of the given FoI and the effective forwarding area of communication. We also believe that this work would motivate further research in estimating critical sensor density problem for heterogeneous WSNs. Note that we assumed the communication range to be 2-D in our analysis. Whereas, our work can also be extended for a WSN consists of sensor nodes with 3-D communication range.

References

1. Kim, J., et al.: Minimizing delay and maximizing lifetime for wireless sensor networks with anycast. IEEE/ACM Trans. Netw. (TON) **18**(2), 515–528 (2010)
2. Kim, J., Lin, X., Shroff, N.B.: Optimal anycast technique for delay-sensitive energy-constrained asynchronous sensor networks. IEEE/ACM Trans. Netw. (TON) **19**(2), 484–497 (2011)
3. Awerbuch, B., Brinkmann, A., Scheideler, C.: Anycasting and multicasting in adversarial systems: routing and admission control. In: Baeten, J.C.M., Lenstra, J.K., Parrow, J., Woeginger, G.J. (eds.) ICALP 2003. LNCS, vol. 2719, pp. 1153–1168. Springer, Heidelberg (2003)
4. Wen, H., Bulusu, N., Jha, S.: A communication paradigm for hybrid sensor/actuator networks. Int. J. Wirel. Inf. Netw. **12**(1), 47–59 (2005)
5. Zorzi, M., Rao, R.R.: Geographic random forwarding (GeRaF) for ad hoc and sensor networks: energy and latency performance. IEEE Trans. Mob. Comput. **2**(4), 349–365 (2003)
6. Liu, S., Fan, K.-W., Sinha, P.: CMAC: an energy-efficient MAC layer protocol using convergent packet forwarding for wireless sensor networks. ACM Trans. Sens. Netw. (TOSN) **5**(4), 29 (2009)
7. Biswas, S., Morris, R.: ExOR: opportunistic multi-hop routing for wireless networks. ACM SIGCOMM Comput. Commun. Rev. **35**(4), 133–144 (2005)
8. Rossi, M., Zorzi, M.: Integrated cost-based MAC and routing techniques for hop count forwarding in wireless sensor networks. IEEE Trans. Mob. Comput. **6**(4), 434–448 (2007)
9. Rossi, M., Zorzi, M., Rao, R.R.: Statistically assisted routing algorithms (SARA) for hop count based forwarding in wireless sensor networks. Wirel. Netw. **14**(1), 55–70 (2008)
10. Mitton, N., Simplot-Ryl, D., Stojmenovic, I.: Guaranteed delivery for geographical anycasting in wireless multi-sink sensor and sensor-actor networks. In: INFOCOM 2009, pp. 2691–2695. IEEE (2009)
11. Wan, P.-J., Yi, C.-W.: Coverage by randomly deployed wireless sensor networks. IEEE/ACM Trans. Netw. (TON) **14**(SI), 2658–2669 (2006)

Resource Management
and Optimization

Effective Capacity in Broadcast Channels with Arbitrary Inputs

Marwan Hammouda$^{(\boxtimes)}$, Sami Akin, and Jürgen Peissig

Institute of Communications Technology, Leibniz Universität Hannover,
Hanover, Germany
{marwan.hammouda,sami.akin,peissig}@ikt.uni-hannover.de

Abstract. We consider a broadcast scenario where one transmitter communicates with two receivers under quality-of-service constraints. The transmitter initially employs superposition coding strategies with arbitrarily distributed signals and sends data to both receivers. Regarding the channel state conditions, the receivers perform successive interference cancellation to decode their own data. We express the effective capacity region that provides the maximum allowable sustainable data arrival rate region at the transmitter buffer or buffers. Given an average transmission power limit, we provide a two-step approach to obtain the optimal power allocation policies that maximize the effective capacity region. Then, we characterize the optimal decoding regions at the receivers in the space spanned by the channel fading power values. We finally substantiate our results with numerical presentations.

1 Introduction

Cooperative communications can provide promising solutions to satisfy the ever-increasing demand for wireless data transmission [21]. Therefore, it has been investigated from several perspectives. For instance, the authors have explored the communication throughput in broadcast channels by invoking information-theoretic tools in [2, 3, 6, 9, 13, 14, 22]. Particularly, considering one transmitter and two receivers, Cover obtained the achievable rate regions [3]. Then, this scheme was generalized to broadcast channels with many receivers in [2]. Furthermore, the authors in [14] defined the ergodic capacity regions for fading broadcast channels considering different spectrum-sharing techniques and derived the optimal resource allocation policies that maximize these regions. Besides, the authors examined parallel Gaussian broadcast channels and obtained the optimal power allocation policies that achieve any point on the capacity region boundary subject to a sum-power constraint [9].

In the aforementioned studies, the authors considered Gaussian input signaling. On the other hand, it is known that many practical systems make use of

This work was partially supported by the European Research Council under Starting Grant-306644.

L. Mamatas et al. (Eds.): WWIC 2016, LNCS 9674, pp. 323–334, 2016.
DOI: 10.1007/978-3-319-33936-8_25

input signaling with discrete and finite constellation diagrams. In that regard, the authors in [7] studied two-user broadcast channels with arbitrary input distributions subject to an average power constraint and derived the optimal power allocation policies that maximize the weighted sum rate in low and high signal-to-noise ratio regimes. Similarly, the authors in [15] considered the mutual information in parallel Gaussian channels and derived the optimal power allocation policies. In addition, the authors in [17] explored the optimal power policies that minimize the outage probability in block-fading channels when arbitrary input distributions are applied under both peak and average power constraints. In these studies, the authors benefited from the fundamental relation between the mutual information and the minimum mean-square error (MMSE), which was initially established in [8].

In another line of research, cross-layer design concerns gained an increasing interest since many of the current wireless systems are to support delay-sensitive applications. Consequently, quality-of-service (QoS) requirements in the form of delay and buffer overflow were studied in wireless communications from data-link and physical layer perspectives. Effective capacity was proposed as a performance metric that provides the maximum constant data arrival rate at a transmitter buffer that can be supported by a given service (channel) process [24]. Subsequently, effective capacity was scrutinized in several different communication scenarios [1, 4, 10, 16, 18, 20]. For instance, effective capacity was examined in one-to-one transmission scenarios in wireless fading channels with feedback information [20], interference and delay constrained cognitive radio relay channels [16], multiple-input multiple-output channels [10], and multi-band cognitive radio channels [4]. Moreover, the authors in [18] studied the effective capacity of point-to-point channels and derived the optimal power allocation policies to maximize the system throughput by employing arbitrary input distributions under an average power constraint. More recently, we explored the effective capacity regions of multiple access channels with arbitrary input distributions and identified the optimal power allocation policies under average transmission power constraints [11].

In this paper, different than the aforementioned studies and our recent study [11], we focus on a broadcast channel scenario in which one transmitter employs arbitrarily distributed input signaling to convey data to two receivers under average power constraints and QoS requirements. We define the effective capacity region and provide an algorithm to obtain the optimal power allocation policies that maximize this region by enforcing the relation between the mutual information and the MMSE. Then, we express the optimal decoding regions in the space spanned by the channel fading power values. We finally justify our analytical results with numerical presentations.

2   System Description

2.1   Channel Model

As shown in Fig. 1, we consider a broadcast channel scenario in which one transmitter communicates with two receivers. We assume that the transmitter is

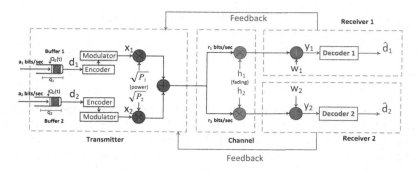

Fig. 1. Channel model: A two-user broadcast channel in which one transmitter communicates with two receivers. The transmitter performs superposition coding, while each receiver performs successive interference cancellation with a certain order. The decoding order depends on the channel conditions, i.e., the magnitude of the squares of the channel fading coefficients, $z_1 = |h_1|^2$ and $z_2 = |h_2|^2$.

equipped with two data buffers each of which stores data to be transmitted to the corresponding receiver. The transmitter, regarding the instantaneous channel conditions and employing a superposition coding strategy with a given order, sends data from both buffers in frames of T seconds. During data transmission, the input-output relation between the transmitter and the jth receiver at time instant t is given by

$$y_j(t) = h_j(t)x_j(t)\sqrt{P_j(t)} + h_j(t)x_m(t)\sqrt{P_m(t)} + w_j(t) \quad \text{for } t = 1, 2, \cdots, \quad (1)$$

where $j, m \in \{1, 2\}$ and $j \neq m$. Above, $x_j(t)$ and $x_m(t)$ are the channel inputs at the transmitter and carry information to the jth and m^{th} receivers, respectively, and $y_j(t)$ is the channel output at the jth receiver. Moreover, $w_j(t)$ represents the additive thermal noise at the jth receiver, which is a zero-mean, circularly symmetric, complex Gaussian random variable with a unit variance, i.e., $E\{|w_j|^2\} = 1$. The noise samples $\{w_j(t)\}$ are assumed to be independent and identically distributed. Meanwhile, $h_j(t)$ represents the fading coefficient between the transmitter and the jth receiver, where $E\{|h_j|^2\} < \infty$. The magnitude square of the fading coefficient is denoted by $z_j(t)$, i.e., $z_j(t) = |h_j(t)|^2$. We consider a block-fading channel and assume that the fading coefficients stay constant for a frame duration of T seconds and change independently from one frame to another. We further assume that h_1 and h_2 are independent of each other and perfectly known to the transmitter and both receivers. Thence, the transmitter can adapt the transmission power policy and the transmission rate for each receiver accordingly. In addition, the transmission power at the transmitter is constrained as follows:

$$\mathbb{E}_t\{P_1(t)\} + \mathbb{E}_t\{P_2(t)\} \leq \overline{P}, \quad (2)$$

where $P_1(t)$ and $P_2(t)$ are the instantaneous power allocation policies for the 1st and 2nd receivers, respectively, i.e., $\mathbb{E}_{x_1}\{x_1(t)\} \leq P_1(t)$ and $\mathbb{E}_{x_2}\{x_2(t)\} \leq P_2(t)$, and $\overline{P}$ is finite. We finally note that the available transmission bandwidth is B Hz. In the rest of the paper, we omit the time index t unless otherwise needed for clarity.

2.2   Achievable Rates

In this section, we provide the instantaneous achievable rates between the transmitter and the receivers given the input signal distributions. We can express the instantaneous achievable rate between the transmitter and the jth receiver by invoking the mutual information between the channel inputs at the transmitter and the channel output at the jth receiver. Given that h_j and h_m are available at the transmitter and the jth receiver and that the jth receiver does not perform successive interference cancellation, the instantaneous achievable rate is given as [5]

$$\mathcal{I}(x_j; y_j) = \mathbb{E}\left\{\log_2 \frac{f_{y_j|x_j}(y_j|x_j)}{f_{y_j}(y_j)}\right\} \quad \text{for } j \in \{1,2\},$$

where $f_{y_j}(y_j) = \sum_{x_j} p_{x_j}(x_j) f_{y_j|x_j}(y_j|x_j)$ is the marginal probability density function (pdf) of the received signal y_j and $f_{y_j|x_j}(y_j|x_j) = \frac{1}{\pi} e^{-|y_j - h_j x_j \sqrt{P_j}|^2}$. On the other hand, if the jth receiver performs successive interference cancellation, i.e., the jth receiver initially decodes x_m and then decodes its own data, we have the achievable rate as follows:

$$\mathcal{I}(x_j; y_j|x_m) = \mathbb{E}\left\{\log_2 \frac{f_{u_j|x_j}(u_j|x_j)}{f_{u_j}(u_j)}\right\},$$

where $u_j = y_j - h_j x_m \sqrt{P_m}$. Above, $f_{u_j}(u_j) = \sum_{x_j} p_{x_j}(x_j) f_{u_j|x_j}(u_j|x_j)$ is the marginal pdf of u_j and $f_{u_j|x_j}(u_j|x_j) = \frac{1}{\pi} e^{-|u_j - h_j x_j \sqrt{P_j}|^2}$.

We assume that each receiver, regarding the channel conditions and the encoding strategy at the transmitter, performs successive interference cancellation with a certain order if it is possible to do so. For instance, if the decoding order is (j, m) for $j, m \in \{1, 2\}$ and $j \neq m$, the jth receiver decodes its own data by treating the signal carrying information to the mth receiver as interference. On the other hand, the mth receiver initially decodes the data sent to the jth receiver and subtracts the encoded signal from the channel output, and then decodes its own signal. Recall that both receivers perfectly know the instantaneous channel fading coefficients, h_1 and h_2, and the decoding order depends on the relation between the magnitude squares of channel fading coefficients z_1 and z_2. Therefore, we consider $\mathcal{Z}$ as the region in the (z_1, z_2)-space where the decoding order is $(2,1)$ and $\mathcal{Z}^c$, the complement of $\mathcal{Z}$, as the region where the decoding order is $(1,2)$. Noting that the transmitter can set the transmission rates to the instantaneous achievable rates, we can express the instantaneous transmission rate for the 1st receiver as

$$r_1(z_1, z_2) = \begin{cases} \mathcal{I}(x_1; y_1|x_2), & \mathcal{Z}, \\ \mathcal{I}(x_1; y_1), & \mathcal{Z}^c, \end{cases} \tag{3}$$

and the instantaneous transmission rate for the 2nd receiver as

$$r_2(z_1, z_2) = \begin{cases} \mathcal{I}(x_2; y_2), & \mathcal{Z}, \\ \mathcal{I}(x_2; y_2|x_1), & \mathcal{Z}^c. \end{cases} \tag{4}$$

The decoding regions can be determined in such a way to maximize the objective throughput.

2.3   Effective Capacity

Recall that the transmitter holds the data initially in the buffers. As a result, delay and buffer overflow concerns become of interest. Therefore, focusing on the data arrival processes at the transmitter, a_1 and a_2 in Fig. 1, we invoke effective capacity as the performance metric. Effective capacity provides the maximum constant data arrival rate that a given service (channel) process can sustain to satisfy certain statistical QoS constraints [24]. Let Q be the stationary queue length at any data buffer. Then, we can define the decay rate of the tail distribution of the queue length Q as

$$\theta = -\lim_{q \to \infty} \frac{\log_e \Pr(Q \geq q)}{q}.$$

Hence, for a large threshold q_{max}, we can approximate the buffer overflow probability as $\Pr(Q \geq q_{max}) \approx e^{-\theta q_{max}}$. Larger θ implies stricter QoS constraints, whereas smaller θ corresponds to looser constraints. For a discrete-time, stationary and ergodic stochastic service process $r(t)$, the effective capacity at the buffer is expressed as

$$-\lim_{t \to \infty} \frac{1}{\theta t} \log_e \mathbb{E}\{e^{-\theta S(t)}\},$$

where $S(t) = \sum_{\tau=1}^{t} r(\tau)$.

Since the transmitter in the aforementioned model has two different transmission buffers, we assume that each buffer has its own QoS requirements. Therefore, we denote the QoS exponent for each queue by θ_j for $j \in \{1, 2\}$. Noting that the transmission bandwidth is B Hz, the block duration is T seconds, and the channel fading coefficients change independently from one transmission frame to another, we can express the effective capacity at each buffer in bits/sec/Hz as

$$a_j = -\frac{1}{\theta_j TB} \log_e \mathbb{E}\left\{e^{-\theta_j TB r_j(z_1, z_2)}\right\}, \tag{5}$$

where the expectation is taken over the space spanned by z_1 and z_2. Now, utilizing the definition given in [19], we express the effective capacity region of the given broadcast transmission scenario as follows:

$$\mathcal{C}_E(\Theta) = \bigcup_{r_1, r_2} \left\{C(\Theta) \geq \mathbf{0} : C_j(\theta_j) \leq a_j\right\}, \tag{6}$$

where $\Theta = [\theta_1, \theta_2]$ is the vector of decay rates, $C(\Theta) = [C_1(\theta_1), C_2(\theta_2)]$ is the vector of the arrival rates at the transmitter buffers, and $\mathbf{0}$ is the vector of zeroes.

3   Performance Analysis

In this section, we concentrate on maximizing the effective capacity region defined in (6) under the QoS requirements for each transmitter buffer and the total average power constraint given in (2). Notice that the effective capacity region is convex [19]. Hence, we can reduce our objective to maximizing the boundary surface of the region and express it as follows [23]:

$$\max_{\substack{\mathcal{Z}, \mathcal{Z}^c \\ \mathbb{E}\{P_1\}+\mathbb{E}\{P_2\}\leq \overline{P}}} \lambda_1 a_1 + \lambda_2 a_2, \tag{7}$$

where $\lambda_1, \lambda_2 \in [0,1]$ and $\lambda_1 + \lambda_2 = 1$. In order to solve this optimization problem, we first obtain the power allocation policies in defined decoding regions, $\mathcal{Z}$ and $\mathcal{Z}^c$, and then, we provide the optimal decoding regions.

3.1   Optimal Power Allocation

Here, we derive the optimal power allocation policies that maximize the effective capacity region (7) given $\mathcal{Z}$ and $\mathcal{Z}^c$. In the following analysis, we provide the proposition that gives the optimal power allocation policies:

Proposition 1.   *The optimal power allocation policies, P_1 and P_2, that maximize the expression in (7) are the solutions of the following equalities:*

$$\frac{\lambda_1}{\psi_1} e^{-\theta_1 T B r_1(z)} \frac{dr_1(\boldsymbol{z})}{dP_1} + \frac{\lambda_2}{\psi_2} e^{-\theta_2 T B r_2(z)} \frac{dr_2(\boldsymbol{z})}{dP_1} = \varepsilon, \tag{8}$$

$$\frac{\lambda_2}{\psi_2} e^{-\theta_2 T B r_2(z)} \frac{dr_2(\boldsymbol{z})}{dP_2} = \varepsilon, \tag{9}$$

for $\boldsymbol{z} = [z_1, z_2] \in \mathcal{Z}$, and

$$\frac{\lambda_1}{\psi_1} e^{-\theta_1 T B r_1(z)} \frac{dr_1(\boldsymbol{z})}{dP_1} = \varepsilon, \tag{10}$$

$$\frac{\lambda_1}{\psi_1} e^{-\theta_1 T B r_1(z)} \frac{dr_1(\boldsymbol{z})}{dP_2} + \frac{\lambda_2}{\psi_2} e^{-\theta_2 T B r_2(z)} \frac{dr_2(\boldsymbol{z})}{dP_2} = \varepsilon, \tag{11}$$

for $\boldsymbol{z} \in \mathcal{Z}^c$. Above, $\psi_1 = \mathbb{E}_z\{e^{-\theta_1 T B r_1(z)}\}$ and $\psi_2 = \mathbb{E}_z\{e^{-\theta_2 T B r_2(z)}\}$, and ε is the Lagrange multiplier of the average power constraint in (2).

Proof. Omitted due to the page limitation.

In Proposition 1, the derivatives of the transmission rates with respect to the corresponding power allocation policies are given as

$$\frac{dr_1(\mathbf{z})}{dP_1} = \begin{cases} \frac{d\mathcal{I}(x_1;y_1|x_2)}{dP_1}, & \mathcal{Z}, \\ \frac{d\mathcal{I}(x_1;y_1)}{dP_1}, & \mathcal{Z}^c, \end{cases} \quad \text{and} \quad \frac{dr_2(\mathbf{z})}{dP_2} = \begin{cases} \frac{d\mathcal{I}(x_2;y_2)}{dP_2}, & \mathcal{Z}, \\ \frac{d\mathcal{I}(x_2;y_2|x_1)}{dP_2}, & \mathcal{Z}^c, \end{cases}$$

and

$$\frac{dr_m(\mathbf{z})}{dP_j} = \frac{d\mathcal{I}(x_j; y_j)}{dP_j} - \frac{d\mathcal{I}(x_j; y_j | x_m)}{dP_j} \quad \text{for } m, j \in \{1, 2\} \text{ and } m \neq j.$$

In the following theorem, we provide the derivatives of the mutual information with respect to the power allocation policies:

Theorem 1. *Let z_1 and z_2 be given. The first derivative of the mutual information between x_j and y_j with respect to the power allocation policy, P_j, is given by*

$$\frac{d\mathcal{I}(x_j; y_j)}{dP_j} = z_j MMSE(x_j; y_j) + z_j \sqrt{\frac{P_m}{P_j}} Re(\mathbb{E}\{x_j x_m^* - \hat{x}_j(y_j)\hat{x}_m^*((y_j))\}) \quad (12)$$

for $j, m \in \{1, 2\}$ and $j \neq m$. Above, $(\cdot)^*$ is the complex conjugate operation and $Re(\cdot)$ is the real part of a complex number. Meanwhile, the derivative of the mutual information between x_j and y_j with respect to P_j given x_m is

$$\frac{d\mathcal{I}(x_j; y_j | x_m)}{dP_j} = z_j MMSE(x_j; y_j | x_m). \quad (13)$$

MMSE and MMSE estimate are defined as

$$MMSE(u; v | s) = 1 - \frac{1}{\pi} \int \frac{\left| \sum_u u p(u) f_{v|u,s}(v|u, s) \right|^2}{f_{v|s}(v|s)} dv$$

and $\hat{u}(v) = \frac{\sum_u u p(u) f_{v|u}(v|u)}{f_v(v)}$, respectively.

Proof. Omitted due to the page limitation.

As clearly noticed in (8)–(11), a closed-form solution for P_1 or P_2 cannot be obtained easily, which is mainly due to the tied relation between P_1 and P_2. For instance, P_1 is a function of P_2 as observed in (8) for $z \in \mathcal{Z}$, whereas P_2 is a function of P_1 as seen in (11) for $z \in \mathcal{Z}^c$. Therefore, we need to employ numerical techniques that consist of iterative solutions. Hence, in the following, we carry out an iterative algorithm that provides the optimal power allocation policies given decoding regions:

Algorithm 1

1: Given λ_1, λ_2, $\mathcal{Z}$ and $\mathcal{Z}^c$;
2: Initialize ψ_1, ψ_2;
3: **while** True **do**
4:     Initialize ε;
5:     Initialize P_1;
6:     **while** True **do**
7:         **if** $z \in \mathcal{Z}$ **then**
8:             For given P_1, compute the optimal P_2 by solving (9) ;

9:          With obtained P_2, compute the optimal $P_1^\star$ by solving (8) ;
10:      **else**
11:          For given P_1, compute the optimal P_2 by solving (11) ;
12:          For computed P_2, compute the optimal $P_1^\star$ by solving (10) ;
13:      **end if**
14:      **if** $|P_1 - P_1^\star| \leq \epsilon$ for small $\epsilon > 0$ **then**
15:          break;
16:      **else**
17:          Set $P_1 = P_1^\star$;
18:      **end if**
19:      **end while**
20:      Check if the average power constraint in (2) is satisfied with equality;
21:      If not, update ε and return to Step 5
22:      Compute $\psi_1^\star = \mathbb{E}_{\mathbf{z}}\{e^{-\theta_1 n r_1(\mathbf{z})}\}$ and $\psi_2^\star = \mathbb{E}_{\mathbf{z}}\{e^{-\theta_2 n r_2(\mathbf{z})}\}$
23:      **if** $|\psi_1 - \psi_1^\star| \leq \epsilon$ and $|\psi_2 - \psi_2^\star| \leq \epsilon$ **then**
24:          break;
25:      **else**
26:          Set $\psi_1 = \psi_1^\star$ and $\psi_2 = \psi_2^\star$;
27:      **end if**
28: **end while**

Given λ_j and ψ_j for $j \in \{1,2\}$, it is shown in [18] that both (9) and (10) has at most one solution. We can further show that (8) has at most one solution for P_1 when P_2 is given, and that (11) has at most one solution for P_2 when P_1 is given. Consequently, we can guarantee that Steps 8, 9, 11 and 12 in Algorithm 3.1 will converge to a single unique solution. In addition, it is clear that (8) and (10) are monotonically decreasing functions of P_1, and that (9) and (11) are monotonically decreasing functions of P_2. Hence, in region $\mathcal{Z}$, we first obtain P_2 by solving (9) for given P_1, and then we find P_1 by solving (8) after inserting P_2 into (8). Similarly, in region $\mathcal{Z}^c$, we first obtain P_2 by solving (11) for given P_1, and then we find P_1 by solving (10) after inserting P_2 into (10). We can employ bisection search methods to obtain P_1 and P_2. In the above approach, when either P_1 or P_2 becomes negative, we set it to zero.

3.2   Optimal Decoding Order

Obtaining the optimal power allocation policies, we investigate the optimal decoding regions in this section. We initially notice that with no QoS constraints, i.e., $\theta_1 = \theta_2 = 0$, the effective capacity region is reduced to the ergodic capacity region. In this case, the symbol of the receiver with the strongest channel is always decoded last [13]. Specifically, when $z_j \geq z_m$ the symbol of the jth receiver is decoded last. This result is based on the assumption of Gaussian input signaling. To the best of our knowledge, no such a result is obtained for broadcast channels when QoS constraints are applied, i.e., $\theta_1 > 0$ and $\theta_2 > 0$, and/or when arbitrary input signaling is employed. In the following, we consider a special case of $\theta_1 = \theta_2$ for $\theta > 0$ and provide the optimal decoding order regions when arbitrary input distributions are employed by the transmitter:

Theorem 2. *Let z_1, z_2 and $\overline{P}$ be given. Define $z_1^\star$ for any given $z_2 \geq 0$ such that the decoding order is (2,1) when $z_2 > z_1^\star$. Otherwise, it is (1,2). With arbitrary input distributions and power allocation policies at the transmitter, the optimal $z_1^\star$ for any given z_2 value is the solution of the following equality:*

$$\mathcal{I}(x_1, x_2; y_1, y_2 | z_1^\star, z_2) = \mathcal{I}(x_1; y_1 | x_2, z_1^\star) + \mathcal{I}(x_2; y_2 | x_1, z_2). \tag{14}$$

Proof. Omitted due to the page limitation.

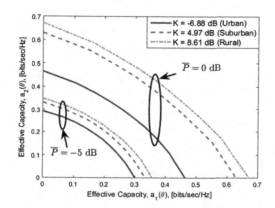

Fig. 2. Effective capacity region boundary when BPSK input signaling is employed for different values of $\overline{P}$ and K. The areas under the curves provide the effective capacity regions.

4   Numerical Results

In this section, we present the numerical results. Throughout the paper, we set the available channel bandwidth to $B = 100$ Hz and the transmission frame duration to $T = 1$ second. We further assume that h_1 and h_2 are independent of each other and set $\mathbb{E}\{|h_1|^2\} = \mathbb{E}\{|h_2|^2\} = 1$. In addition, we assume that signals transmitted to both receivers are independent of each other, i.e., $\mathbb{E}\{x_j x_m^*\} = 0$. Unless indicated otherwise, we set the QoS exponents $\theta_1 = \theta_2 = 0.01$. We finally assume that both receivers have the same noise statistics, i.e., $\mathbb{E}\{|w|^2\} = \mathbb{E}\{|w_1|^2\} = \mathbb{E}\{|w_2|^2\} = 1$, and we define the received signal-to-noise ratio at each receiver with $\frac{\overline{P}}{E\{|w|^2\}} = \overline{P}$.

In Fig. 2, we initially consider binary phase shift keying (BPSK) employed at the transmitter for both receivers and investigate the effect of channel statistics on the effective capacity region in Rician fading channels with a line-of-sight parameter K, which is the ratio of the power in the line-of-sight component to the total power in the non-line-of-sight components. The empirical values of K are determined to be -6.88 dB, 8.61 dB and 4.97 dB for urban, rural and suburban environments at 781 MHz, respectively [12]. Considering these K values, we

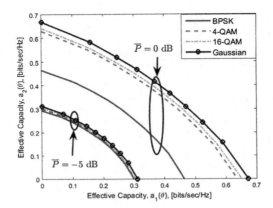

Fig. 3. Effective capacity region boundary with different modulation techniques and signal-to-noise ratio values when $K = -6.88\,\mathrm{dB}$.

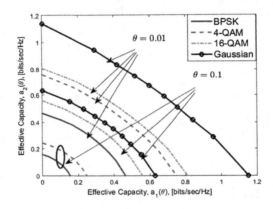

Fig. 4. Effective capacity region boundary with different modulation techniques and decay rate parameters, $\theta = \theta_1 = \theta_2$ when $K = -6.88\,\mathrm{dB}$ and $\overline{P} = 5\,\mathrm{dB}$.

obtain results for different signal-to-noise ratio values, i.e., $\overline{P} = 0$ and -5 dB. We can clearly see that the effective capacity region broadens as K increases because the line-of-sight component becomes more dominant with increasing K. We also observe that the effect of K is more apparent when the signal-to-noise ratio is greater.

Subsequently, setting $K = -6.88\,\mathrm{dB}$, we investigate the effect of different signal modulation techniques with different signal-to-noise ratio values in Fig. 3. We consider BPSK, quadrature amplitude modulation (QAM) and Gaussian input signaling. We can easily notice the superiority of the Gaussian input signaling over the others, while BPSK has the lowest performance. However, the performance gap is reduced with decreasing $\overline{P}$. Lastly, we explore the effect of the QoS exponent θ on the effective capacity performance in Fig. 4. We set $\overline{P} = 5$ dB and $K = -6.878$ dB and plot results for different modulation techniques. Increasing θ results in a smaller effective capacity region as the system is subject to stricter QoS constraints.

5   Conclusion

In this paper, we have examined optimal power allocation policies that maximize the effective capacity region of a two-user broadcast transmission scenario with arbitrarily distributed input signals. We have invoked the relation between MMSE and the first derivative of mutual information with respect to transmission power. We have proposed an iterative algorithm that converges to optimal power allocation policies given decoding regions under an average power constraint. Obtaining power allocation policies, we have further characterized decoding regions for successive interference cancellation at the receivers. Through numerical solutions, we have substantiated our results. In general, there is an apparent superiority of Gaussian input signaling over the other modulation techniques, whereas the gap between Gaussian input signaling and the others decreases with decreasing signal-to-noise ratio. Therefore, it is reasonable to employ simple modulation techniques in low signal-to-noise ratio regimes.

References

1. Akin, S., Gursoy, M.: On the throughput and energy efficiency of cognitive MIMO transmissions. IEEE Trans. Veh. Technol. **62**(7), 3245–3260 (2013)
2. Bergmans, P.P.: Random coding theorem for broadcast channels with degraded components. IEEE Trans. Inf. Theory **19**(2), 197–207 (1973)
3. Cover, T.M.: Broadcast channels. IEEE Trans. Inf. Theory **18**(1), 2–14 (1972)
4. Elalem, M., Zhao, L.: Effective capacity and interference analysis in multiband dynamic spectrum sensing. Commun. Netw. **5**(2), 111–118 (2013)
5. Gallager, R.G.: Information Theory and Reliable Communication. Springer, Heidelberg (1968)
6. Gallager, R.G.: Capacity and coding for degraded broadcast channels. Problemy Peredachi Informatsii **10**(3), 3–14 (1974)
7. Gündüz, D., Payaró, M.: Gaussian two-way relay channel with arbitrary inputs. In: International Symposium on Personal Indoor and Mobile Radio Communications (PIMRC), pp. 678–683. IEEE (2010)
8. Guo, D., Shamai, S., Verdú, S.: Mutual information and minimum mean-square error in Gaussian channels. IEEE Trans. Inf. Theory **51**(4), 1261–1282 (2005)
9. Gupta, G., Toumpis, S., et al.: Power allocation over parallel Gaussian multiple access and broadcast channels. IEEE Trans. Inf. Theory **52**(7), 3274–3282 (2006)
10. Gursoy, M.: MIMO wireless communications under statistical queueing constraints. IEEE Trans. Inf. Theory **57**(9), 5897–5917 (2011)
11. Hammouda, M., Akin, S., Peissig, J.: Effective capacity in multiple access channels with arbitrary inputs. In: IEEE International Conference on Wireless and Mobile Computing, Networking and Communications (WiMob), pp. 406–413 (2015)
12. Jeong, W.H., Kim, J.S., Jung, M., Kim, K.-S.: MIMO channel measurement and analysis for 4G mobile communication. In: Lee, G., Howard, D., Kang, J.J., Ślęzak, D. (eds.) ICHIT 2012. LNCS, vol. 7425, pp. 676–682. Springer, Heidelberg (2012)

13. Jindal, N., Vishwanath, S., Goldsmith, A.: On the duality of Gaussian multiple-access and broadcast channels. IEEE Trans. Inf. Theory **50**(5), 768–783 (2004)
14. Li, L., Goldsmith, A.J.: Capacity and optimal resource allocation for fading broadcast channels. I. Ergodic capacity. IEEE Trans. Inf. Theory **47**(3), 1083–1102 (2001)
15. Lozano, A., Tulino, A.M., Verdú, S.: Optimum power allocation for parallel Gaussian channels with arbitrary input distributions. IEEE Trans. Inf. Theory **52**(7), 3033–3051 (2006)
16. Musavian, L., Aïssa, S., Lambotharan, S.: Effective capacity for interference and delay constrained cognitive radio relay channels. IEEE Trans. Wireless Commun. **9**(5), 1698–1707 (2010)
17. Nguyen, K.D., Guillen i Fabregas, A., Rasmussen, L.K.: Outage exponents of block-fading channels with power allocation. IEEE Trans. Inf. Theory **56**(5), 2373–2381 (2010)
18. Ozcan, G., Gursoy, M.C.: QoS-driven power control for fading channels with arbitrary input distributions. In: IEEE International Symposium on Information Theory (ISIT), pp. 1381–1385. IEEE (2014)
19. Qiao, D., Gursoy, M.C., Velipasalar, S.: Achievable throughput regions of fading broadcast and interference channels under QoS constraints. IEEE Trans. Commun. **61**(9), 3730–3740 (2013)
20. Tang, J., Zhang, X.: Quality-of-service driven power and rate adaptation over wireless links. IEEE Trans. Wireless Commun. **6**(8), 3058–3068 (2007)
21. Tao, X., Xu, X., Cui, Q.: An overview of cooperative communications. IEEE Commun. Mag. **50**(6), 65–71 (2012)
22. Tse, D.N.: Optimal power allocation over parallel Gaussian broadcast channels. In: IEEE International Symposium on Information Theory (ISIT), p. 27. Citeseer (1997)
23. Tse, D.N.C., Hanly, S.V.: Multiaccess fading channels. I. Polymatroid structure, optimal resource allocation and throughput capacities. IEEE Trans. Inf. Theory **44**(7), 2796–2815 (1998)
24. Wu, D., Negi, R.: Effective capacity: a wireless link model for support of quality of service. IEEE Trans. Wireless Commun. **2**(4), 630–643 (2003)

Throughput Improvement Using Partially Overlapping Channels in WLAN with Heterogeneous Clients

Sreetama Mukherjee[1] and Sasthi C. Ghosh[2]([⊠])

[1] Department of Information Technology, Jadavpur University, Kolkata, India
sritmukh@gmail.com
[2] Advanced Computing and Microelectronics Unit,
Indian Statistical Institute, Kolkata, India
sasthi@isical.ac.in

Abstract. We consider a realistic wireless local area network (WLAN) consisting of a number of access points (APs) and a number of clients of heterogeneous types (IEEE 802.11 b/g/n). Although, activating APs using only non-overlapping channels (NOCs), which is very limited, can help us achieve interference-free environment, but the achievable throughput may not be optimized. So, partially overlapping channels (POCs) may be used along with NOCs in the most optimized manner, in order to improve the achievable throughput up to certain extent while satisfying the interference criteria. We present an effective greedy algorithm that makes the most desirable configuration by appropriately selecting a subset of APs for activation using NOCs as well as POCs and associating the clients with the selected APs in the most optimized way. Our simulation results show a significant improvement of the aggregate throughput obtained by using NOCs as well as POCs, over using NOCs only.

Keywords: Heterogeneous clients · Channel interferences · Non-overlapping channels · Partially overlapping channels · Maximum aggregate throughput

1 Introduction

We consider an IEEE 802.11 wireless local area network (WLAN) which consists of a set of APs and a set of heterogeneous clients (IEEE 802.11 b/g/n). A client can send data frames via an AP only when it is associated with that AP. This requires a client to AP association. An AP can serve its associated clients only when the AP is activated with a frequency channel. The 2.4 GHz frequency spectrum has a total of 11 channels $[1, 2, \cdots, 11]$ available for this purpose. The central frequencies of each channel is separated by 5 MHz. Two channels are known to be non-overlapping channels (NOCs), if and only if they have a

© IFIP International Federation for Information Processing 2016
Published by Springer International Publishing Switzerland 2016. All Rights Reserved
L. Mamatas et al. (Eds.): WWIC 2016, LNCS 9674, pp. 335–347, 2016.
DOI: 10.1007/978-3-319-33936-8_26

separation of 5 channels or more. So, accordingly, there can be maximum of 3 NOCs 1, 6 and 11 having channel separation of 5. All other channel pairs having separation of less than 5 channels are known to be partially overlapping channels (POCs). Often a dense deployment of APs is required to improve the capacity and throughput of the WLAN. Due to the limited number of NOCs, all APs in a given area may not be activated with NOCs only. As a result, many clients, which are close to a particular AP, may or may not be able to associate with that AP. This may lead to enormous reduction in maximum achievable aggregate throughput of the network. So, assigning only NOCs to the APs would definitely ensure minimum or no interference. However, practically, it is not feasible to assign NOCs to each of the large number of APs as it introduces co-channel interferences. This has to be dealt with properly in order to measure the actual achievable throughput of the clients as well as the aggregate throughput of the network. Throughput achievable in the presence of interferences is found to be much less than the theoretical maximum throughput obtained in the ideal case involving no interferences. Thus we can infer that using only NOCs, we can achieve ideal condition undoubtedly, but the aggregate throughput may not be optimized.

This problem may be resolved to a certain extent using the POCs. It is observed that, certain APs, which could not be activated using NOCs only, can be activated with POCs. This, at the end, may lead to increased aggregate throughput, if we can carefully select a subset of APs for activation with POCs. However, this does not indicate that all the APs must be activated using either NOCs or POCs to achieve the improved throughput. Such possibility may even lead to a reduction of the throughput instead of increasing it as POCs will lead to an increased level of interference with the APs activated with NOCs. Our results reveal that in case all APs are activated, the aggregate throughput achieved is not maximum, in some cases, even less than the aggregate throughput obtained using only NOCs. Thus, POCs can be used to our benefit if and only if they are used optimally and carefully.

In this paper, we consider a heterogeneous client environment where IEEE 802.11 b/g/n types of clients are present in the network. Our primary aim is to make the most optimized use of POCs for AP activation and associations of heterogeneous clients, while taking care of the effect of interferences to determine the actual achievable aggregate throughput. To achieve this, we develop an effective greedy algorithm which finds an appropriate association and channel assignment using NOCs as well as POCs in the most optimized way. Our algorithm works as follows. Initially, NOCs are used as far as possible considering the interference and the number of available NOCs. The heterogeneous clients are then temporarily associated with the APs activated so far with the NOCs only and the current maximum achievable aggregate throughput is calculated. The unassigned APs are then considered for assignment with POCs. For an unassigned AP, we choose a POC that causes minimum interference with the existing assignments and temporarily assign that POC to the AP. We recalculate the aggregate throughput after assigning a POC to an AP by taking care of the interference effects. If such a temporary assignment of POC causes improvement in the aggregate throughput then only we consider the concerned POC to be permanently assigned to the AP, otherwise, that AP is kept unassigned. Then again, the clients are reassociated with the activated APs considering the newly activated AP. Our simulation results show a significant improvement of the aggregate throughput obtained by using both NOCs as well as POCs over using NOCs only.

2 Literature Review

Recent studies on heterogeneous clients include [1–3] where study has been conducted to show the effect of legacy clients (IEEE 802.11 a/b/g) on IEEE 802.11n clients. With CSMA/CA medium access control, clients with lower data rates tend to dominate, whereby, all other clients tend to have the same lower throughput. Moreover, least-load AP association also does not seem appropriate for IEEE 802.11n WLANs. This is mainly due to the fact that IEEE 802.11n clients have much higher data rates in comparison to legacy clients and exhibit frame aggregation. So, they present various AP association algorithms that would mitigate the problems related to high data rate to a large extent. However, the entire work has been conducted in an interference-free environment. In our work, we have included the effect of interference to present a more realistic situation. In our study we have considered both the co-channel and adjacent-channel interferences while assigning channels to the APs and their effect on achievable aggregate throughput. We have used the concept of *interference factor* reported in [6], in order to determine the amount of interference caused due to POCs. In [4], interferences have been considered while calculating the throughput, but they have considered the IEEE 802.11b clients only.

As argued in [5], POCs can be highly beneficial as far as spatial reuse is concerned. The POCs not only allow spatial reuse, but also encourage multi-channel communication in mesh networking environment. It has been reported that interference decreases with increasing channel separation. Interference with channel separation more than or equal to 5, has minimum or no interference. However, using only NOCs, does not always guarantee the most optimized channel assignment. So, in our work, we aim to use POCs together with NOCs, which may lead to the most optimized channel assignment resulting in maximum achievable aggregate throughput. Thus in our study both co-channel as well as adjacent channel interferences have been taken care of, for the improvement of the aggregate throughput. In [9], the POCs are exploited to improve the per user throughput and the channel utilization, but they have considered only homogeneous clients. In [10], although POCs have been considered, there all links are assigned channels mandatorily. But in our work, we have assigned a POC to an AP subject to the condition that they improve the maximum aggregate throughput. If assigning a POC to an AP results in reduction in the aggregate throughput, that AP is left unassigned. This aspect has not been taken care of in [10]. In fact, as per our findings, if all APs are activated, the aggregate throughput achieved may not be optimum, in some cases, even less than the aggregate throughput obtained using only NOCs. In [6], the POCs have been used, but their main consideration was load balancing. So, here, we have approached in a different aspect where POCs are used only if that is beneficial with respect to the achievable aggregate throughput. So, we have focused in performance improvement rather than load balancing.

3 Calculation of Throughput in the Presence of Interference

First we calculate the individual throughput that a client will get from the AP to which it is associated, when only NOCs are used and hence no interference is involved here. Then, using NOCs as well as POCs, the throughput calculation is considered where the effect of interference has been taken into account. After computing this individual throughput obtained by the clients from their respective serving APs, we calculate the aggregate throughput of the network.

3.1 Individual Throughput Obtained by the Clients

In order to calculate the power received by a client from an AP, the model used here is Two-Ray Ground Propagation Model [11]. In this model, the signal power attenuates fast as the transmission distance increases. Define P_t as the transmitting power and d as the distance between the transmitter and its receiver. In such a model, the receiving power P_r is given by:

$$P_r = \frac{(G_t G_r h_t^2 h_r^2) P_t}{d^k} \tag{1}$$

where G_t is the antenna gain at the transmitter side, G_r is the antenna gain at the receiver side, h_t is the antenna height at the transmitter side, h_r is the antenna height at the receiver side and k is the path-loss parameter typically having a value between 2 and 4. The maximum transmission ranges are taken as 450 ft for 802.11b clients, 325 ft for 802.11g clients and 250 ft for 802.11n clients as given by CISCO in [12,13]. Individual throughput obtained by the clients depend on their distances from their respective serving APs which are limited by their maximum transmission ranges.

Throughput Calculation When There Is No Interference: No interference is involved when only NOCs are used. Let P_r be the power received at the client from its serving AP as calculated using Eq. (1). The individual throughput perceived by a client from its associating AP can be expressed by using Shannon's throughput limit as:

$$T_{max} = W \log_2 \left(1 + \frac{P_r}{W N_0} \right) \tag{2}$$

where W is the channel bandwidth in Hz and N_0 is total noise power density in Watts/Hz.

Throughput Calculation When Interference Is Involved: Interference is involved when NOCs as well as POCs are used. To model the interference we have used the metric *interference factor* defined in [6]. The interference factor IF_{ij} between two APs operating on channels i and j is defined as [6]:

$$IF_{ij} = \begin{cases} \frac{IR(\delta)}{d_{ij}} & \text{when } 0 \leq \delta < 5 \text{ and } d_{ij} < IR(\delta) \\ 0 & \text{otherwise} \end{cases} \tag{3}$$

where $IR(\delta)$ is the interference range for channel separation $\delta = |i - j|$ and d_{ij} is the distance between the two APs operating on channels i and j.

Two APs will interfere to each other if they are within the interference range of each other and their channel separation is less than 5. That is, two APs operating on channels i and j are *interfering* if $0 \leq \delta < 5$ and $d_{ij} < IR(\delta)$ where $\delta = |i-j|$. Note that $IF_{ij} > 1$ if the concerned APs are interfering and $IF_{ij} = 0$ if they are non-interfering. To measure the interference ranges for different channel separations, we have used the experimental results reported in [6–8] as shown in Table 1.

For calculation of the throughput perceived by a client from a particular AP, we have calculated the channel separation between the concerned AP and all other APs interfering to that AP. Then, taking the distances between the particular AP and the APs with which it is interfering, the interference factors are calculated using Eq. (3). Accordingly, the total interference received at the client is calculated and then Shannon's throughput limit is used to obtain the throughput.

Table 1. Interference ranges

δ	0	1	2	3	4	5
$IR(\delta)$	13.26	9.21	7.59	4.69	3.84	0

Suppose a client is served by an AP which operates on channel i. Let I_{ij} be the interference that the client will receive from another AP operating on channel j. Let P_r^i and P_r^j be the powers received at the client from the APs operating on channels i and j respectively. Obviously, the client will not receive any interference when the concerned APs are non-interfering. That is, $I_{ij} = 0$ if the APs operating on channels i and j are non-interfering. The received interference at the client is given by $I_{ij} = (1 - \frac{1}{IF_{ij}})P_r^j$ if the concerned APs are interfering. Note that $0 < (1 - \frac{1}{IF_{ij}}) \leq 1$. Also, with increase in IF_{ij}, the fraction $\frac{1}{IF_{ij}}$ decreases and accordingly, the term $(1 - \frac{1}{IF_{ij}})$ increases, as expected. Now let us assume that there are ℓ APs operating on channels $j_1, j_2, \cdots, j_\ell$ which are all interfering to the AP operating on channel i. The total interference received at the client served by the AP operating on channel i is then given by:

$$I_i = \sum_{x=1}^{\ell} I_{ij_x} = \sum_{x=1}^{\ell} (1 - \frac{1}{IF_{ij_x}})P_r^{j_x} \tag{4}$$

Note that P_r^i and $P_r^{j_x}$ $\forall x = 1, 2, \cdots, \ell$ can be computed using Eq. (1). Now for throughput calculations, we have used the Shannon's throughput limit stated in Eq. (2) where P_r and WN_0 are replaced by P_r^i and $WN_0 + I_i$. Hence the throughput obtained by a client from an AP operating on channel i is given by:

$$T_{max} = W \log_2 \left(1 + \frac{P_r^i}{WN_0 + \sum_{x=1}^{\ell} (1 - \frac{1}{IF_{ij_x}}) P_r^{j_x}} \right) \tag{5}$$

3.2   Aggregate Throughput of the Network

Suppose there are n clients and let $T_1, T_2, \cdots, T_n$ be the throughput obtained by them from their respective serving APs as calculated using Eq. (2) or (5) depending on the case. The aggregate throughput of the network is defined as the logarithmic sum of individual throughput obtained by the clients. That is, aggregate throughput is given by:

$$T = \sum_{i=1}^{n} \log_{10}(T_i) \tag{6}$$

Our objective is to maximize the aggregate throughput T.

4   Motivational Example

In this section we present few examples in order to explain our idea in detail. For these examples, we assume that each AP can detect the transmission of data packets by the other APs, regardless of the client positions. The interference relationship between the APs considered in these examples are comparable to the type-4 conflict situation as reported in [4]. Clients associated with an AP gets the maximum achievable throughput as calculated using Shannon's throughput limit as stated in Eq. (2) or (5) depending on the applicable case. The aggregate throughput is then computed using Eq. (6).

For the first example, we consider the association between 7 clients C_1^g, C_2^b, C_3^n, C_4^b, C_5^g, C_6^n, C_7^n and 5 APs AP 1, AP 2, AP 3, AP 4, AP 5 as shown in Fig. 1(a) where grey colored APs denote active APs and C_y^x denotes that client y is of type 802.11x. Here AP 1, AP 2 and AP 3 are activated with NOCs 1, 6, and 11 respectively and AP 4 and AP 5 remain inactivated. The label [a] associated with an AP represents that channel a is assigned to that AP. An edge between a client and an AP represents that the client is associated to that AP. The weight d of an edge between a client and an AP represents that the client is at distance d meters from its associated AP. Since all 3 activated APs are assigned NOCs, so there is no adjacent-channel interference. Also, each activated AP is assigned a distinct NOC so there is no co-channel interference too. Hence each pair of

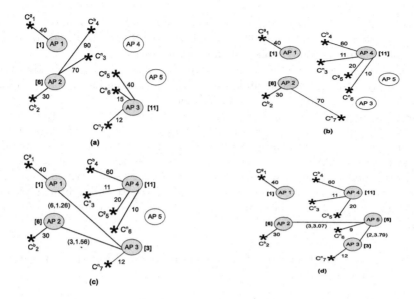

Fig. 1. Different associations between the clients and the APs

activated APs is *non-interfering* to each other. For this association, the aggregate throughput becomes $AT_1 = 11.37$ Mbps. For this and all other examples, we have used pathloss factor as 2, the value of N_0 as 7.9432×10^{-14} Watts/Hz, the transmission power of each AP as 20 dBm and the channel bandwidth as 20 MHz.

For the second example, we consider a different association of the clients and the APs where AP 1, AP 2 and AP 4 are activated with the 3 NOCs 1, 6, and 11 respectively as shown in Fig. 1(b). Here AP 3 and AP 5 remain inactivated. In this case, the aggregate throughput becomes $AT_2 = 11.49$ Mbps.

So, from Fig. 1(a) and (b), it is seen that the aggregate throughput in the second association is greater than that in the first one. It shows the fact that the aggregate throughput depends on both the selection of APs and the association between the clients and the selected APs even when only NOCs are used.

For the third example, we consider another association of the clients and the APs where AP 1, AP 2, AP 3, AP 4 are activated but AP 5 remains inactivated as shown in Fig. 1(c). But, since there are only 3 NOCs available and all APs are within the interference range of each other, so one of the APs must be assigned a POC. Here, AP 1, AP 2 and AP 4 are assigned with the NOCs 1, 6 and 11 respectively. Thus AP 3 must be activated with a POC in $[1, 2, \cdots, 11]$. Since both NOCs and POCs are used, interference is involved in this case. In Fig. 1(c), an edge between two APs indicates that the corresponding APs are interfering to each other. Considering the interference ranges $IR(\delta)$ shown in Table 1 the IF_{ij} values are computed and shown in Fig. 1(c) where the weight (d, IF_{ij}) of an edge between two APs indicates the distance in meters and the interference factor IF_{ij} between them. Here POC 3 is assigned to AP 3 as it produces minimum interference for this case. Aggregate throughput obtained in this case is $AT_3 = 12.02$ Mbps which is higher than both the previous examples. Thus, it clearly shows that using POCs together with NOCs can be advantageous in increasing the maximum achievable aggregate throughput.

In the forth example, all 5 APs are activated as shown in Fig. 1(d). But, since there are only 3 NOCs available and all APs are within the interference range of each other, so two of the APs must be assigned 2 POCs. Here, AP 1, AP 2 and AP 4 are assigned with the NOCs 1, 6 and 11 respectively. It is seen that POCs 3 and 5 produce minimum interference for this case and hence POCs 3 and 5 are assigned to AP 3 and AP 5 respectively. The aggregate throughput obtained in this case is $AT_4 = 10.63$ Mbps which is even lower than the throughput obtained using NOCs only (first example). So it is found that activating all the 5 APs with NOCs and POCs actually reduces the aggregate throughput instead of increasing it. Thus, POCs can be used to our benefit if and only if they are used optimally and carefully.

5 Proposed Algorithm for Throughput Maximization Using POCs

In this section we describe our proposed greedy algorithm to select an appropriate subset of APs for activation using NOCs as well as POCs and to find an association between the clients and the selected APs in the most optimized way.

The proposed algorithm works as follows. It first computes the maximum achievable throughput of each client from each AP. The APs are then sorted based on their potential contributions to the aggregate throughput. The available NOCs are then assigned to the APs one by one following this order. If no NOC is available for an AP that AP is left unassigned. The clients are then associated with the APs activated so far based on their obtained throughput from the APs. The maximum achievable aggregate throughput is then calculated for this configuration. This is the present maximum aggregate throughput and is marked as maxThr. Then, the rest of the unassigned APs are assigned with the most appropriate POC causing minimum interference. Now, every time a POC is assigned to an AP, the aggregate throughput is recalculated. This is marked as CurMaxThr. The value of CurMaxThr is then compared with the maxThr value and the POC is assigned to that AP permanently if CurMaxThr is found to be greater than maxThr. If so, maxThr is updated by maxPOCthr. Otherwise, that AP is left assigned. Every time a POC is assigned to a particular AP, then it is compared with the current maxThr value and accordingly, that AP is assigned or kept unassigned. Formally the algorithm is presented below.

Input: set of APs S_A; set of clients S_C; set of NOCs S_N and set of POCs S_P.

Step 1: Initialization
Let S_{AA} be the set of activated APs. Let A be the association matrix where $A_{ca} = 1$, if client $c \in S_C$ is associated with AP $a \in S_{AA}$ and 0, otherwise. Initially no AP is *activated* and no *association* has been done and thus $S_{AA} = \emptyset$ and $A_{ca} = 0$ for all $a \in S_A$ and $c \in S_C$. Let $F = (f_a)$ be the frequency assignment

of the activated APs, where $f_a \in (S_N \cup S_P)$ denotes the frequency assigned to AP $a \in S_{AA}$. Initially no frequency has been assigned to any AP.

Step 2: Sort the APs
Calculate the maximum achievable throughput of each client from each AP using the Shannon's throughput limit as stated in Eq. (2). Let r_{ca} be this throughput obtained by client c from AP a. Let R_a be the logarithmic sum of the throughput provided by AP a to all the clients in S_C. Here R_a represents the maximum aggregate throughput that can be obtained by the clients if only AP a is activated. This measures the positional importance of AP a with respect to the positions of the clients. Compute $R_a = \sum\limits_{c \in S_C} \log_{10}(r_{ca})$ for all $a \in S_A$. Sort the APs according to descending order of their R_a values. Let AP 1, AP 2, ..., AP m be this sorted ordering. The time complexity of this step is $O(mn + m \log m)$ where n and m are the number of clients and APs respectively.

Step 3: Assign NOCs as far as possible to the APs
Consider the APs in the order as obtained in Step 2 above and assign NOCs to them one by one. For AP a assign the *least* NOC g in S_N that is *safe* to be assigned at that AP and update $f_a = g$ accordingly. A NOC is safe to be assigned at an AP if the NOC is not being assigned to any AP which is *interfering* to that AP. Leave an AP unassigned if no NOC is safe to be assigned at that AP. Let S_{AA} be the set of APs assigned and $S_{UA} = S_A \backslash S_{AA}$ be the set of APs which are left unassigned by considering the NOCs only. The worst-case time complexity of this step is $O(m^2 s)$ where s is the number of NOCs available.

Step 4: Associate the clients to the APs in S_{AA} and compute the maximum achievable aggregate throughput
Associate the clients one by one to the APs activated so far. Associate a client to an AP from which it gets the maximum throughput among the set of APs in S_{AA}. That is, associate client c to AP a' if $r_{ca'} = \max\{r_{ca} : a \in S_{AA}\}$ and update $A_{ca'} = 1$ accordingly. After associating all the clients, compute maxThr, the maximum achievable aggregate throughput obtained by the clients in S_C from the APs in S_{AA}. That is, maxThr $= \sum\{\log_{10}(r_{ca}) : a \in S_{AA}, c \in S_C$ and $A_{ca} = 1\}$. The time complexity of this step is $O(mn)$.

Step 5: Assign POCs to the unassigned APs in S_{UA}
Consider the APs in S_{UA} according to the order as obtained in Step 2 above and assign POCs to them one by one. Suppose an unassigned AP u is temporarily activated by POC p. Compute $TempMaxThr_{up}$, the maximum achievable aggregate throughput obtained by the clients in S_C from the APs in $S_{AA} \cup u$ using Step 4 above by replacing S_{AA} by $S_{AA} \cup u$. For this computation, since POCs are involved here, Eq. (5) instead of Eq. (2) is used for calculating the values of r_{ca} for all $a \in S_{AA} \cup u$ and $c \in S_C$. Compute $TempMaxThr_{up}$ for all $p \in S_P$. Let p' be the POC for which $TempMaxThr_{up'} = \max\{TempMaxThr_{up} : p \in S_P\}$. Define CurMaxThr $= TempMaxThr_{up'}$, the current maximum aggregate throughput. If CurMaxThr > maxThr then activate AP u with POC p' and update

$S_{AA} = S_{AA} \cup u$, $S_{UA} = S_{UA} \backslash u$, maxThr = CurMaxThr and $f_u = p'$ accordingly. Otherwise, leave AP u unassigned and update $S_{UA} = S_{UA} \backslash u$. Repeat the process by considering each unassigned AP in S_{UA} until $S_{UA} = \emptyset$. The worst-case time complexity of this step is $O(m^2 nq)$, where q is the number of POCs.

Output: the set of activated APs S_{AA}, the frequency assignment F of the APs in S_{AA}, the association A between the APs in S_{AA} and the clients in S_C and the maximum aggregate throughput maxThr.

Time complexity: The overall time complexity of the proposed algorithm is $O(mn + m \log m + m^2 s + m^2 nq) = O(m^2 nq)$ as usually $q > s$, where n, m, s and q are the number of clients, APs, NOCs and POCs respectively.

6   Simulation Results

In our simulation setup, we have considered the same WLAN environment as in [6] where, a number of APs and a number of clients are uniformly placed in a $100 \times 100 \, \text{m}^2$ area. The number of clients is 200. The number of APs is varying from 50 to 80 with a step of 5 to represent different AP densities. Number of available NOCs is varied from 2 to 11 to reflect different spectrum availabilities. In our simulation setup, the clients are of heterogeneous types. We have considered 50 % of total clients as 802.11b, 25 % of rest of the clients as 802.11g and rest 25 % as 802.11n. Type of each client is selected randomly. One possible placement of 50 APs and 200 clients of different types is shown in Fig. 2.

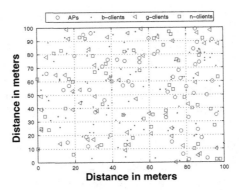

Fig. 2. Uniform placement of 50 APs, 100 b-clients, 50 g-clients and 50 n-clients

With this simulation environment, we evaluate the performance of the proposed algorithm in terms of aggregate throughput obtained under three different scenarios. In the first scenario (NOC only) we measure the obtained aggregate throughput where only NOCs have been used to activate the APs. In the second scenario, we consider the use of NOCs as well as POCs (NOC+POC). In the third scenario we measure the aggregate throughput that can be achieved if the effect of interference is completely ignored (Without interference). Results show that a significantly higher aggregate throughput can be achieved by using NOCs as well as POCs, as compared to the case when only NOCs are used. Results obtained by ignoring the interference can be considered as a naive upper bound of the aggregate throughput as the number of available NOCs is actually very limited. We have conducted different experiments to show the effect of number of NOCs and number of available APs on aggregate throughput for all three cases. In all cases we have considered 100 different runs and reported the average results to mitigate the effect of randomization. In our setup, 100 runs may be considered as good enough as the standard error of average was found to be lower than 0.0776 in all cases. Clearly this deviation is insignificant compared to the magnitude of the average aggregate throughput obtained by different runs.

In Figs. 3 and 4 the relationship of throughput variation with number of NOCs are shown. Our results depict that with increase in the number of available NOCs, the curves using NOCs only and using NOC+POC merge upwards. This is very realistic as, if number of NOCs is large, the selected APs can easily be activated using NOCs only. But, if number of NOCs available is less, POCs must also be used to achieve the maximum aggregate throughput. In Figs. 3 and 4, the number of APs considered are 50 and 75 respectively. As we can see in the two curves, the curves using NOCs only and using NOC+POC merge at NOCs equal to 6 and 5 respectively. This indicates that availability of more APs increases the flexibility to choose the appropriate APs and thus require less number of NOCs to obtain the maximum achievable aggregate throughput.

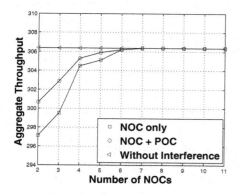
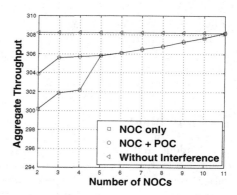

Fig. 3. NOCs vs throughput for 50 APs   **Fig. 4.** NOCs vs throughput for 75 APs

In Figs. 5 and 6, the variation of throughput with increase in number of APs is shown, where the number of available NOCs are 2 and 3 respectively. As the number of APs increase, the throughput increases for all three cases and almost saturates at some point. An increased number of APs must increase the overall aggregate throughput as, most of the clients will get the opportunity to be served by most appropriate APs. Also, the NOC only curve is at the lowest level indicating that using only NOCs does not provide the maximum

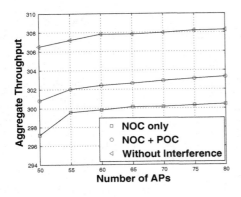

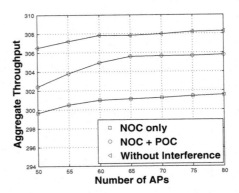

Fig. 5. APs vs throughput 2 NOCs

Fig. 6. APs vs throughput for 3 NOCs

achievable throughput. The without interference curve is at the highest level, which shows the throughput for the ideal case (without any interference) which may not be achievable in practice as the number of NOCs available are limited. So, the NOC+POC curve (intermediary to the above two curves) depicts the most optimized curve, which is the maximum achievable throughput range in practical situation. Note that when number of available NOCs is 2 (Fig. 5), as the number of APs increase, the aggregate throughput saturates earlier as compared to the case where number of available NOCs is 3 (Fig. 6). These results clearly indicate that the availability of NOCs play a very significant role in increasing the aggregate throughput. The POCs are meant to improve the aggregate throughput only as an aid to the NOC, when used appropriately. Thus, POCs along with NOCs result in the overall improvement of aggregate throughput when used in the most optimized manner.

7   Conclusion

It is evident that proper AP selection, proper frequency assignment and proper client association are the pre-requisites for obtaining the most optimized aggregate throughput. Also, using only NOCs is not always beneficial. Using POCs together with NOCs is found to be most advantageous. However, all APs must not necessarily be activated altogether with the hope to increase the throughput. This may even reduce the throughput instead of increasing it. Hence POCs must be used very carefully and optimally.

References

1. Gong, D., Yang, Y.: On-line AP association algorithms for 802.11n WLANs with heterogeneous clients. IEEE Trans. Comput. **63**(11), 2772–2786 (2014)
2. Gong, D., Yang, Y.: AP association in 802.lln WLANs with heterogeneous clients. In: Proceedings of the IEEE INFOCOM, Orlando, FL, USA, pp. 1440–1448, March 2012

3. Jun, J., Peddabachagari, P., Sichitiu, M.: Theoretical maximum throughput of IEEE 802.11 and its applications. In: Proceedings of the IEEE NCA, Cambridge, MA, USA, pp. 249–256, April 2003
4. Mishra, A., Brik, V., Banerjee, S., Srinivasan, A., Arbaugh, W.: A client-driven approach for channel management in wireless LANs. In: Proceedings of the IEEE INFOCOM, Barcelona, Spain, pp. 1–12, April 2006
5. Mishra, A., Rozner, E., Banerjee, S., Arbaugh, W.: Exploiting partially overlapping channels in wireless networks: turning a peril into an advantage. In: Proceedings of the 5th ACM SIGCOMM Conference on Internet Measurement, Berkeley, CA, USA, pp. 29–35 (2005)
6. Hoque, M.A., Hong, X., Afroz, F.: Multiple radio channel assignement utilizing partially overlapped channels. In: Proceedings of the IEEE GLOBECOM, Honolulu, HI, USA (2009)
7. Feng, Z., Yang, Y.: How much improvement can we get from partially overlapped channels? In: Proceedings of the IEEE WCNC, pp. 2957–2962 (2008)
8. Feng, Z., Yang, Y.: Characterizing the impact of partially overlapped channel on the performance of wireless networks. In: Proceedings of the IEEE GLOBECOM, pp. 1–6 (2008)
9. Cui, Y., Li, W., Cheng, X.: Partially overlapping channel assignment based on 'node orthogonality' for 802.11 wireless networks. In: Proceedings of the IEEE INFOCOM, Shanghai, pp. 361–365 (2011)
10. Ding, Y., Huang, Y., Zeng, G., Xiao, L.: Channel assignment with partially overlapping channels in wireless mesh networks. In: Proceedings of the 4th Annual International Conference on Wireless Internet, Brussels, Belgium (2008). Article No. 38
11. Rappaport, T.: Wireless Communications: Principle and Practice. Prentice Hall, Upper Saddle River (1996)
12. http://www.cisco.com/c/en/us/products/collateral/wireless/aironet-3600-series/white_paper_c11-688713.html
13. Florwick, J., Whiteaker, J., Amrod, A.C., Woodhams, J.: Wireless LAN design guide for high density client environments in higher education, CISCO Design Guide, November 2013. http://www.cisco.com/c/en/us/products/collateral/wireless/aironet-1250-series/design_guide_c07-693245.pdf

Optimal Link Deployment for Minimizing Average Path Length in Chain Networks

Zeki Bilgin$^{(\boxtimes)}$, Murat Gunestas, Omer Demir, and Sahin Buyrukbilen

General Directorate of Security, Gumushane, Turkey
{zbilgin,mgunestas,odemir,sbuyrukbilen}@egm.gov.tr

Abstract. This study considers chain-topology networks, which has certain inherent limitations, and presents an optimization model that augments the network by the addition of a new link, with the objective of minimizing Average Path Length (APL).

We built up a mathematical model for APL, and formulated our problem as Integer Programming. Then, we solved the problem experimentally by brute-force, trying all possible topologies, and found the optimal solutions that minimize APL for certain network sizes up to 1000 nodes. Later on, we derived analytical solution of the problem by applying Linear Regression method on the experimental results obtained.

We showed that APL on a chain-topology network is decreased by the proposed optimization model, at a gradually increasing rate from 24.81 % to asymptotic value of 41.4 % as network grows. Additionally, we found that normalized length of the optimal solutions decreases logarithmically from 100 % to 58.6048 % as network size gets larger.

Keywords: Chain networks · Average path length · Link deployment

1 Introduction

Many industries, today, prefer chain topology on their networks comprised of nodes connected each other consecutively throughout both long and narrow deployment areas like railways [1], highways [2], underground mines [3,4], as well as in some special type of wireless sensor and mesh networks [3–7] and backbones of telecommunication systems [8]. Similarly, it is also a well-known implementation to connect (wi-fi) routers in daisy-chain topology to provide internet access at each floor in towers or high buildings.

A major disadvantage of chain networks is to have high *Average Path Length* (*APL*) relative to network size, unlike many other types of networks owning the properties of "small-world" networks [9]. *APL* is generally desired to be *small*, and is investigated analytically and numerically in many studies related to network design and optimization [10–18], social networks [15,17,18], computing [19], and logic design [20].

© IFIP International Federation for Information Processing 2016
Published by Springer International Publishing Switzerland 2016. All Rights Reserved
L. Mamatas et al. (Eds.): WWIC 2016, LNCS 9674, pp. 348–359, 2016.
DOI: 10.1007/978-3-319-33936-8_27

In this paper, we examine *APL* for chain networks, and propose an optimization model based on an additional link deployment to the network, with the objective of minimizing *APL*. We derive analytical formulation for *APL* prior to and subsequent to optimization process, as well as obtain numerical results which precisely agreed with analytical analysis.

2   Network Model

Suppose we have a chain-topology network with n nodes, containing bidirectional links between consecutive nodes. This network can be represented as a path graph, P_n, with undirected edges[1] as depicted in Fig. 1.

Fig. 1. A path graph representing a chain-topology network with n nodes

Suppose, we aim at augmenting this network further by adding a new performance enhancing link between a certain pair of nodes on the network[2] as illustrated in Fig. 2. We should notice at this point that the augmentation process (i.e. adding a new link) is intentionally confined by just one new link in order to keep the optimization cost minimum, and that the implementation cost of such a new link can be assumed fixed regardless of the distance between connected nodes, which is true especially for the leased lines obtained from ISPs.

Fig. 2. Adding a new enhancement link (i.e. edge) connecting v_x and v_y

We are now ready to ask our optimization problem:

Main Problem: Which nodes should be connected to reach the objective of *minimizing average path length (APL)* on the network?

Not only does the proposed optimization model minimize *APL*, but also it improves robustness on chained networks by means of generating alternative routes, as well as reduces cost of packet transmissions.

3   Related Work

3.1   Chain Networks

Given the side effects of unbalanced energy consumptions at nodes in chain networks used in underground mines or on trains, the studies of [1,3,4,6] proposed

---

[1] The edges are undirected because of bidirectional transmissions between nodes.

[2] This could be realized via several ways like obtaining a leased line connection from an ISP between the two points of interest, or using a long-range radio link.

different protocols or node deployment strategies, aiming to provide balanced energy consumptions at nodes in order to increase network lifetime.

Agbinya [2] discussed a specific application of chain networks on highways, and addressed certain characteristics of the network such as interference level, coverage area and path loss; on the other hand, Zhou et al. [5], in a recent study, considered Chain-typed Wireless Sensor Networks (CWSN) deployed in coal mines, and proposed a source-aware redundant packet forwarding scheme for emergency information delivery in CWSN.

Leu and Huang [7] proposed a mathematical model that calculates the maximum throughput of a Wireless Mesh Network in chain-topology, dealing with signal interference, hidden nodes and STDMA time slots among nodes.

Flammini et al. [8] considered the construction of wireless ATM layouts for a chain of base stations, and showed that the problem studied was NP-complete for special instances, and provided optimal solutions for certain cases.

3.2   Average Path Length (APL)

Several researchers derived analytical formulation of *APL* for different type of networks. For instance, Kleinrock and Silvester [21] considered random graphs; Fronczak et al. [18] and Guo et al. [14] studied a large class of uncorrelated random networks with hidden variables; Zhang et al. [17] examined Apollonian networks; Peng [16] dealt with Sierpinski pentagon; Gulyás et al. [13] focused on the networks with given size and density; Chen et al. [11] investigated Barabási–Albert scale free model; Zhi-guang et al. [10] discussed belt-type networks; and Gao et al. [22] analysed Sierpinski gasket in a recent article.

In the field of logic design, Butler et al. [20] studied *APL* of binary decision diagrams by deriving the *APL* for various functions, and showed that the *APL* for benchmark functions is typically much smaller than for random functions.

Mao and Zhang [19] considered the computation problem of *APL* for large scale-free networks, and presented a dynamic programming model to solve the load-balancing problem for coarse-grained parallelization. Yen et al. [12] presented an efficient method for updating the closeness centrality of each vertex and the *APL* of a network, where edges change dynamically as in the case of social networks. In a recent study, Reppas et al. [15] introduced rewiring rules to tune *APL* on a network while keeping the degree and clustering coefficient distribution unchanged.

To the best of our knowledge, ours is the first study to propose an optimization model aiming to minimize *APL* for chain networks by optimal deployment of an incremental link.

4   Mathematical Model

4.1   Pure Path

Average path length, *APL*, of a network is an important parameter showing the efficiency of information transmission on the network, and can be calculated by finding the shortest path between all pairs of nodes, adding their lengths[3] up, and then dividing by the total number of pairs.

To find the mathematical expression for APL of a chain network, let P_n be a path graph including n vertices indexed in sequence from 1 to n, like $v_1, v_2, ..., v_n$, as depicted in Fig. 1. It is obvious that the shortest path between a certain pair of nodes on a path graph is the *subpath*, having no alternative, between this pair of nodes. Moreover, the length of such a subpath is equal to the number of edges on itself. Thus, since the vertices are indexed in order, length of a subpath (PL) between vertices of v_j and v_k on P_n can be stated rigorously as follows.

$$PL_{(v_j,v_k)} = |k - j|$$

Then, the Eq. 1 gives the sum of path lengths for all (unordered) pairs[4]

$$\sum PL_{(AllPairs)} = \sum_{i=1}^{n-1}\sum_{k=1}^{n-i} k \tag{1}$$

After rewriting the Eq. 1, and dividing by the number of all pairs, which is $\frac{n(n-1)}{2}$, we find the APL for the path graph of P_n as given in Eq. 2.

$$APL_{P_n} = \frac{\sum PL_{(AllPairs)}}{\frac{n(n-1)}{2}} = \frac{n+1}{3} \tag{2}$$

According to Eq. 2, the APL for a chain-topology network is linearly proportional with the length of the chain or the number of nodes, i.e. $O(n)$, and almost equal to one third of network diameter.

4.2 Path with an Additional Edge

Let P_n' be a graph obtained by adding a new edge (v_x, v_y) to the path graph P_n as depicted in Fig. 2. Rigorously,

$$P_n' = P_n \cup (v_x, v_y)$$

To built a general mathematical expression for APL on P_n', we first studied on small networks (e.g. around 10 nodes), manually calculated APL, and produced a sketchy formula for APL. Then, we extended our work with larger networks, as repeatedly checking accuracy of the formula, and revised it when needed until the formula persistently gave correct values for all networks investigated. This process yielded Eq. 3. Yet we also verified its correctness via experiments as described in the following sections.

$$APL_{P_n'} = \frac{\sum_{i=1}^{t-1}\sum_{k=1}^{t-i} k + (h-1)(\sum_{i=1}^{x} i + \sum_{i=1}^{n-y+1} i) - 1 + R}{\frac{n(n-1)}{2}} \tag{3}$$

---

[3] The length of a path is measured here in terms of hop count.

[4] By all pairs we mean all unordered pairs because the edges are undirected, and for this reason, it is enough to count path lengths in only one direction.

where $h = y - x$, $t = n - h + 1$, and

$$R = \begin{cases} (2n - h - 1)\sum_{i=0}^{h/2} i - h(n - h + 1) + 2, & \text{if } h \text{ is even} \\ (2n - h - 1)\sum_{i=0}^{(h-1)/2} i + \frac{(h+1)^2}{4} - \frac{(h-1)(n-h+3)}{2}, & \text{if } h \text{ is odd} \end{cases}$$

Thus, we obtained analytical expressions for APL prior to and subsequent to additional link attachment into a path graph, as in Eqs. 2 and 3, which allows us to formulate our problem in the form of *Integer Linear Programming (IP)* as follows:

$$\text{minimize } APL_{P'_n}$$
$$\text{subject to n, x, y are integer}$$
$$x < y$$
$$1 \leq x \leq n$$
$$1 \leq y \leq n$$

where $APL_{P'_n}$ is given in Eq. 3.

It is known that *IP* is NP-hard [23], which implies that there is no known polynomial-time solution for *IP* problems. Yet, in the following sections, we will solve certain instances of the problem above by experimentally in the first place, and then, construct a general analytical solution for any value of network size (i.e. n) by means of linear regression method.

5   Finding Optimal Solutions

5.1   Numerical Solutions by Experiment

To find optimal solutions for certain cases of the problem introduced, we prepared an experimental set-up shown as pseudo-code in Fig. 3.

In the experiment, we incremented network size from 3 nodes to 1000 nodes, and varied attachment points (i.e. vertices) of the additional link for all possible

---

```
1: for n ← 3 to 1000 do                              ▷ Varying network size
2:      Enter Adjacency List of the Graph    ▷ Defining network topology for all cases
3:      function APL(Graph)
4:      Find the minimum APL among all calculated values at each step of n
5: function APL(G)                                    ▷ Determines APL for G
6:      c ← 0                                         ▷ Counter
7:      APL ← 0
8:      for all Pairs (v_i, v_j) in G do
9:          function DIJKSTRA(v_i, v_j)               ▷ Runs Dijkstra
10:             return Shortest Path (SP) between v_i and v_j
11:         APL ← (APL * c + Length(SP)/(c + 1)
12:         c ← c + 1
13:     return APL
```

Fig. 3. Experimental setup for determining APL

cases as a brute-force approach. At each step of network size, we first defined network topology by entering adjacency list for the network, for all possible deployment of the additional link as varying variables of x and y, which represent the relative location of vertices v_x and v_y. Then, for each topology, we found the shortest paths for all pairs by implementing Dijkstra's well-known shortest path algorithm [23,24]. Notice that Dijkstra determines the shortest path between only one pair of nodes, and for this reason, we iteratively employed it for all pairs in the graph (i.e. topology). After calculating lengths (i.e. hop counts) of the shortest paths for all pairs, we took average of them, and thus found APL. Finally, we identified the minimum APL among all calculated APLs yielded as varying locations of v_x and v_y. This experimental process was repeated for certain network sizes of 3, 5, 10, 20, 50, 100, 200, 500 and 1000 nodes.

Table 1. Experimental results obtained by brute force computation

Network Size (n)	APL for Path P_n	APL for Ring $P_n \cup (v_1, v_n)$	Min APL (Optimal) $P_n \cup (v_{x\_opt}, v_{y\_opt})$	Optimal Solutions (x_{opt}, y_{opt})
3	1.33	1.0	1.0	(x=1, y=3)
5	2.0	1.5	1.5	(x=1, y=5)
10	3.66	2.77	2.53	(x=2, y=8)
				(x=3, y=9)
20	7.0	5.26	4.5	(x=4, y=16)
				(x=5, y=17)
50	17.0	12.75	10.37	(x=10, y=40)
				(x=11, y=41)
100	33.66	25.25	20.13	(x=21, y=80)
200	67.0	50.25	39.66	(x=41, y=159)
				(x=42, y=160)
500	167.0	125.25	98.24	(x=104, y=397)
1000	333.66	250.25	195.87	(x=207, y=793)
				(x=208, y=794)

Table 1 contains some of the numerical results acquired in the experiments, including optimal solutions that minimize APL as well as results belong to ring topologies (i.e. the cases in which the first and the last nodes of paths are connected each other by the additional link). The first column in the table includes network size in terms of the number of nodes, while the second and the third columns contain APL for *pure path* (P_n) and *ring topology* (i.e. $P_n \cup (v_1, v_n)$) respectively. Notice that *ring topology* occurs when the first and the last nodes on a path are connected each other. The fourth column involves minimum APL which appears when the additional link is placed optimally (i.e. $P_n \cup (v_{x\_opt}, v_{y\_opt})$). The last column shows optimal values of (v_x, v_y) that *minimize APL*.

Figure 4 shows experimental results in the form of 3-dimensional color mapping when network size equals to 100 nodes. As can be seen in the figure, APL has the minimum value (i.e. dark blue color) at around $x = 21$ and $y = 80$, or equivalently, vice versa. Notice that the red area from left bottom corner to right upper corner represent *Path* topology, whereas the points both at the left up corner and at the right down corner produce *Ring* topology.

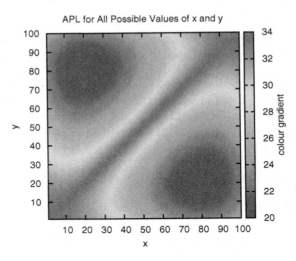

Fig. 4. APL for varying values of x and y, when network contains 100 nodes (Color figure online)

Verification of the Mathematical Model: One might doubt the accuracy of our mathematical model presented in Sect. 4, i.e. Eq. 3. To verify correctness of this mathematical expression, we first computed APL values by using Eq. 3 as assigning all possible values to the variables up to network size of 1000 nodes, and then searched out the instances giving minimum APL for each network size. Afterwards, we compared minimum APL values computed in Eq. 3 with the APL values yielded from the experimental calculations for certain network sizes as listed in Table 1. We eventually observed that both the mathematical model and the experimental calculations give precisely the same outcomes for APL, which shows the consistency between these two different approaches.

5.2   Analytical Solution by Linear Regression

Table 1 contains numerical results of optimal solutions for certain network sizes. However, to make a comprehensive analysis including asymptotic behaviour of optimal solutions and other variables, we need to establish analytical relations between these variables. For this purpose, we applied a linear regression method on the numerical results at hand, based on least square technique, and consequently, found the following relations.

$$APL_{P'_n}(n) = 0.195331 * n + 0.559447 \tag{4}$$

$$x_{opt} = Round(0.207174 * n - 0.0251311) \tag{5}$$

$$y_{opt} = Round(0.793222 * n + 0.0497688) \tag{6}$$

where $Round(z)$ is a function which returns the *nearest integer* to z.

In fact, Eqs. 5 and 6 give precise answers to the main problem asked at the beginning of this paper. Equation 4, on the other hand, yields exact outcome for APL when an optimal solution is applied.

6 Discussions

6.1 Average Path Length (APL)

Figure 5 depicts APL for both P_n and P_n' when optimal values of (v_x, v_y) is applied, as network size varies from 3 nodes to 1000 nodes. As seen in the figure, APL linearly increases for both cases as network size grows. However, notice that P_n has higher slope than P_n', which means that adding extra edge reduces APL on a network.

Notice that there is also model fit (i.e. regression line) which is obtained by linear regression. Goodness of fit can even be visually evaluated in Fig. 5, as the fitted line and numerical data exactly matches each other.

6.2 Improvement

Figure 6 exhibits the *Improvement*, i.e. the rate of decrement, on APL when an additional edge is placed to the network at optimal positions. As can be followed in the figure, the improvement rate begins with a slow growth at around 24.81 % when $n = 3$, followed by a period of moderate growth, and then back to a period of slow growth asymptotically approaching to 41.4 %, which is consistent with the analytical analysis below.

$$Improvement = 100 * (APL_{P_n} - APL'_{P_n})/APL_{P_n}$$
$$= 100 * \frac{(\frac{n+1}{3} - 0.195331n - 0.559447)}{(n+1)/3}$$

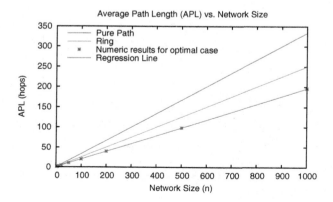

Fig. 5. Average Path Length (APL) for different topologies as network size grows

$$= 300 * \frac{0.138n - 0.226114}{n + 1}$$

$$= \frac{41.4n - 67.8342}{n + 1}$$

$$\lim_{n \to +\infty} Improvement = 41.4\,\%$$

6.3 Optimal Solutions

Equations 5 and 6 are optimal solutions in *analytic form*, while values on the fifth column in Table 1 are *numeric* solutions for certain network sizes. Thanks to Eqs. 5 and 6, one can readily determine optimal values of (v_x, v_y) for any network size. It is interesting to observe that the optimal solutions, when $n = 3$ and $n = 5$, are two end points of the path (i.e. (v_x, v_y) equals to (v_1, v_3) and (v_1, v_5) respectively) . As network size grows, the optimal values of v_x and v_y slide gradually towards the center of the network. This observation motivated us to investigate normalized length between two end points (i.e. v_x and v_y) of optimal solutions in the next part.

Another observation here is that there is only one (i.e. unique) optimal solution when the network size (n) is odd, whereas there may emerge many optimal solutions when n is even, as can be observed in the fifth column of Table 1. We discovered that alternative optimal solutions for the same network yield isomorphic graphs when they are applied.

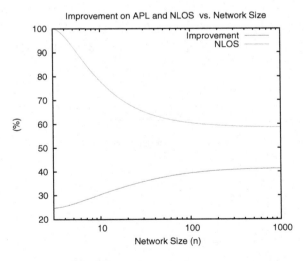

Fig. 6. Improvement on APL and normalized length of optimal solutions (NLOS) as network size grows (smoothed)

6.4 Normalized Length of Optimal Solutions (NLOS)

$NLOS$ represents the normalized distance between two end points (i.e. v_{x_opt} and v_{y_opt}) of optimal link deployments that minimize APL. The normalization process is performed with respect to network size. Figure 6 includes $NLOS$ as network size logarithmically grows. It can be deduced from the figure that the $NLOS$ is reduced logarithmically beginning from 100 % to around 58.6 %, which is consistent with the analytical analysis below. This means that the optimal solutions occur at around two end points of chain-topology when network size is small, whereas attachment points of optimal solutions move away from this end points as network size grows.

$$NL = 100 * \frac{|y_{opt} - x_{opt}|}{n - 1}$$
$$= \frac{Round(58.6048 * n + 7.48999)}{n - 1}$$
$$\lim_{n \to +\infty} NL = 58.6048\,\%$$

7 Conclusion

Chain-topology networks performs poorly in certain performance metrics such as throughput, robustness, energy efficiency in data transmissions [1–7]. This is mostly due to fact that average path length (APL) in chain-topology is extremely high, which is almost one third of network size as we showed.

In this study, we aimed at compensating this deficiency by presenting an optimization model in which incremental link deployment was considered, with the objective of minimizing APL on a chain network. For this purpose, we first discovered mathematical expression of the objective, as well as formulated it in the form of Integer Programming (IP). Then, we prepared an experimental setup in order to determine $APLs$? of all possible topologies generated by placing an additional link to varying locations on a chain-topology network. Thus, we found optimal solutions that minimize APL for specific network sizes up to 1000 nodes, and also verified accuracy of our mathematical model. Through the experiments, for each specific network size, we implemented Dijkstra's shortest path algorithm for all pairs, and took average of their lengths in terms of hop count to calculate corresponding APL values. Afterwards, we derived analytical solution by implementing Linear Regression method on the data obtained experimentally, which allowed us to see asymptotic behaviour of the solutions.

Our analyses showed that the optimization model proposed was able to reduce APL on chain-topology networks at a rate of between 24.81% and 41.4%, with gradually increasing ratio as network size grows. Moreover, we found that normalized length of the additional link for optimal solution asymptotically approached to 58.6% of network size.

Besides contribution of such an additional link optimally implanted for minimizing the APL, further research is required to improve other performance characteristics of chain-topology networks, such as ensuring load balancing.

References

1. Kim, S., Kim, J., Yoo, Y.: Container security device chain network for safe railway transportation. Int. J. Distrib. Sens. Netw. **2014**, 12 (2014). doi:10.1155/2014/767802. Article ID 767802

2. Agbinya, J.: Design considerations of MoHotS and wireless chain networks. Wireless Pers. Commun. **40**(1), 91–106 (2007). http://dx.doi.org/10.1007/s11277-006-9103-0

3. Haifeng, J., Jiansheng, Q., Yanjing, S., Guoyong, Z.: Energy optimal routing for long chain-type wireless sensor networks in underground mines. Min. Sci. Technol. **21**(1), 17–21 (2011). (china). science/article/pii/S1674526410000219

4. Yuan, Y., Shen, Z., Quan-fu, W., Pei, S.: Long distance wireless sensor networks applied in coal mine. Procedia Earth Planet. Sci. **1**(1), 1461–1467 (2009). http://www.sciencedirect.com/science/article/pii/S1674526410000219

5. Zhou, G., Zhu, Z., Zhang, P., Li, W.: Source-aware redundant packet forwarding scheme for emergency information delivery in chain-typed multihop wireless sensor networks. Int. J. Distrib. Sens. Netw. **2015**, 10 (2015). doi:10.1155/2015/405374. Article ID 405374

6. Chen, Y., Ren, T., Liu, Y., Zhou, Y.: Lifetime maximization algorithm for chain wireless sensor networks. Inform. Technol. J. **12**(4), 656–663 (2013)

7. Leu, F.Y., Huang, Y.T.: Maximum capacity in chain-topology wireless mesh networks. In: Wireless Telecommunications Symposium, WTS 2008, pp. 250–259, April 2008

8. Flammini, M., Gambosi, G., Navarra, A.: Wireless ATM layouts for chain networks. Mob. Netw. Appl. **10**(1–2), 35–45 (2005). http://dx.doi.org/10.1023/B3AMONE.0000048544.06992.f7

9. Watts, D.J., Strogatz, S.H.: Collective dynamics of 'small-world' networks. Nature **393**, 440–442 (1998)

10. Xu, Z.G., Zhu, L.J., Shi, Y.S., Jiang, H.: Research of scalability of the belt-type sensor networks. J. Shanghai Jiaotong Univ. **17**(2), 237–240 (2012). (Science)

11. Chen, F., Chen, Z., Wang, X., Yuan, Z.: The average path length of scale free networks. Commun. Nonlinear Sci. Numer. Simul. **13**(7), 1405–1410 (2008). http://www.sciencedirect.com/science/article/pii/S1007570406002383

12. Yen, C.C., Yeh, M.Y., Chen, M.S.: An efficient approach to updating closeness centrality and average path length in dynamic networks. In: 2013 IEEE 13th International Conference on Data Mining (ICDM), pp. 867–876, December 2013

13. Gulyás, L., Horváth, G., Cséri, T., Kampis, G.: An estimation of the shortest and largest average path length in graphs of given density. ArXiv e-prints, January 2011

14. Guo, D., Liang, M., Li, D., Jiang, Z.: Effect of random edge failure on the average path length. J. Phys. A: Math. Theor. **44**(41), 415002 (2011). http://stacks.iop.org/1751-8121/44/i=41/a=415002

15. Reppas, A.I., Spiliotis, K., Siettos, C.I.: Tuning the average path length of complex networks and its influence to the emergent dynamics of the majority-rule model. Math. Comput. Simul. **109**, 186–196 (2015). http://www.sciencedirect.com/science/article/pii/S0378475414002456

16. Peng, J.: Average path length for sierpinski pentagon. Int. J. Adv. Comput. Technol. **5**(5), 724–732 (2013). http://search.proquest.com.mutex.gmu.edu/docview/1400499426?accountid=14541

17. Zhang, Z., Chen, L., Zhou, S., Fang, L., Guan, J., Zou, T.: Analytical solution of average path length for apollonian networks. Phys. Rev. E **77**, 017102 (2008). http://link.aps.org/doi/10.1103/PhysRevE.77.017102
18. Fronczak, A., Fronczak, P., Hołyst, J.A.: Average path length in random networks. Phys. Rev. E **70**, 056110 (2004). http://link.aps.org/doi/10.1103/PhysRevE.70.056110
19. Mao, G., Zhang, N.: Analysis of average shortest-path length ofscale-free network. Int. J. Appl. Math. (2013)
20. Butler, J., Sasao, T., Matsuura, M.: Average path length of binarydecision diagrams. IEEE Trans. Comput. **54**(9), 1041–1053 (2005)
21. Kleinrock, L., Silvester, J.: Optimum transmission radii for packet radio networks or why six is a magic number. In: Proceedings of the IEEE National Telecommunications Conference, vol. 4 (1978)
22. Gao, F., Le, A., Xi, L., Yin, S.: Asymptotic formula on average path length of fractal networks modeled on sierpinski gasket. J. Math. Anal. Appl. **434**(2), 1581–1596 (2016). http://www.sciencedirect.com/science/article/pii/S0022247X15009312
23. Cormen, T.H., Stein, C., Rivest, R.L., Leiserson, C.E.: Introduction to Algorithms, 2nd edn. McGraw-Hill Higher Education, New York (2001)
24. Dijkstra, E.W.: A note on two problems in connection with graphs. Numer. Math. **1**, 269–271 (1959)

Author Index

Printed in the United States
By Bookmasters